THE SINGING ELMS

To Christine & Tony
with love and
With best wishes from
Laurie Elms

and from
Graeme Elms de Graaf

PREVIOUS VOLUMES IN EMINENT MUSICIANS OF AUSTRALIA
Available from Bowerbird Press

VOLUME 1
Dearest John. The Story of John Lemmoné, Flute Virtuoso,
and Nellie Melba
Simson Master Clarinettist. A Search for the Man and His Music
Donald Westlake

VOLUME 2
From Me To You. The Story of Clive Amadio
Donald Westlake
Compact disc: From Me To You. The Music of Clive Amadio

THE SINGING ELMS

THE AUTOBIOGRAPHY OF LAURIS ELMS

BOWERBIRD PRESS
Eminent Musicians of Australia
Volume 3

Bowerbird Press
35 Burraga Ave, Terrey Hills,
NSW 2084 AUSTRALIA
Fax (02) 9450 0430
Email: bowerbrd@ozemail.com.au

Typeset in Garamond by Laura Danckwerts
Made and printed in Australia by McPherson's Printing Group
Cover design by Joy Lankshear

National Library of Australia
Cataloguing-in-Publication data:

Elms, Lauris, 1931-.
The singing Elms : The autobiography of Lauris Elms.

Includes index.
ISBN 0 9577790 3 8 (paperback)
ISBN 0 9577790 2 X (hardback)

1. Elms, Lauris, 1931- . 2. Contraltos - Australia -
Biography. 3. Women singers - Australia - Biography. I.
Title. (Series : Eminent musicians of Australia ; v. 3).

782.68092

Contents

List of Illustrations

Foreword

Lauris Elms was one of an extraordinary generation of Australian singers who, in the years after the war, took the operatic world, and especially the English operatic world of Covent Garden and Sadlers Wells, by storm: Joan Sutherland, Elizabeth Fretwell, Marie Collier, Sylvia Fisher, Elsie Morrison, June Bronhill, John Shaw, Ronald Dowd and most renowned of all, except for Joan Sutherland, that enduring star of the Paris Opera, Lance Ingram (Albert Lance). Lauris Elms worked with all these great contemporaries and grew up with some; most of them were her friends. They are the close companions of her working world and she writes of them with great affection and a generous sense of the reality of other people's lives; never more humorously, or with so much affectionate wonder, as in her account of her first teachers, the Modestis. The picture she paints of this amazing pair would alone make her book worthwhile.

Utterly in thrall to the Voice, whose richness and beauty it has been her life's responsibility to cultivate and care for, she writes in a way that is rare of what it means to be the keeper of such a wayward angel.

This is a far cry from the usual romance of the artist's life. Her wonderful detailed account of her childhood and growing up at Springvale records the emergence of a distinctively Australian sensibility and a nature that is at once determined, humorous, irreverent, often angry, sometimes rebellious and at all times refreshingly down-to-earth.

The thread that runs through all is her dedication to her difficult and demanding art. There is an insistence on the highest professional standards, and a demand, sometimes at a cost, as we see in her relationship with the Australian Opera, that others observe them as well. Most of all what she insists on is the wholeness of life, and it is this that makes her account of her life here – work, marriage and family, and friends – so moving, and has allowed her to retire from stage and concert-platform, as she does in the final pages, regretfully, but with such a sense of fullness and with so much dignity and grace.

David Malouf

Preface

Lauris Elms has given us an autobiography of endearing frankness. This is the story of a truly Australian career, and Australian by choice. As a girl growing up in the country south of Melbourne, a student of violin and a talented painter, she brings the era to life and shows us the provincial music scene with its problems and charms.

After her studies in Paris with her adored Modestis she was engaged at Covent Garden where she appeared in: *A Masked Ball, The Trojans, The Tales of Hoffmann,* Handel's *Samson, Elektra, The Walkyrie, The Dialogues of the Carmelites, Rigoletto* and *Lucia*. Her voice was a true contralto, a great and beautiful instrument, and was much admired. I can remember her inspiring performance as Micah in *Samson* as if it were yesterday. Her worldwide career loomed ahead and Covent Garden offered her further work. She gave it all up to return to Australia to be with her academic husband. The world's loss was Australia's gain.

She spent the next thirty years as a musical pioneer in Australia singing not only the great warhorses of Handel, Bach and Beethoven, but championing the works of Mahler and introducing music unknown to Australia for the first time, notably Berlioz' *Beatrice and Benedick* and Schoenberg's *Gurrelieder*.

She tackles all sorts of institutions very forthrightly and is not frightened to give her views on the Opera, the Australian Broadcasting Commission, the Union, etc. Severe in her self-criticism, if her views tend to be somewhat rosy regarding her colleagues, she can be praised for her generosity. She never took the easy route and sang frequently for miserable fees in less than palatial venues. Her interest was solely in music and she championed many Australian composers such as Dorian le Gallienne, Margaret Sutherland and Larry Sitsky.

Australians were fortunate to hear her in a large concert repertoire as well as a wide range of operatic roles which included Gluck's Orpheo, Handel's Giulio Cesare and Bradamante, Rossini's Arsace, Bizet's Carmen, Wagner's Erda and Fricka, Verdi's Azucena, Amneris and Mistress Quickly, Saint-Saën's Dalila, Puccini's Frugola, Principessa and Zita, Berlioz' Dido and Beatrice, and Bartok's Judith.

In renouncing the bright lights of Europe she had the

happiness of a full life with her husband and seeing her daughter grow up to become a brilliant clarinettist. Dear Lauris, may you have many days of happy painting and sailing.

Richard Bonynge

Acknowledgments

A wonderful life of music, blessed by having loving parents who encouraged me and were financially able to indulge me, meant that I had many reasons to be grateful for a long career.

After my farewell Sydney recital, I adjudicated the Melbourne Sun Aria. This singing competition begins in Ballarat, Victoria, where the preliminary heats take place over four days. I flew down from Sydney and a couple of hours later, on a very cold September Monday morning, was installed in the comfortable hotel room where I had stayed with my mother when I had been a competitor in the Sun Aria of 1954.

What should I do with myself during these days, waiting for the preliminary heats to begin each evening at 6pm? When I had had to fill in time as a singer on tour, there had always been words to learn, new repertoire to study and the necessity to conserve energy in rest and concentration, preparing for the evening's performance.

That day it was cold outside, and my life as a singer was over. I had so many memories and the years had seen such changes during the time my own career had developed. Perhaps I could write the story of my life, which would also cover the history of post-war opera in Australia? I wanted to tell young singers what it had been like for me and my colleagues, and I thought that the best way to heal my own sense of loss might be to write about it.

It worked. I enormously enjoyed writing about this other life of mine. I have moved away from grieving, to an amazed and amused contemplation of that life which seems increasingly distant. Now comes the hard part, as I try to remember all the people who have lovingly helped me along the way with advice, encouragement and information.

I wanted most of all to honour the memory of the beloved Modestis, who gave me my career and my voice, and the support I needed as a young girl living in a foreign land, away from loving parents and home for the first time.

I am grateful to David Malouf who, with his great love of opera, wrote pages of corrections, suggestions and alterations, (few of which I adopted), as well as a tribute in the foreword which I treasure. Rosemary Harle, who corrected and checked the very first rough draft for spelling of names of musicians and composers, both early and contemporary, spent hours of her time in the first year of my writing. Our friend Maurice Wright talked and wrote to me about style. Jill Hickson liked the book so much she tried to find me a publisher, and encouraged me in that first year. Richard Davis, whom *I* had helped find a publisher, also gave me encouragement and advice. Nancy Clarke took on the arduous task of proofreading.

Philip Sametz carefully edited the manuscript. His professional approach improved the book, and took away pages of boring descriptions of unimportant events.

Moffat Oxenbould gave me invaluable information, corrected facts and the spelling of colleagues' names. David Garrett and Robert Allman both generously responded to frequent requests for information.

Brent Thomas spent hours of his convalescence after a serious illness scanning the photos, and my darling daughter Deborah Nelson gave me both love and practical help with the illustrations. The unknown photographer from *The Border Mail* in Albury has my gratitude for the splendid cover photo. My thanks to The Royal Opera House, the Victoria and Albert Picture Library, Opera Australia, the Victorian Opera, the State Opera of South Australia and Mrs Gordon Clarke for the use of other photographs.

Dame Joan Sutherland and her husband Richard Bonynge have my admiration and affection for their help and advice, and all that song over the years, and at this time have given me such support in bringing this book to fruition. Sir Charles Mackerras who gave me the gifts of his great music and the opportunity to sing with him, now includes words of praise for my book, for which I am grateful.

Those whom I have forgotten and whom I should have thanked, please forgive me, as this is my debut in a new role. Any mistakes are mine alone, and you who know me know that I have strong opinions, not always soundly based on fact. Please remember that all of you have my thanks for your support and love over the years.

I am forever indebted to my dear Laura Danckwerts, friend and editor, for bringing these hundreds of separate leaves together in the present form of a book you can hold in your hand. And to Graeme de Graaff I can only say that the good fairies who gave me the wonderful gifts I had at my birth, included (or threw in) at a later time a husband who encouraged and shared this life of mine with a sense of adventure, understanding, humour and good advice. The good fortune to have his company and friendship down the years has filled me with pleasure and eternal gratitude.

Lauris Elms, Sydney 2001.

1. Springvale

Every night the big goods train hooted as it chugged up the hill, carrying coal from Gippsland to Melbourne. The night seemed so still after the train had passed, but at last came the sound of the milkman's horse trotting along Lightwood Road, then the metal milk billy being filled. Soon the magpies would begin to sing in the pine trees on the corner and the sky would lighten, and I would fall asleep again until the rest of the house stirred.

First the alarm would ring, then the sound of my father's voice, then Betty would wake and the day would be bright behind the blinds, with motes of dust dancing on the shafts of light streaming into the darkened room.

The house was built of dark-stained weatherboards, with a wide brick-pillared veranda around the front. It faced the main railway line from Gippsland to Melbourne. The landscape looked flat, but the slight rise between Noble Park and Springvale made the goods trains strain under their heavy weight of coal.

Opposite the line was Rocla Industries. The view there was of huge concrete pipes, like some surreal painting. But the house maintained its dignity behind a splendid ti-tree hedge. The buffalo lawn in front was centred with a West Australian flowering gum tree, which marked the beginning of the Christmas season by producing a crown of scarlet flowers. Dad really loved this tree. He was proud of the ti-tree hedge too, but had to trim it back two or three times a year, and the side hedge was two metres high, and nearly as wide. We children used to walk along this high road on top of the hedge occasionally, which would make Dad growl at us.

There was a small hill which ran up from the corner of the paddock. We loved to play along the unmade road, with its dividing twin tracks winding through the soft grey sand. There was a grove of wattles, and in the misty days of late winter and early spring there were 'eggs-and-bacon,' sarsaparilla and tiny green slipper orchids hiding in the long damp grass. More rarely, there were tall stands of white and red heath to pick and arrange in glass jam-jars in the cubby-houses we made between the stunted trunks of the wattles. Then my sister and I would have elaborate tea parties, pouring make-believe tea under the indigo clouds of the winter sky and sheltering from the downpours when they came, under the great pine trees on the corner of View Road.

The old house had a neglected orchard on the western side in which stood apple, quince, pear and cherry-plum trees. Beyond the orchard stood a grove of twisted quince trees, growing close to the high ti-tree hedge. We two children, with Gladys and Peter from next door, would squeeze in amongst the twisty trunks and I would tell scary ghost stories while the autumn wind banged and rustled and tossed the branches. The other children seemed very frightened by my stories, although they knew I was just pretending. Wailing loudly, they ran complaining to Mum. It was bewildering. It was only 'made-up' stories, I told them!

Under the quince trees were the fowl pens. The hens were Mum's favourites. She looked after them with passion. There were always ten laying hens. If a chook looked droopy around the eyes, Mum would grab the axe and chop off its head, and there would be the special treat of chicken for dinner. The chooks were so used to coming when Mum called "Chook, chook, chook" that she could easily catch them. Dad could never bring himself to do the dreadful job of beheading!

I do not remember a time when I was not singing some melody under my breath, and when I was not aware of sounds and of the music played by my mother, grandmother, aunts, uncles and, as she grew up, my little sister Betty.

But one day I became aware of a machine which made music. It was a wooden box with a gloriously shaped horn arising from it. Our Uncle Lindsay began an elaborate ritual, sharpening to needle-point a piece of bamboo which was then screwed into a heavy metal head. Then, after he wound the handle and placed the heavy breakable record on the turntable on top of the box, out of the horn came the most extraordinary sounds which, with shrieks of laughter, my sister and I labelled 'the egg-laying competition'. This convulsed us throughout our childhood, and it was not until the opera season of 1966 that I stopped giggling at the 'chook, chook' noises made at the beginning of *The Anvil Chorus* from Verdi's *Il trovatore*. Thirty years later, the 'egg-laying competition' became the prelude to my singing Azucena's first aria, *Stride la vampa*, and now it still produces the pre-natal tension all singers feel before delivering their first notes on stage.

There was always a feeling inside me that one day I would be someone! Reading Arthur Mee's *Children's Encyclopaedia* every Sunday at Grandma Elms', I would be inspired by the stories of great heroines like Joan of Arc and Grace Darling. I was transported into another world by Deanna Durbin singing *Waltzing in the Clouds,* and would swing myself ever higher and higher on the swing, singing every song recently heard on the radio.

When I lay in bed at night, I imagined I was growing longer and longer, like 'Alice' in my favourite story, growing bigger and taller. When I was three, I was very ill in hospital at Christmas-time, Dad used to come every day to read me *Alice in Wonderland*. It was hot and through the open window came the sound of tennis balls plopping on the gravel court next door, behind the Presbyterian Church. At night Sister Williams or Sister Coleman slept on the floor beside my narrow hospital bed. They were waiting for 'the crisis'. After that night, when the pneumonia man had passed (riding by, looking like the Knight in the Dürer print), I was able to go home again to the house that I loved so much.

I was born on October 20th 1931, in the private hospital at Springvale. When it was time for my young mother to take me home, Auntie Ede, Dad's sister, came to help her.

"Where will the baby sleep?" Auntie asked.

They found an old suitcase and removed the lid and I slept peacefully in this makeshift crib for several months. The family believe that from this beginning comes my love of travel.

Springvale was a sleepy country town, in the middle of the plain that stretched from Mt Dandenong to the sea at Edithvale. It was a typical small Victorian community. Although now it is a busy suburb of Melbourne, then it related much more to the prosperous market town of Dandenong. The railway line crossed the main street at a level crossing, where manually operated gates were closed to allow the passing of infrequent trains. There was a triangular vacant lot on the corner opposite the station, neglected and full of long dry grass, then a row of small tile-fronted shops: a newsagent's, a bakery, a haberdashery, then another vacant block and on the other side, Burden's large grocery store on the corner, a milk-bar, and more gaps like missing teeth before another group of very old weatherboard shops.

The small town was caught in a time warp as if the Depression had stifled a dream of prosperity that would finally arrive thirty years later. It still had a blacksmith's, and on drowsy afternoons going home from school we children would hang around the door of the smithy to watch the sparks fly upwards, as the smith bent the red-hot metal into the curve of the horseshoe. The patient horse would stand with his back to the street, swishing the flies away with his tail, and the smith would cradle his huge foot in one gentle hand while he hammered the shoe carefully on the hoof.

The blacksmith's was opposite the most handsome and largest building in the town. It stood on the left of the main street, built of brick with a red-tiled roof, a date palm in front and a large asphalt yard where the children gathered every morning.

This was 'State School no. 3507'. Behind it was a large paddock of long grass and three or four beautiful, drooping, grey river-gums. The boys played football or cricket in this lovely place. The girls played basketball on the asphalt in the front, hoping not to fall over and skin their knees.

In 1937 there was an outbreak of polio in Victoria, and all schools were closed for many months. My little sister Elizabeth and I could both read. We had taught ourselves, I think, by reading comics called *Chick's Own* and later, *Film Fun*. Remembering these comics, they seemed such innocent papers that they might have come from another world. Books were expensive and treasured, but those weekly papers were our delight. That year I should have started school, but, with all the other children, was kept at home. So I had an extra year of play, before the serious business of going to school and the end of innocence that the school playground brings.

My grandfather Halford, a Presbyterian Minister, died when I was about five, and my dynamic little grandmother ruled her family with a rod of iron. My mother, the eldest daughter of Grandfather's second family, was lively and good-looking. She and her six siblings were the grandchildren of Professor James Halford, the first Professor of Medicine at the University of Melbourne, a fact they were never allowed to forget! They had amongst their ancestors a famous Victorian artist, Briton Rivière, who was much admired by Queen Victoria. Hardly mentioned, because of her scandalous behaviour, was the equally famous soprano, Madame Anna (Rivière) Bishop, who had left her husband Sir Henry Bishop and run away with the French harpist, Nicolas Bochsa. Queen Victoria heartily disapproved of Madame Anna Bishop!

My father's father had been a pioneer in Gippsland, selecting land from a plan in the Melbourne office of the Lands Department, then driving a bullock team through the swamps of Koo-wee-rup, to find the prehistoric rainforest engulfing the steeply rounded hills of this part of Gippsland. In his chapter of the book, *The Land of the Lyrebird*, he makes an interesting comment on the effect of clearing the forest upon the rainfall of this part of Gippsland. He kept a record of the annual rainfall over a period of ten years, and it shows that for each year of clearing the trees there is a one-inch drop in the rainfall. Visiting this area now it is hard to believe it was once a dense forest.

My father Harry was handsome, strong and funny. He teased everyone, but was also puritanical and a workaholic. My mother and father met each other at their cousin's farm at Lancaster near Kyabram in 1929. My father was leasing a property with his cousins at Lake Urana, and when he fell in love with mother she thought she would be a farmer's wife. It was not until

4

her wedding that she found she was going to live in the little town of Springvale on the outskirts of Melbourne, because drought and the Depression had forced the cousins to sell up. My father found work in a Grain and Produce store in Noble Park and later became the owner of this business. Dandenong was our large town, a market town, serving the dairy farms of Gippsland, and the market gardens of Dingly Dell and Keysborough. Tuesday was market day in Dandenong. Here were the wonderful and terrifying saleyards, where huge bulls were paraded majestically and pretty little poddy-calves cried for their mothers. The noise was tremendous as the huge auctioneer roared, the bulls bellowed and the farmers and 'cow-cockies' shouted their bids. It was so exciting. This was an entirely male world. Both the animals and men seemed monstrous to two small, wide-eyed girls peering through the rails, between the boots of the Gippsland farmers.

The days Dad took us to the market were the most exciting and dramatic of our lives. It was always hot and smelly. We would go for the whole day with Dad, taking jam sandwiches in brown paper bags. We would start the day in a small street of tiny 'dollshouses'. These were the sales-offices of salesmen who, like my father, took orders from the Gippsland farmers for their grain and timber requirements. The tiny box-like houses had an irresistible charm for my sister and me. We regarded Dad's as 'home' and would set out 'exploring', never going too far. It was a long time before we discovered the other side of the market where, under the corrugated iron roofs, there were trestle tables piled high and festooned with hanging coloured clothes which people bought and sold.

On other days my father would be up and at work by six in the morning, helping to load the heavy bags of wheat and bales of hay onto the trays of the trucks, for delivery all over the district. He then spent the rest of the day driving around, taking further orders, each day covering a different area. He worked tremendously hard at this time of his life. When he was later able to buy the business, he was able to give up the labouring side of his work.

As young children we often spent summer, and sometimes our winter holidays, at *Delamere* or *The Mount*, the homes of the Bonwick family. In my memory, the light at San Remo in these two old houses was always at that moment between day and night, when the lamps were lit and huge shadows grew upon the yellowed pine walls. The Aunts were Great-aunt Elsie, with a wicked grin and frizzy white hair, and Ethel, severe and practical, who always seemed disapproving.

They lived in a very old guesthouse, which had been built to provide an income for my widowed Great-grandmother, taking in 'paying guests' in the summer. Built of pine, it was insulated by seaweed tightly packed into the walls and the roof. The seaweed had been collected from the beach facing out into Bass Strait by long-forgotten builders. The house was cool in summer with its high ceiling, and on hot summer days you could catch the breeze blowing through the hallway, from the open front and back doors. Her daughters carried on looking after 'guests' into our childhood, when they were well into their eighties.

Behind the house was a cool dark place where a round topped brick well sat like a sleeping frog. Outside on top of the hill behind the house, was a communal four-seater lavatory. Sitting and talking to other little girls on the four wooden seats with the door open, while looking out over the tremendous view below, was a perfect beginning to those summer mornings. Up on the very top of the steep hill slept the old cemetery where, amongst the crumbling rabbit-burrows which undermined the elaborate metal guard-rails and granite tombstones, my father's ancestors, the Bonwicks, lay in peace. Gorse and blackberries grew everywhere, withstanding the Bass Strait gales and under the straggling pine trees mushrooms grew in their season. The view over the bare paddock out into Bass Straight and looking towards Cape Woolami took my breath away. I was glad the Bonwicks had such a beautiful resting place.

In winter, the wind blew in gales straight from the Antarctic. Up higher on the unmade road was a cluster of old pines where Old Brit had lived. This was my father's great-uncle, Henry Britton, who had been a journalist and historian. The empty tumbledown shack under the trees looked spooky, and I wondered how an old man could have survived in those bitter winters. My aunts took his food up the hill three times a day throughout his old age.

Aunt Elsie Dickie was a joy, for she never patronised us but treated little children like people, although she never had any children of her own. Funny, gay, her snow-white frizzy hair was her special beauty. Though unfashionable at the time, despaired of and mocked at by her relatives, her hair was wonderful to me. In later years her untidy derelict home was the refuge for all her nieces and nephews when they needed a holiday. We descended in family groups on the old house, enjoying its eccentric and generous occupant through the endless hot days of those remembered summers. Once we went to stay in an unbelievably wet wild August school holiday with my mother's two younger sisters. The candles and lamps would be lit at 4.30pm, our cupped hands shielding the match's flickering flame from the draughts sweeping through the house. In the gloaming we would stumble down the steep hillside to the village of San Remo, taking care not to fall into the decaying rabbit burrows hidden in the gorse bushes, which later on in September would clothe the hillside with gold.

As we grew up there were annual summer-long camping holidays at Cape Woolami on Phillip Island. A fishing boat, laden with heavy tents and provisions, would be taken from San Remo to the place at the end of the great sand dunes where the camp was to be. Heavy army tents would be erected, Uncle Alf would dig holes for the supporting posts, and as if by magic elaborate dining tables were made from the railway sleepers and ti-tree branches which were always to be found washed up on the beach. Permanent campfires made under old spreading ti-trees would be provided for my mother to somehow cook meals for large numbers of people. Alf also built a pit toilet, surrounded by tall saplings and enclosed by hessian, into which one had a dread of falling. Mother endured without complaint the hay fever brought on by flowering wattles and the smoke from her campfire, while we played and swam and never gave a thought to the morrow. As teenagers we spent six weeks every summer in this paradise.

My father's mother's sisters, my great-aunts, were all characters, some more eccentric than others, and they all loved to play the piano. They would sit down to play at any hour of the day, dash through some four-handed duet, then rush away to complete their next domestic chore. On winter evenings they would light the candles of the piano candelabra, and giggle and quarrel their way through Schubert's *Marche Militaire*.

I have been told that in the late 19th century there were more pianos in Australian homes than in any other country in the world. When one imagines the pioneers hauling their bullock-teams through the mud of Gippsland, one realises how much music meant to them in their lonely new lives.

My father's grandfather, Walter Bonwick, was the first Inspector of Music in the Victorian State Education System and wrote the first schools' music book ever used in Victoria. In 1867 there was a great celebration when Prince Alfred, the Duke of Edinburgh, laid the foundation stone of the Melbourne Town Hall. Walter Bonwick conducted a huge choir, out-of-doors, on the corner of Swanston and Collins Streets. For this event he had to marshal, organise and conduct a choir of thirteen thousand school children. He spent his life teaching music, mostly in schools.

My earliest memories are of singing little songs under my breath, and joining in the singing around the piano on Sundays. This was a ritual at both my grandparents' homes, where the aunts and uncles sang and played hymns and ballads, as well as the music of Schubert, Brahms, Mendelssohn and Gounod, on flute, violin and piano.

Too young to be able to read the words in the hymnbook,

7

I often 'made up' splendid poems about fairies, singing the hymn tunes all the time. I remember my embarrassment at Church one Sunday when some well-meaning lady bent down to say, "I really enjoyed your singing today, dear."

My mother was impulsive, courageous and full of energy. She played the piano very well and had been invited to accompany the duet singers, Viola Morris and Victoria Anderson, on a tour of New Zealand. Her father James Halford, the Presbyterian Minister, would not allow her to go, and she always regretted this lost opportunity. She was a born performer, and I suppose she lived out her ambition in my career.

When I was five, my sister Betty and I began to have ballet lessons. Mother was engaged to play for a ballet school in the city run by Miss Aytown. We travelled to the distant city, all three sitting neatly knitting, side by side. From a very early age we copied our Mum, whose fingers were never still. So there we sat for the hour it took to get to Melbourne in the train. Together we walked up the wooden stairs to the bare, wooden-floored, mirror-walled studio which seemed beautiful in its spacious emptiness. We stood at the *barre* in our 'best' dresses, (with tied sashes at the back, and Peter-Pan collars around our throats) and were astonished at the other children's little 'tights'. How curious they looked to my eyes. We watched, amazed at the others' movements, but gradually learned to point our toes, arch our arms and turn out our feet into the 'five positions'.

As I stood at the end of the line behind the children in their strange clothes, I listened as if for the first time, to the music of Chopin and Tchaikovsky that Mother was playing.

That year, our first at school, was a year of colds and measles, and we were so often ill that our mother got her sister, Auntie Nonie Knox, to take her place as the ballet-class pianist, and only now do I realise that this was probably a big disappointment for our Mum. Auntie Nonie was a very good pianist, and Mother never went back to play for Miss Aytown's classes.

Soon our lives were changed by the great world outside. My sister remembers that, on the way home from school one day, we saw the hoarding at the newsagents announcing the outbreak of war. I burst into uncontrollable sobbing and cried all the way home. I had seen pictures of the Napoleonic and Boer Wars in the *Children's Encyclopaedia,* and could not bear the thought of so much death and suffering.

As the war began, we stayed at home in Springvale, never going into the city. Now we were sent to a dancing class in Dandenong, where the Fallow sisters, Pat, Lal and Kal, taught us tap-dancing, classical ballet and high-kicking 'numbers'.

Betty was good at dancing, but I was always chosen to be the Fairy Queen, and given songs to sing like *I'm Always Chasing Rainbows.* The fact that I was always chosen to *sing* in these concerts meant, to me, that I was no good at dancing and this filled me with a secret shame. However on the understanding that dancing might strengthen my flat feet, I was beginning my theatrical training.

My mother wanted me to learn piano, and tried hard to teach me, but I resisted, longing to produce the legato singing sounds of Uncle Lindsay's violin. With hindsight this was one of the big mistakes of my life. The violin did give me the phrasing and 'line' I needed to follow in my singing, but the piano would have given me the ability to learn my music, with the harmonies and chords underlying the melody.

I began learning the violin at school in a group of five-year-olds, sawing away on borrowed quarter-sized violins.

When my violin teacher was called up for his military service, Mother sent me to have lessons with a newly-arrived resident of Springvale South, the prettiest part of my world, with its undeveloped sandy tracks winding through the delicate coastal wattles and ti-trees. Stella and Paul Nemet had fled Europe, arriving in 1940. Paul had been a Doctor of Laws in Poland and Stella a concert violinist. They had bought a poultry-farm and my father, through his business selling chicken feed, quickly became friends with Paul. Mother began to play the piano for Stella, and so found me my new violin teacher.

Suddenly my dreams of what another culture would be like were realised. I walked into a small fibro cottage, like any other in the district, to find it furnished with beautifully designed, light-coloured furniture. The floors were of bare polished wood, with wonderful rugs on them. On the walls hung prints by Van Gogh and Cezanne. I was so excited by the strange lunatic asylum of Van Gogh's painting that I found it hard to drag my eyes away from the wall above my music stand during my weekly lesson, and to concentrate on what Mrs Nemet had to say. As a young child of seven or eight, I could not articulate the feelings I had for the exotic European interior I discovered at the Nemets'. It was an escape from the drab landscape I inhabited. I began to be very interested in the violin, and loved the two-mile bike ride to Mrs Nemet's every Saturday. The violin was strapped across the handlebars of my bike, and I would set off, sometimes in streaming rain, to arrive panting hot.

Mrs Nemet was small and quick-moving, like most violin players. She cajoled me, and began to shape my musicianship. My mother would comment on my artistic interpretation, and like all daughters, I argued with her and disagreed, preferring the advice of my teacher. Phrasing seemed different on the violin from the piano, and the ability to shape a long legato, with the bow biting into the string was a physical sensation I have always retained, and tried to reproduce when singing.

Stella and Paul Nemet were founding members of Musica Viva in Melbourne. Stella played in the Astra Chamber Orchestra for many years. Their daughter, Mary Nemet, became a concert violinist and had a wonderful career as a performer and teacher, both here and overseas.

As I grew I became 'dreamy', preferring to sit and read or draw, while the rest of the family loved *doing* things. What I wanted to do was to be an artist, and every spare moment I filled in with drawing, copying in pencil from children's books, and trying to make drawings of my own. I was a large child, always taller than average, and from the age of eight I seemed to be always falling over, spraining my ankles, or breaking my arms. My father teased me for my clumsiness, and I began to hate the thought of any physical exercise, because I dreaded hurting myself. In a family of small-boned, quick-witted jokers, I was the slow and dreamy butt of their humour.

During the war we would eat early 'tea' at six o'clock, then the four of us would sit in a line facing the wall with a loom Dad had made, and weave camouflage nets for our 'war effort'. It was fun doing this together as a family. We also played marathon games of Chinese checkers, and listened to *Dad and Dave* and *Martin's Corner* on the wireless. We followed the war with the rest of the nation with passion and commitment. The war, having begun in Europe, was our war because we were British, and gallant little Britain was 'home'.

I remember the feelings of surprise and outrage that the bombing of Darwin invoked in us all. The Japanese attack on Pearl Harbour, which began the Pacific War, gave us powerful allies, but to ordinary people in Melbourne at that time it was inconceivable that we were under any real threat. For Elizabeth and me, watching our father dig an air-raid shelter in the backyard (which rapidly filled with water and was never used), or hiding under the desk at school with corks in our mouths (to prevent biting our tongues in a 'direct hit'), it was all a dramatic and exciting game.

My mother threw herself into working for the Red Cross, the Australian Comforts Fund and the VAD (Voluntary Aid Detachment), and this as well as her interest in the local Presbyterian Church and the local Health Centre, made her life extremely busy. In the middle of the war, an American Army camp was created in an area of bush at Sandown Park, and my mother began to play for dances for the troops in the local Mechanics Hall. She loved this, and was out nearly every night of the week. On Sundays we often had a few American soldiers come for the evening meal.

Every Monday morning we had a ceremony in the schoolyard swearing allegiance to King (George VI) and Country, and singing *God Save The King*. Almost all the teachers were women for the 'Duration', but we were blessed by having the most wonderful male teacher. Mr Jenkins was retired but came back into our school, inspiring all sixty of his pupils with devotion, and managing that huge class of small boys and girls with a gentle authority. Each Friday afternoon he took us into the bush at Sandown Park, showing us how a creek had started as a plough-furrow and pointing out frogmouth owls sitting motionless in the trees near a dam, at what is now the Sandown Park Race Track.

At last Elizabeth and I, who had sat in the same class for seven years and were inseparable, were to go to Dandenong High School. Betty had been the other half of my life. Now we began to grow apart and find our own differing interests. Elizabeth was always in trouble at school for talking, and when we changed schools she discovered that life was not easy for those who held strong opinions.

At the end of 1944, in the Dandenong High School Speech Day Concert in the Dandenong Town Hall, I was chosen to sing the solo in *Land of Hope and Glory*. As I stood waiting on the curving stairs rising up to the stage from the dressing rooms below, one of the boys filing past smiled at me, and I recognised the son of one of my father's Rotarian friends. He was Graeme de Graaff, who was to become the major influence and the love of my life.

2. Presbyterian and Other Ladies

Our parents had put our names on a waiting list for the Presbyterian Ladies College in Melbourne, and we were able to start there in the second year of our secondary schooling in 1945. We two girls set off to school in the city. It was a major change in our lives, and our very different and complementary personalities became more apparent. We were given intelligence tests before being placed in our new classes. Betty was put into Middle IVA, and I into Middle IVB. This was a blow to my pride, to be the elder, but in the 'lower stream', but I think we both benefited by being separated and able to make our own friends. I found this more difficult than Betty. She found a friend in Faye Mishael, and her sister Elaine, who was in my form, became my friend.

The announcement of the end of the war came one morning during a Geography lesson in my first year at PLC. I scratched into my ruler, 'The war ended today, August 15, 1945'. We went home early through jubilant crowds, hurrying through the beautiful Treasury Gardens, down the long lines of singing elm trees, to Flinders Street station. So much pain and drama had ended. In Melbourne, far from the war, we had been suspended in time. "Wait till the war's over," had been said every day during those years.

Now, at last, it was over! And we, too young to have suffered, were filled with anticipation for a brave new world, which we were going to build ourselves.

To be a teenager in 1945 was to stand in my life at the same point as Australia seemed to be, at a time of change and growth, preparing for the excitement of maturity, yet a little apprehensive at the burgeoning future. The static society ended when war restrictions were over, and suddenly our country was pushing and reaching towards prosperity and change, after the rigours of the Depression, and then of the war. The anti-nuclear movement, the dissatisfactions of women, which gave rise to the women's movement, and even the environmental movement, all had their beginnings at this time.

Travelling to PLC each day involved a one-hour train journey each way. After the train arrived at Flinders Street, we either caught a tram, or walked the whole length of Flinders

Street and on through the Treasury Gardens. We were always worried about being late. To go to school in the city, and have pressures of academic achievement added to the ridiculous disciplinary rules of the school, was all overwhelming. I loved the academic discipline of the classroom, but hated the restrictions and pressures put on us by petty rules. The correct wearing of gloves, hats, ties, belts and stockings was inspected morning and evening at the gate by the Prefects, and to be seen talking to boys was practically a hanging offence!

I was *always* losing my gloves!

Miss McConchie was the school Head of Music. I changed violin teachers and had lessons at the school. I became a member of the school orchestra. I was not a good sight-reader, and this exercise of counting bars of rests was extremely good for me. I made friends with Anne Grieve and Lucie Fouvy and we played trios together, Anne the pianist and Lucie the cellist, giving a string trio recital on 'Young Australia' in 1945, my very first broadcast for the ABC. This was a performance of the first movement of Haydn's 1st String Trio.

I remember singing in the school choir a strange, beautiful unaccompanied song about swallows sitting on telegraph wires, by C Armstrong Gibbs. The eerie harmonies reproducing the singing of wind in the wires stay with me even now. This was music I had never heard before, and we were making it with our voices.

Melbourne at that time was still very 'proper', but one knew the world was changing. Women had held responsible positions during the war. The returning servicemen rightly expected jobs, but the women who were being displaced were not going to give up their newly won independence easily. At PLC we felt we were being prepared for careers and professions. We were never made to think that 'a woman's place is in the home'.

In my second year at the school, I joined the newly formed Junior Symphony Orchestra. John Bishop had the vision to establish an orchestral group of young people, who came together each Saturday morning in the gloom and shadows of Melba Hall at the Melbourne Conservatorium. The Con had dreadful 'vibes' from the annual violin examinations I did each year, but in the very back desk of the second violins, sawing carefully through the Ballet Music from *Rosamunde,* I tried to escape notice and keep counting, hoping to arrive at the end of the music when everyone else stopped. I was secretly astonished when, a year or so later, I was made the leader of the orchestra! The conductor was now Basil Jones, and for a year I sat just below his baton and learned to follow the beat of the orchestral conductor.

As we grew into our developing bodies, I think I always

felt physically tired. I was late in menstruating, and in developing an interest in boys. Amongst many of the girls at school, boys were the overwhelming interest, but I was not so 'driven' and was able to concentrate on schoolwork and music.

Like most girls, I was irritated by the regular monthly 'period' and felt it was unfair that girls had to put up with the inconvenience, and sometimes pain and embarrassment, of menstruation. Before I started the cycle, I always felt terribly lethargic, and just wanted to lie still and sleep all day. To talk about 'the curse' as it was called, was 'not done'. But later, as a woman singer, it was to be an extremely important part of my life, as it is of all women's lives. The terrible enervating lethargy on the day before my period began meant that later, when I had to sing and rehearse on 'those days', I found I needed more concentration to compensate for the 'dopey' feeling which engulfed me. I noticed that I had a tendency to sing flat, and my voice had a husky quality, lacking its normal brilliance.

I have rarely heard anyone talk about these matters, but one singer told me that before the Second World War it was customary for the top women singers to give their 'dates' to their agents, so that managements would not ask them to perform on those days when they were 'unwell'. I wonder if this is true? Did opera seasons then revolve around the moon cycles? Another belief was that sexual intercourse would improve a woman's performance. Yet another was that it caused mucous, and created huskiness on the vocal chords. I have a friend who says she can tell if a woman is taking 'the pill' by the quality of her voice. I wonder if these things will one day be studied scientifically? As far as I know, there has been no research into any of this, and for women singers it could be of importance. Does the use of hormones cause the vocal cords to coarsen and the quality of the voice to darken? We women have always been secretive about 'women's business' and singers retain this personal modesty, but throat specialists and vocal experts should make this information more readily available.

There are other less delicate subjects for myth making about what is good for the voice. For instance, Melba is reputed to have always drunk French champagne when she was singing. I'm sure this is not true. This would have wrecked my voice, as it would have dried it out. I always ate segments of a mandarin during performances, if my mouth was dry. I suspect that all singers have their own superstitions.

Although school was important, we still maintained our involvement with the local Presbyterian Church and our Springvale community. On the weekends we played basketball in the inter-church competitions. A remarkable Scot named Alec Wilkie started a youth club, which attracted a group of teenage boys and girls who met and played games, and went on camping trips. It was an achievement for Wilkie to persuade the Elders of our Presbyterian church to allow dancing, and we had ballroom dancing lessons in the little wooden church building.

One windy Sunday morning I set off for church on my bicycle. Riding straight into the strong wind and wearing a hat, I kept my head down and pedalled hard, hoping not to be late. Near the Health Centre, the bike came to a stop and I sailed gracefully over the handlebars, sliding down the 'boot' of a parked Vauxhall on my nose. It was badly broken and I later found it had been badly set by the doctor. This accident meant that I had difficulty breathing through one nostril, and it was always blocked when I had a cold. It did not seem important at the time, but created problems later when I became a singer.

Now I began to be envious of my little sister Betty. She had already met the boy she would love all her life, and eventually marry. Laurence (Laurie) Hart Brown was the son of Dad's business partner Alf Brown, and Elizabeth had first met him when she was twelve. Laurie, at sixteen, was six feet tall, dark and handsome. The two children looked at each other, and from then on were a couple. It was wonderful to see such commitment, but I said that I had no intention of marrying! I would have a career as an artist. I was still determined to become a book illustrator, and drew and painted as often as I could in my spare time.

Although I was still far removed from romance, now I was introduced to the erotic. Sensuality entered my life in a less than joyous way. The red thing dangling between the legs of the old man sitting opposite me in the empty train rattling between the stations of Clayton and Springvale was a thought to put to one side, and to examine in the silence of the night, before going to sleep. To see it several times out of the corner of one's eye when travelling home on the train, usually while doing mathematics homework, was very disturbing! No wonder I had problems with maths.

I was growing into a rebellious teenager. I became snobbish about the family furniture when my father, who had sold the Grain Store and bought a furniture shop, brought home new veneered furniture without consulting my mother. He threw out all the comfortable solid things we had always had, and this enraged me.

I argued with him about his politics. He was a devoted follower of R G Menzies, the Prime Minister at the time, and he worshipped Lord Casey (the Bengal Tiger!) whom he had met. He said people were only poor because they were lazy and didn't work hard enough.

At the age of fourteen, I was reading George Bernard Shaw and H G Wells, and was beginning to question the right-wing conservative values of my parents. During this emotional turmoil our family became firm friends with the Mishaels. Bert Mishael was editor of *The Age* newspaper. He was a marvellous raconteur, with fascinating tales of the time he had spent in China during the Sino-Japanese War. My father and mother began to play 'solo' with Bert and Hazel Mishael, and we girls often went to the Hartwell Presbyterian Church socials with their daughters Faye and Elaine.

We had begun to read about the Cold War at that time, when one day a plain-clothes detective came to the door and told my father that Bert was suspected of being a Russian agent. Dad had invited Bert to be a guest speaker at the Dandenong Rotary Club, to talk of his years spent in China. Dad was shocked and devastated. I don't know if Bert ever knew he was under a cloud, but we were told we were not to see the Mishael girls any more. I was furious, and said I would be friends with whomever I pleased. So we continued our friendship. On the train travelling home from school, we talked and did our homework with a couple of Dandenong boys who were going to Caulfield Grammar, one of whom was Graeme de Graaff. He got on the train at Caulfield in the afternoon, and I began to look out for him on the way through the station. By the time the train got to Carnegie most of the carriages were empty, and we would talk comfortably about the state of the world, or other more important matters, like the School Formal. A good-looking serious boy, he made me think and talk about issues that were never discussed in my busy, hedonistic family. Together we talked about 'the meaning of life' and tried to solve the big questions of the world; dismay at the nuclear race, injustice and political corruption in high places, the lack of cultural life, and the boredom of living in Melbourne at that time.

Moving up through the school, I decided that my Intermediate year would be my last at PLC. I wanted to go to Swinburne Technical College and study art. I was in a hurry to get on with 'living' and thought I should begin my chosen career. When the Headmistress, Miss Nielson, was told, she called my mother in and said she would be very upset if I left, as I should go on to University. Another battle with my poor father ensued. I don't think he cared at all about my going to University, but he did think that going to Art School was a terrible waste of money. However, he was generous enough to let me go to Swinburne, and he gave me an allowance sufficient to buy paints, paper, canvas and a 'New-Look' skirt, which he truly loathed.

And so in 1948 I began my four years as an art student. The first year was devoted to a rather unexciting syllabus, as we learned Mechanical Drawing (drawing the threads on screws, etc) and drawing and 'rendering' in pencil the plaster busts of Julius Caesar and other ancient Romans, which stood on the high shelves running round the room. The class that year comprised not only nice little girls coming straight from school, but a group of ex-servicemen who had served in New Guinea. Often they were away from classes, returning with the yellowed complexion

16

of a recent malaria attack. Their presence made one aware of the seriousness of life, and of their desire to achieve great things in a short time, to make up for the years they had lost.

We did some pottery for a year, and in second year began watercolour, life drawing and oil painting. I began a course called 'The Art of the Book', which was my real interest. I learned the techniques of woodcut, etching, lithography, bookbinding and a little about typesetting. The days flew by.

At home, I was looking for more exciting friendships. Riding on the back of a motorbike, I enjoyed the sensation of flying and the leather jacket to which I clung, as we wound around corners, leaning dangerously. I had two boy friends who had motorbikes, to my father's disapproval and rage.

The local Presbyterian minister, dour old Mr Goble, all hell-fire and damnation, was replaced by gentle Mr Billings, who had a sweet wife and two children. Their daughter Helen was our age and had been with us at PLC, and her elder brother Bob was at University. He seemed so handsome, grown-up and sophisticated, and I developed a 'crush' on him. I heard that he was learning singing. I decided to stop having violin lessons, as my days were so full, and mother suggested that I, too, have some singing lessons, just for fun. Together we had been to see Bob sing in the Hawthorn Light Opera Company production of *The Gondoliers*. We were pleased he sang well, but were absolutely enthralled by the talent of the leading soprano, Marie Collier. I decided I wanted to learn from her teacher, Katherine Wielaert.

One late winter afternoon I walked up the 'Paris end' of Collins Street, the bare branches of the plane trees reflecting in the shining puddles from the lights of Jonas' Fruit Shop. Climbing the narrow flights of stairs on that first afternoon was a strange experience. I had never been nervous about singing. I had sung all my life, without thought, often unaware I was making a sound. Now I was to learn to do something I had always done naturally. The door at the top of the stairs was opened by a frail little woman who said, "Come in and wait please." After a short time Madame Wielaert called me, and I entered the large studio-sitting room in which she taught. She was a short, stout, tightly corseted little woman with steel-grey hair cut severely short in an Eton crop, and she had remarkable, rather prominent blue eyes.

"Now Lauris, sing this scale," she said, seating herself at the upright piano.

She took me up and down the scale a few times, then higher and higher, then lower and lower, then I sang some long slow notes, and at last she said, "I'll accept you as a pupil. You will come at 4.30 each Thursday."

So my first singing audition was passed.

I lived the next year in a kind of dreamy vacuum. I spent the hours and days between my classes at Swinburne learning to develop vocally, and yet still wishing to draw and illustrate books, before anything else. On Thursday afternoons after my art class I made my pilgrimage to Madame Wielaert's studio. I was always both excited and fearful. When my mother first suggested I learn to sing, I sang as a child, with a small clear voice, without thought. Now I had to sing 'long notes' and exercises, which always sounded the same to me, but which my teacher said were either good or bad, or right or wrong; I had no way of telling which was which. It all seemed a mystery, and my scales, arpeggios and 'long notes' stretched from one Thursday to the next. I was stopped at the same places every week, and I never knew when it *was* right or wrong.

But one day an enormous, frightening sound came from my mouth, and I felt a resonance in my body, and a sensation like a counter-weight inside me. It was a different and new adult sound I was making. After a time, this strange new voice, short of breath and unpredictable as to pitch, began to take wings, and I could sing my first songs, Handel's *Ombra mai fu* and Brahms' *Sapphic Ode* with some degree of control and pleasure. I remember the loss of singing as a natural part of me. From now on, it was always to be worked on, learned and worried about; a challenge and a discipline, my Doppelgänger, 'The Voice'. Forever now, I was hooked like an addict, to my beloved art.

Madame Wielaert taught a method of singing which I now believe to be dangerous, at least for me. She taught her pupils to 'groove' the tongue, pulling the tongue down at the root, so that, on looking in a mirror, one could see the tongue looking like a perfect heart-shape. Mario Lanza, starring in the film *The Great Caruso* at this time, sang with this perfectly shaped tongue, and was held up as our model. I now think some people do this naturally when they sing, but it was really difficult for me to pull the tongue down in such an unnatural way. The introduced strain at the root of the tongue meant that most of Madame Wielaert's pupils had difficulty with their top notes. But she developed great strength and beauty in my voice at the right time.

In my second year of singing, at her suggestion, I entered in a few sections in the Dandenong Festival. I have a memory of sitting in the Dandenong Town Hall listening to other people singing. My first hearing of *The Willow Song* from Verdi's *Otello* reduced me to hysterical giggles, as the poor girl singing "Weee-low" so softly, suddenly let out a gigantic squawk with which she finished her aria. Of my own performance I have no memory at all, and it was only recently, on finding the adjudicator's report, that I even knew I had taken part.

I began to go to Saturday classes at the National Theatre in the old hall at St Peter's, Eastern Hill. Founded by Gertrude Johnson before the war, these classes in stagecraft and drama provided a wonderful training ground for the remarkable crop of singers in Melbourne at that time. The National Theatre also

1. The courting couple, my
parents, Harry Elms with Jean Halford.

2. Four generations. Standing, Grandmother Halford
with her daughter, Jean Elms, and great-grandmother
Carter holding baby Lauris on her knee.

he Halfords, my mother's
ily. L to R, standing: Stan,
e, Marjorie, George,
, Lindsay and Jim.
ed: the Rev James Halford
randma, Elsie May Halford.

4. Our house, Athol, at Springvale.

5. Betty and Lauris about 1935.

6. Lauris, Mother and Betty about 1945.

7. L to R: Lauris, Harry (Father), Betty and Jean (Mother) dressed for a wedding.

8. Ernest and Isabel de Graaff departing to fly to Southport,
for a golfing holiday with Jean and Harry Elms.

9. The Elms' camp at Cape Woolami, about 1949. L to R: Lauris, Harry, Edith, Jean, Alf, Murraie (Forster) McFarlane, Leigh Matthews, Betty and Geoff Haw.

10. My departure from Port Melbourne on the *Strathnaver* in December, 1954. Mother, Betty, Lauris and father.

11. Dolly and Dominique Modesti.

12. The Modesti studio in 1955. L to R, standing: Barbara Wilson, Robert Allman, Lance Ingram (Albert Lance) and Elizabeth Fretwell, who was visiting Paris. Seated: Nance Rassmussen, a coy Lauris Elms and Dominique Modesti.

13. Madame Daïan and Lauris striding out on the Champs Elysées.

14. My first role at Covent Garden in 1957 was as Mlle Arvidson in Verdi's *Un ballo in maschera*. Here I am in the same role, in the Australian Opera's production in Sydney in 1985, where I am called Ulrica. Photograph by Branco Gaica, courtesy of Opera Australia.

15. Mrs Sedley in *Peter Grimes* of Benjamin Britten,
the photo of his fiancée Graeme showed his friends when he was at Oxford.
Courtesy of the Theatre Museum © Victoria & Albert Picture Library.

16. As Anna in *The Trojans (Les Troyens)* of Berlioz at The Royal Opera House, Covent Garden in 1957. Courtesy of the Theatre Museum © Victoria & Albert Picture Library.

17. As Micah in Handel's *Samson*. Courtesy of the Theatre Museum © Victoria & Albert Picture Library.

mounted a short professional opera season each year. Miss Johnson gave Melbourne, and Australia, an operatic heritage which has still to be properly acknowledged. There was no full-time opera company, and singers like Elizabeth Fretwell, Marie Collier, Justine Rettick, Morris Williams, Keith Neilson, Neil Warren-Smith, Robert Simmons, Lance Ingram and Robert Allman had their first stage experience here.

We started classes on Saturday mornings about ten o'clock, learning music, and in the afternoon we were given some individual instruction in stage movement, and then brought together in scenes from opera, directed by Stefan Haag.

One of the first things I sang was the Susanah-Countess duet from *The Marriage of Figaro,* which I performed with great difficulty, as I found it incredibly high! We all loved these classes, and I remember many of the young singers there with great affection, in particular a tall young baritone named Leonard Delany. Len and I began going to concerts together, and staying in the city to have dinner, when we could afford it. Len lived another life as a milkman; he found that working at night and early in the morning gave him time during the day to work on his voice, and learn repertoire. He was very ambitious, had a much greater knowledge of opera than I, and contributed to my musical and operatic education.

That year I saw my very first professional opera, a marvellous performance of Verdi's *Aïda,* sung by Betna Pontin, with the great dramatic soprano Marjorie Lawrence as Amneris, at the Princess Theatre in Melbourne. Betna Pontin also studied with my teacher, who was a fervent Christian Scientist. At the end of this, my second year with her, she arranged for me to sing a religious solo once a month at the First Church of Christ, Scientist, in St Kilda Road. This was a very good way for me to gain experience and confidence, she said. I was given a small fee, which helped to pay for my coaching. I was beginning to work regularly on repertoire with National Theatre coach Paul Arndt, and he helped me learn the new music I was studying.

I was still at Swinburne, now in my third year, and somehow balancing my love of both artistic activities, when Madame Wielaert persuaded me to enter radio station 3KZ's 'Swallows P&A Parade'. The show was performed 'live' on a Sunday evening, in front of a small audience in the station's theatrette.

My memory of performing up to this time is very hazy. Like many young singers, I was not yet secure in my technique and still unsure what sound was going to emerge under stress. On that Sunday afternoon before my first appearance (or 'heat'), my sister Betty travelled with me to Madame Wielaert's studio in the grey winter's afternoon, so that I could have a 'warm-up' before going down to the radio station. We clattered up the dark staircase above the fruit shop to be welcomed by my teacher and her sister. Madame sat down at the piano and I stood up to sing, but NO SOUND CAME OUT. I did not have any cold or sore throat. Madame did not believe in illness, and she used every possible trick to get me to sing, as well as sternly talking to me about her Christian Science beliefs, but nothing happened.

I think I was so petrified with nerves that my throat just seized up. Many years before, I had seen a film in which this had happened to my idol, Deanna Durbin. Did some memory of this influence me?

The radio station had to make an announcement that I was 'indisposed', which we were in time to hear broadcast on the radio when we got home to Springvale by train. But was I ill? I did not have any voice for a week afterwards. 3KZ were kind enough to let me appear in the 'Newcomers' Section' four weeks later. In the successive heats of the competition I sang *Danny Boy, My Ain Folk* and *Knowest thou the land?* from Thomas' opera *Mignon*. At the end of the year I won this 'Newcomers' Section', singing for the first time with an orchestra.

One of the other winners of the 'P&A Parade' that year was Johnny O'Keefe, singing in the 'Pop Section'.

At the end of 1952 I was asked to sing in 'Carols by Candlelight' in the Botanic Gardens. Looking out over the thousand lights from the candles of the crowd there that night, I felt for the first time the mystery of holding an audience in the palm of one's hand, even for a brief moment. The conductor of the orchestra was Hector Crawford, an important figure in Melbourne music, and later in Australian television. His wife, Glenda Raymond, had one of the most beautiful soprano voices in Australia and sang in the long-running radio series, 'The Life of Melba'. Hector ran 'The Mobil Quest', the most important talent quest for operatic voices on radio. Hector Crawford was to become a powerful television production company owner.

Also singing that night was Marie Collier, in a performance of *The Holy City* that I have never forgotten. She brought passion and drama to everything she sang, and as I stood watching in admiration from the wings, I was appalled to see a moth hover around her opened mouth. "Hosanna in the highest" she sang, her black eyes raised to the starry sky. The moth flew into her mouth and out again on her wonderful long top note!

For the first of many times, I became aware of the terrors associated with outdoor performances. They may be wonderful for the audience, but they are always nerve-racking for the performers.

After the publicity surrounding my win in 'The P & A Parade', 1953 saw my debut as a performer, and my other life came to an end. I completed my fourth year at Swinburne, easily the least enjoyable. With hindsight, I suppose I was realising my true vocation as a singer. I was no longer enjoying the 'routine' of my Art classes. The spark had gone from me, and my joy in drawing. We had to spend time drawing from life and painting in oils, when I would rather have been etching, and learning about book illustrating and print-making.

At the end of the year I was not awarded my Diploma, because, although I had achieved very good marks in all other subjects, I failed in Life Drawing. It was a terrible blow to my pride.

So it was time for me to look for a job. With my folio under my arm, I set off each day with no success. It was very depressing, and after a time I took a job at Murfetts, the greeting card manufacturer. I was ushered into a dark basement, where I sat in front of a screen, rather like a computer screen, on which was thrown up an enlarged black and white negative of a greeting card. The print comprised thousands of minute dots, and I was there to fill in any dots or flaws which had been missed by the negative printer. I was to place the smallest possible spot on what was a blank place. After four years intensive training as an artist, this seemed a truly miserable place to end up.

My real life began after dark, when I sang. I began to receive engagements, one of my first being a concert with the Myer Choir in the Myer Mural Hall. At that time Myers Department Store had a wonderful choir which rehearsed regularly and performed concerts with an orchestra several times a year, conducted by Leslie Curnow.

Madame Wielaert's son, Tristan (known un-operatically as Bill), was the Electricity Commission's chief engineer in Mt Beauty, and he invited me to sing for the local Music Club. My fellow artist was the Aboriginal singer, Harold Blair, who was also a pupil of Madame Wielaert. I sang *Down in the Forest* by Landon Ronald, *My Dear Soul* by Wilfred Sanderson, and *Softly Awakes My Heart* from Saint-Saëns' opera *Samson and Delilah,* in English. Our accompanist was my mother, Jean Elms.

With the ABC Dance Band, conducted by Frank Thorne, I sang *Beautiful Dreamer,* by Stephen Foster, and *I Heard a Forest Praying,* by Peter De Rose, in a program called 'My Song Goes Round the World' in January 1953. This was my first appearance for the ABC with an orchestra, and the program went 'live to air'. These songs, and the others previously mentioned, were my entire repertoire at this time. As I began to sing in public, I had to search for new songs, and finding songs with a very low tessitura to suit my contralto voice was always difficult.

In March that year came my momentous operatic debut. I was engaged to sing five performances of Vera Boronel in the opera *The Consul* for the National Theatre. I found it exciting and nerve-racking when I had to do a complicated little dance in the opera's dream sequence.

This piece was still very topical at the time, and was

produced by Stefan Haag in a tremendously dramatic production. My idol, Marie Collier, was Magda Sorel and the conductor was Joseph Post. John Shaw was the sinister Police Inspector, and the cast also included Robert Simmons, Dorothea Deegan, Justine Rettick, Joyce Simmons, Robert Allman, Elizabeth Fretwell and Lorenzo Nolan as the Magician who produced a rabbit from a hat and doves from his cuffs. Wilma Whitney was Vera Boronel, and I was to alternate in five performances of this role in the season. Stefan Haag himself played the small role of Assan. The designer was Louis Kahan. As dramatic as any play or film of the day, its potent message of displaced persons in Europe at that time was heartbreaking. The whole production was the sensation of the National Theatre's 1953 season.

All the singers in the Company were part-time professionals, having to earn a living for most of the year, and getting 'time off' from their daytime jobs to sing with the Company when an opera season was in progress. Some of Australia's greatest singers began their careers hurrying from office, bank or schoolroom to the theatre, to put on make-up and appear in operas for these National Theatre opera seasons.

After *The Consul's* success, the National decided to take it on tour throughout Victoria. Many of the singers resigned from their jobs and went on tour, for the present becoming 'full-time' singers for the first time of their lives. I was asked to join the tour, but decided not to do so. I was still very insecure vocally. The company needed two casts in case of illness, and I would have 'covered' (understudied) The Secretary, as well as singing half the performances of Vera Boronel.

The conductor Eric Clapham took the production around country Victoria where it was played in cities large and small. On the tiny stages of places as remote as Numurka and Colac, the brilliant set of Louis Kahan and the superb production of Stefan Haag seemed to work just as well.

There were many stories about this tour. When the live rabbit grew too big for Lorenzo to hide in his sleeve, it mysteriously disappeared to be replaced by a smaller new one. The cast very much enjoyed a rabbit stew on those days!

Playing in small country halls meant adapting the larger orchestra to a chamber ensemble, and Harry Jacob cleverly arranged the parts, giving the second clarinet all the parts that were not covered by the existing instruments, except for the timpani part which was played on the piano by Max Olding.

The most extraordinary moment on tour occurred when Magda Sorel, at the tragic climax of the drama, contemplates suicide by gassing herself. Sitting on the floor in front of the open gas-oven door, she sings sadly, "I never meant to do this." One night, on the steeply-raked stage of the little country hall, the dreadful gas stove began to roll down-hill towards the horrified orchestra seated below, with Marie Collier (Magda), her head in the oven, hurrying after it on her knees, trying to catch it, and catch up with it, before it crashed over the edge!

Left behind at home in Springvale, I was feeling my way in my new vocal world, and exploring and finding my voice as each week went by. I still had difficulty singing any note above the stave, and really did not know how to achieve a secure top note; it was mostly a matter of luck if I did! I was flattered to be asked to go away on the tour, but I knew it was too soon. I really still needed my regular weekly lessons. Stefan Haag was annoyed, and perhaps this had later repercussions for me.

At this time I was asked to appear as a guest soloist on the ABC program 'The Village Glee Club'. After my first appearance, I was asked to join the show on a weekly basis as the singer, Mrs Sharpshott, whose 'speaking voice' was that of distinguished actress Agnes Dobson. Each character, except solo soprano Kathleen Goodall, had two people performing, one a singer and another to speak the lines of the script, which portrayed a regular village choir practice, with an amusing narrative running through the dialogue. Pompous Mr Crump, the Choirmaster, would gossip or flirt with the other characters. This popular ABC program ran for thirty years. Dan Hardy was the resident ABC choral conductor, and conducted The Melbourne Singers who became the Choir of the little Glee Club for this program. This group included some of Melbourne's best voices. I remember the memorable operatic bass voice of Fred Collier rolling out like an organ week after week. Fred may have been over seventy years old at the time, but still made a magnificent sound. Charles Skase was the baritone. The tenor was Herbert Brown, comic patter was rattled off by Syd Hollister, while Joan Arnold was one of the sopranos. The strikingly beautiful Muriel Luyke was one of the contraltos, and she replaced me as the solo voice of Mrs Sharpshott when I left.

Each of the principal characters was given a solo to sing in the show. We also had distinguished overseas and local soloists on the program, and it was wonderful to hear the great baritone Peter Dawson, who was probably nearly seventy when he sang one afternoon on the Glee Club.

I received a fee of three guineas (£3.3.0) for the afternoon's work of about two hours. I had to learn a song, generally an English ballad, and was given a copy of the music on each Tuesday for performance in the following week's show. We read through the script and rehearsed the show once, and then went to air, finishing a recording about 4.30pm, for re-play at 7.30pm.

I was not a quick sight-reader, and found it took me some time to have a song prepared to my liking. I believe that one must have a song 'sung in', and sight singing is always

23

disappointingly apparent to me in other people's performance. There are some eminent performers who rely on picking up the music at the last moment, and I think their performance is sadly short-changed by the lack of actual vocal practice. While being a good sight-reader has many advantages, it is not a substitution for solid practice, which results in the sound being 'placed'. I practised even the simplest ballad, until it was physically 'sung in' as well as I could make it. The voice learns, with its muscles, how to place the next note, and prepares, before the act of singing it, to make the adjustment. Singing is an athletic experience, involving both the great muscles of breath-control in ribs and lungs, and the tiny organs of the throat and larynx. The 'art' comes in making the voice sound completely natural when these different actions are combined to produce the sustained sound we call singing. The few times in my professional life that I had to sing something 'at sight' were a disaster, both vocally and artistically.

The experience of singing every week on radio, with the professional members of the ABC Singers critically listening to my every note, was invaluable. Dan Hardy and Colin Crane, in particular, liked to offer me their vocal advice, and said I would not sing for much longer if I continued with my present habits! I was already becoming insecure about my singing technique, and this had the effect of making me very defensive of my teacher and her methods.

My singing life was going ahead, but my work as a visual artist was at a stalemate. After carrying my folio to many studios, I still could not find work, and in the middle of the year I applied for a job in the Art Department at the Methodist Ladies College in Glenferrie Road, Melbourne.

I was interviewed by Dr Wood, whom I later discovered was held in awe by all Melbourne Methodists. I did not know of his standing in that particular church community, and to me he seemed to be a kind and charming old man. I found that I was required to teach only Craft and not Art and because of my four years at Swinburne, was given a teacher's salary. My first teaching project was to get the girls to make cane thermos baskets. This involved soaking the cane in cold water until it was pliant, in the winter term. Preparing the cane each morning was agony, and the Melbourne winter proceeded to give both teacher and pupils a fine crop of chilblains on our hands. Maybe this was why it became so difficult to get some of the girls to finish their baskets. Ten years later, I saw one of these dreadful objects for sale in an opportunity shop window in Glenferrie Road. In the Studio were three young apprentice teachers, all ex-MLC girls, who were teaching Craft. They had much more skill in their subject, and were also attending teacher-training classes. They were kind enough to give me instructions day by day, in order to keep me one step ahead of my pupils. Claire Rigby in particular became a life-long friend.

The staff were very kind to me as my singing career developed. They helped to ease my load, went to concerts I was in and listened to me win the radio competition at the end of the year.

In 1953 Dr Schildberger from the National Theatre conducted the Brighton Choir in a performance of a cantata by Schumann called *The Pilgrimage of the Rose,* and I sang the contralto solos. I wonder if this was a 'first performance' in Australia?

To celebrate the young Queen Elizabeth's impending visit, the Myer Choir, conducted by Neil Curnow, put on a performance of *Merrie England.* I sang for the first time *O peaceful England,* the solo given to Queen Bess by the composer Edward German. I sang this again a short time later with George Logie-Smith conducting. George was to become an important part of my life, as he gave me many engagements and helped to shape my attitude towards singing in oratorio. He founded the Astra Chamber Music Society and taught music, first at Geelong College then at Scotch College.

At the end of the year the ABC engaged me for my very first *Messiah* in the Melbourne Town Hall, in a performance called 'The Citizens Take Part', conducted by Clive Douglas with the Melbourne Symphony Orchestra. Concert singing in a vast hall like the Melbourne Town Hall, alone with one's voice and the orchestra, presenting the great solos of Handel, was a new and confronting challenge. This was the most important engagement I had so far attempted. It was one of four *Messiahs* I sang that year – the others were in Ballarat, Bendigo and Geelong.

The opera had given me an opportunity to work with some really great local singers. The director Stefan Haag was wonderfully demanding, but acting was standing in another character's shoes, which gave me a mask to put on and wear, and to hide behind. The experience of standing alone on stage to sing is quite different to being part of the shifting and moving operatic stage. To learn to convey passion and commitment solely with one's voice and artistry is very lonely, and one feels completely exposed and vulnerable. All my life, I found the musical quality of the concert repertoire was more satisfying intellectually than the operatic, but opera was more fun, because one was part of the ensemble.

It was George Logie-Smith who taught me how best to approach the music of *Messiah.* He believed that the work had the sweep of any great dramatic narrative. The biblical texts demand the same style as any operatic performance. George shouted and raged at his choirs, demanding their total attention and commitment for every second of the rehearsal and performance. And beside me stood the fiery-haired Robert Payne, singing of *The Refiner's Fire* with his splendid baritone voice. Here was a model to emulate, as he declaimed his recitatives with all the passion of a great preacher, added to his stylish singing voice.

Messiah's contralto solos seemed to be written for three different voices. The first, *O thou that tellest good tidings to Zion,* seemed much lower in range than *He shall feed his flock,* and for me, then and ever afterwards, the easiest vocally was *He was despised.*

Singing *Messiah* was a trial at Christmas time, as it was always hot. Tradition demanded that the female soloists wore long white dresses, looking like a pair of brides at a wedding, whilst I, singing quite truthfully, *Behold, a virgin,* wished we did not have to wear long white suede or satin gloves! It was hotter still for the men, in their formal 'tails'! Air-conditioning was not common at that time, and at the end of each concert everyone was bathed in perspiration.

On those breathlessly hot summer nights, I found that most of the audience would doze off during the *Pastoral symphony.* The men in particular seemed unable to stay awake, and I would have bets with myself as to which one would actually snore out loud first.

This quiet and gentle music at first nearly reduced me to sleep too, and I realised I had to develop a technique to stay awake myself during the long breaks between my solos. I found that if I concentrated on the music as if I were playing it on my violin, I enjoyed it much more and I was never bored. At that time, *Messiah* was always given with the biggest possible choir, sometimes with an organ, sometimes with a large orchestra. Most of these orchestras were amateur and bad, but the choirs were almost always very good.

Our new Queen Elizabeth visited Australia in 1954. The whole nation was gripped in a fever of admiration for her youth and beauty. The National Theatre presented a wonderful production by Stefan Haag of Offenbach's *The Tales of Hoffmann,* to which the Queen and Prince Philip were invited.

I was engaged to sing The Voice of the Mother in all performances, except for the Royal Performance. I felt upset, but it was explained to me that Justine Rettick, who would sing this role only once on this special occasion, was a long-standing member of the company, and it should be her 'right' to sing before the Queen.

So I got on with learning the great trio in the opera, and also the tiny role of Annina in Verdi's *La traviata,* with Barbara Wilson in the lead as Violetta. The tenor in *Hoffmann* was Lance Ingram; Barbara sang Olympia; Marie Collier, Giullietta; and Elizabeth Fretwell, the beautiful role of Antonia. It was always a thrill for me to sing with her, as our voices blended so well. The timbre and quality of her voice seemed a higher extension of my own.

Lennox Brewer was the producer of *La traviata* that season. The principals were Barbara Wilson and Raymond Macdonald. After the very 'tight' direction of Stefan Haag, and with my lack of experience on stage, I dreaded standing in the background while Violetta and Alfredo 'got on' with the end of the opera.

"What do I do while they are singing?" I timidly asked Len.

"Oh da-a-arling" he drawled, "just do a little bit of business in the corner!"

The magnificent costumes by Louis Kahan, with which the *Hoffmann* production was dressed, and the surprisingly low attendances for the Royal Opera Season, made the National Theatre bankrupt that year. We were all devastated. The season had been such a huge artistic success! It was said that the people stayed away because they had lined the streets in the daytime to see the Queen and the Duke, and were too tired to go out at night to the opera!

The temporary demise of the National Theatre was a tragedy, and many young singers began to plan to go abroad to further their careers.

A permanent worry was the condition of my teeth. My parents had both worn dentures from an early age. It was quite common for country people who suffered toothache to have all their teeth out! This solved a problem for life. When I was a child, there were no chemical trace elements in our very pure water in the district around Dandenong. One effect was a high incidence of thyroid deficiency, caused by a lack of natural iodine in the water, and another was a very high rate of tooth-decay.

There was no dentist in Springvale when we were children, and consequently I had seldom been to a dentist in my life. When a young man set up a practice for the first time in Springvale, I went along to be told that I had to have dozens of fillings. I was then in my late teens. I spent many hours in the dental chair looking out of the window at the sky, while a very old-fashioned drill whirred away in my head. My teeth were to be an ongoing problem for the rest of my life.

I was also facing a personal crisis with my singing at this time. I now knew that Madame Wielaert taught a method of singing which was dangerous for my voice. I began to find, after my first successes, and as I became busy with my new career, that now in my fourth year of singing, my throat grew hot and my voice tired quickly. I needed to find a new teacher before any permanent damage was done.

But how could I do this without hurting Madame Wielaert, who had given me such a new direction to my life? She had changed my ambitions when she unlocked my voice. She had made me aware of a pleasure I never knew existed, and that I had possessed as an unknown gift. I owed her so much, yet I knew I would not be able to sing for long if I continued to sing in this way. There was no other teacher in Melbourne that I would trust with my newly-discovered treasure, and I had no-one I could confide in. The busy winter days passed, while I secretly wondered how to escape to another life.

3. The Modestis

One day the telephone rang, and a friend of my mother asked if I would like to audition for some French people who were in Melbourne on a visit, and who wanted to hear a contralto. The voice of Kathleen Ferrier had impressed Madame Modesti, and she was keen to find another voice of this kind, if such a singer existed. Contraltos were, and still are, a rare voice type.

This friend of my mother knew Linda Phillips, music critic for *The Sun* newspaper. Linda asked her to contact me, as she remembered my voice from the 'P & A Parade'. So one wintry afternoon, after teaching at MLC, I took the tram down Glenferrie Road to the Toorak Road corner, and walked into the lives of the Modestis.

I was shy and nervous standing before these two impressive people, but Madame Modesti, with her direct questions about my aims and present situation, managed to put me at ease in her very businesslike way, so that after a few minutes I was singing, unaccompanied, all my not very large song and operatic repertoire. Monsieur Modesti sat at the piano, like a huge bear, stabbing out the first note I had to sing with one finger, and speaking in a strange mixture of French and English. At the end of about an hour Madame brought out some of her own music and I tried to sight-read some of these songs. Monsieur Modesti took me through some exercises and the room grew dark. The lights were turned on and the curtains were drawn, and still they wanted me to sing.

I knew it was getting very late. What would my father and mother say? We always had 'tea' at six o'clock! They would be worried. I was so shy before these sophisticated French people that I didn't even ask to ring my parents to let them know I would be late! Finally, about eight o'clock, they asked me to go to Paris. I would have free lessons with Monsieur Modesti for a period of two years.

Madame said in her loud voice, "You are to go in the 'Sun Aria' and win it," (just like that, I thought with an inward smile) "and you must now try to gather as much money as you can. Living in Paris will be very expensive."

It was very late when I got home that night, and mother and father were sitting up in their bed, waiting for me. I rushed into their bedroom and gasped, "Can I go to Paris?"

And my dear Dad said, "Of course."

The Modestis departed for Paris, and I was left to ponder the decision I had made. Madame Wielaert was not very pleased that I was going away "to study with those French people."

At the back of my mind there was a notion that Frenchmen were all wicked libertines and this large man who was from another world might well qualify, with his wicked black eyes and strange garbled speech. I wondered what had I got into? Perhaps they were white slavers, these two large strangers? But I knew I had to get out of Melbourne and away from my present life, and never for one moment did I confess my fears to anyone. I discovered that two other Melbourne singers were also going to Paris to study with Modesti. That was reassuring. There was safety in numbers.

A year later, leaning against the sink in Madame Modesti's tiny kitchen, postponing my departure from the studio in Paris after my lessons, I heard the story of the lives of the Modestis. My dark suspicions about Dominique Modesti could not have been further from the truth.

How these two people changed the lives of three Australian singers, and influenced the lives of many others, is an extraordinary story.

On January 6th, 1898, Dominique Modesti was born in Setif, in French Algiers, into the Corsican family of a minor customs official; and nineteen days later at the opposite end of the world in Sydney, Australia, Dorothy Violet Smith was born.

As Norma Smith she attended Abbotsleigh School, and was sixteen when the family moved to Melbourne. There she attended the Albert Street Conservatorium, hoping to have a career as a pianist. But she discovered that she had a fine voice and started singing lessons at the same time as Gertrude Johnson. She also had a few lessons from Melba, on one of her visits to Melbourne.

When she was only seventeen, she married into the wealthy Gadsden family. The young couple had two beautiful children but their marriage did not work out and, at twenty-two, Norma Gadsden decided to leave her husband and her two children, and see if her voice held the key to her future.

She travelled to Paris, where she found lodgings in the same 'pension' as Marjorie Lawrence and began her singing studies with Dinh Gilly. She hoped that Lawrence, the newly emerging star, would help another young Australian, but Lawrence was installed as the girl-friend of the family's son, and had no intention of giving any quarter of her privileged position to a potential rival. Besides, I suspect Dolly was too good-looking for Marjorie to want her staying in the house for long. She was the most strikingly beautiful woman; blue-eyed and statuesque, she looked the perfect Wagnerian soprano.

Madame Modesti, singing under the name of Norma Gadsden, worked for a year in Breslau studying German and the Wagnerian repertoire with the great coach Markovitz. With her warm voice, placed between a mezzo and a soprano in quality, she attracted the notice of the conductor von Hoesslin and the director Teichen, who engaged her to sing Sieglinde in *Die Walküre* for her Monte Carlo debut on January 2nd, 1937. On January 29th she sang her first *Walküre* Brünnhilde, conducted by von Hoesslin. It seems to me a remarkable achievement for a young soprano to sing these huge roles for the first time, in the same month. She sang Brünnhilde in Brussels on September 11th that year. Over the next few years she sang most of the great Wagnerian roles, singing all three Brünnhildes in *The Ring,* appearing at the Festival of Zopperter in Belgium, and at Aix-la-Chapelle. Von Hoesslin subsequently persuaded her to go to Germany to audition, and she sang Waltraute in *Götterdämmerung* at the Bayreuth Festival under the baton of Furtwängler, and Marina in *Boris Godunov* opposite the greatest Boris of all time, Chaliapin, in his last performance just before his death. She also created the role of Marie-Louise in *L'aiglon* of Honneger.

Dolly met her future husband when he had to go to a singing engagement at some distance outside Paris. Dolly had a car, and Madame Gilly asked her to drive him. On the way, the car broke down with a flat tyre. Dolly told Dominique to go and change the tyre, and he, looking helpless, confessed he hadn't the faintest idea how to do this. So Dolly did it herself. This was the beginning of a relationship that lasted 60 years.

The boy Dominique attended the 'lycée' in his home city of Algiers, and had completed two years of a teacher training course when he was drafted into the army during the 1914-18 war, aged seventeen. He described his very first day in the trenches, when his commanding officer sent the young boy with his 'copains' over the top. On that horrendous day, as they attacked out of the trench, his best friend fell mortally wounded beside him.

The war, or his part in it, ended and he returned to Algiers, and soon began teaching at a primary school. Someone noticed his gifts as a painter, and arranged for him to go to Paris to study art.

In the French capital he began to enjoy a vibrant social life. One evening he was singing at a party when the pianist turned to him and said, "You have a really wonderful voice. You should be a singer, not a painter." She was a voice teacher and gave him free lessons for a year, at which point he decided to audition for the Paris Opéra.

A painter friend said to him, "You're mad to want to be a singer. It is hard enough being a painter! My father-in-law is an administrator at the Paris Opéra. I'll arrange an audition and that will soon show you how hard it is to have a career as a singer, when you encounter the competition and the heartbreak of all the rejections you will face."

The audition was arranged. The Paris Opéra immediately offered Modesti a full scholarship with Dinh Gilly. He says that the audition panel were so impressed by his range that they believed he could be either a heldentenor or a baritone. He spent a year with Gilly, who was the reigning French baritone of the day. The Paris Opéra then heard him sing again, and explained that although they thought his singing was splendid, they could not engage him immediately as he had no stage experience and the principal opera house in France demanded 'stars' with major reputations on its stage. "Go into the provinces and get some experience, and we will have you sing for us then."

After auditioning in many provincial houses, he appeared at Bordeaux where he sang major roles including Donner in *Das Rheingold,* in French; but he was constantly being told everywhere that he would be engaged immediately if only he had more experience, and if he had sung in Paris.

At last Dominique Modesti was successful in obtaining a contract. The then Director of the opera of Monte Carlo was a passionate lover of Wagner, and had translated *Parsifal* into French. By having performances of his translations staged, he hoped to have all his Wagner translations sanctioned for use in all the French opera houses. At this time most operas were sung in French in metropolitan France and at Monte Carlo, but no well-known German Wagnerian baritone would agree to sing the huge role of Klingsor in French.

When this Director heard Modesti's phenomenal voice, he knew he had found his French Klingsor at last and engaged him, giving him a contract for one year to learn the role. With his magnificent and powerful voice, Modesti was singing in a major opera house at last. It was surely a 'make or break' choice for a first role. His next role in Monte Carlo was equally challenging, Telramund in *Lohengrin.*

"If I hadn't been so inexperienced, I should never have attempted it," he said. "I didn't know how terrifying it would be. I had a naturally placed voice, and after learning the notes, thought that was all there was to going on stage to perform."

Dominique sang this role opposite Norma Gadsden as Ortrud. These two beautiful, strong and passionate people, who had been born at the opposite ends of the world in the same year, then raged at each other as Tosca and Scarpia. Eventually they married.

Dominique Modesti sang Lord Henry Ashton in *Lucia di*

Lammermoor many times with the great Lily Pons. The flamboyant role of Mephistopheles in Berlioz' *The Damnation of Faust* was one of his favourites. His Rigoletto, and Athanaël in *Thaïs* became famous all over France.

He had a voice which was made for Wagner and he now began to be pressured to sing in German. But he hated singing in that language, for he could neither memorise nor understand it. He said ruefully that he just could not get his tongue to pronounce it! At Monte Carlo he had to turn down some performances of Wagner because he refused to sing in German.

It was in Bayreuth in that year, when Dolly went to sing the *Götterdämmerung* Waltraute, that the Modestis met their life-long friend Friedelind Wagner, the grand-daughter of Richard, and the rebellious Anglophile of the Wagner family. Dolly told me that after the first performance of *The Ring* with Furtwängler conducting, there was to be a dinner reception for all the cast, at which Hitler was to be the principal guest, or perhaps the host. Dominique, being very dark and a Corsican, was not invited. Dolly refused to go. This was to be her first and last time at Bayreuth.

Dolly's daughter Georgine Gadsden was staying with the Modestis at the outbreak of the war of 1939. During that long drawn-out period when nothing seemed to happen, all Frenchmen were obliged to register for military service. Dominique returned to Algiers to do so. Dolly, with their one-year-old son, young Dominique, and Georgine, followed. For six months they lived in a hotel in Algiers. Almost as soon as the army was formed the fighting began, and six months later France fell. With the armistice, Modesti was demobilised.

Dolly, Georgine and the baby Dominique Modesti, who were travelling on British passports, were able to go to Casablanca, and from there they bought a passage on a banana-boat going to Lisbon. Eventually Dolly decided that Georgine must go back to Australia, and sent her away by boat from Lisbon, across the Pacific. She was sick with fear for herself and for all three of them, but eventually her husband was able to join her and together they sailed, by way of South America, to New York.

In New York an audition was arranged for Dolly at the Metropolitan Opera. She was very ill, but even though she had developed a boil on her side she decided to sing. As she sang, the boil broke. Nothing came of the audition.

They decided to travel to Australia for Georgine's 21st birthday, and Dolly was briefly reunited with her two Gadsden children. During this period, Modesti went by train into Central Australia to the Hermansberg Mission, where he lived for several weeks, painting portraits of the young aboriginal boys at the Mission and some wonderful landscapes of the Centre. He held an exhibition and subsequently sold all these pictures at Georges'

Gallery in Melbourne.

They then returned to New York, where Dominique hoped that he would be engaged to sing the great French baritone roles at The Metropolitan, but the reigning French baritone was not prepared to allow any new-comer onto this famous American stage.

The careers of both Dolly and Dominique were destroyed by the war and politics. At the height of their vocal powers the opportunities for performing were denied them, and soon it was too late for them to sing any more.

The tragedies that followed for the Modestis were so profound that one can scarcely believe they could come to the same family. In 1943 one of Dominique's two sons from his first marriage was killed. Shortly after, Dolly's children were killed too. Her beloved daughter Georgine was lost in the snow on a skiing holiday at Mt Bogong, and at the end of the War her son John, who was in the Air Force, was killed in an air crash at Mildura.

Dominique said that Dolly nearly went mad. He did not speak of his own suffering.

The months drifted by, and Dominique went to Mexico to paint. In New York in December 1944 he held a successful exhibition at the Arthur Newton Galleries.

In 1946 they decided to sail back to Australia, where they spent a year or two living in Melbourne with Dolly's mother. Mrs Smith detested her son-in-law and the feeling was mutual. She believed he had married Dolly for her money, and finally he could stand it no longer. He hated the slow dragging days in Melbourne and they now decided to return to France.

To prove to the Smith family that he really was not a 'gold-digger' after Dolly's fortune, he decided that he would divorce her! Under French law he would have no rights to her property, and so they both decided that Dolly would seek the divorce. They knew that the presiding Judge was a passionate lover of Wagner's operas. Dolly was asked on what grounds she wished to leave Modesti.

"I am a Wagnerian soprano. My husband will not allow me to sing the music I love most." The divorce was granted.

Later that year they were quietly remarried in a civil ceremony in Paris. Modesti had proved his point. But their lives seemed aimless, and time hung heavily. As the months went by, they thought of a plan, a memorial to their children.

Modesti had started to teach singing, and they decided to see if they could find someone with a really beautiful voice in Australia, whom they might launch on an international career. This person would receive lessons free of charge, but would have to find their own living expenses in Paris.

They sailed to Melbourne, and asked advice from Dot Jones, the woman who ran the Melbourne 'Sun Aria' Competition.

One winter evening in Glenferrie Road, Toorak, a soirée was held at the Smith's home, and the best of the younger resident singers were invited to sing for the Modestis in front of an invited audience of important musical critics. They chose the tenor, Lance Ingram.

Also present that night were the baritone Robert Allman and his wife Margaret. Margaret begged the Modestis to take Bob as well, and said she would work to earn their keep in Paris. She promised they would never regret it if they let him go too. Madame was doubtful about the wisdom of allowing a married couple to travel, because of the insecurity of their finances, but Bob had such a wonderful voice they finally agreed. A month later I was drawn into this magic circle, by the merest chance of a contact with Linda Phillips. I did not meet the other singers at this time.

With my departure for France not far away, I began to have some French conversation lessons, in a vain attempt to arrive speaking the language.

I was persuaded to enter the 'P and A Parade' in the Vocal Section this time, on the advice of Margot Sheridan and Eddie Balmer, and won. And I entered the Ballarat Eisteddfod. Mother had been at school at Clarendon College in Ballarat, and was delighted to come with me. Although I won some sections, what I recall most vividly was a terrible afternoon when I was preparing to sing on stage and suddenly knew I *had* to immediately climb down the steep outside back staircase to the 'dunny' in the overgrown back-yard of the hall! I raced through the long grass in my good evening dress, and just made the old wooden seat before the entire contents of my weekend's meals were discharged over it. Oh, the shame of it!

I went back into the old hall, sang like an angel and won a place in the finals of the 'Sun Aria' to take place a few weeks later in the Melbourne Town Hall.

Singing *Che farò* from Gluck's *Orfeo* and *Softly Awakes My Heart* from Saint-Saëns' *Samson and Delilah* (both in English), I was given second prize in the finals. I was delighted. It was the first time I had entered this competition and I had never been in so big an event. Secretly, I was surprised that people thought I had a good voice and sang well. I always knew I had so much more to learn and so far to go.

It would have been nice to have won the big prize, to help pay for my coming years in Paris, but my father was very generous and said he would give me a monthly allowance for the two years I was to be studying.

My little sister had married her Laurie in the previous year. Dad had bought a dairy farm and installed the two young people in the beautiful country near Berwick as farmers. So the family's situation had changed in these past two years, and my parents were suddenly going to be left alone.

The rest of 1954 drifted by for me, lost in a dream of what was to come.

I was getting a lot of engagements, both in Melbourne and in the country. In July I sang in a curious work called *A Tale of old Japan* by Coleridge-Taylor, with the Victorian Postal Institute Choir, in Wangaratta and Bendigo. In October I sang for the Quartet Club in Broken Hill. I was treated like a 'star' and felt that I sang well, as I trotted out my old ballads yet again.

My 'farewell recital' in the Dandenong Town Hall was a wonderful help to my finances. With the proceeds I bought my single fare on the *Strathnaver* for £90. I sold my precious violin.

On the day before my departure, my father arranged that I sing for the Dandenong Rotary Club Friday night dinner, to thank them for their help. During the morning my beautiful black cat was run over on the road outside the house. It seemed like the final parting to all my former life, that my funny little black friend should be gone. He used to sit at my feet when I practised the violin, and gently scratching my leg with his claws, try to attract my attention and break my concentration. (Perhaps he was also gently trying to tell me something about my violin playing!)

For the rest of the day I was a tearful wreck. My cat's death opened the floodgates of weeks of nervous tension, as I inwardly contemplated leaving my secure and loving home and parents for the unknown foreign shores of France. Mum and Dad did not know what to do with me, nor how I was to sing at the dinner, so they wisely set off without me and arranged that Graeme de Graaff should come back in their car to get me when they judged the time was right for me to sing. Alone, I managed to compose myself. My calm and kind friend arrived, put me in the car and drove me to my last Australian engagement.

In my photo album there is a large picture of my father gazing into my eyes, while I, holding a sheaf of flowers, look at him through half closed eyes. My sister gazes up in admiration and my mother stands to one side tentatively, while we all wait for the photographer to catch the moment of farewell on the ship that would separate us, perhaps forever.

I left Melbourne on a warm day. The streamers joining the ship to the wharf, stretching from my parents' hands to my fingertips, showed the transience of my family relationship which in fact never did resume the closeness of our early life together. And there were a few friends who came to see me off, amongst whom was Graeme de Graaff. We had played tennis occasionally and been to a friend's 21st birthday party, but that was all really, but I was astonished to see 'de', as his friends called him, on the pier at Port Melbourne. His letter a few days later in Adelaide astonished me even more, as he confessed his regret at letting me go to Europe without having spoken of our relationship becoming closer. I replied saying that I would write regularly to him, and this I did for the next two years.

4. Paris

The sea voyage from Melbourne to Marseilles was drifting into a strange no-man's land of loneliness, boredom and longings, filling the days with pointless activity and envying Donald Hazelwood, a young violinist who practised from morning till night in his cabin, preparing for his study year at the 'Conservatoire'. There seemed no point in my practising when I was going to have to change everything. I sang madrigals each morning with a group who gathered in the ship's lounge. I was ashamed of my inability to read 'at sight' as well as the others did.

We arrived in Colombo on New Year's Day. I still remember the smell of spices and strange fragrances in the air as we tied up in the harbour. Sari-clad women picked tea in the plantations, and men with hessian bags over their heads because of the cool misty rain, swept the paths in the beautiful tropical gardens. Fifty years ago we did not have the images of television to educate us as to what we might expect to see in the East. When we sailed through the Suez Canal, with the flat-topped levee banks of mud and the dhows sailing by, I realised how much I had taken my own culture for granted.

The warm lazy days gave way to cold winds, windows and portholes were closed, and we passed the glowing cone of Mt Etna erupting on a dark, bitter afternoon. The next day we were in Marseilles and I disembarked.

I was very fortunate to have the company of the serious young violinist whom I had hardly seen on the voyage. Don Hazelwood spoke French and seemed to know where to go and what to do; going through Customs was made easy by his presence. I disembarked with five large suitcases containing all my worldly possessions. I believed I might stay in Europe for the rest of my life. Don and I left Marseilles by train and travelled through that long day to Paris.

My memory of the train journey was an unreal view of endless still water, stretching to the horizon, in which red-roofed, two-storey, stone farm houses and poplars, in lines like skeletal fingers, stood with their feet in water, the reflections of the grey skies stretching for hundreds of miles. This was the south of France in flood that January of 1955.

Talking to Don Hazelwood recently, I was surprised to

hear that he remembered an elderly couple sitting opposite us, who talked French to him and shared their picnic lunch with us. He had no recollection of the spectacular flood which covered southern France that year. And I had forgotten that elderly couple. It seems remarkable to me that we have such different memories of the same moment in time.

In Paris I said goodbye to Don, and there was a fur-clad Madame Modesti waiting in the cold winter's night with smiles and a great bear hug.

My shyness evaporated before her generous kindness. Everything about Dolly and Dominique was larger than life-size. The first thing she said was "Now you are going to see Paris by night." And she drove madly through the maze of strange, spoke-shaped Paris streets at breakneck speed. After the square grid of Melbourne, the impression of narrow streets opening out into the grandeur of the Champs Elysées, the Arc de Triomphe shining in a diamante haze of electric brightness and the temple-like grandeur of the Paris Opéra, all kindled a love that I've never lost for Paris. I felt at last that I had found my 'land', like Goethe's Mignon, that I had been here before. Madame Modesti took me back to their studio apartment in Montmartre, and to bed at last in the city of my dreams. I woke next day as if I had awoken from a sleep that had lasted for twenty-three years.

The Ile-de-France begins in the centre of the Seine, which conceived and nurtured the egg-shaped centre of the nation, and radiating in cobweb patterns from the river, the dark narrow streets always open out into dazzling light; always open out into the great squares and the famous vistas which are even more impressive in reality than in photos. To come from a narrow dark alley onto the Place de la Concorde, or see the length of the Seine divide, curving round the base of Notre Dame, framed by the bare black trees of that first winter, filled me with delight. As the days lengthened and the trees began to show their first tinge of green, the Boulevards came alive with colour, but no one could describe the wonder of the chestnut trees in flower along the Champs Elysées.

At the same time I was shocked at the shabbiness and air of decay of most of Paris at that time. Later I realised that the city was still recovering from the war. Ten years was not long in the eyes of Europeans, used to a longer view of history than my impatient antipodean viewpoint.

My first lessons with Dominique Modesti were strange. I had to learn to sing again. He was wise in that he never actually said, "I am going to completely alter the way you sing." I realised later that this is what he did. Subtly and slowly I felt the sensation in my body and throat changing. My body was becoming more involved in my singing. All singers feel that 'the voice' is in an 'other', a separate entity within the persona. I began to feel this 'other' for the first time, a child to protect and nurture and cherish, in the way that a woman feels a fierce jealous protectiveness for her child.

I knew this 'other' voice would grow into a strong and wonderful 'organ'. Monsieur and Madame Modesti were always talking about 'the organ' which often made me giggle, but they were right. This is what singing felt like now, a great instrument lodged within my whole body. Monsieur Modesti was only interested in developing the operatic voice. I had practically no knowledge of any other vocal music at this time. For two years, every day except for the summer holidays, I began my lessons with vocal exercises for about twenty minutes. Then out would come the score of *Samson et Dalila* and I would sing through *Printemps qui commence,* always being stopped at the same places every lesson, gradually working through the song. Then I learned *Mon coeur s'ouvre a ta voix (Softly awakes my heart)* in French, again stopping at every error of French pronunciation, and also every subtle fault of tone and breath. It was irritating and frustrating, but worthwhile of course.

Occasionally M Modesti would be enraged, and sometimes I would burst into tears with frustration and impatience.

Both Dolly and Dominique were full of ambition for their pupils. They were able to arrange free tickets for the opera from time to time. I was able to hear truly great singers like Régine Crespin, Rita Gorr and Nicolai Gedda, and the baritones Rene Bianco and Ernest Blanc. I also heard a lot of poor singing in the Paris Opéra then.

The renewal of interest in baroque music was only just beginning and the first baroque opera I ever saw was a magnificent production at the Paris Opéra of Rameau's *Les Indes galantes*. It was a revelation, with Nicolai Gedda in the lead, and contained wonderful baroque ballets. The Modestis thought it was a huge bore; it was not one of the 19th century romantic operas they loved and was probably rather ahead of its audience then.

I stayed with Dolly and Dominique for a week or more and Dolly gave up her days to help me find a comfortable place to live. We met a young Australian pianist, Lyall Duke. Lyall was studying with Marcel Chiampi. Dolly decided that I should not live there because the noise made by two musicians practising in the same house might well be intolerable! However, Lyall and I have remained friends to this day, and she still is for me, one of Australia's great pianists.

We found a large shabby room in a huge apartment taking up the entire fourth floor, where a sad old widow and her cheerful old Spanish maid, Agathe, lived together on the corner of the Rue Condorcet, in the 9th 'arrondissement', in a building dating from the last quarter of the 19th century. In a tiny cupboard-like flat on the ground floor lived the concierge and her husband and child. Together they watched all who came to the building, took in the mail for distribution to the occupants, lit the heating on October 1st for the winter, made sure the fire in 'la cave' was maintained until April 15th and delivered messages to the dwellers of the building. It was wise to give them a sum of money from time to time, as they depended on the generosity of the residents for their living and they could become difficult if they felt they were not appreciated.

To the right of their rooms was the entrance to the main residential apartments, with a grand staircase rising through a large stairwell. Inside the stairwell, the lift was a wire cage and one pulled on a cable to make it go up or down. The speed of the lift was a fast walking pace, so that one could converse with people who preferred to climb the grand but very dark staircase on foot, as many did!

The door to the apartment opened into a substantial hallway with wooden floors, and indeed all apartments had bare and beautiful wooden floors. I never saw wall-to-wall carpet in all the time I lived in France. The walls had been papered many, many years before, so that they now matched the dark brown floors except where an occasional shred of wallpaper hung in tatters.

I had the use of the room which had been my landlady Madame Daïan's 'salon' in more affluent times, before she had to let her rooms. Next to the 'salon' was a little 'bureau' and then a large dining room, all connected by double doors, so that in grander days these large main rooms could have been opened into a huge salon. Every day we would eat a magnificent 'déjeuner' of several courses, in the French style, prepared by Agathe, who slaved in the kitchen when she was not cleaning the parquetry floors with her feet, by shuffling along with steel wool placed under polishing cloths beneath her old slippers.

Agathe cooked and then served the large mid-day meal, as we two sat in splendour in the dining room at the polished table. Agathe ate alone in her tiny cupboard-sized kitchen, often not sitting down, but running in and out with entrée, soup, main course, dessert, cheese and fruit. Then Madame and I would go into the study (bureau) to drink coffee and listen to an old fashioned 'opéra-comique' which was broadcast daily on the radio.

At that time there was a two-hour period when all offices were closed to allow the white-collar workers of Paris to go home and have their mid-day meal (the most important of the day) and a 'snooze', before resuming work until about 7pm. So I would make conversation with Madame Daïan for half an hour before going off to my singing lesson.

Living with Madame Daïan was a bit like being a schoolgirl again, because my day was structured by time and very restricted. Although there had been no mention of it, she expected me to be her companion for these hours. It was very good for me because, as Madame spoke no English, I was obliged to learn French as quickly as possible. I also began to feel less lonely and disorientated.

After my lesson of an hour-and-a-half, or two hours (and a gossip with Dolly in the kitchen to postpone my departure), I would walk down the steep stairs to Anvers, passing by the tiny fenced garden there, always cold, sand-strewn and dog filled, to Rue Condorcet and my room on the fourth floor. I could see the white domed Sacré Coeur if I stood by the side wall of the room. I hired a terrible piano for a very small sum and had a rather beautiful old table with drawers, which was my desk. Here I did my daily homework for Alliance Française, where I went every morning to classes from 8am till 12 noon, learning to speak and read French.

I enjoyed the class enormously and it was great to meet people of my own age from all over the world. Once I was asked to a formal dinner by a rather grand German boy who was training to go into the Diplomatic Corps, but I was so shy and self-conscious that I made a miserable companion for him. I did not know how to behave in this sophisticated new-old world, and felt like the gauche young girl from Springvale who ate 'tea' at six o'clock. When I told Madame Modesti about this 'date', she made it quite plain that she disapproved of any fraternising with 'les Boches', even ten years after the conclusion of hostilities.

Madame Daïan, my landlady, was Jewish and her late husband had been a schoolteacher. I gradually learned that Agathe, who had been born in Spain, had travelled with her employers to Paris many years before the war, and when 'les Boches' took the city they all fled to the south of France, where the two women and Madame's daughter hid for the rest of the war. Madame's spaniel-like eyes always filled with tears when she spoke of this time and I believe that her schoolteacher husband had been taken away and shot. But I never asked her about her war experiences.

Her handsome and light-hearted daughter, a schoolteacher, often came to visit with her three little children. Her son-in-law, who was much older than Adeline and nearly as old as Madame, came to 'déjeuner' every Monday, after which he would sit in the 'bureau' going through Madame's weekly accounts, always giving her a tongue-lashing for her extravagance with the food bills. I began to know this very conservative family very well. I think I was lucky, as it was rare for a foreigner to become so much a part of the family.

At the end of my first year in Paris I received a certificate from Alliance Française, of which I was very proud. I could speak reasonably well and understand French, and felt at home. But I have never forgotten the terrible feeling of mental fatigue which I experienced at the end of each day during my first few months in Paris. Madame Modesti had quite rightly maintained that I should try to hear and speak English as little as possible, and had insisted I find a 'pension' where no-one spoke the language. This certainly hastened my attempts to speak French, but it was very lonely. It gave me an understanding of the emotional pressures that non-English speaking migrants to this country experience.

Madame Daïan must have understood my loneliness and in her kindness sometimes invited Don Hazelwood to dinner, and several times she asked Lance Ingram to one of Agathe's famous meals.

At this time I hardly knew Lance. He was having a very difficult time adjusting to the sophisticated city of Paris and learning to speak French. He retreated into himself and, following the strict advice of Madame Modesti, he distanced himself from us other three Australians. It was only recently that I learned the story of the boy who came from nowhere to become one of the top tenors of his day in Europe. He was born in Adelaide in 1925 and at the age of four was 'fostered out' to a woman who ran a dairy farm to the north of Adelaide. He was expected, with other children in her care, to milk the cows and help with the general farm work. At the age of eleven the truant officer caught up with him, and Lance then attended school until he was able to leave again at the age of fourteen. A relative in Adelaide then employed him in a factory making chrome chairs, grinding the metal smooth before the finish was applied.

When he was about sixteen he got a job as wire-man and circus hand with the 'Flying Colleanos' and travelled with the circus for a year or two. Someone gave him a record of Caruso and he played it over and over, finding that he could sing along with his idol, floating his voice effortlessly to the top C at the climax of the aria.

He joined the Tivoli Theatre circuit, touring first as tenor in a Barber Shop Quartet, then becoming a soloist with his own 'spot', surrounded by pretty girls and singing *Pedro the Fisherman*.

He had singing lessons with Horace Stevens in Melbourne, and joined the National Theatre Opera School, where Paul Arndt gave Lance his first lessons in reading music. He had a great sense of fun and was a skilled cartoonist, drawing his colleagues with amazing insight. Paul Arndt helped him to learn the role of Cavaradossi in *Tosca,* and at the end of 1952 he was judged ready to give a matinee performance.

Always cautious, conductor Joseph Post was suspicious of his ability and asked Ronald Dowd to be in the theatre, ready to replace Lance if he were unable to complete the role. Lance had a triumphant debut and went on to become the lyric tenor star of the National Theatre in Melbourne until his departure for France.

From that time he worked tirelessly to perfect his French accent, to speak and sing in flawless French and to succeed in a way that few foreigners ever have in France.

Dominique and Dolly occasionally took Lance Ingram or Bob and Margaret Allman and myself away on short trips to the country. We were all stunned by the beauty and history of France, of which we knew so little. We began to expand our knowledge of the culture and 'la Civilization Française'.

As the weeks went by, I found myself going more and more often to visit the Allmans, who lived in a tiny apartment on the Quai des Grands Augustins on the banks of the Seine. They had been told that their two rooms had once been the love-nest of Louis XIV, the end of a secret passage leading over the narrow street into the royal apartments of the King.

Certainly the bathroom and kitchen had been little changed since those days, as Margaret bitterly observed on freezing winter days, when she hung the week's washing over the stove in the kitchen. She would hoist it high on a pulley, where it would hang for a week before drying. Sometimes it froze solid. Their double bed was a broad shelf in the wall, hidden from the rest of the room by a tattered old red brocade curtain.

We were able to go to many wonderful concerts and operas by joining Jeunesse Musicales. On looking through my diary for 1955, I see that I went to hear Georges Tzipine (with whom I often sang in Melbourne later on) conducting the great American mezzo, Nan Merriman, in concert. I heard Victoria de los Angeles and Marian Anderson in recital, and went with Donald Hazelwood to hear the Philadelphia Orchestra conducted by Eugene Ormandy, with William Warfield as the soloist. And I saw *Aïda* with different casts, a work at that time I never contemplated being able to sing myself. Incredibly, I now have only hazy memories of these artistic pinnacles: I was dazed by the richness of the music I was hearing for the first time, in such splendid theatres and dazzling surroundings. But I do remember first hearing the music of Berlioz, in a wonderful performance of *Roméo et Juliette* in the Cour du Louvre.

During the year Margaret Allman asked if a friend of hers could stay with Mme Daïan for a couple of months. It appeared that the National Bank was sending some of its staff to London for extra training. Peter Allender was selected to go and wished to take his wife, but the Bank stipulated that no wives were to be taken on the training program. Betty and Peter Allender had no children at that time and Betty conceived the plan that when Peter had a spare weekend he could slip over to Paris and they would have a wonderful time together.

Mme Daïan had a tiny back room, near Agathe's bedroom, and was delighted to let it. So I met the lively Betty, whose wicked ways and amusing tongue enlivened my stay for a time. My progress in speaking French was halted for eight weeks! Betty delighted in making derogatory remarks about Mme Daïan's fur capes. Mme Daïan wore very old short capes over her shoulders when she was sitting in her bureau doing her accounts, or listening to the radio. She seemed to have about four of them and apart from being very old, they really were unusual. It was Betty who drew my attention to the fact that they were not only dreadfully moth-eaten, which I had noticed, but that they were made of cat-skin fur. She would announce in a loud voice, "Another moth-eaten moggy model today, I see," and I would collapse into giggles. Poor old Mme Daïan would anxiously ask me why we were laughing at her. "Elle se moque de moi," she would say to me. "Non, non," I would say, trying to soothe her ruffled feathers.

It was a relief when Peter Allender came over to Paris, which he did as often as possible, and took Betty off to a hotel. I did manage to repair my damaged 'standing' with Mme Daïan, when Betty went after eight weeks.

During that year I had studied a good number of the *Arie Anthiche (Early Italian Arias)* published by Ricordi. Modesti believed that they were an important part of vocal training, that these works served the same purpose of focussing and training as the exercises of Concone or Vaccai, and at the same time the student was learning a beautiful song which could become useful performance repertoire. I think he was quite right.

I began to hear for the first time the songs of the great French composers like Duparc, Debussy and Fauré. I saw the premiere of Milhaud's opera *Christophe Colomb* at the spectacular Palais de Chaillot.

I saw the stage play of *The Dialogues of the Carmelites* in French, in the year the play was written, and found it profoundly moving. I had no knowledge of the Catholic faith and began to realise how many strands of culture can colour human religious belief. What gulfs were revealed between the Irish Catholics of my home town and the French 'rékligieuses' of that convent in the days of the 'Terror'.

I remember a heated discussion with Mme Daïan's ninety-year-old Aunt Jeanne, who insisted that I was of an enemy race because Napoleon had been defeated at Waterloo by the British, and because I was British I too was an enemy. In vain I tried to explain that I was proudly Australian, with no sense of involvement in that distant time. She seemed to me to still live with the shame of an event which took place at the time of the settlement of Australia. I think that France lived in a dream of past grandeur as no other nation then did.

I was privileged to hear the first performance in Paris by a German opera company after the Second World War. The bitter memories of the German occupation were fresh enough for there to be demonstrations against the conductor and Wieland Wagner. There was a sense of danger in struggling through the demonstrating crowd to get to the sold-out performance of Beethoven's *Fidelio*. The performance was thrilling, because it introduced me to a new style of production where the effects were achieved by lighting, rather than elaborate sets and costumes. I think that the economy of those performances, enhanced by great singers and conductors, were made memorable because there was less distraction in the theatrical effects.

In September lessons began again for all of us and this latter part of the year began to bring changes. One of my Australian friends, Barbara Wilson, left to go to London, then at the end of this year Lance auditioned for the Paris Opéra and was immediately engaged as principal tenor. The following year he sang Cavaradossi with Callas as his Tosca, and a magnificent Faust, and his unforgettable Don José, Hoffmann and Werther at the Comique. I began to study this Massenet opera and loved the drama of Charlotte's music, but thought her an irritatingly foolish girl to marry someone because her mother wished it! The 'mores' of Goethe's world seemed unbearable to me, with my Australian directness and disregard for the conventions of more distant times.

In the new year, Bob Allman auditioned for Covent Garden and he and Margaret left for London when he was given a contract. He was impatient to begin his career and begin earning a living. Margaret had a job that had been supporting them both while he was studying in Paris, and she was anxious to start a family. The Allmans were a great loss to me, for they had generously provided the Australian home I missed. Whenever I grew homesick, which seemed to increase as the days shortened and darkness and cold descended on the boulevards, I had been accustomed to go down to their apartment and the winter gloom would disappear in the fug of the little flat and the warmth of the Allmans' gossip. In the beginning, I had been too afraid of not learning to speak French quickly (I was, and still am, a Puritan at heart), but as time went on I began to allow myself the luxury of these visits. Eventually Mme Daïan complained that I was neglecting her. Bob and Margaret were to go away and I would now be on my own for the first time, without their company.

I decided to go to London for a few days while the Modestis were away. This was my first visit to England. I did the kind of things excited young tourists do and heard Elizabeth Fretwell sing at Sadler's Wells as Musetta in *La Bohème*. She was then beginning her best years as a great spinto soprano at Sadler's Wells and Covent Garden. I shall always remember her Tosca and Butterfly as truly great performances. I regret that I never heard her sing Ellen Orford in *Peter Grimes,* which was one of her greatest roles. She sang it all over Europe with Ronald Dowd.

In early January I went back to Paris, never having seen the sky during the days I spent in London. I remember my disbelief that people could spend the winter in gloom and fog without complaint. This was at the end of the 'pea-soup' fogs, before the clean-air act made London a lighter city. Three o'clock in the afternoon seemed as black as midnight and the horrible dark-brown smelly air made breathing difficult. The experience made me appreciate the light and air of Paris even more and I was grateful that I did not have to live in London.

In Paris, Lance was settled in his career, with his magnificent vocal prospects before him. He decided to change his name and sang as Albert Lance from that time on. He was to remain in France for the rest of his life and still lives there. Decorated with the Légion d'Honneur by de Gaulle, he became a French citizen. It was a great shame that his own country never heard his wonderful tenor voice at the height of his international career. Those of us who heard him in Melbourne as Hoffmann in 1954, or in *Tosca* or *Butterfly*, will always remember his radiant sound, with its effortless top C.

I sat at the window of 43 Rue Condorcet, looking out at the grey skies, snow on the edge of my balcony, wondering what I should do and what would become of me; feeling sorry for myself. Each week I wrote to my mother and father and often I wrote to Graeme de Graaff more than once a week, pouring out my frustration. Modesti said I was not ready to audition yet and needed another year with him. He wanted me to enter the Concours Internationale de Genève, where I would be heard by international agents who would immediately engage me. This major competition had launched Mattiwilda Dobbs only a year or so previously.

So I began work on my program with M Maurice Picard from the Paris Opéra, who was a friend of Dolly's. I also started 'mis-en scène' (acting) classes with a Mme Chereau, which I felt were a great waste of time and money. In a wonderfully decaying room I learned to express emotion. Grief demanded both hands clutching my breasts, despair was shown by leaning one's head back, with the right hand pressed to the forehead, and rage was represented by flinging both hands to the sky with fingers fully extended. (This was at the time of the Actors' Studio in New York, and Marlon Brando and James Dean were becoming well known!)

Mother and Father decided it was time to do 'the world trip' that all Australians of that time felt obliged to make. They would come to London in May, in time for the Chelsea Flower Show, then hire a car and drive through Europe later, in time to hear me sing at Geneva. I began serious work on repertoire, beginning on the role of Amneris in *Aïda* and the role of Charlotte in *Werther*. For Geneva I prepared five different songs which I have always loved and sung ever since: Vivaldi's *Un certo non so che* was my early Italian aria; Duparc's *La Vie Antérieure* was my French song; and *O Tod*, the third of the *Four Serious Songs* of Brahms, was the one M Picard and I chose, after I had learnt this greatest of the German cycles. I also prepared *Che farò* from *Orfeo* in Italian (having learnt the role in French in that year) and *Mon coeur s'ouvre a ta voix*.

During the time I was in Paris, the Melbourne Olympics were being staged, and there were daily reports of the events in the conservative paper, *Le Figaro*, including some very biased complaints about the judging, claiming that French athletes were being discriminated against by the dreadful Australian judges.

I wrote a letter in French, which was published by *Le Figaro* (to Mme Daïan's amazed amusement) expressing my disapproval of the biased attitude of the reporters. This was my first letter to a newspaper.

This second year in Paris was much harder. The novelty of life was smoothed into routine and the Allmans were gone. Periodic Australian visitors seemed a distraction and meant time lost in study.

Then my parents arrived in May, seeming so young and handsome and excited by their adventure when I caught up with them in their comfortable hotel in Green Park in London. We spent a wonderful week of warm, beautiful spring days. The Chelsea Flower Show made me doubt my earlier first impressions of life in London. Together we heard Bob Allman sing Donner in *Das Rheingold* at Covent Garden. I said goodbye to my parents as they went off to tour Britain in their hired car, while I returned to Paris to finish my two years with Modesti before presenting my program in Geneva.

At last the summer came and Mum and Dad arranged to stay in a cheap hotel near me in the Place d'Anvers. Like all my other Australian visitors, they were dismayed by the strangeness of things foreign. They resented having to pay extra for a bath and having to have the bathroom unlocked seemed barbaric! The difficulty of obtaining a nice hot cup of tea was a constant complaint and the coffee was so strong as to be undrinkable. Towels of linen with the absorbency of paper were also a trial, while the public 'stand-up' toilets were unbearable. The deep brown peeling wallpaper of Mme Daïan's apartment meant that the rooms had been papered sometime in the 1930s and that she was too poor to have it renewed. I agreed with all these complaints, but still loved France because of its great beauty and history and tried to show them that the comfortable life of suburban Melbourne could be exchanged for different values for a short time without too much pain. (After all, they both enjoyed the discomforts of camping each summer).

The worst mishap during their stay occurred on a trip to Chantilly by train one Sunday morning. The European platforms left a wide gap between the train and the very low platform. As we raced to catch an infrequent train and jumped the wide space, Mum missed and landed with a horrible crash on her bottom, leaving her legs suspended between the train and the platform. We pulled her to her feet just in time, got into the train and spent the day sightseeing.

We had a month together, going through the Loire to the south of France and on up the Rhône to Switzerland. I think that we all had an unspoken feeling that this might be the last time I would spend time with them both.

At the end of a wonderful time, we travelled on to Geneva and I began rehearsals with the shy and gifted Swiss woman who was the official accompanist for the Concours International, and I passed from the preliminary sections into the semi-finals and then into the finals.

The pretty Conservatoire was the venue for us singers. Again I felt that strange disembodied sensation, floating, of my voice not being under my control, so that I have no memory at all of how I sang, or for that matter what the place was like where I sang. I seem to remember that the Salle was rather like the old hall at the Melbourne Conservatorium, but beautifully proportioned and carefully maintained.

When they arrived, my parents loved this clean and prosperous-looking city and we enjoyed taking a trip to Chamonix by train one day and taking trips on the lake. The days between my appearances were filled with exploring the old city of Geneva with its steeply curving, crooked paved streets and admiring the very new and modern United Nations buildings and the famous fountain, which my father loved watching as it played on the lake in the wind. By this time they were beginning to long for Australia and were waiting with impatience to hear me sing again, after nearly two years.

At last the day of the finals came. I sang well and was pleased to hear that I was awarded a medal, which I still treasure. As I hold it in my hand, I remember saying goodbye to my parents amid floods of tears at the 'Gare', before travelling back to Paris by train. My mother and father continued on their journey south to Italy and embarked from Naples for Australia.

I turned away from their loving security to face an unknown future and returned to Paris.

The year came to an end. I watched the grey sky above the apartments of the Rue Condorcet darken and saw the snow decorate the railing of my tiny balcony once again. I wondered how soon it would be before I might do some more auditions and how to go about beginning my career.

My friend Graeme de Graaff wrote that he had applied for scholarships to two of the provincial universities in France, Montpelier and Aix-en-Provence and been accepted by both. As he spoke no French, his work as a philosophy graduate would be made very difficult, at least until he learned to communicate. I thought it was brave and perhaps foolish for him to try to come to France, but this news did cheer me on those days of gloomy grey.

I decided I should try to earn some money. Mme Daïan had a great-niece who had two little children and I agreed to work as their nanny while the young mother went on with her career. I loved the children, but not taking them out to the park in the depths of winter, and I was really too young and inexperienced to make a success of this role.

The winter that year seemed very long and cold. I missed my good friends. I was lonely. The Modestis went away for Christmas, so a week or so without lessons made me doubly miserable. Then one morning the telephone rang. It was Bob Allman ringing from London to ask if I would go over as soon as possible to audition for the role of Ulrica in *Un ballo in maschera (A Masked Ball)*. The woman who had been engaged to sing the role had cancelled and they needed someone urgently.

I packed and caught the night train and ferry, and next morning was taken up to the Crush Bar, the quaint upstairs foyer of the Royal Opera House, Covent Garden. This was where preliminary auditions took place. Under the magnificent chandeliers, an elfin man sat at an upright piano, which was tucked under the staircase, and another young man ranged up and down the length of the long room, gloomily listening to me sing.

What a difference from the lofty marble magnificence of the Paris Opéra! This room was like a rather tatty drawing room in a large house. There were fake candles with imitation wax dripping from the electric fittings, just like at home. I sang the *Re del abisso* with Robert Keys playing the piano. Then the other young man snarled at me, "Come down onto the stage. We want Sir David to hear you."

Someone led me into a narrow passage, and I walked out into the centre of the stage.

5. Covent Garden

Why do all theatres smell like this, I wondered: a smell of old candle grease, hemp and sawdust, mice-droppings, cooked cabbage, burnt bakelite. A piano was wheeled out on to the stage; Robert Keys sat down again and played the sinister opening bars of the aria. I stood on the stage under the harsh lights and sang the short first part of the scene.

"Will you please continue," said the voice from the dark.

"I don't know the second part from memory," I stammered.

"Read it then," said the voice, which I later discovered belonged to Edward Downes.

So I read the dramatic second part of the aria over the pianist's shoulder. Then I think I sang *Che farò*. Another voice called, "Please come to my office. Miss Barnes will show you the way."

So I followed Wendy into the old-fashioned office of Sir David Webster.

"Will you come to London to learn the role and be prepared to open on tour in Cardiff in four weeks time?" he said. "The tour goes from Cardiff to Southampton and then to Manchester. Your conductor will be Edward Downes, and you'll be expected to learn the role in two weeks and then go into production with the staff producer, Christopher West, and the other principals."

Here was the dream!

The Greeks say one feels emotion in the stomach. It was my head which felt empty and light as I looked at the round-faced man with the prominent blue eyes who faced me across the desk. In my nervous excitement he seemed aloof and cold. He held the reins of one of the great opera houses of the world. As time went on I came to realise his English manner concealed his intense desire to enhance the company and look after all its members. It was then a repertory company and the singers were rather like a large family. There were many Australians at Covent Garden at that time, certainly more than half the principal singers. Almost all the men in the chorus were Welsh.

I went home to Paris, to say goodbye to Mme Daïan and leave my room in Rue Condorcet. I hugged the Modestis and Dolly said she would come over to see me soon. I returned to London in January, surely the worst month to arrive in that city, and arranged to stay for a while with Elizabeth Fretwell in her big house at Swiss Cottage until after the tour.

I caught the tube on those dark mornings and when I finally left the Opera House in the evening, night had fallen so there had been no 'day' in the theatre world I was now entering, but I felt so happy and busy. I loved learning the rest of the music in the role of Ulrica, which I did with the help of staff coaches (repetiteurs) Robert Keys and Albert Knowles. The opera was to be performed in English, which made memorising it easy.

Then I began work on production with the staff producer, Christopher West. A gaunt homosexual, he seemed to be aggressively antagonistic. He worked quickly, plotting out the moves with me, at first alone in a small room, then on the set with all the huge Covent Garden chorus watching. I had been told by the Modestis to pretend that I was an experienced performer, but I probably should have confessed my lack of skill straight away. He finally lost his temper as he explained a move to me for the umpteenth time, and in front of the chorus shrieked at me, "Can't you get that into your little *antipodal* mind?"

Shaking and near to tears I would try to remember once again, with more success each time I was humiliated. In fact, I think it was good for me to be driven like that. But for about three months I was unable to eat properly, and grew thinner and thinner, as I lived on my nerves. I knew, but hoped that nobody else would, that the top of my voice was still very insecure. In fact the *A flat* I sang at the climax of the little aria was the highest top note I had ever safely managed at this time. The other problem, which I never resolved in all my working life, was that as soon as I had to take stage direction, the words *and sometimes the music* of the role would fly out of my head. Even when the music was completely embedded in the voice, something happened to my concentration when I began to 'move' at the beginning of stage rehearsals.

After a time Christopher West became a friend, and would insist on buying me a daily glass of stout at the bar in the canteen, in order to 'build me up'. I hated stout, but everybody told me that I needed to put on weight in order to support my large and still developing voice. Later on Christopher was incredibly kind to me, spending long hours of extra time helping me develop the characters of some of the roles I played.

So I went off on tour to Cardiff with two other newcomers to the company; in fact we had all signed contracts with The Royal Opera House on the same day. Jon Vickers and Joseph Rouleau were both Canadians. Vickers with his magnificent tenor voice was to sing Gustavus, his Amelia was Amy Shuard, the great English soprano, and basses Joseph Rouleau and Michael Langdon were the conspirators.

The role of Oscar on tour was sung by Edna Graham and she kindly took me under her wing, letting me share her digs. Here I met my first Welsh Dogs. Sitting on each side of the mantelpiece in the tiny Cardiff terrace house where we were boarding, they seemed breathtakingly ugly. Edna's admiration for these almost life-sized china monsters made me aware of a great cultural difference between the British and the Colonials.

The meals on this tour were truly terrible. After Agathe's culinary triumphs in the Rue Condorcet, I was not used to the 'stodge' of post-war England. My stomach rebelled, and I ate less and less.

After Cardiff, and very good debut notices for us all, we went to Southampton and Manchester before returning to London. I was invited to become a permanent member of the company and went to live with Elizabeth Fretwell. Sharing the comfortable house were Barbara Wilson and Gracie Sutherland, who had been Lance Ingram's girl friend. She was now working for the Australian Trade Commission, travelling around demonstrating Australian dried fruits. This meant that she was not staying at Swiss Cottage all the time, but when she *did* come back there was always a big party, with lots of wonderful cooking, especially fruit cakes. She and Barbara were lively, talkative and amusing, while Elizabeth Fretwell was ordered, dedicated, disciplined and quiet. How she put up with the disruption of the other two girls I don't know, but maybe their gaiety repaid her generosity in having us all living there. So I now had a home with these expatriate Australians who, except for Gracie, were not well off.

We did four more performances of *Un ballo in maschera* in London. One night, I was visited backstage by an elderly woman, who introduced herself as a relative of mine. In fact she was the wife of the brother of my aunt's husband. As an opera lover, she claimed me as her own, and invited me to visit her home in Suffolk at the earliest opportunity. This was the beginning of a warm friendship with a remarkable woman.

Her husband had come from a large Yorkshire family. Chosen by his uncle at the age of sixteen to go out to India, he had become an engineer and a successful tea-planter, and returned to England to marry Doris.

The young girl went out with her husband to the remote high country of Assam. Her days stretched endlessly in her busy husband's absence, until she found that she was pregnant. But her baby died, and then another, and in her grief she decided that she had to 'go home' to have her children. In these waiting times of her life she, who had smoked smart little cigarettes in another land and could not get them in the remote hill station, turned to smoking a pipe. Pipe tobacco was easy to get! On my first visit to Woodbridge I was astonished to see my dear, sturdily-built, middle-aged, very 'county' Maw, as I called her, stand by the marble mantle-piece, and carefully select her pipe from an elaborate number in a pipe rack, and begin puffing away.

How courageous those Englishmen and women were, in those days so far removed from ours! Her three children were sent to school in England while she returned to stay with her husband in Assam until it was time for him to retire to the Suffolk town of Woodbridge.

When I caught the train for this my first visit to the country, spring had arrived. I found this land very different from the French country I knew and loved so well. The cosy landscape of the Home Counties was enlarging to distant horizons. From the subtle grey plains, square Flemish churches rose occasionally into grey skies. There was a kind of spaciousness I remembered from Australia, but rendered in monotone. Later, my uncle-by-marriage took me to visit nearby Aldeburgh and I saw the Britten village. On that first wintry visit, the view of marshy river-mouth and the stern shingle beach gave me the flavour of Peter Grimesl, before I knew him in his profoundly complex character, in the opera based on George Crabbe's poem.

There were five of us who all shared a dressing room in *The Trojans,* my next opera. The other young principals were Joan Carlyle, Noreen Berry, Iris Kells and my particular friend and vocal rival, Josephine Veasey. We were all about the same age and engaged to sing whatever roles the opera house needed, but looking back I now see that Sir David and the casting staff were very astute. When they gave us large roles, these were always well within our capabilities. For instance, the role of Ulrica was a very big sing for a very short time. I could not have survived an Amneris at that point of my development, but the short dramatic scene in which Ulrica appears was a perfect vehicle for my dramatic contralto.

Anna was the secondary part of Dido's sister in *The Trojans.* She has some beautiful little solos, duets and ensembles to sing, and my reviews after the opening night were extremely flattering. The producer, Sir John Gielgud, bathed the opening scene in Part 2 with space and light, and the glory of the opening chorus gave me a love of Berlioz which has lasted all my life. Sir John gave me a pretty antique pendant on opening night, as was the custom in those days, with a card saying that this was the start of a major career. The opera was conducted by the Musical Director, Rafael Kubelik, whom I adored.

Dido was sung by the great American mezzo, Blanche Thebom. She introduced me to the world of the mink-coated Prima Donna. She had had a wonderful career as a dramatic mezzo, but the beauty of her voice was now beginning to show signs of wear. Her talent as an actress and her magnificently long dark hair, which had never been cut, were great features of the publicity photos. However the sets were not to her liking, and she refused to wear the costumes designed for her. (When we got on stage and saw the costumes, I realised she was probably quite right). She had some completely different dresses made for herself, so that all the other women's costumes seemed truly ugly. We were all astonished that she got away with it. She persuaded Sir John that she should 'let down' her magnificent hair, two metres long, at the end of the opera in the scene when she takes her own life, and this 'stole the show'. Amongst the cast there was also a certain amount of interest and amusement in the representation of the profile of the under-belly of the Trojan horse, with its realistically portrayed appendages, which formed the proscenium arch in the opera's Part 1, *The Taking of Troy*.

But nothing could upstage the new and exciting voice of Jon Vickers as Aeneas, or indeed the work itself, which took London by storm that year. The music of Berlioz was the secret to the success of that production, which was never overshadowed by the producer's desire to tamper with the composer's intentions.

Blanche Thebom was used to being 'feted' in America, and behaving like a Great Singer did not go down very well in the dreary world of post-war London. English singers in English opera houses tended to live rather ordinary domestic lives, and partying and socialising was 'not done' when one was working as hard and paid as poorly as we were then. As a newcomer to London myself, I was happy to fill in time taking in the tourist sights with Blanche. She was very kind to me and 'treated me' on several occasions, taking me to tea at the Savoy where she was staying. To this naive young Australian, still finding my way around English customs, 'tea' still meant the evening meal in my vocabulary, so I was surprised at the hour she suggested. We became good friends, although I was in awe of her glamour and sophistication.

During the latter part of July, I opened in the tiny part of The Voice of the Mother in *The Tales of Hoffmann*, with Ted Downes conducting. This was the role I had sung in Melbourne in my previous life. It involved climbing up a steep ladder to stand in the dark behind a gauze representing a portrait painting of the mother of Antonia (sung in this production by Joan Sutherland). I always found standing in the dark curtained alcove at the top of the ladder strangely claustrophobic. I would wait for the light to shine on my face, which gave the cue that the painting of the Mother is coming to life. I was always nervous before I began singing the wonderful melody that starts the trio. Five years earlier, at the performances in Melbourne, it had seemed perilously high for me and I still found it difficult, as the climax moves inexorably higher and higher. And I so wanted to impress Edward Downes! A nervous, highly-strung young man with a reputation as a ladykiller, he hid behind immensely thick-lensed glasses and yet I found him obsessively attractive.

Friedelind Wagner found me a very comfortable and pretty bed-sitting room in Primrose Hill. My landlady was Madeleine Smith, the widow of Cecil Smith, the American-born music critic of *The Daily Express* between 1951 and his death in 1956. Madeleine knew everyone in the music and operatic world and took an impish and mischievous delight in theatrical gossip. When I was studying with Modesti, I had met Friedelind several times in Paris and sung for her. Friedelind was one of the sisters of Wolfgang and Wieland Wagner and she had turned her back on Nazi Germany before the war, going to live in America, where she had written a book of such invective against the other members of her family that they would not speak to her. She was a fascinating, tempestuous and impulsive person, whose physical resemblance to her grandfather was extraordinary.

Friedelind came to see *The Trojans* and we had tea together. She discovered that I was looking for a flat. Almost the next day I was installed in two pretty rooms in Madeleine's house and I found that I was an object of great interest to my new landlady. From her I learned that I was an immensely promising singer, and that I should make up my mind to marry Edward Downes, or at least have an affair with him!

As I had never had an affair with anybody, I was surprised that my life should be so promptly preordained, but I listened with interest. Madeleine told me that Ted had been married, and was now going to re-marry a talented soprano, but that I should stay in the picture and in the fullness of time I would find true happiness with him.

What little I already knew about Ted Downes convinced me that Madeleine was a madly interfering gossip, or perhaps just mad. I knew that Ted was *definitely* not interested in me as a sex object, but I did admire his musicality and the passion and commitment of his conducting. However Madeleine's prodding made me hideously ill at ease with Ted and my relationship with him was always uncomfortable after that.

Friedelind came to see my new 'digs' and invited me to be her guest at *Wahnfried* in Bayreuth, during the forthcoming Bayreuth Festival. Already the Bayreuth Festival held a place in my mind akin to Olympus!

So at the end of the season, after two weeks of singing lessons in Paris, I went by train to Bayreuth, where Friedelind met me, and took me to *Wahnfried,* the family home built by Richard Wagner. It was a beautifully proportioned classical house. The grounds were shaded by silver birch trees bordering the gravel paths, and the property was enclosed by a high stone wall. We did not drive up to the house, but stopped and entered the cottage near the gates, which was probably a gatehouse in former times. It was a substantial two-storey building and Friedelind was the occupant, well separated from the rest of the family.

The next day, walking in the blazing sun about three o'clock along a white gravel path to the entrance of the Festspeilhaus, I looked with astonishment at the simplicity of the classical facade of this famous theatre. It seemed an odd time of the day to begin this journey into mythology and music. Trumpeters appeared on the balcony above the crowd and played their wonderful fanfares. The theatre, with its rather stark interior and extraordinary acoustic, seemed to proclaim the right to be a temple to Richard Wagner. It had neither the baroque grandeur of the Paris Opéra, nor the cosy fustiness of Covent Garden. The interior was functional, so that all attention was focused on the proscenium. The seats were simple, wooden, hard, severe. "No lounging about here," they proclaimed. "To attend *this* ceremony of worship, all must stay awake for however many hours the opera takes!"

On that first afternoon we had the best places in the family box. I did not know then of Friedelind's strained relations with the rest of the family, but thought it strange that when we took our seats the other people seated in the box there neither spoke to her, nor looked at us. When I later read her book called *The Royal Family of Bayreuth,* so critical of her family's attitude to the Nazis, Hitler and the war, I understood.

The audience, the men all in dinner jackets and the women in black or white with their mink coats, sat expectantly with a reverential air of worship in this shrine of German culture. Continental women never wore the bright coloured clothes I had been used to in suburban Australia and I was still surprised at the sober colours of the gowns these women wore, even after living for two years in France. As if in church, the audience stood waiting reverently for the conductor. There was a moment's pause as he took his place on the podium, then with the great clatter of two thousand wooden seats, the audience sat down. There was no air-conditioning, so that on those hot summer evenings, the frequent temptations to nod off were thwarted by my concentration on the wonderful music, great voices and hard seats.

There followed a strange labyrinth of jumbled days and long hot sleepless nights. Performances began at 4pm, and I entered the Festspielhaus at the height of a hot summer afternoon to emerge at 10pm in a daze of glory, to join the throng who went to dinner in the restaurant. There we discussed the performance in every detail and watched the great singers slough off their god-like personae and begin to eat and drink like other mortals. Friedelind reserved a table in the restaurant each night and we watched and occasionally met with the great performers of that generation. Then a walk home to bed, a late brunch in the hot still dusty summer noon, before returning to the continuing saga.

I had read the stories as a child in a school prize book of my mother's, *Stories from Wagner.* With its wonderful sepia illustrations of wing-helmeted Brünnhilde riding through flames to her 'immolation', it had always been part of my romantic dream world. But I had never heard Wagner performed on stage until I saw *Rheingold* at Covent Garden, with Robert Allman singing *Donner,* when Mother and Father came to London in 1956.

The first of my Bayreuth operas was *Die Meistersinger,* surely the most enchanting way to begin an exploration of the works of Wagner. The conductor was the great André Cluytens, with Otto Wiener as Hans Sachs and the glorious Elisabeth Grümmer as Eva.

Then came what is, for me, the most problematic of Wagner's operas, *Parsifal.* George London and Ramón Vinay were remarkable, but *Parsifal* has never been my favourite, and when I came to sing in the Garden production later in that season, I found the music so distressing that I almost became ill. Whilst I loved most of Wagner's operas, Parsifal filled me with disgust. I was repelled by the thought of the wound which would not heal, because it evoked the picture of Christ with his exposed bleeding heart. The theology of the Christian church seemed to be mingled with some pagan blood sacrifice, against which I rebelled. The suffering of Amfortas was portrayed in dreadful chords which expressed these ideas musically. In my own life I had no wish to have someone suffer and die for me. In most of the operas I performed I was able to suspend disbelief and enjoy the theatrical. But not in this opera.

Then *The Ring* at last.

Astrid Varnay was Brünnhilde; Hans Hotter, Wotan; Sieglinde, Birgit Nilsson; and the conductor was Hans Knappertsbusch. The production by Wieland Wagner was always breathtakingly simple; I was never distracted from the musical content by the producer's effects or the designer's fantasies.

After the four days of *The Ring,* dazed by the powerful music, the lack of sleep and the general atmosphere of reverence for the music of Wagner, I found time at last to walk around to the tiny baroque opera house and the museum in Bayreuth.

Friedelind was a kind and generous hostess, more American than German. She lived much of her life in the States, but eventually founded an Opera School attached to an industrial city in the north of England. I regret that I lost touch with her. I have never forgotten her kindness to me at the beginning of my singing career. The short lazy hot days and endless nights of music of the Bayreuth Festival remain a kind of fantasy memory drifting down the years whenever I hear Wagner's music.

After these days I left Nürnberg by train, standing in the corridor or sitting on my suitcase, on the long journey to

Salzburg, where I met up with Barbara and Gracie. We spent a night there before going on to Vienna, where we were met by Eric Troyna and Leonard Delaney. Vienna seemed to be closed for the summer. I remember a wonderful picnic in the Wienerwald and the palace of Schönbrunn, but the Opera was closed, alas. We three girls set off for Innsbruck, where we stayed two days, and then went on to Venice which was another kind of revelation. Cradle of European art, so different from any other city in the world, one feels the waves of the eternal sea underlying the great monuments of men. At that time of the year, so long ago, I still remember most the smell of ozone overwhelmed by rotting garbage. I have never been back and wonder if the smell still lingers on the lagoons on hot summer days.

Returning to London, the next opera I began to prepare was *Die Walküre,* with Rudolf Kempe conducting. The role of Grimgerde, one of the Valkyries, was great fun, as I was singing with some really great voices in the *"Hojotoho."* We spent much time learning to run up the fibreglass rocks with our spears at the precise angle required to avoid injury to the Valkyrie in front, and still have the long spears balanced so that the fulcrum was ready to slide through the hand and the spears stand on end, in time to allow us to sing on cue. Many a poke in the behind was a reminder that you needed to move a little further and faster up the slope. Amy Shuard and Joan Sutherland were part of the splendid team of 'girls' that year, as well as a new friend, the Australian Una Hale.

In September I began to learn the Strauss opera, *Elektra.* The soprano was the unknown Gerda Lammers, replacing the scheduled singer at short notice. The opera's cruel story is compounded by its sustained and highly involved vocal writing. I had never heard such music. After the first brutal whip-lash chords, singing the role of The First Maid, I began the opera, "Wo bleibt Elektra?" and it seemed as if that lash whipped on through the whole opera, except for the ecstatic dance of triumph before my next entry. In this production, grimly brown and always dark, I was required to come alone out of the shadows, having crossed the stage behind the set, and place a flaming torch in the bracket on the door of the supposed castle. Lammers' voice dipped and soared, and the orchestra conducted by Rudolf Kempe played the rich, sticky chords of Strauss' dance. I then had to go off and lead the other four Maids on, in the second of their frantic dashes onto the set. You will know by now that I was an incurable dreamer. I was always a bit vague about time, and one night, well into the run, I spent too long dancing to Elektra's song behind the stage. Horrified to hear my cue for the entry of the Maids being played by the orchestra, I ran like the wind in time to see the other four

59

girls running on stage, frantically looking over their shoulders for me, as they tried to pick up their 'cues' without my first notes. Kempe called a rehearsal for the Maids and I apologised to everyone. I had learned a lesson. There is no place for dreaming during a performance.

During a subsequent revival of *Ballo,* Jon Vickers told me that he blamed me for being responsible for his not getting an engagement at Bayreuth in the 1958 season! He had auditioned sometime that summer in Bayreuth and had *not* been engaged and had thought it must be because I had said something against him, while I was staying with Friedelind. I tried to say that I had absolutely no influence and had never even spoken to either of the brothers Wagner, but he refused to believe me. I was sorry that our relationship always remained strained after that, as his voice was one of the most beautiful tenors I have ever heard. He had a warm baritone quality, but the price he paid for his 'dark' sound was a difficult top to his voice and sometimes a devastating cracking on his top notes, so that you often held your breath as he approached the climax of the aria. But he went on to have a formidable career and sing the great heldentenor roles at Bayreuth, as well as recording *Peter Grimes* and many other operas with Colin Davis.

In September, my friend Graeme de Graaff arrived. In 1950 Graeme's father and mother had let him go to England when he had matriculated at the age of sixteen. He had travelled with three friends and worked in the Festival of Britain office for a year. His most permanent memory was a long held dislike for brussels sprouts on his return to Oz. Food rationing was still in full force in Britain and to achieve the necessary protein the boys decided to become vegetarians. This entitled them to more eggs, cheese, etc (instead of one chop per week), but the only vegetable that was readily available was brussels sprouts, which they ate for that whole year.

He returned to study at Melbourne University, where he later completed his Master's degree in Philosophy. When I went away to Paris, he applied for and won scholarships to France, but his mentor, Professor Gibson, nominated him for a scholarship to Oxford. 'Gibby' now paved the way for our romance by arranging for Graeme to take up the Simms Scholarship at Balliol College.

And now Graeme was returning to live in England. He was a stranger to me. Although we had written so many letters, I found that we had grown up in different ways. For one thing, he had become prematurely bald, so his appearance was different from the boy I remembered. Before leaving Melbourne he had been to see my father to say that he wanted to marry me. My father had been less than kind.

"I've invested a good deal of money in Lauris' career," he growled, "And I don't want her to marry some *pink professor* or long haired academic!"

Graeme was angry, as you can imagine, when he reported this conversation to me. I told him he was not to worry, as he was definitely not a long-haired academic! We would see what happened over the next few months. In retrospect, I can see that I was very insensitive to the needs of this sober young man who had come so far on my account. Immersed in my own exciting new career, I was not very aware of his financial and academic difficulties at this time.

He arrived in a damp autumn in England and went off to the marshes of Oxford, after spending a week in London. During that week he stayed with his old landlady from his previous visit, whom he called Mrs G (Mrs Gardener). She lived in the working class suburb of Tooting. When I eventually met this lively, witty old lady, I enjoyed her company enormously.

He decided to buy a Lambretta motor scooter, so that he could travel up and down from Oxford frequently to visit me. He had to traverse the whole city to get to Primrose Hill. I loved this area. Standing on the top of the hill, overlooking the whole of the city, we could pretend we were miles away as we sat on the grassy slope looking out over the distance to the dome of St Paul's and the distant City, under the blue-tinged, Turner, turning clouds.

We spent that week getting to know each other again, finding both strange differences and real affinities. I enjoyed talking about things not related to singing. Singers are incredibly self-centered and only talk about subjects related to their discipline. Now G and I began again to talk about the world in which we lived and the politics of our time. He loved literature and we talked books, writing and the newly emerging writers of the day, including Lawrence Durrell's great *Alexandria Quartet,* which had just been published. We sat on the grass in the long twilight on top of Primrose Hill, holding and kissing each other, as the light faded and night fell. G went off to Oxford at the end of that week to begin his term at Balliol.

Almost immediately my friend, Len Delaney, arrived from Vienna, to audition at Covent Garden and Sadler's Wells. It was a strange thing to have both these young men in London in the same week. The passionate kisses made me light-headed and stupid with the drunkenness of young love. I found myself weighing them up, trying to come to terms with these two very different people. It was a relief when Len left and I could return to the serious and cloistered life which had been my habit until all the emotional turmoil of those short northern summer nights had started.

One result of his visit was that my decision was made. My life would be with Graeme de Graaff.

At the Garden I was plunged into a busy schedule of rehearsals and performances. The new season began for me with the *Walküre*. The Wagner season began in September, with Birgit Nilsson as Brünnhilde, Hans Hotter as Wotan, the tenor Ramón Vinay, and the bass Gottlob Frick. To stand in the wings and hear these legendary people singing at the height of their powers was miraculous. And it was great fun to sing "Hojotoho" with the other girls, who all had wonderful big voices. When we all sang together, the result set up vibrations within our heads and hearts that made me dizzy. It was thrilling, as was watching Kempe coaxing his rich sounds from the marvellous orchestra with barely visible hand gestures and the merest darting glances from his deep-set, narrowed eyes. His conducting was the least 'visible' of any person I have ever worked with. By contrast, Kubelik really seemed to elicit the sounds, leaning forward with graceful, long-armed, arching gestures. Ted Downes (now Sir Edward) was all vertical bounce it seemed, with no grace, but lots of energy.

Every day I would prepare the new works that I would sing later in the season with the excellent repetiteurs provided by the company to teach the music to the resident singers. These great musicians are the unsung heroes of the opera house. They taught the style and shaped the music, without interfering with vocal technique, were always supportive and tactful, and the welfare of the young singers' voices in the company was always protected by their special knowledge of their young 'pupils' weaknesses and strengths. The season was planned so far in advance that I began learning the music months before the production rehearsals commenced, so that a role was completely 'sung in' by the time I started to move on the stage. In this way I began to learn Poulenc's opera *The Dialogues of the Carmelites,* which I had seen in Paris as a play two years earlier.

G came back to London for the vacation and we began to spend every moment together when I was not rehearsing or performing. I discovered for the first time his misery at the treatment he had received in Oxford. After spending a week or more getting himself settled in, he found that the money for his accommodation at Balliol had not been sent from Melbourne and he was obliged to borrow money. And there was worse to follow! The person he had come to work with on his thesis for two years had left for the USA for a two-year period. So G had to find someone else. He was fortunate to find the great Gilbert Ryle and in fact believes that he benefited wonderfully in having this change of his supervisor. But his spirits were low. He hated the grey skies and damp cold, and longed to go home to Australia. He found the ingrained class system, the rules of the college and the whole system of the hierarchical university life deeply offensive to his democratic ideas, and the treatment 'colonials' got in Oxford was rude, to say the least.

When he arrived at Holywell Manor, the annexe to Balliol

where he was to live, he was told that the building was locked at midnight. He explained that he would be spending a certain amount of time in London going to the Opera, and would like a key to get in when the gates were locked. The Praefectus laughed and said, "I'm afraid that's not possible. You'll just have to climb over the chapel roof, like all the other fellows." As a senior postgraduate, he didn't know whether to laugh or cry.

He hated the meals and the obligation to eat horrible food 'in Hall' five times a week. But he liked, respected and enjoyed Gilbert Ryle, who was very kind to him. He made some good friends amongst the other 'fellows' in Holywell Manor, who have remained close in spite of 'the tyranny of distance'. Many of them had similar problems in their settling into life in Oxford, as most of them were, like G, postgraduates from overseas countries or from 'red-brick' universities. His room-mate, Maurice Wright, was a graduate from Nottingham University. He made another close friend, Graeme Clarke, travelling on the same ship to England. Clarke became Classics Professor at the University of Melbourne and later the Director of the Humanities Research Centre in Canberra.

The winter was wet and dreary and we enjoyed snuggling up on the cosy rug by the fire in my flat. It was Australia Day, January 26, 1958 and we were listening to a BBC broadcast made by Australians in London to celebrate the day. Richard Bonynge had asked me to sing with Joan Sutherland, Raymond Nilsson and David Allen in the quartet from *Rigoletto*. The program was introduced by Keith Michell, and amongst others in the show were June Bronhill, John Cameron and William Herbert. The program had been pre-recorded at the BBC on the 17th January.

As we sat listening, G suddenly said, "I'm going to Spain in the summer on the motor scooter, with Graeme Clarke."

"Can I come too?" I said.

"Not unless you marry me!" said G.

So it was arranged! Graeme Clarke did *not* go to Spain.

But there was a condition to marrying Graeme. G had decided to accept an offer of a position as Vice-Master at his old college, Queen's College, and a Lectureship in Philosophy at Melbourne University. He very much wanted to be part of the growth and development of Australia and said to me that he felt sure there was a great need for talented young trained people to contribute to the life of our country. It was a time when all young Australians wanted to go to London and when everyone with the slightest ambition was to be found in Britain or on the Continent. As I have already mentioned, many of the best singers at The Garden were Australians.

The Elizabethan Theatre Trust had just been formed in Sydney in 1956, and G said he was sure there would be a place for me there and that I should be part of the development and flowering of Australian opera. I was not too enthusiastic about returning home when I was enjoying my singing career so much. I think I believed that it would be a long time before G would complete his degree, and I hoped he might change his mind about going home. After all, he still had another year at Oxford.

We decided to marry at the end of the Covent Garden 1958 summer season, in July, and planned a wonderful honeymoon on the Lambretta travelling through France and Spain.

I also had another exciting offer to look forward to. Kubelik asked me to go to Israel to sing in the 10th Anniversary Celebrations of the founding of the Israeli State. At first Kubelik thought he might do Mahler's 2nd Symphony and I bought a pocket score, my first encounter with the music of Mahler. But he then decided to conduct Beethoven's Ninth. The other singers were to be the Australian-born Elsie Morison, David Kelly, the Scottish bass baritone, and the tenor, Waldemar Kmentt from the Vienna State Opera. We were to sing in Hebrew, as the German language at that time was forbidden in Israel.

And it was now that I had my first chance to hear the music of Benjamin Britten. For months I had been preparing the role of Mrs Sedley in *Peter Grimes*. The part was a challenge for a very slim young girl, and Christopher West decided to capitalise on my appearance by making the twisted old lady poke and point her umbrella and be pointed in her movements. He worked me very hard, trying to unlock the character's nasty prying ways, and I grew to love playing the crazy old bat and feel the compassion for her that one must, when one is acting a character in a great play, as I believe *Grimes* is. The opera filled me with awe. Britten's understanding of the human condition adds another dimension to the terrible story.

The searing beauty of the *Now the Great Bear and Pleiades,* when sung by Pears, was a nightly miracle. And the risks of the difficult ensembles falling apart every night also added a dimension of danger and excitement to each performance!

In early February that year there was a revival of a very old production of *Rigoletto,* in which I had the tiny role of Giovanna. The sets were said to be 100 years old. The heavy, dark old 'flats' with the paint cracked and fading could not dim the extraordinary talent of the Gilda, Joan Sutherland, and her golden voiced tenor, my friend Albert Lance, who came over from Paris to sing the Duke. The Rigoletto was another Australian, John Shaw, who had sung with Joan Hammond in Australia the year before. She had been so impressed that she had told Webster about him and he had been engaged *without audition* to sing this huge role. John's portrayal of the twisted hunchback with the broken heart was so moving that I often wept for him, and I remember him with tears in his eyes and in his voice, at the end of the opera.

At The Garden we were now in full production rehearsals for *The Carmelites* with the great director, Margherita Wallman. She was a stern little middle-aged woman, walking with an elegant cane and a pronounced limp. She demanded great acting from the principals in the cast and the rehearsals were long, and for us minor principals, very boring. The set by George Wakhevitch, representing the convent cloisters, was 'cut away' to show two floors, upstairs and downstairs, with colonnades where the 'minor' nuns walked in the background during much of the singing by the major principals. In the wings was a table on which a beautifully bound set of the novels of Sir Walter Scott was laid out, so that at one point we went off-stage, picked up a book, then paced through the colonnades at the back of the set, pretending to be reading our 'breviaries'. My companion nun, Josephine Veasey, possessed a lovely mezzo voice and a wicked sense of humour and we were often cast as alternatives for the same roles. We were also becoming firm friends, even though we were rivals.

Josie and I would pick up our books and read in whispers to each other such gems as, "Gadzooks, quoth Sir Blodwin, drawing his sword from the scabbard ..." and gradually become helpless with giggles as we clung to each other in the twilight gloom at the back of the stage. The serious gravity of the story we were involved in only seemed to make our laughter more uncontrollable. At last, one afternoon Margherita Wallman noticed our misbehaviour and stamping her foot angrily, told us to behave ourselves or leave the set and the production! That soon brought us to our senses!

Kubelik conducted and Elsie Morison headed the cast as Blanche, the child born in fear, who goes through her life in fear until her weakness is conquered in the triumphant manner of her death. Joan Sutherland played Mère Lidoine. The opera was sung in English, with Sylvia Fisher giving a memorable performance as the inflexible Mère Marie, John Lanigan, David Allen and Robert Allman were other Australians in the cast. I never failed to be moved by the final scene; and the scene played by Jean Watson where she dies 'a bad death', by taking on the 'fear' of Blanche for her own passage to her God, had such power that I longed to play this role myself one day. Alas, this was to be one of my unfulfilled ambitions.

In this opera I was playing Mère Jeanne, the oldest nun in the convent, supposedly a hundred years old. As I re-read a remarkable essay on the opera by Peter Heyworth published in *The Times* when this production was mounted, I wonder why I remember this opera with such affection? It was a small role I had to play, yet it stays in my memory.

The opera was written between 1953 and 1955 and this was its first production. Sitting in the darkened theatre at the final rehearsals was the composer Poulenc, with his extraordinarily long pale face. We were all aware that this was a rare event, to be delivering a first performance in the country, with the composer present, of a new work which may live forever.

When the Ballet season began a short time later, we were on tour again and I went to Manchester and Oxford, where I was for the first time introduced to G's new friends. I was only in *Carmelites* on this tour, so that apart from preparing future new roles with the staff coaches, I could go to some of the performances I had not seen in London. I heard Marie Collier sing *Aïda* in the New Theatre in Oxford. The stage was tiny after Covent Garden and the principal male dancer in the ballet scene in Act 2 was performing his circle of *grands jetées* splendidly around the perimeter of the set, when he ran out of space! To his embarrassment and the audience's huge delight, he suddenly dropped over the edge of the stage, landing amongst the timpani with a loud bang. The performance was enhanced by the sight of his neat bottom scrambling up over the footlights and back onto the stage, to howls of laughter. Ah, the joys of touring!

In Manchester Noreen Berry, another of the young singers who became a great friend, showed me an enjoyable and inexpensive way to spend an hour or so in a strange city.

"We'll go and look at hats," she said. And that is what we did. For a whole afternoon on a grey and gloomy day, we went from one to another of the grandest shops we could find, trying on hats we had no intention of buying.

Finally the tour ended and the company returned to London. We were given some phonetic coaching in Hebrew pronunciation for the forthcoming concerts with the Israel Philharmonic, and we had a 'sing through' with Kubelik, before flying out to Tel Aviv.

The flight touched down at Athens and I saw for the first time the ancient Greek ruins, and the Acropolis. It was a hot and dry landscape that we were seeing, after the green years of Europe. For the first time I was homesick for Australia as we flew into the desert-dry, red-coloured country which reminded me of the Mallee.

The Israel Philharmonic owned two houses right on the beach, each staffed with a cook and a housekeeper, where we would be based during our eighteen-day tour. Mrs Kubelik and their son came too. We were within a stone's throw of the beach, separated only by sand dunes, so we went swimming each day before going to the new Frederick R Mann Auditorium for the orchestral and choral rehearsals.

Beethoven's Ninth does not require a lot of singing for the contralto, so I had a very enjoyable holiday. The soprano, tenor and bass have much more responsibility as they all have exposed and difficult solos. I had never heard the Ninth performed live, so had no comparison by which to judge the singing of my colleagues, but having sung the work many times since then, I believe the three other voices in those nine performances were probably amongst the finest you could hear at that time. Elsie Morison floated her voice through the top Bs of the end of the quartet with an ease that I have never heard again, and the two men were equally secure in their solos.

The audience, listening to the short solos at the end of the last movement of this symphony, rarely know how difficult it is to sit quiet and still through the music of the first three movements. There is always a discussion about where the soloists should be placed in relation to the choir and the orchestra. On that occasion we were put in front of the orchestra, in a line behind the conductor's podium. If the stage is too small or narrow, the soloists are sometimes put at the back of the orchestra, below the choir. The hall was very like the London Festival Hall, with its wooden interior, and had a warm and generous acoustic, as does our Concert Hall in the Sydney Opera House.

It was a pleasure to sing there and we gave four concerts in Tel Aviv, then three in Jerusalem and two in Haifa, in twelve days, to sold-out houses. We were delighted to read in the local press that the critics thought the soloists' Hebrew diction was better than the choir's!

Once we had rehearsed and done our first concerts in Tel Aviv, we set out for Jerusalem which was then a divided city. We drove for about three hours, on narrow unmade roads, through hilly, dry country so like outback Australia in both climate and appearance. From our suites in the King David Hotel we gazed across a deep valley to the ancient city on the opposite hilltop, in the Arab zone, where a column of smoke spiralled lazily upwards into the cloudless blue sky, day and night for the whole time we were there. We were told the smoke was from a Jewish library of thousands of ancient books being burnt in the Arab occupied section of the old city.

We were not allowed to visit Bethlehem, but were enchanted by a lazy day spent swimming in the Sea of Gallilee, after a wonderful outdoor fish luncheon eaten from trestle tables in the shade of an ancient grapevine. The restaurateur assured us that the fish, caught that morning, were the same kind that the disciples would have eaten.

After another long hot drive we were at last approaching the ancient city of Haifa, where Kubelik, who had visited the country frequently, pointed out the ancient ruins of a castle stretching out along a sea wall into the calm blue sea. "The Crusaders built that. It's said to have belonged to Richard the Lion Heart," he said.

The hills outside these ancient towns were of a beautiful rose and ochre colour, and as I walked over them I discovered that pebbles and stones lying in the grass were actually shards of ancient Greek and Roman pottery.

In Haifa, we went with Kubelik to a local market where he bought amber and, with his help, I bought an ancient Yemen necklace. The narrow stalls and the bargaining of the street vendors were exciting and exotic. In this ancient city the hall was old and we were less comfortable performing, as the temperature inside the hall soared without the benefit of air conditioning.

Back we went to Tel Aviv for the final concert, and Kubelik took us to visit friends who lived in a modern apartment in the centre of the city. "I want you to meet this family," he said. "The fourteen year old son is a prodigy, who will one day be famous throughout the musical world." I looked at this young boy from the experience of my own twenty-five years, wondering how Kubelik could assess and know his future so well. His name was Daniel Barenboim.

The whole tour was an experience I shall never forget. Israel was then a new country with a tremendous feeling of hope and idealism, and there was such joy in the achievement of building a prosperous and united society in those first ten years. It was inspiring to be there to help them celebrate their anniversary.

Returning to London, there were lots of exciting things to contemplate. Our wedding in July was approaching and we had to plan our honeymoon on the Lambretta. We would have a very small wedding with only twenty-six guests.

Covent Garden revived *Elektra* and a further five performances of *The Trojans,* and we began stage rehearsals for *Peter Grimes* which Kubelik would conduct with Peter Pears in the title role.

On June 10th, 1958 the Royal Opera House celebrated the centenary of the present building. A Gala concert was given in the presence of the Queen and the Duke of Edinburgh. The great Australian soprano, Sylvia Fisher, opened the evening by singing *God Save The Queen* with the Opera House orchestra and chorus. It is rare to hear such a commonly-heard piece of music performed by a singer of this stature and it set the tone for the whole evening, which has become one of my unforgettable memories.

Joan Sutherland and John Lanigan sang *I dreamt I dwelt in marble halls* and the following duet, *O love whom alone I adore,* from *The Bohemian Girl;* The Royal Ballet presented *A Birthday Offering* with Margot Fonteyn partnered by Michael Somes and some of the other great dancers from the company. I took part in the night scene on the beach from Britten's *Peter Grimes.* But I think the highlight of that night was the performance by Callas in a scene from *I Puritani.*

"The skill with which she varied the colour and weight of

her voice to suggest *Elvira's* fluctuating moods, the grace of her florid singing and the dramatic intensity of her whole representation revealed a singer in whose art the tragic actress and the musician are equally powerful." These words by Martin Cooper in *The Daily Telegraph* sum up the performance on that night and my feelings about Maria Callas, the singer. I saw her several times at The Garden in those years as Medée, Tosca and Violetta in *Traviata,* and hoped that one day I would learn to sing with her passion and dramatic commitment.

After the Gala we were all lined up backstage and presented to the Queen and Prince Philip. *This* was one of the nights I was glad to be a part of!

6. Marriage and Home

When Graeme was in London in 1950, he had worked as a volunteer for the West London Mission at Kingsway, run by Dr Donald Soper, who now agreed to marry us. We arranged to have the service in the Little Chapel at the back of the church. We found the formalities of the marriage interesting. We had to have all our parents' birth certificates, and then publish 'the Banns', displaying our intention to marry, for four Sundays prior to the wedding.

We arranged to move my few belongings from Primrose Hill to the Cannonbury flat we had now leased from my friend Faye Mishael and her husband, John Bailey. I had no furniture except for my very old twangy upright piano. I bought it when I saw a hand-written notice advertising it in a shop window. It was a genuine antique, with red satin cloth covering the strings above the keyboard, beautifully carved fat legs and brass candlesticks; I loved its appearance even while I deplored its tone. Now, looking back, I believe that it may really have been a forte-piano, as it was very old and made the sound that is now fashionable in early music.

Madame Modesti flew over especially on the day from Paris for the wedding. In 1958 people rarely travelled by plane, so we were doubly thrilled. This dear friend arrived with a huge pale blue Lalique 'Coupe de Marriage' under one arm and a bottle of champagne under the other. We were told to drink the champagne from the cup on our first wedding anniversary.

On the day, we rang Australia for the first and only time we lived abroad. This was an unheard-of extravagance. Our four parents were all upset at not being able to come to the wedding and to celebrate, so they went to see *Salad Days* together at Her Majesty's Theatre in Melbourne, on the night we got married.

Our simple service went smoothly in the Little Chapel, with Trevor Hubble standing behind G, and Robert Allman 'giving me away'. He was so kind that day. The terrible doubts that creep through one's dreams on the last night before the wedding, and the responsibility of the vows to be taken overwhelm everyone at this moment. Bob held my hand firmly in the taxi, and patting it gently, read me a little homily, and generally behaved as my own Dad would have done if he had been there.

Our life together had begun magnificently, with a honeymoon so memorable that we still ask each other, "Is it as beautiful as Aigua Blava?" when we see a beautiful place. Aigua Blava, just north of Barcelona, was our Arcadia.

Our return to London was made easy by the kindness of Gordon and Vivian Signy, our new landlords. G began working on his thesis each day at John Bailey's desk, and soon it was time for him to return to Balliol and the second year at Oxford.

After his constant company for over two months, it was strange to be alone again. It seemed as if we should always be together and had been created for each other. But my life was busy and full of excitement, with wonderful new work to prepare and perform in one of the greatest opera houses of the world. The joy of singing with an orchestra is indescribable, for the voice is supported and held, swimming in a warm pool of sound. Difficult high areas of my voice were easier to achieve. I had never been so happy and fulfilled.

This year I had a magnificent piece to sing, which suited me down to the ground, Handel's *Samson*. I was thrilled to be given the role of Micah, with Raymond Leppard conducting a staged performance of this great oratorio. My Samson was Jon Vickers, and the sound of his voice singing *Total Eclipse* has stayed with me for the rest of my life. The work was produced by Herbert Graf and the bass Joseph Rouleau was also in the production. It was remarkable that we three who had come into the company together on the same day were always cast in the same operas.

The 'opera' was to be performed in the Leeds Centenary Festival, in the presence of the Queen and Prince Philip, in the Leeds Grand Theatre and Opera House. The theatre itself was all old red-plush and gilt, and the beautiful Oliver Messel set was designed to complement these surroundings.

The soprano, Elisabeth Lindermeier, was an attractive singer who had a soft-grained voice and an English pronunciation which made me smile. When she sang her first aria, I wondered what "The scoos" meant, until I looked at the score and saw, "Thus coos the turtle-dove alone" as the first words.

The role of Micah was beautiful to sing and I was on stage all night as Vickers' alter ego. I loved standing near him, acting the young man who is his conscience and inspires him to brave deeds. The great words of Milton were an inspiration, and I was given a recitative and aria called *Then long eternity shall greet your bliss,* full of long cadenzas, which was not in the old Novello score. I discovered I loved singing this music and had the flexibility to manage it well. I became aware of the different demands Handel's florid music placed on the voice and the fact that I had an ability to sing it.

In Melbourne I had sung Handel's *Messiah* often, but somehow in my years with Modesti, he had only worked on the range, power and line of my operatic sound, trying to build the Verdi voice which was to come to me later, and for which I am so grateful. We did little work on the song repertoire or music of other periods. Meanwhile, the musical world was re-discovering the appropriate performance style for baroque music, and ornamentation was beginning to become fashionable, after more than two hundred years of neglect. Raymond Leppard was the lively young conductor who had just finished his research into this area in Cambridge, and he brought a breath of fresh air into the conducting of Handel. I enjoyed the opening night very much, acting to the best of my ability in the longest role I had so far sung on stage.

On that first night, my astonished ears heard Joan Sutherland sing *Let the bright seraphim* as only an angel could have sung it. (I did not remember having heard her during the rehearsals. Perhaps she did not rehearse with the cast, before the opening night?) The audience rose to its feet and gave her the ovation of the night, in spite of Vickers and Lindermeier and Rouleau (not to mention myself) having delivered fine sounds and sung all night long! There was no doubt in my mind that this was the most ravishing singing I had ever heard!

After the performance we were presented to the Queen and the Duke of Edinburgh, then we changed into our most glamorous evening clothes and went to the Mayoral Reception in the Civic Hall. The plates and cutlery were of gold, the glasses of finest crystal; I have never attended a grander function. Lord and Lady Harewood were there with the Princess Marina, as well as many other distinguished guests, to celebrate the centenary of Leeds, the great manufacturing city. The memory that stays most vividly from the dinner was the music played by a simply dressed girl playing an Irish harp and singing in the sweetest natural voice. Who she was I don't know, but the memory of her song has persuaded me that she must have been famous in her own field of music, so different from my own.

In January 1959 the members of the cast of *Peter Grimes* were to record the opera for Decca. Every morning we travelled out to Walthamstow Town Hall to record what has become an historical recording. Britten himself conducted and Pears was Peter Grimes. (At Covent Garden, Kubelik had been the conductor). It was the depths of winter and snow made travelling difficult. Iris Kells, who sang one of the 'nieces', lived nearby in Cannonbury. She picked me up each morning and we drove out to Walthamstow through deep slush, to the unheated Town Hall. During the recording sessions we all sang in heavy overcoats, hats and gloves.

The producer of the recording was the legendary John Culshaw. The floor of the Town Hall was marked out in numbered, segmented, concentric circles and we were directed to move from one to another, as if moving in a stage production. This was one of the early attempts at stereophonic sound in recording. With hindsight, this was probably the most important work I did during my time in London. Certainly it was the most enduring.

After each 'take' the composer/conductor went into the makeshift control room at the back of the stage and listened with headphones to the result, to see if the section should be re-done or if we could go on. The chorus were seated on the stage, with their own microphones, and when we principals were singing with them, as in the 'hunt' chorus, we sat with them. When recording other scenes, we moved on the floor of the hall, from one numbered segment to another, as we made our entrances and exits, as in the opening of the 'Pub' scene. It was a wonderful experience to have the composer conduct his own work with his own tempi and interpretative ideas, and it was amusing to hear Britten mutter to someone one day that if he had known he was ever going to conduct this work, he might have made some of it a bit easier! (He was, of course, a superb conductor).

The resulting record is, in my opinion, the definitive performance. The fine recording of Colin Davis, with Vickers in the lead, seems a different piece of music for me.

The next role I learned was the tiny role of Alisa in *Lucia di Lammermoor*. I was to share this role with Margreta Elkins, who had just joined the company. I had no idea of the importance of this opera, as it was only a 'bit part' for me to sing, until I began to attend the production calls in the theatre. I sat in the dark, waiting and watching, and as the producer occasionally called from the stalls or raced up onto the stage, I was aware of an extraordinary metamorphosis.

My colleague Joan Sutherland was becoming a great actress, and her wonderful voice was only a part of the artistic power in her portrayal of the mad Lucia. She was developing the 'charisma' all great artists require to hold the audience. The man in the darkened theatre was, of course, the legendary Zeffirelli, and when the Covent Garden orchestra was conducted by Tullio Serafin the magic was complete. Margreta Elkins sang in the opening performance, and I watched from the theatre as the new star from the 'South Land' was made. I went backstage afterwards to offer my congratulations, and as I burrowed through the narrow passages to the dressing room, I saw Maria Callas ahead of me, smiling and embracing the new young diva. Flashlights erupted, and the famous photograph of the encounter of the two great bel canto sopranos was born before my eyes.

I sang in many of the Sutherland *Lucia's* that season, but

also had the pleasure of singing with Mattiwilda Dobbs in that same production, as well as another great Australian soprano, June Bronhill. June had the advantage of having attended many of the stage rehearsals conducted by Zeffirelli, so she knew the director's intentions very well and was a wonderful actress. Dobbs only came into the production after the opening, and sang the role with her exquisite voice, grace and beauty, but having missed the production rehearsals she lacked the insight into the role which Zeffirelli demanded.

I was privileged to hear Callas sing on many occasions at the peak of her career. I heard and saw her great Tosca with Tito Gobbi. She sang this role with my friend Albert Lance (Ingram) in Paris, a performance of which has been shown in Australia on SBS. I saw her *Traviata,* and for the first time *believed* in the fragile courtesan. Until that time I had always regarded the opera as an excuse for some great singing, but now I saw Violetta, the vulnerable woman, with all her humanity and her life's dilemmas. In *Medea,* for the first time, I watched a singer stand facing upstage, with arms outstretched, as if she were being crucified, delivering the whole of her great opening aria with her *back* to the audience. Her portrayal of Medea's obsessive madness was riveting, but it was her ability to colour the voice, changing the quality to match the dramatic action, which I loved most in her performances. It was a revelation to me that sometimes an ugly sound was dramatically important. Until then I had striven to produce only beautiful sounds, but I saw now that the word, or the mood, demanded its own special colour. And I saw that Callas could achieve great acting by stillness, *being the still centre,* while her charismatic presence dominated the stage in the midst of frenetic activity. She was not a perfect singer in the way that Sutherland and that other great soprano Tebaldi were, but her dramatic ability made every role she sang unforgettable. She was a supreme actress, even without her extraordinary voice.

The major production in the latter part of this season was a wonderful *Don Carlos,* with Boris Christoff, Gré Brouwenstijn, Vickers, Grace Hoffman, Geraint Evans, Michael Langdon and Rouleau. The conductor was Giulini and Visconti was the producer. The production was lavish, complete with ballet and the Fontainebleau Act, which is often cut. I was fortunate to see this beautiful opera presented so early in my career because, years later, I had the opportunity to sing Eboli.

At the end of the regional tour to Oxford and Manchester in March, we returned to London. It was the custom for us to be each called in to see Sir David to discuss contracts for the end of the year, in this case the 1959/60 season, starting the following September. I had been rather upset that 'my' Ulrica had been sung in this latter part of the year by Margreta Elkins, which meant I had not been given so many performances this season. Like the silly child I was, I thought perhaps the Garden was dissatisfied with me and that I would not be re-engaged. And I had not breathed a word to anyone that G and I were intending to leave London to return to Australia.

Imagine my feelings when, as soon as I was seated in front of Sir David's desk, he said in his cool English voice, "We are very pleased with your development. We want you to accept a study scholarship for a year in Italy."

My eyes filled with tears and I stammered "I can't."

He looked at me with astonishment. "Why ever not?" he asked.

"Because I'm going to return to live in Australia," I whispered. "I meant to tell you before this, but I wasn't sure if you were intending to renew my contract."

"Well!" he said, "I'm sorry you're leaving, and wish you good fortune in your future life ... Goodbye, Miss Elms ... I think you'll be back in six months ... perhaps a year."

I stumbled out of the room and down the twisting stairs to the green-room, where I burst into uncontrollable sobs. "Whatever is the matter?" said my friend Josephine Veasey.

When I told her the story, a delighted beam spread across her face. "That's great news for me," she laughed. "You've always been my greatest threat. Now I can get on with my career without a worry!"

I had to laugh at this. She was such an open, honest and cheerful person that I could only thank her for saying the right thing to put this situation into perspective. After all, it *was* my own decision, and I must look forward to the future without regret.

G had submitted his thesis and had been awarded his degree. He began to make plans for our return to Melbourne and Queen's College, excited at the prospect of his new life as the Vice-Master. The College had engaged one of Melbourne's top architects to design a town house attached to the new wing being built on the side of the College. We would have a brand new, modern little house to live in at the beginning of 1960.

G wrote to Robert Quentin, the director of the Elizabethan Theatre Trust (the forerunner to Opera Australia) and received an enthusiastic reply. Quentin was delighted to hear of my return, and asked that we should meet as soon as I was back, to discuss the roles I would like to do. He wrote that he really needed a voice like mine in the new company.

We also wrote to the ABC, which sent a contract by return mail for a concert in November in the new Festival Hall in Melbourne.

I got to work on the arias for this Melbourne concert with my friends at Covent Garden, the repetiteurs Robert Keys and Albert Knowles. It was Robert Keys who suggested *Bel Raggio Lusinghier,* the aria from *Semiramide.* I'd never heard of Rossini's *Semiramide,* but enjoyed the challenge of a really high tessitura aria with lots of dazzling coloratura.

The beautiful summer days began in London as the season drew to a close. We began packing our possessions, mainly books and music, and sent them off by sea. At dinner at Ronald and Elsie Dowd's house, Ron and John Shaw shook their heads, bewildered at the thought of my leaving Covent Garden and London. Newly arrived Jenifer Eddy was more positive. Revealing a pattern of thought which stood her, and later on the Australian singing world, in good stead, she said, "You'll have the stage to yourself in Australia, Lauris."

As we began to think of our return to Melbourne, we had a letter from Graeme's mother saying they were planning a big 'welcome home' party for us. The family were so excited to have us coming home to live in Melbourne, that they asked all the relatives and friends they could think of. At this time, travel overseas from Australia was almost always by the civilised ocean liner and we were very advanced to be returning by air. Our families had no idea of the phenomenon of jet lag. We had already done sufficient flying to know that arriving in Melbourne at about 5pm after an overnight flight would make us zombies.

However, we were to take about six weeks to come home. Athens and five days in Greece preceded an extraordinary four-week trip around Ceylon with an old friend of G's. Ceylon was a quiet and magical country and this visit was a strange pause in our lives, between the hard work and happiness I had known in London and the dread I felt about returning to the Melbourne life that I had left five years before.

I was rather more apprehensive than excited about the prospect of the family party. I was also aware for the first time of how much I had grown away from my very close-knit family, with its intense interest in everyone else's business. I had learned to enjoy my independence and make my own decisions, for good or ill. So I worried about my return to Melbourne. We arrived at Essendon on a cold damp afternoon, where we disembarked into an icy, corrugated iron shed, where a small fire burned in an open fireplace. But the loving warmth of the welcome by both sets of parents helped to take some of the chill out of our bones. As we drove through the flat streets of Melbourne to Dandenong, I couldn't help thinking how low the buildings were and how wide and spread-out the streets, as if some giant had ironed all the wrinkles out and flattened the world I had known. There was so much space everywhere!

And how tiny Isabel and Ern's house was. I had forgotten, too, that central heating did not exist in domestic houses and how *cold* it was, even with the gas fire burning in 'the lounge'. But the party was a huge success and we stayed awake for a suitable time, until all the guests had departed.

We spent the next week or so at Dandenong while we looked for a temporary flat until our new residence at Queen's

College was completed. In the end we found a quaint set of rooms in the top turret of a big old house in Hawthorn, near the tram depot. Here we made our nest amongst griffins and gargoyles, like the storks amongst the red roofs in an old fairy story.

7. Queen's and the Blues

As soon as we found somewhere to live, we contacted the Elizabethan Trust Opera to arrange an appointment to talk to Robert Quentin about my operatic future.

"I'm sorry," said the voice at the other end of the phone, "Mr Quentin is no longer here."

There had been the first of the many power struggles in the history of the Opera Company while we were having our long holiday travelling home.

Stefan Haag had replaced Quentin and he told us curtly that there was nothing for me in the forthcoming season, and also made it clear that he thought I had returned to Australia because I was a failure overseas.

I was devastated!

G was excited and looking forward to his new job enormously and I, who had been more apprehensive about returning, was now proved only too right. As I tried to hide my anger and disappointment, it seemed important to create work for myself and to be as busy as possible. The Dandenong Town Hall was the first place in which I demonstrated my newly found vocal skill. With Christopher Kimber and his pianist brother William, I presented a joint recital in aid of the local Rotary appeal for the new Dandenong Hospital. It seemed so strange that this should be my first concert back in Australia. I had sung in Dandenong on my last night in Melbourne. It was coming full circle, and yet, and yet ...

Mme Modesti was there, by some strange quirk of fate, to hear me sing in my homeland and home town.

The local newspaper said, "Unspoiled by her success, Lauris is as natural and friendly as ever."

If only people could have known! I *was* changed by my success. However humble the venue, I was going to prove that I was the best singer in this provincial city and country that these people were ever going to hear, if I could. I made this arrogant pledge to myself out of my rage and frustration. I loved music and singing so much. I could not bear mediocrity and I believed that to spend my life making mediocre music would not only diminish me, but also demean music which I loved above everything else. I must continue to grow and develop as a performer in my own country, even if I could not do it on the world stage. And I must try to sing music of more value than the current local singers were accustomed to performing. I had, after all, come back to an environment in which music from all countries was generally sung in English and Edward German was one of the most popular composers. There were some really first-class singers in the country, but so often they were expected to perform with less than the best accompanists and to sing music which was frankly unworthy. Well then, let me sing *everything* to the best of my capabilities. *This* was my ambition now.

Mother suggested a recital at the tiny Berwick Hall. I prepared a mixed program of opera and lieder with the help of my conductor friend from the National Theatre, Eric Clapham, who played the piano for me. I learned the lovely Dvořák *Gypsy songs* especially for this and began a life-long policy of learning something new each time I sang a recital. We really enjoyed preparing and presenting this concert together.

Eric Clapham was at a crossroads in his life. The impermanence of his conducting with the Elizabethan Opera meant he had to find another way to make a secure living to support his young and growing family. He was beginning to conduct musicals for the commercial theatre managements of Garnet H Carroll, who had 'bought out' the Benjamin Fuller chain of theatres. Eric agreed to do a major tour of *The Most Happy Fella* with Inia Te Wiata, the great Maori singer, around Australia and New Zealand. When I knew he was going away, I asked whom he could recommend as a coach. He immediately suggested Gwen Halstead. Gwen had gone abroad a little earlier than I, and had returned with her husband, Eric Brooker, to live in a house they were building for themselves in North Balwyn. She was a very good coach and she wanted to accompany singers as much as I wanted to sing. I began working with her regularly and we became very close friends.

I had been asked to sing in the newly-built Festival Hall in Melbourne by the ABC. They wanted to see if this new venue would be suitable for their concerts, and I carefully chose a program designed to show my new found coloratura ability. With Clive Douglas conducting the Victorian Symphony Orchestra at this free concert on that Sunday afternoon in November, I sang Rossini's *Bel Raggio* from *Semiramide, Traüme* from the *Wesendonk-Lieder* by Wagner and the Dvořák *Gypsy songs,* all of which I'd prepared with coach Robert Keys in London. As I gazed around the boxing stadium from which the Festival Hall had come, I felt I was back in a frontier town. The acoustics were abominable and the audience was tiny and very restless. I felt I sang badly, having chosen unsuitable repertoire for this venue. I was at a low point in my life.

This seemed to be as good a time as any to 'start a family'. G and I found ourselves suddenly very excited at the prospect of a baby, to be born after we were in the new Queen's College flat. But I was very nervous about becoming pregnant because I still wanted to sing professionally, and the ABC was talking about giving me work in the following year. I knew that becoming parents would completely alter our lives.

Almost as soon as I stopped taking 'the pill', I went off to the local doctor to have the test, and I found I was pregnant. It was a memorable day. Sharing this new secret in the marriage is a private and momentous happening. It is akin to those other most important, deepest and happiest moments in a shared life: marriage, birth, the weddings of your children and the birth of grandchildren.

I consulted the local GP about how soon he thought I would be able to sing after the birth of our baby. "Oh," he smiled, "You won't want to do *that* any more. You'll be content to stay home and feed your little baby, like a contented cow."

This tactless advice made me *even more uneasy* about our decision to have a child at this time. How *dare* he suggest that I would feel like a cow, contented or otherwise!

And what if he were right? How awful!

It made me angry that this man, who knew nothing about me, or singing, or music, for that matter, should tell me what I would or should feel! Naturally I changed doctors and went to one of the top gynaecologists in Collins Street, who did his best to reassure me that I would be able to fulfil the following year's singing engagements.

Driven by this passion for singing, I looked forward to my next concert with Dr Schildberger, who had been one of the conductors at the National Theatre before I went away. With his nose twitching like a tiny frightened rabbit, he seemed so old and frail when I met him again after five year's absence, for the rehearsal of Handel's *Samson* in concert, with his choirs, the Camberwell and Brighton Philharmonic Societies.

The concert was in the Independent Church in Collins Street, a lovely place with good acoustics. But the dreadful freelance orchestra playing for us that night filled me again with despair, and Doc Schildberger was no Raymond Leppard! The future seemed a downward spiral of mediocrity. The nice thing about that performance was that my colleague Robert Allman, on a visit to Melbourne from Germany for the Elizabethan Opera Company, was also singing.

I was asked to go to Korumburra to sing a *Messiah,* and this was a special journey for me as it was the country where my grandparents had farmed a hundred years earlier. My grandfather, Arthur Elms, founded the butter factory there.

Robert Allman and I met again a few weeks later when we sang in my first ABC *Messiah* for five years. The conductor was the redoubtable Sir Bernard Heinze. This man had driven the musical life of Melbourne for thirty years, manipulating politicians and helping to create the Melbourne Symphony and the other ABC symphony orchestras, in spite of rivalry and obstructions. He introduced great new music to concert audiences for the first time. He had been ruthless in his ambition to achieve his place as the principal conductor in Melbourne, and to gain his knighthood, often destroying equal or greater talents on the way to achieving his ambitions. But he was always ready to help young talented performers and had an eye and an ear for recognising the musically gifted. He was very kind to me and for many years always asked for me to sing in his concerts, most often in *Messiah*.

He had many faults as a conductor. One was a difficulty getting started. His tempi were likely to be 'flexible' so the initial down beat need not necessarily indicate or set the tempo for the rest of the work, or even the first few bars! I remember a performance when, with quivering jowls, he raised the baton, and cried, "Go!"

I sang again in Hector Crawford's 'Music for the People' concert on Christmas Eve, 1959, in the Myer Music Bowl. This was a wonderful experience, to look across the thousands of glittering candles, into the starry night.

Sometime in that December we left our curious little flat, high amongst the gargoyled roofs of Hawthorn, and took up residence in the smart little flat at Queen's College, an all-male Methodist residential college within Melbourne University. We loved its grey/black walls and matching carpet. We even had a spare room, which would be suitable for the 'nanny' I would need if I were going away to sing.

We felt this was a new year full of promise when we would both begin our new lives. Graeme had a door from his study, at the end of the flat, which opened into the corridor of the new wing of the college. We looked forward to having students drop in and I began to practise the new skills of serving afternoon tea to the undergraduates.

The centre of the city of Melbourne was always beautiful to my eyes, with its wide tree-lined streets and magnificent public gardens. But the flat and dreary suburbs stretching around the crescent of Port Philip Bay did not enchant me. My heart was always away in south Gippsland, near the racing waters of Western Port bay, where the old Bonwick house looked down on the Bridge and where the ghosts of my great-aunts laughed their way through the windy nights and long hot summer days of my memory. That first summer after our return to Melbourne, we returned there and joyfully spent a week or so at my family's camp at Cape Woolami. I was three months into my pregnancy and feeling very well. The family had been enlarged whilst I had been away. In five years my little sister Elizabeth and her husband Laurie now had three children: Marvyn, Stuart and three year old Linda. Uncle Alf, his son Bill, and numerous other younger boys and friends of Laurie's were there.

The magnificent campsite was in the curve of the bay below the rocky headland of Cape Woolami, where mutton-birds nested and squabbled all night on the bracken-covered mountain. The headland sheltered the bay from the constant cold winds of the south, and stretching away to the west were great sand dunes, constantly moving and changing, like an echo of an Arabian Night's dream. As if we were still children, we were compelled to climb these dunes and slide down in the sand to the bottom.

My uncle and father went fishing nearly every day from the rocks at the outer end of the Cape. It was a dangerous place where enormous seas from Bass Strait broke over the mountainous granite boulders. To get there we had to trudge over the top of the Cape and then scramble down the side face of the promontory.

I remembered a family joke from my girlhood, when one morning my father asked me if I wanted to fish or swim. I usually disliked fishing, but on this occasion I said "Fish."

"Well, you've got to swim," he scowled. That meant staying home at the base camp and spending the day lying about reading, swimming and sun-bathing, walking over the grassy sea bed at low tide to look at the little fish trapped there, and walking out along the old partly-wrecked granite wharf some earlier inhabitants of the bay had built, in order to transport the great stones which were used in the beautiful buildings of the old wealthy and gracious city of Melbourne. Those golden and red granite stones glowed with an inner fire, and seemed like living jewels on the hot still afternoons.

The camp site itself was situated over the edge of a low marram-grassed sand dune, separated from the beach, just above high water. Behind this sheltered space was the steep climb up to the top of the headland itself, and running into the shallow narrow valley, a permanent spring of sweet water meant that we were always able to camp there, even in the driest summers. This was the place of my father's and uncle's romantic boyhood adventures and they willingly returned to their youth each year as to some ancient rite.

This holiday was my husband's initiation into this very special secret family paradise. He hated it! He hated the flies, the sand, the constant smell of wood-fire smoke, the lack of privacy, sleeping in the communal tent with the other men and, worst of all, the communal open pit toilet surrounded by a hessian bag and a cloud of flies, which was beaten back by throwing a spadeful of sand into the pit.

I spent a rather tense week, trying to enjoy my own holiday in this beautiful place and divided in my sympathies with G, who came in for the usual family teasing, which we both hated.

We decided that we would not repeat the experience and that we needed a refuge of our own for weekends and the long University vacations. I would have loved to go to San Remo but it was too far away to spend one night a week. We began to spend time with 'Isanern', the warm and loving parents of my husband, at their home in Somers, which was about half the distance to travel from Melbourne. Isabel and Ernest owned an old house behind the General Store. It was a wonderful holiday house, possessing its own 'live-in' friendly ghost. A white-haired lady, she liked to sit on the veranda, watching the deserted tennis court opposite.

Finally holidays and the summer were over. Autumn came, and the University year began. The Prime Minister, R G Menzies, opened the new residential addition to Queen's College. Gazing down from the upper floor on to our tiny terrace garden, he cried jovially, "A fine place in which to drink beer." The Methodists who surrounded him at that moment gasped with horror.

On April 9th, 1960 I sang my first *St Matthew Passion,* in English. I had heard this work once before in a fine performance in Oxford, where Helen Watts had been the contralto soloist. In Melbourne the conductor was Henri Krips, "who conducted in a style proper to Johann Strauss, and fatal to Bach," said the unkind critic. However, I received wonderful notices and John Sinclair in *The Melbourne Herald* said: "The one great consolation was Lauris Elms, who sand (sic) the aria *Have mercy Lord* not only with a glorious voice, but as though she really understood and loved the music."

I *did* love this music. I was having to learn and perform my new repertoire so quickly, but I felt as if I must sing this music in a pure, instrumental way, trying to achieve a depth of sound as I would have wished to play it on the violin. I was at last able to make the sounds I heard in my heart and mind, and here the words were not the important thing. It was the music that mattered. The duet with the violin in *Have mercy Lord (Erbarme dich)* was my greatest pleasure, as the two instruments wove their intricate melodies together.

The most difficult solo part is that of The Evangelist. The tenor has to sing music which is almost entirely recitative. Trying to make the words clearly audible for some singers means that they are really reduced to speaking the texts from the Bible. I listened with admiration to the tenor singing this part, and with relief that I was not faced with the dilemma of making a good sound and maintaining a 'vocal line' and still trying to make the beautiful words meaningful in English. The choir for these concerts was the formerly great Royal Melbourne Philharmonic Society, which was beginning to decline and now no longer exists. The Philharmonic at this time was a choir of elderly people, and the grey and balding heads were the same ones I had seen ten years earlier, beating time with their music, and rocking to and fro as they sang. The choir was very large and sang in the style of the day, full-throated, strained on the tenor's lines and rather stodgy. But, because of its long history, I have always regretted its demise.

I knew nothing about baroque style at that time and there were very few people in Australia who did. Later on, when I moved to Sydney, it became a passionate interest of mine when Dorothy White became my close friend and coach. This music could fill me with as much joy as singing in opera. Concert singing was a new experience and I was ready to become deeply involved in it.

The life of a College Warden's wife, living within an all-male University college, created demands too. There was a protocol to be learned and the rules had a certain quaint logic. For example, women were not permitted to dine 'in Hall' except by special invitation once or twice a year, whereas G was obliged to 'dine in' every night, except at weekends. We usually had lunch together. G loved his job, which was really to be a counsellor in time of trouble and a go-between, within the college and university disciplines. Hopefully, the rejection and dislocation he had experienced in Oxford would never happen to the young men in Queen's, at least while he was there. As well as being ready to give advice, or just listening at any hour of the day, or more usually the middle of the night, he was lecturing full time within the Philosophy Department in the University of Melbourne. It was exciting at last for him to feel fulfilled and we enjoyed making new friends amongst lively young men and listening to the worries of the quieter and more introspective fellows.

I decided I had to learn to drive, so that I could make the journey to work with Gwen Halstead during the day, while G was so busy. As my *tummy* expanded, I needed to push the seat back to fit behind the wheel and I, who had been so slim, began to grow accustomed to being a larger size.

I was asked to do a lot of concerts in the suburbs and in the country and Gwen was always my accompanist at this time. We giggled together as we surveyed our profiles in the mirror. Our babies were due to arrive within two weeks of each other and I went on and on accepting engagements in places as far afield as Bendigo and Wangaratta until Gwen said, "Really, we begin to look too ridiculous, waddling out on to the stage together. I shall call a halt, even if *you* want to go on."

So we hid our developing, Raphael-like figures for the next two months, whilst I went every day to Gwen's, preparing my future work. This was a happy time, waiting for our baby to arrive. We were convinced it was a boy.

As we settled into Queen's, there were visits from some of my friends from the world I had left behind. Elsie Morison, against all tradition, arrived with a gift of a fine set of kitchen knives. The Barenboims passed through. And Sir John Gielgud visited Melbourne to play in *The Seven Ages of Man*. I invited him to lunch, and to my delight he accepted. I was so proud of our modern little home, and when he arrived he was charming to us both. I had also invited Louis and Lily Kahan to lunch with him, hoping Louis could sketch him, but when they arrived the Kahans seemed to become overwhelmed by the occasion. Sir John became more and more withdrawn, while we became more and more embarrassed. It then emerged that his companion, of whose existence we had not even been aware, was wandering about the University grounds waiting for this interminable lunch to end. There never was a Kahan drawing of Sir John on that day.

We saw a good deal of the Master of the College, Raynor Johnson. He had been a distinguished physicist before coming to Melbourne from the UK. He and his wife Mary were gentle and kind and G was very fond of 'Sam', as he was called by everyone. They lived in the College grounds, in a large two-storey house built sometime in the fifties. Beryl, their eldest daughter, who was married to G's best friend Trevor Hubble, was still living in Bury St Edmunds in England. We were aware that the Johnsons were experimenting in psychical research at this time. 'Sam' was less and less involved in the day-to-day running of the College, and G thought he was wasting his considerable intellect on this peculiar branch of research.

Then it was second term. The College Formal would be on August 3rd. I had a black satin evening dress made in an Empire style in 'The Block', Collins Street, for the recent concerts I had been singing. It was very expensive at the time, very beautiful, and hid my growing child from view. I would go to the Queen's Formal in this dress. The night came and G and I danced together all night. I was not prepared to dance with anyone else at this stage, even if they had asked me! We had to keep very much at arm's length!

At dawn next morning I was up, feeling very uncomfortable, and shortly after, standing at the kitchen sink filling the kettle for a cup of tea, 'the waters broke'. I flooded the kitchen floor, and as I never knew this was a possibility until the moment it happened, I think I was amazed and rather amused. Looking back, I seem to have always drifted along, coming to know things after the event. The next few hours were likely to be full of action and G had a full day's teaching, so he took me straight into the Jessie Macpherson Hospital, where we said goodbye for the moment and I sank into a drifting time, until the labour really started.

I had attended the antenatal classes run by the hospital and always wanted to stay awake to see my baby born. But as the long hours dragged by, it was obvious that I was too tired to last the distance and when G came, at the end of his long day, I was being given oxygen, and at last they 'put me under'. I felt a deep sense of failure. Perhaps my breathing had been wrong, or I had not exercised properly? But I was too tired to care.

I awoke to hear that we had a little girl. This was a real surprise, as we had always expected a boy. She was perfect, a beautiful nut-brown little honeybee, one of the meanings of the name we gave her, Deborah. There had been Deborahs and Isabellas in Graeme's mother's family for over four hundred years, so the choice of her name was easy.

She was a beautiful baby I thought, as I gazed lovingly at her, lying beside me in the hospital bed. I prepared to feed her for the first time, cradling her in the crook of my arm as I placed her to my breast. With the other hand I picked up the book I was reading. In bounced the Sister, snatching the book away as she cried, "That's enough of that, my lady. You have to concentrate good and hard to do this job properly!" In fact, the baby preferred to sleep and was what was then called a 'lazy feeder'. I had to spend time in the The Queen Elizabeth Hospital for Mothers and Babies, just across the road from Queen's College, learning how to make sure my precious bundle was getting sufficient food. They weighed her before and after each feed, to try and find out why she was not gaining weight. It was an interesting time for me, who had assumed that having a child was the end of the affair.

It was the beginning, of course. Life is never the same again and I was never an individual again. I think you are always one half of another after you marry, but when you have a child, that creation is always living within you for the rest of your life. No matter how old the mother is, her child is always to be protected and nurtured. And the child, even in middle age, struggles to be free of the cobwebby, wrap-around love of the mother, 'until the third generation' when often the grandchild is able to bridge the generations.

Deborah Louise Elms de Graaff was born in early August. Gwen Halstead Brooker's baby, Paul, was born two weeks later. We both stayed quietly at home. I was learning how to be a mother, a new area of study, and one I found very interesting, but also very stressful. How did you fit in the feed times? They took a long time and often seemed to run into one another, as mother and baby dozed together. The night feeds were the worst, trying to stay awake in 'the wee small hours' was agony.

At last the baby was putting on weight and I had a concert to prepare. We engaged a young girl to come and help me when I was rehearsing. She would live in from time to time, when I needed her to look after the baby.

This concert was devoted to a work which was to become another of my favourites. In *The Herald,* John Sinclair wrote of the performance, "Beethoven's *Missa Solemnis* ... is famous, but greatly neglected, and this was only the second performance by the [Royal Melbourne] Philharmonic Society since its formation in 1854."

Does this really mean it was only performed twice in 100 years in Melbourne? I find this incredible, looking back at the earlier appreciation and knowledge of music in Australia. Surely it means that the early Victorians were more adventurous than their grandchildren in their music making. At least *they* were prepared to produce the operatic works of Verdi and Wagner as soon as they were written. The conductor of the *Missa* was Sir Bernard, demonstrating that he did a great deal for the introduction of neglected and important music in his time.

By far the most memorable performance of the year, and perhaps one of the most important in my entire concert life, was on December 3rd.

Shortly before Deborah was born, sometime in June 1960 perhaps, I met a man called Paul Smiley at a function. He was a Viennese immigrant who had founded the Mahler/Bruckner Society in Melbourne. Paul's aim was to hear the works of both composers performed live by the Victorian Symphony Orchestra. Through Paul, I met Margaret Schofield and began work with her on some of Mahler's wonderful songs. Here was a new composer I could die for! Margaret Schofield (Bunty) was a wonderful pianist and had a profound influence on my approach to the singing of Lieder and Art Song. Demanding and musically sensitive, she honed my operatically trained voice, with its tendency to burgeon and swell on all the climaxes, to the more intimate skill of expressing emotions by colouring the quality of the sound. I found working with her on my first performance of *The Songs of a Wayfarer (Lieder eine fahrendes Gesellen)* for one of Paul Smiley's forthcoming soirees, a revelation. Bunty's fingers sketched the orchestral languor of the songs at the keyboard and together we charmed the small audience, while in the corner of the suburban sitting room, my friend Louis Kahan made a marvellous drawing of me singing.

Paul Smiley then asked me if I would sing in the first Melbourne performance at the end of the year of Mahler's *Das Lied von der Erde (The Song of the Earth)*. The first Australian performance had been given in 1955 with Goossens, Max Worthley and Florence Taylor in Sydney. The concert was given jointly by the ABC and the Victorian Government, to celebrate the centenary of Mahler's birth. It was conducted by Henri Krips and the tenor soloist was Kenneth Neate, a distinguished Australian heldentenor who made his career principally in Germany, and who spent his life there, teaching in Munich after his retirement from the operatic stage. He died in Munich, in 1997.

The experience of coming to the music of Mahler, with my limited knowledge of German, brought me into a fresh world of poetic and musical romanticism which I had never known before. As I stood on the stage in the concert, cradled by the sounds of the forest and of nature, I was filled with wonder that a composer could reproduce the cry of a bird on an oboe, or that a flute could sing a bird's song so faithfully; and that he could say things about humanity and human life in his music that no words could ever express, which touched the heart with a silver pointer. Filled with longing for the unattainable, I responded to both the poetry and the sweetly sour harmonies of his songs with passion.

8. Equilibrium

I was busy singing ballads with the small suburban music clubs and choral groups and going to Gwen Halstead to learn the new concert works I was being asked to perform. But the desire to sing great music stayed with me. There were always a few major ABC concerts with orchestra, which gave me such pleasure and demanded increased volume and musicality of my voice. I was trying to find an equilibrium between my domestic life, my passion for work and the frustration eating at my heart after the full-time career I had enjoyed so briefly in London.

Working with Margaret Schofield from time to time introduced me to a different musical milieu. I met Felix Werder, Margaret Sutherland and Larry Sitsky, and heard the difference between the conservative music of Linda Phillips and Alfred Hill, and the avant-garde sound. The cream of Melbourne's musical talent was far removed from the ballad and opera singers of my youth. Through Bunty (Margaret Schofield) I met Jack and Sibyl Glickman, and was introduced to the wonders of both listening to and performing in chamber music. Musica Viva brought me exciting new work, and people were beginning to explore the new music being written in Australia after the hiatus in ideas in our musical world caused by the war.

In June 1961 I was asked to undertake a long tour of New Zealand by John Hopkins. He was then the conductor of the National Orchestra and the Director of Music for the NZBC. I was to begin the tour in Wellington with Mendelssohn's *Elijah*, then travel around the islands presenting two different solo recital programs for the Chamber Music Federation. At the end of the tour I was to sing in two concerts of the Verdi *Requiem*, one in Christchurch and one in Wellington. This was a huge undertaking for me. I had to learn these orchestral works from scratch and a lot more music besides this for the recitals, and leave G and little Deb for seven weeks. How could I bear to do this? G said I must and the singer in me desperately wanted to, but the new mother inside me cried out that I should stay with my baby and my husband. It was arranged at last. Graeme's sister Lois Williams would have Deb stay with her for the time I was away. She had two children of her own, Julie and little Ray who was only four years old. Deborah was not yet a year old. I would be back home for her birthday in August.

So I went to Wellington. Knowing that the weather would be very cold, I took as my one and only coat, a sheepskin garment which had been given to me as a farewell gift when I first went to Paris. It was a close cropped soft brown fur called Beaverine. I still have it, it still looks beautiful, and it must be at least sixty years old. It weighed a ton and was very bulky, and when I arrived in Wellington the weather was mild. I thought I had made a terrible mistake and it would be a nuisance for six weeks, carrying this great animal about with me. But soon the weather changed and by the time I was ready to work with my pianist, Margaret Nielsen, I knew I was going to need that coat every day. Margaret was a very good pianist and when I began rehearsing for the tour we soon developed the 'rapport' needed between singer and accompanist.

Wellington was then a small city and rather pretty, as all the wooden houses climbing higgeldy-piggeldy up the slopes were painted in lollipop colours, so that from a distance the city looked like an illustration from a child's picture book. But the great mountain behind the city created up-draughts, and in June it seemed that there was always a force ten gale blowing. To get to rehearsals at Victoria University, where Margaret was teaching in the music department, I took the cable car, like the 'téléferique' of my Paris days. I spent about ten days in Wellington and was incredibly homesick. Every time I saw a man who resembled my husband, or a baby who was a even a little like my baby Deborah in the street, my heart would turn over with longing for them both.

I sang *Elijah*, with John Hopkins conducting me for the first time. He was a slight, serious young man of about my age who had come from the BBC Northern Orchestra. We became great friends and established a rapport which was always present whenever we worked together. I found him a wonderful 'singers' conductor'.

After this auspicious concert, with wonderful 'notices' behind me, Margaret Nielsen and I set off to present recitals in Wellington, Wanganui, Nelson, Timaru, Hamilton, New Plymouth, Napier, Dunedin and Christchurch. Margaret was a perfect travelling companion and a sensitive and rewarding accompanist, supporting but never dominating, and a woman with similar interests to my own. The beauty of New Zealand took my breath away, with its spectacular mountain scenery. The rural dairy farms of the rich green North Island, with its rolling hills, reminded me of a lusher Gippsland, with a backdrop to every view of a single great volcanic mountain peak. But the grandeur of the Southern Alps was something I had never imagined. The cold also took my breath away; the snow was deep on every mountain. Central heating in New Zealand was for the future, and the small fires then in hotel lobbies did little for country dining rooms. The concert halls were always icy, except for the then new and glorious Wanganui Auditorium.

The tour went very well. We had glowing reviews and I was sad to say goodbye to Margaret in Christchurch, where she left me to return to Wellington.

I was overjoyed to be performing the Verdi *Requiem* for the very first time under John Hopkins, who had been so sympathetic in *Elijah*. And although I did not know it then, to sing this Verdi suddenly revealed to me that this composer was to become one of my great strengths and loves. The soloists assembled on the afternoon of Wednesday for a piano rehearsal with the conductor, when I met the New Zealand tenor Jon Andrews and the bass Noel Mangin for the first time. The soprano was a fellow Australian who had been flown over especially for this concert.

Anyone who knows the Verdi will realise that it is a huge work to sing, ranking with the greatest of Verdi's operas as a tour de force for both soloists and chorus. Vocal power and strength are demanded of both. The three lower voices all enjoyed the sing-through, but it was obvious that the soprano did not know her part! I think I had been responsible for recommending her to John Hopkins, so I felt very embarrassed about her singing. I have never heard anyone before or since arrive at rehearsal seemingly so unprepared.

John Hopkins was trying to get a replacement within New Zealand by the end of the rehearsal. It was too late to get anyone else across from Australia in time for the concert. The next day the orchestra would fly down from Wellington to rehearse with us in the afternoon and we would then have a full choral and soloists rehearsal in the evening. The choir was the Christchurch Harmonic Society, trained by the young William Hawkey. This impressive choir was to travel to Wellington with the orchestra to give the same concert on the following night. It was a mammoth undertaking to travel both orchestra and choir up and down the two islands.

On that afternoon the impressive organ tones of the young Noel Mangin were very subdued. He complained of an agonisingly sore throat, so John Hopkins said, "Mark, [ie sing softly] don't sing. Save it."

With the concert the next day, we were all now feeling nervous. Noel did not come to the evening dress rehearsal, and by that time, after singing the Requiem through three times with great delight, I realised that *my* throat was suddenly a burning and raging furnace.

With the soprano incapable, and us two 'heavies' unable to even *croak* on the morning of the concert, *the two performances were cancelled,* and the hideous expense of the air flights of soloists, orchestra and choir had to be written off.

I had been given a charming room in the Christchurch hotel, which was reputed to be the room used by the young Queen Elizabeth on one of her recent visits to the Dominion. Next morning, as I lay groaning in my hot sweaty bed, with alternating raging fevers and icy chills making life such a misery that death would be a welcome release, the house-keeper brought in *The Christchurch Star.* The front page showed photographs of Noel and me with the headline, "Concert cancelled. Opera stars in bed."

I was too ill to laugh, but Noel and I always felt we had a very special bond ever after that. But I felt so miserably guilty about cancelling these concerts.

I had been away from home for so long, but I was really so very ill that I had to stay on in bed in the hotel and wait a few days till I was well enough to travel.

On the earlier part of the tour I had fallen in love with the beauty of New Zealand. When I got home and felt a little better, I wrote to the NZBC suggesting that if they would fly me back to repeat the concerts the following year, I would sing for no fee. However they asked me to do the concerts again and paid me, so they were very generous.

The next month saw me travelling to Adelaide to sing with one of the great conductors of our time, Karel Ancerl. After his imprisonment under the Nazis during the war, he was appointed to be conductor of the Czech Philharmonic. This truly great man was an idol to all who ever worked with him, and it was inspiring to sing in Dvorák's *Stabat mater* with him. The choir and orchestra were splendid and I met and sang with the great Australian singer, Arnold Matters.

In October 1961 I made my first visit to Sydney. Having grown up in Melbourne, I had been to Adelaide several times and travelled widely in Victoria but had never been to Sydney. I had no particular wish to see the Harbour Bridge, which my father said was Sydney's main claim to fame. But the ABC wanted me to sing in one of its earliest TV productions, Saint-Saëns' opera, *Samson and Delilah.* I was thrilled to be asked to sing the role of Delilah, and the only sorrow was that I would have to be away from Graeme and Deborah yet again for a long period. The music and orchestral rehearsals would last about two weeks, before recording the entire sound track, and then we would begin production for the telecast which would be transmitted live to air on November 22nd.

My Samson was an old friend, Raymond MacDonald, and the role of the High Priest was to be sung by Ronal Jackson. The conductor would be Joseph Post who was then the Assistant Director of Music at the ABC and one of Australia's best operatic conductors.

I asked my friend Adele Salmon - who had given me that sheepskin coat all those years ago - if I could stay with her for the four weeks I would be in Sydney. She agreed, though it would be a tight squeeze in their little house near the ferry wharf at Mosman.

As soon as I saw this city I knew I would love it. No one had prepared me for the stunning beauty of the harbour, studded with blue water inlets dotted with white sails, and the steeply climbing roofs, hiding glimpses of sleepy coves and rocky headlands. I came at a time when the jacarandas were in bloom, dropping their own blue seas of petals on the wet pavements.

The Salmon's house clung to the side of the hill above Mosman Wharf, amongst gum trees which they told me were called Angophoras, and which I did not remember having seen before. With their twisting pink limbs, these trees climbing up the back of the house were anthropomorphic and primeval. There was a huge rock above the house, which sheltered tree ferns and formed a cave in the back garden. Two minutes walk to Mosman Wharf took you to the harbour and the view painted by Streeton in the 1890s.

For two weeks that November the skies were grey and the rain plunged down, flooding the gutters and requiring urgent canals to be dug under the Salmon's house to help drain the water over the big rock on which the house stood. To a Melbourne girl, it seemed incredible that one could be clad in shorts and, barefoot in driving rain, still be warm!

There was a decadence about the area of King's Cross where the old ABC orchestral studios were. You entered the building above the Pink Pussycat strip club and went along a narrow corridor above Woolworths. I could not believe the ABC leased such a tatty old building, after the formal facade of the purpose-built Melbourne studios on the corner of King and William Streets (now replaced by new premises in South Melbourne). But it was here that we rehearsed the score of *Samson and Delilah*.

ABC buildings were scattered all over the centre of Sydney, with rehearsal rooms in old stone churches and recording studios in William and Forbes Streets. I loved singing in a very old sandstone church in Bourke Street, which had a beautiful polished wooden gallery around three sides. For acoustic reasons, a hessian cloth was stretched across from one side of the gallery to the other, but the building, with its beautiful classical exterior, had a marvellous feeling of dignity and age. I think it was here that I worked for the first time with Robert Pikler and Marie van Hove. We rehearsed there, then presented 'live to air', a TV program on Sunday November 12th, at 4pm.

There was another old church in Forbes Street which was smaller and rather 'boomy' to sing in, which was used for rehearsals. As a stranger to Sydney, I sometimes found it difficult to arrive in time for these rehearsals at different places, and when I did, I would often batter at the wrong door to gain entry, cursing the ABC for not giving me the proper instructions about these mysterious venues. It was invariably on a hot, wet Sunday afternoon when, after trudging up hills to a telephone box, I would be unable to find anyone who could give me the information I needed. Sydney seemed a very big and raffish place and had a dangerously exotic feeling, quite unlike my own home town.

The rehearsals for the sound track of the film were completed and we recorded the opera with the Sydney Symphony in that studio above Woolworths. My colleagues all had splendid voices and I believe the quality of that recording was very good. The opera was sung in English. The chorus was trained by Ivan Rixon, who was the chorus master for the Hurlstone Choral Society.

I sang a free concert in the Sydney Town Hall on that Sunday afternoon. The following week we began production calls for the telecast. This was a very ambitious opera to put on, with elaborate ballet scenes and the destruction of the temple as the finale. There was a great deal of excitement about the end of the opera, as we had to perform 'live to air', without the luxury of being able to rehearse the destruction of the temple. A difficulty for me was my relationship with my Samson. Ray MacDonald was short and I was tall. He was stout and I was thin. We were very good friends and Ray was great fun to work with, as he was very funny and always managed to make me giggle. It was going to be difficult to achieve any semblance of romantic realism.

In *The Sydney Morning Herald,* Roger Covell wrote: "The planning of movement and gesture during Delilah's singing of *Softly awakes my heart* was poor, and the result more awkward than passionate, and Raymond MacDonald's ... obviously false beard and hair gave him an old fashioned nautical look, like an essentially jolly but slightly apprehensive pirate."

Alas, both these comments were true. My miming to my own singing was not good either. It was hard for me to seduce my delightful and funny fat tenor, even if he did sing like an angel. I needed a much tougher director than Peter Page, who did a wonderful job on the crowd scenes and the camera, but who treated me very gently. As a matter of fact, I think I always performed better with a director I hated! I should have, and perhaps could have, done better. I was very aware of, and wary of the camera, and the new medium of TV made me uneasy because I thought I was not good-looking. I had the feeling that I was trying to see myself through the eyes of the viewer, as if I were directing myself. This was *not* a good idea if I were trying to portray a personality so far from my own character. I believe I am now a good actress, but there were definite moments of disaster in that *Samson*. As I bent my knees to achieve eye contact with my lover, his eyes would twinkle and another passionate moment would be lost!

But most of the critics were kind and the print of the film, which still exists, shows a splendid and heroic Samson pushing the pillars of the temple apart to bring down an avalanche of huge stones and pediments, under which we had been working for at least four weeks in the ABC's Gore Hill studios. Talcum powder made appropriate dust and the frantic crowds in the film had to hide their amusement as the polystyrene foam stones bounced into the air in a most implausible way.

"It looked marvellous," I was told.

When I got home to Melbourne, I fell into my husband's arms with relief and a new appreciation of his generosity towards my career. How understanding he was to me. I was not easy to live with. When I was performing there was always a worry about getting colds. It is terrible to spend weeks or months learning some wonderful music and then wake up on the day of the performance with a sore throat. My colds always ended up as bronchitis.

The other recurring problem I had was dental. Chalky and small, my teeth were constantly having to be filled. Nearly every month I was forced to make a visit to the dentist. I had been told to try to keep the teeth I still had left *at all costs,* as a full denture would alter my 'bite' (the distance between my upper and lower jaws). So I kept a little plastic plate with its four front teeth, needing to have it repaired every few months as it wore away and I finally bit through it.

I believe that every person's facial structure affects the way the sound of the voice is produced. In fact, the acoustic you have inside you is God-given and inbuilt. It can be altered and improved with teaching, but the sound you make is there at birth and will always be basically the same. A tall thin person will probably have a low, rich voice. A small thin person will either be a coloratura or a high tenor. A robustly built male will be either a baritone or a dramatic tenor, while a dramatic soprano will probably be more heavily built. The various shades of soprano sound can also be determined by the shape of the body and the shape of the face. Singing is a physical and athletic exercise on which the artistry of the performer is superimposed.

Every successful marriage demands some sacrifice of self and a step towards the centre from the poles of two viewpoints. Like all new parents, we found it a huge adjustment to have our baby. We were learning to adapt to each other's character and to enlarge our little family to three, and incorporate our two separate families into our marriage. I knew that G loved his sister Shirley more than any other person, although he never talked about this. I knew too how fond he was of Trevor Hubble, at that time living in England. He adored his father and mother, but he never spoke much about them. My husband was taciturn in comparison to my own loquacious family. He was becoming more withdrawn as the demands of his several jobs became more onerous. Incredibly conscientious, he gave himself unstintingly to his lectures and to the counselling of the residents of the College in his spare time. We tried to maintain an open house so that they would feel welcome to drop in whenever they chose. This meant we had less time to enjoy the closeness of our courting days.

We found living in College exciting and exhausting. There was rarely an evening when we were at home alone. There were College and University functions to attend and as the weeks went by, more and more students 'dropped in' to have coffee and talk to my wise young husband. Often the bell would ring at 2 or 3am and some terrible crisis would present itself at our door, which opened into the student's wing. We were sympathetic to the really serious events demanding our help, but often were very thin-lipped to find that some young undergraduate had simply been out on the tiles and forgotten or lost his key.

We decided to spend more time away at the weekends. After all, the Master, Raynor Johnson, and all the theological Professors were in residence across the gravel driveway. The 'men' could go *there* when they needed help at the weekend!

We would spend our holidays, the university vacations, at Somers. Our little girl was growing up. She was a delight to Graeme's parents, Isabel and Ern, with her independence and charm. Ern would quote her quaint words to every listener, chuckling at his granddaughter's cleverness. We learned that his older grandchildren were 'pretty fed up' with hearing of Deb's latest exploits, but we doted on her, with her solemn brown eyes and curly hair.

We found that G's parents were spending more and more time at Somers and asking their own friends to stay, so we decided to buy a block on a side street of the same development, in order to build as near to them as possible. We would be free to come and go when we needed a time away from the city ourselves. In this way we would have an investment.

The whole of the Mornington peninsula is very beautiful. In 1961 it was covered with stands of tall ti-tree all along the coast on the Western Port side, and from there the land rose steeply beyond the coastal sheep grazing properties to the centre of the peninsula, where the soil suddenly became a deep red and tall pine trees grew along the crests of the steep hillsides, making shaded avenues of the roads. I could always see in my mind, as in a map, the two great bays like different key-holes, Port Philip with its pointed end, and the wider rounded Western Port with its two sleeping islands, French and Philip, resting like drawings of birds in the arch of the circle.

We often went across the peninsula, taking the long straight road due west, then up the hill into a steep climb. We would be in Red Hill where apple orchards replaced the gentle lower rises of the Western Port side. Now we were descending towards the town of Mornington where Graeme's family had holidayed as children. I was moving from my family's background into his. To please my husband and to move into this new part of my emotional life, I was giving away my love of San Remo and of my father's family, the Bonwicks, and the Cape Woolami holidays. I was giving up my secret inner dreams, to the present of the ti-tree and the pasture of the sheep-grazing property on the hill.

9. Wayfarer with a Toddler

In 1962, I fulfilled two ambitions: to sing with John Pritchard and the London Philharmonic Orchestra, and to perform at the Adelaide Festival. I was engaged by the ABC to tour with the LPO and John Pritchard, beginning at the Adelaide Festival on March 20th and then travelling to Melbourne, Sydney and Brisbane. The major work on the program was Walton's 2nd Symphony, then quite a recent piece, and I sang de Falla's *El amor brujo (Love the magician)* for the first time, in Spanish. To work with John Pritchard was a great honour. I had admired his performances of Mozart at 'The Garden', and singing with this truly great orchestra was a revelation.

John became a good friend, and we enjoyed each other's company on this tour. In Brisbane, I rehearsed in the morning in the Town Hall with its very boomy acoustic. We noticed the unusual circular shape of the building, with the stage built across a quarter of the diameter. The performers enter in full view of the audience. In the evening, as I prepared to make my entry, John said jokingly, "Be careful not to trip as you come on." Immediately, as I walked to the top step, I ended up on my hands and knees, *almost crawling* on to the stage. "It was all *your* fault!" I told John later, with a grin.

In the winter I returned to New Zealand to finally sing the Verdi *Requiem* for the NZBC and hopefully repay my debt for the previous year's debacle. With its sweep and drama, the *Requiem* contains some of Verdi's greatest operatic writing. On this visit I also sang in recital with Margaret Nielsen again in Hamilton, Lower Hutt, New Plymouth, Timaru and Hastings between July 2nd and 9th, before rehearsing the Verdi in Christchurch. The conductor was once again John Hopkins.

In Wellington we gave the second New Zealand performance of Mahler's *The Song of the Earth,* in English. This now seems a strange idea, but in those days it was quite common to perform in translation. This always gave wrong accents to the shape of the phrases in the music, where text and melody were set by great composers. I often re-arranged the English text to suit my own wishes, to the distress of critics following the words on the printed page. I figured that if some non-singer could do a translation which did not suit the music, I could be forgiven for trying to accommodate the words to the music in a way I found more comfortable to sing. Sometimes the words in the old-fashioned translations bore little resemblance to the actual meaning, as the translation attempted to make rhymes and verse.

My next concert this year was the Australian premiere of Arthur Honegger's *Joan of Arc at the stake*. It was given in English, with Georges Tzipine and the Victorian Symphony Orchestra, in the Melbourne Town Hall. The tenor soloist was the distinguished William Herbert, returned from Europe to live in Australia. The wonderful young St Joan was Beverly Dunn, recently returned from London, who gave a performance of passion and beauty that all who heard will never forget. She has a very beautiful speaking voice, which she uses with great skill, and a great love of language. She became one of my dearest friends. When we meet now, we seem to re-establish the old rapport that we felt on our first meeting in the Melbourne Town Hall so long ago. Another close friend I made at this concert was the soprano Nance Grant. She became a colleague with whom I sang for many years.

It was a memorable concert for me, working with the large cast of actors, singers and a huge choir, and establishing a friendship with Georges Tzipine, with whom I sang frequently from then on. And to think I had first heard him conducting in Paris when I was a student!

In September I was able to sing Mahler's *Lieder eines fahrenden Gesellen (Songs of a Wayfarer)* again, this time in German, in an all-Mahler program at the Assembly Hall in Collins Street for the Victorian branch of Musica Viva. The baritone Brian Hansford sang *Kindertotenlieder (Songs on the death of children)* in the same concert, and some of the songs from *Des Knaben Wunderhorn (The Youth's Magic Horn),* while I sang several of the *Rückert Songs* for the first time. It was a pleasure to work with Margaret Schofield again. The critic of *The Sun,* John Sinclair, wrote that I achieved a performance which "rose above the level of competence and became magical." Composer Dorien Le Gallienne was the critic for *The Age* and also reviewed the concert, saying I "possessed a voice with the greatest lustre, and with a fine sense of line that was particularly telling in the *Songs of the Wayfarer.*"

This concert was my first for Musica Viva, I think. Some memorable names in the musical world of that time were involved with this great organisation. In Melbourne, Arnold Teague, I G Spira and Dr Paul Nemet (my beloved violin teacher's husband) were all influential early members.

In Sydney at that time, but not yet known to me, were the manager Regina Ridge, who was later to become an important and good friend; Kenneth Tribe, one of the most influential people in music in Australia; the violist Richard Goldner, and A K Wenkart, W A Dullo, Charles Berg, Dr Ernst - the list is impressive. Musica Viva has made such a contribution to the life of Australia that we, from this distance, forget how provincial our musical world was then, until this organisation was born in the minds of a very few people, more than 50 years ago.

Later in the year I took part in another memorable event. I remembered a Broken Hill concert for the Quartet Club which I gave before I went to France. The Quartet Club had brought music to this outback community for many years and had started, I believe, as a Barber Shop Quartet. I was invited to go back for their 206th concert.

I remembered the parched earth of the tarmac as the little plane rolled to a stop in the mining capital of Australia. The door opened and the flight steward lowered the steps to the ground. As I disembarked, the dry heat rose up to hit me and I could only feel admiration for the men and women who chose to live in this harsh place.

As I walked towards the tin shed terminal, two men in dark blue suits advanced towards me, beaming a welcome. They introduced themselves as the president and secretary of the Society, whom I had in fact met on my earlier visit five years before.

"Welcome back," they cried. "You've been a long way since we last met."

"Yes," I smiled.

"You've sung with June Bronhill?" (I knew June had been born in Broken Hill and the city was very proud of her, and had helped her to go overseas to pursue her career).

"Yes indeed," I nodded.

"And you've sung with Joan Sutherland?"

Once more I agreed.

"How wonderful to have sung with those people who sing so much better than you do," they shouted at me into the dust and the wind!

The concert was a mixed program, with local soloists of duo-pianists, bass-baritone, soprano, a splendid cornet player, the choir of the Quartet Club and myself as the visitor, accompanied on the piano by the local pianist. He and I rehearsed together and then I was taken to view the town, where they proudly showed me the beautiful gardens and brilliant greens of the Bowling Club, which were watered by artesian bore water. This was indeed a remarkable sight to see, as the surrounding desert gave no hint of the possibility of green gardens and lawns.

They told me, as on the previous visit, that no visitor was allowed to view the mine, the thing I wanted to see more than anything.

The items I chose were the *Lieder eines fahrenden Gesellen (Songs of a Wayfarer)*, in German, and the Dvořák *Gypsy songs,* in English. I think the audience were disappointed with these 'highbrow' contributions, which sat oddly with the pieces by May Brahe, Cole Porter and Arthur Sullivan which the other performers offered. I suppose I should have sung the ballads and operatic arias I now disdained as second-rate music.

I had become a musical snob.

At the end of the year I took part in the first Sydney performance of the Watkins-Shaw edition of Handel's *Messiah*. Conducted by Sir Bernard Heinze, the performance used a reduced orchestra for the first time, with strings, oboes, bassoons, trumpets and drums, and without the extra wind instruments which were added in Victorian times to increase the sound for the huge choirs then in fashion. However, the Hurlstone Choral Society was not reduced and the fine-tuning required to produce a more baroque sound did not occur – perhaps it was not even possible. Instead, the tenors in particular came in for a 'serve' from the critic Roger Covell in *The Sydney Morning Herald,* who described their tone as something between "the cry of an approaching bottle-oh and the neigh of a distant horse."

The other soloists were Rosalind Keene, William Herbert and Alan Light, all great singers with wonderful voices. Commenting on the difference in this performance to the Victorian traditional *Messiah,* Covell also observed that *But Who May Abide* was sung by a contralto instead of the customary bass, that the *Rejoice Greatly* had become a light-hearted jig, that the soloists occasionally indulged in an unwritten ornament, and several other comments. I proudly kept a hand written card from the Hurlstone Choral Society celebrating my association with the choir in that *Messiah* of 1962. I think this performance marked a beginning of an Australian interest in baroque performance practice, which had begun much earlier in Europe. And it was here that I first met my great friend and teacher, Dorothy White, who was playing cembalo. She had studied baroque music before the war in England and was one of the few authorities in this field in Australia at that time.

The same month saw Dean Dixon for the first time as a guest-conductor in Sydney, having completed a season in Salzburg. He conducted a Mozart Festival of three concerts on December 12th, 15th and 18th. The leader of the SSO was Ernest Llewellyn and the other soloist was Neville Amadio in Mozart's *Flute Concerto in D,* K314. I sang the concert aria *Ombra Felice* and the *Per pietà* from *Così fan tutte.* It was Joseph Post who chose *Per pietà* for this concert. I had never heard it sung and wondered how he knew that this soprano aria would suit me. The price of the tickets is interesting now: 17/9 ($1.79) and 12/9 ($1.29).

After the obligatory Melbourne *Messiah* performances with Sir Bernard, and Christmas with our families, G and I packed up the VW, and went to our little house in Somers for the month of January.

I was already engaged to sing in a performance of Elgar's *Land of Hope and Glory* with a choir and the Victorian Symphony Orchestra in the presence of the Queen and the Duke of Edinburgh, on a Sunday afternoon in February 1963. The ABC was presenting the concert in the Myer Music Bowl. During our holiday period at Somers, a telegram arrived from Melbourne asking if there was a photograph of me *in the dress I would wear for the forthcoming Royal performance.*

Here was a dilemma! I did not want to go back to Melbourne just to have a photograph taken for a newspaper article. But I discovered that a friend from my student days at Swinburne Technical College was now living in Somers. Pauline had married Rod Nuske, who was working as a photographer at the Flinders Naval Base. We had become good friends, so I asked Rod to take a photo of me in the living room of our house at Somers in my "new, prune-coloured chiffon dress, with a softly draped bodice and a bell-shaped skirt," which in fact I had had for some time! Rod Nuske's photograph of me appeared in the Women's Page of *The Melbourne Herald,* together with an article about Nance Grant, the other woman soloist, and "what we would wear for the great occasion." *The TV Times* also had a full-page spread about our 'worry' over the dresses we should wear! How journalism has changed. It is a very long time since I have seen this kind of article, or for that matter, a women's page of this sort in a newspaper!

My own concern about this concert was singing "Wider still and wider shall thy bounds be set ..." I think Elgar's *Pomp and Circumstance* music is wonderful, but I was personally uncomfortable singing before the Queen about the 'boundless Empire', which I knew was beginning to shrink and vanish. After all, this was during the years when former Empire countries were becoming independent. I thought the words of the song inappropriate, and wished I could sing something else entirely. As it was, the program chosen was a strange mixture of what I now regarded as 'rubbish' and some fine operatic arias from Nance Grant. The *Easter Hymn* from *Cavalleria Rusticana,* with choir, *Ah, fors e lui* from *La traviata,* and Neil Warren Smith's magnificent bass voice, in arias from's *Faust,* had my approval because of my interest in opera. But I felt that W G James' *The Sun God* and Linda Phillips' *The Droving Song,* sung by this noble voice, were a big let-down at the end of the afternoon. "Let down the slip rails" was a commentary as well as the refrain!

I had sung for Her Majesty twice in England. Perhaps I was *blasé* about this honour, but I was already aware that there was something wrong in the attitude of a young and vigorously growing Australian society towards the then young and handsome woman, whom we still call Queen Elizabeth. I suppose I was beginning to be a Republican way back then in 1963!

While the music chosen for that concert was somehow not worthy of the day, I don't know what I would have chosen instead. The really great younger generation of Australian composers were not yet writing and our musical life was still very much geared to the 19th century. We were in a musical time warp, with such composers as Robert Hughes, Felix Werder and Margaret Sutherland struggling to break out of the cobwebs.

The concert was televised and broadcast nationally and headlined "Huge audience will hear Australian Compositions." Maybe I was quite wrong, but the critic Dorien Le Gallienne also thought "the concert did not make for a coherent program." He said that "the sound shell was not a suitable venue, for some of this [music] demanded careful listening."

In May that year, I sang for the first time a work which was to become one of my favourites, Béla Bartók's *Bluebeard's Castle*.

For this performance my conductor was the young John Hopkins, who was leaving New Zealand to take up his position as the ABC's Director of Music. He was to be very important to me as a singer, and also very influential in the development of music in this country. Over the years he engaged me for a huge number of important concerts, and greatly helped my development as an artist by introducing me to new repertoire like this wonderful one-act opera. (During my singing career I almost never selected an orchestral work of my own choice, but was usually engaged to sing something chosen by others, which I would not have known at the time, like Mozart's *Per pietà*. However I almost always chose my own recital repertoire).

Three concerts were given in Sydney, and my Bluebeard was the extraordinary bass Alan Light, whose voice was magnificently rich and sonorous. The narrator was James Condon.

As I grew to know this music, it resonated in me. The myth of Judith, the inquisitive wife who wishes to possess her husband's innermost secrets, gave me a message about my own marriage. I must not delve into the inner space of my husband's secret life. I longed to know what G thought and felt about everything but the more I probed, the more remote and taciturn he became. At last the message was delivered in the searing chords and slashes of sound that Bartók gave to his anti-hero: "Leave well alone!" I found this command a response to my curiosity. For G and I were following such divergent careers and were so busy that we did not have time to delve into the hidden parts of our very different souls. Bartók held the answer in his wonderful opera about one aspect of the human condition, at least within my own marriage.

In June the New Music Ensemble gave some first performances of local composers' new works, and I then set off on a tour for the ABC going to Brisbane with visiting conductor

Massimo Freccia, giving my first performances of Wagner's *Wesendonk-Lieder* in German. I then went to Tasmania with Georges Tzipine to sing Berlioz' *Les nuits d'été (Summer nights)* in French. In an interview in the Tasmanian paper, I see the reporter had me saying, "Australia would become one of the world's centres of operatic art once it had a permanent opera house."

In September I sang the first Australian performance of Lennox Berkeley's *Four Poems of St Teresa of Avila* with the newly formed Victorian String Orchestra, conducted by Maurice Claire, and at the end of this extremely busy year I sang in the first Australian performance of Benjamin Britten's *Spring Symphony,* a work I love and which seems to be very rarely performed.

It was a year of travel and much new music, all of which I had learned with Gwen Halstead at her North Balwyn home with our two toddlers, Paul and Deborah, playing in the garden together.

10. Living Together and Apart

Our little girl was now three years old, and with the help and support of Graeme I was able to travel and fulfil myself as a singer. He must have been exhausted by his responsibilities. It was he who stayed home, working at the University by day. At night he played mother and father to Deb, helped the students who dropped in and put up with the different and sometimes difficult housekeepers we engaged to look after Deb whilst I was away.

We had naively thought that the taxation rules for live-in child minders would be similar to those in England. My female colleagues in London were able to claim the expense of employing an 'au pair girl' or nanny if they were working. When G filled in our tax return the year after Deb was born, he claimed for a housekeeper during the periods when I was away on tour.

One morning at eight o'clock, I answered the telephone and a male voice said, "This is the Taxation Department. Is Mr de Graaff there?"

When G took the call, the person asked, "Do you live with your wife?"

Puzzled, G replied, "Yes, why do you ask?"

"Don't you know," came the irritable reply, "The term 'housekeeper' is a euphemism for mistress? If you live with your wife, you can't claim on a housekeeper."

It was vain to point out that I could not go away to sing without someone to care for our baby during the day.

As I travelled more and more, I slowly learned to 'screen out' the longing I had for my husband and daughter and began to enjoy the 'work and rest' regime of a full-time singer. I enjoyed being released from the burden of housekeeping, planning and preparing meals, and the loneliness I often felt as a young mother with only a small child to talk to. I really enjoyed rehearsing with my pianist, learning new repertoire and singing all day. I also enjoyed staying in the good hotels I was booked into on these journeys and being waited on. When I was away, I would have a short sleep on the afternoon of a performance, a thing not always possible at home, with a telephone and my small daughter, and I really enjoyed the challenge of honing my voice in new works, in new venues, with different acoustics, different conductors and new pianists.

My voice was very sensitive to heat and cold, humidity and dryness, and I learnt to try not to let these things affect my performance. I nearly always got good reviews for my work and I tried to make my next performance better than the previous one, in my own opinion. I was pitting myself against myself, trying not to take notice of the local music critics, who in general seemed to know next to nothing about the art of singing and the use of the voice. I was making and keeping to my own standards.

At the end of the year I took part in a memorable performance of *Messiah*. George Logie-Smith and the Astra Chamber Orchestra gave a performance in a small hall near Melbourne University, in which his chamber choir sang impeccably with a true baroque style and the local critics for the first time understood the clarity that a very good small choir and orchestra can bring to the great music of Handel.

It was time to pack up and move to Somers for the summer.

Left at home while I was away, Graeme had been just as busy as ever and really needed a holiday. The Master of Queen's College was doing less and less within the life of the college. At G's suggestion, the College Council made the Vice-Mastership a full-time position, but G did not want it. He was tired of living in College, with constant visitors and the disturbed evenings we seemed to endure. We left Queen's at the end of 1963 and bought a tiny, newly-built flat in North Melbourne, on the opposite side of the University campus.

G decided to become a full-time lecturer within Melbourne University's Philosophy Department. He really enjoyed lecturing and tutoring, but there was always a good deal of pressure to publish from within the Department and the University. It seemed a shame that his great talents as a teacher and counsellor were not so important to the heads of the department. I knew how restless and dissatisfied he was feeling.

Our new flat was very small and cramped, given that we often needed to have a housekeeper living in to look after Deb when I was away. This year was proving to be a mess. But we were lucky to have Lorna Monro ('Auntie Lorna', my mother's best friend) to come and sleep on a settee whenever she was needed.

I did a tour of country Victoria and went to Tasmania for the ABC with Georges Tzipine. I loved working with him and I was able to sing some wonderful French repertoire. But my workload was too little to keep me happy. I have found all through my professional life that there were long periods of no work, when it seemed as if I would never sing again. Then suddenly, a month would change everything, and I would have to learn and perform three different new works in one week.

How I longed then for a less erratic career!

About this time G saw a short article in *The Age* about Richard Bonynge and Joan Sutherland returning to Australia for J C Williamson. This would be Joan's first visit 'home' since her phenomenal success. The article said they were to bring some of the world's best young singers, in the tradition of previous J C Williamson tours. I immediately wrote to Richard, saying that although I was enjoying singing in concerts, I would dearly love to take part in his opera season, because I loved singing opera.

He wrote by return mail. He was delighted to hear I was available and offered me seven roles in the season. As I had never performed in five of the works he mentioned, with the exception of Marthe in *Faust* and the tiny role of Annina in *La traviata,* I really had no idea how much work was involved. The other operas were *La sonnambula, Eugene Onegin, Lucia di Lammermoor, L'élisir d'amore* and Rossini's *Semiramide.* Most people did not even know how to pronounce the name of this last opera. I did, because I had been singing *Bel Raggio* as a party piece for some years, but no one here knew the opera.

I was ecstatic. At last I had a chance to sing opera again!

At this time fee structures were set by the hiring body. The ABC made their own assessments of their artists' values, with an elaborate scale of fees; organisations like Musica Viva or the big choral societies usually wrote a personal letter offering a fee, instead of negotiating formal legal contracts between the artists and management. Instrumental musicians were *very* poorly paid, which meant that they did not want to give enough time to rehearse properly. Singers were lumped into this category. I had evolved my own rehearsal schedule, which was very demanding, and I worked my repetiteurs as hard as myself, demanding several sessions of one-and-a-half hours or more. I paid for these long rehearsals out of my earnings, and I often ended up out of pocket with G underwriting my career.

We waited for a contract to come from J C Williamson's, and nothing happened. Writing to Richard, we found that all the other principal singers were coming from overseas, and their contracts were handled by their agents. He suggested we contact Sir Frank Tait ourselves. We did.

"What! You live in Australia? We don't know anything about you, and we won't pay you any more than the local chorus singers!" he shouted angrily.

He was annoyed that Richard Bonynge had a 'local' singer in this company of distinguished overseas artists. Williamson's were running the opera season as a commercial operation, so I suppose they were entitled to try and cut their costs to a minimum. We consulted a young lawyer, John Hicks, who had been a student of G's in Melbourne, who said he knew nothing about musicians' contracts but would go away and find out. He drew up an acceptable contract for us and eventually it was signed by all parties. Without Richard Bonynge's and John Hicks' advice, I would not have been paid a principal's salary.

The future for me began to look more hopeful. The season would commence with a six-week rehearsal period in Melbourne and then a six-week opera season at Her Majesty's Theatre in Melbourne, before travelling to Adelaide, Sydney and Brisbane.

Within a month or so, life for G and our small family suddenly took on another perspective. The Master at Queen's College, Raynor (Sam) Johnson, was retiring and G applied for this position. He was not appointed. He decided to apply for several jobs as College Principal around the country. He was offered two jobs interstate, in cities which were not very attractive to us. Then an invitation came to create the new International House at the University of Sydney! He would be working from the beginning with the architect, Walter Bunning, on the planning of the building and the creation of a model Hall of Residence. The site of the new International House would be very small, and there would be no room for a residence for us on site. This was a 'plus' as we really did not want to live within a University College any more. Once G accepted the job, we knew that the end of the year would release us from the claustrophobic North Melbourne flat and we would begin an exciting new life in another city. Ever since my first visit, I had decided that Sydney was the city I would choose to live in. Headquarters for the ABC, it was the most important centre in Australia for a musician to work in at that time. And the harbour, with its estuaries and hills and sandstone rocks and cliffs, was so beautiful!

Before the end of this year I went to Christchurch, New Zealand, to sing for the first time as soloist with the Royal Christchurch Musical Society. This visit became one of many over the years and began my real love for the city and its people.

Christchurch at that time was remarkable for having two marvellous choirs. For a comparatively small city, musical life was extraordinarily strong with great rivalry between the Royal Christchurch and its conductor, Robert Field-Dodgson, and the Harmonic, conducted by William (Bill) Hawkey, who would later come to live and work in Australia. Both conductors were charismatic and attracted the adoration of the women and the respect and admiration of the men in the choir.

I have noticed during my working life as a singer that this quality of great personal charm is an essential quality for all the great choral conductors. It is not a requirement for an orchestral conductor, who must gain the respect of his orchestra by showing exactly what he wants from an intellectual perspective, knowing the score intimately, hearing it in his mind, and then working in a straightforward manner, without talking about it. I have endured some bad moments when inefficient conductors go through a work, *talking* about interpretation, and pointing out where dynamics and rubatos should occur. If the parts have been properly marked, the good conductor does not need to talk about his interpretation. He does this by his clear indication with his baton, and with his eyes.

Back in Melbourne I took part in an ABC Television production of *Peter Grimes.* This had been one of Ronald Dowd's greatest triumphs in England and Europe, and he gave a superb performance. The ability of the camera to focus in close-up on the emotions of the driven and stricken Grimes tore at my heart. My good friend Eric Clapham conducted the VSO, and I remember Keith Neilson's noble singing in the role of Balstrode. There were some other great performances, but unfortunately some miscasting. The Ellen was inadequate when singing some of the music with the fine soprano clarity this exposed and difficult role demands. I sang the role of Mrs Sedley, as I had in London, and enjoyed the old woman's gossipy wickedness once more.

It was Christmas. The end of the year had come. We three de Graaffs travelled to Sydney in the second week of January, with our VW Beetle loaded to the hilt. We arrived to see Churchill's funeral on the television. G was to start work on February 1st, in one of the narrow terrace houses in City Road, belonging to the University, which he would use as an office while International House was being built. It was expected that this would take eighteen months and G was to go to America and England to look at some of the International Houses there before work on the project was started.

On arriving in Sydney we booked into an old-fashioned boarding house on Kurraba Point. As we stood on the cliff looking out onto the Harbour that first Saturday afternoon, we smiled, looking into each other's eyes. The blue water of the whole harbour was dotted with white sails.

"Well, we'll just have to learn to sail, won't we?"

The harbour in all its wonderful variety sparkled in the warm sun. We decided we would buy a house with a harbour view. During his interview with the Vice-Chancellor, Sir Stephen Roberts, and Harold Maze, the Deputy Principal, G asked where Sydney University staff usually chose to live. The answer was, "Ninety percent of University staff live between Chatswood and Turramurra, on the North Shore." This seemed strange to us when we consulted Gregory's Street Directory, but as G said, "Intelligent people must have a good reason to live so far from their place of employment."

We discovered that the areas of Glebe and Chippendale, near the University, were full of derelict, dingy houses belonging to the Anglican Church. In that very week there was a child abducted and murdered in Glebe. We also discovered that a house with a harbour view was beyond our budget. We were determined to find a place to live in quickly, as we could not afford to stay in the boarding house for long. On the first morning we found a pretty little house in a quiet street between Chatswood and Roseville. It was a 'battleaxe' (a name we had never heard before) and was as far away as possible from neighbouring windows on any surrounding suburban property. We believed the noise of my practising would be less of a problem to our surrounding neighbours if we were down the back of their yards. We walked down the long path toward the house and felt we were entering a different kind of dwelling from the red brick houses up on the street. We saw a cherry-plum tree spanning the drive and when we walked into the house, the bare wooden floor covered in rugs and a cello leaning against a large Viennese oak 'armoire' gave me a feeling of coming home.

We were installed in this house before G started work at Sydney University on February 1st!

We found that Deborah, now aged four-and-a-half, could go to Roseville College which was only two or three streets away, and we thought she would enjoy the company of other small girls. It touched our hearts to see our baby in school uniform for the first time and I remember gloves that had impossibly long fingers for her tiny hands and a little face totally obscured under a mushroom of a hat.

In spite of my joy at being in Sydney, I was aware that it might be some time before I could expect to be given local engagements. I had met Dorothy White during a previous visit and perhaps it was she who recommended me to Norman Johnson, conductor of the Sydney University's Oriana Choir. At any rate, I was asked to sing in my second performance of the *St Matthew Passion,* in the Sydney Town Hall on Good Friday. To a girl brought up in conservative Melbourne, it seemed a very daring thing to give a concert on Good Friday, the most sacred day of the year. No longer a visitor, it was important for me to impress and perform at my peak. I was in the company of some of the finest freelance players in Australia, gathered and rehearsed with great care by Norman Johnson. There were two choirs: the Oriana, and the St Andrews Choir trained by a very young Winsome Evans. Two orchestras seated on opposite sides of the stage, two harpsichords and a portative organ made this performance different. As always on a special occasion, I had no idea of how well I performed, only the feeling of floating on the music stayed with me.

I had to begin work on the music for the Sutherland-Williamson Opera Company and I had to find a coach. I was incredibly fortunate to remember Marie van Hove. She lived only two suburbs away, in Gordon. For two months, after seeing

Graeme take Deborah, protesting, off to school on his way to the University, I would climb into the 'beetle' and drive up the Pacific Highway to Marie, to spend three wonderful hours with her. Singing faultlessly in her high treble, she would go over and over each phrase, until it was embedded in my brain. I found all the opera scores, even the obscure *Semiramide,* in second-hand music shops in Sydney, and discovered that most of my roles were tiny; servant maids and old women, the usual voices for contralto. But Olga in *Onegin* was a young girl, and after I got the score of *Semiramide* and started to underline my role with a red pencil, I was amazed and excited to see how big it was. Arsace was a young man and a General! I wondered if there was a mistake.

Each morning Marie van Hove sang the role Joan Sutherland would later perform so wonderfully. We sailed through Rossini's notes as if the opera would never end and we would together, General and Queen, conquer the score, Sydney and the world! It was such fun learning this opera with Marie, not like work at all.

The weather that year was superb, as each day of blue sky and warm sun succeeded the previous day. Driving up the North Shore in my little VW, I remembered autumn in Paris, London and Melbourne, and wondering if it would ever rain again, decided that Sydney was paradise. G had bought the Penguin book, *How to Sail Small Boats,* by Peter Heaton, and each night would sit reading this textbook with all the attention of a serious academic. The major decision was what kind of small boat we should buy.

By day he went into the University and selected his staff. He found Rosalie McCutcheon, his live-in Deputy Director, almost immediately; she was to become one of the most important people in his life. Rosalie was one of those remarkable women whom one is glad to have had the privilege of knowing. G had first met her at the Student Christian Movement when he was a student at Melbourne University. Rosalie had been widowed after only a year or so of marriage when her missionary husband died in India, leaving her there with her baby son Kim. She had the experience of counselling and wisdom in dealing with young people, and best of all a sense of fun and adventure. Together they set up their office and laid down there the concepts of what a utopian student residence should be. Both idealists, they were practical enough to see the possible pitfalls of opening the first ever 'mixed' residence in Sydney.

The idea of men and women living in the one college was anathema to the other older established colleges of the University, and there were dark mutterings amongst the aged heads of these venerable institutions. Graeme was far younger than them all, and at thirty-two years of age was regarded by them as a mere boy. Many of these men had been Wardens or

Principals forever, and we were invited to each college in turn to meet the rest of the fraternity. An exception to this dreary social life was to meet the women Principals of Sancta Sophia. Over the years these women were always exceptionally able, warm and charming people. Often the Wardens of St John's were also different from the other principals, being friendly and amusing. The Catholic College principals were changed frequently, whereas the other colleges held onto their old 'heads'. We became great friends with Doreen Langley, then principal of Women's College. All of the University Colleges were huge, gloomy buildings, built in a style vaguely resembling the Oxbridge Colleges.

I found fitting in as a 'University wife' extremely difficult. As a young woman who had a career of my own, I found many of the older women and men of the University narrow-minded and provincial. When invited to a dinner party at a private house in those days, it was customary for the wives of university people to be ushered into the master bedroom and place their handbags and gloves on the bed. After suitable small talk, 'the ladies' would have drinks in the 'sitting room' before proceeding in to dinner, with age and authority taking some kind of precedence. I was amazed when, after dinner, the ladies would all go and sit on the bed in the bedroom, one by one in turn going off to 'powder their noses' as it was always called. In small suburban houses, this attempt at upper class English manners struck me as pretentious and I began to refuse the offer to join 'the ladies' because I enjoyed the small talk of the men much more than the domestic gossip of the women. Most of the women were years older than I and exchanged recipes, discussed their cleaning ladies and the cost of meat and vegetables. Whilst they were waiting for the ladies to come back and join them, the men would be offered port or Scotch, in the tiny sitting room. I stayed with the men and so forced the other women to come and join their husbands. The men probably hated me cutting short their drink time, but G never told me off. I think he thought this a lot of nonsense, too.

11. The Sutherland/Williamson Opera Season

As I travelled more in my career, it became terribly important to me to have not just basic comfort, but some semblance of attractive surroundings. So often the rented flats were carpeted with grubby stone-coloured feltex and curtained with basic grit-coloured cotton, hanging over windows which had never been cleaned. In the '60s, finding decent places to stay was very difficult. I took a dreary flat in Albert St, East Melbourne, because I could walk to Her Majesty's Theatre past the old church, St Peter's, Eastern Hill.

Coming back to this part of East Melbourne filled me with nostalgia. In this wide street, with its central aisle of bluestone kerbed grass, I had walked with my sister to and from school, through the Treasury Gardens and down the great avenues of elms to Flinders St and the station. Now the school had gone. The old bluestone building was still there, but was being used by the ABC as a music library. Here was a strange coincidence. The ABC, so influential in my life, was now filled with the ghosts of Henry Handel Richardson, Melba and other women from PLC.

The red brick facade and stout wooden doors of the old National Theatre presented other memories to me, as I crossed the tram lines swinging round past St Patrick's Cathedral and the Dental Hospital. Here I had learnt my first opera roles and performed in *Traviata,* in the same small role I would sing again with Sutherland in a few weeks time.

At first we were so busy that all we needed for accommodation was a bed to sleep in at night. The moment we began rehearsing, days and nights ran into each other with only time to eat at the little cafe next to the theatre between 'calls'.

Norman Ayrton, a charming and talented man, was responsible for directing five of the operas in the season. The rehearsals were scheduled to be in the rooms above Her Majesty's. On the first morning, the cast for *Lucia di Lammermoor* was assembled in a barn-like warehouse area situated above and behind the stage, opening onto Little Collins Street. Introductions were made and Norman explained that we would all have to work day and night to get the operas on in time. There were five weeks in which to rehearse and mount seven operas. It seemed an impressive feat of management at the time, and viewed from thirty years later, still appears to be a near impossibility if not a miracle. Norman made a lot of this possible. His great gift was that he knew exactly what he wanted, every move was economical and afterwards very little was altered.

The rehearsal studio is always a large empty room, roughly the size of the stage, and with a minimum of 'props'. Perhaps there will be a chair or a bed, if this is an essential part of the action, and the floor is often marked out with chalk to give the dimensions of walls or doorways.

Against the raw brick walls, chairs lined the outside perimeter of the room, and those not actually 'on the set' were told to sit quietly until they were called. I was amused when the chorus ladies began to get out their knitting, and were told by Norman that the movement of the busy hands was too distracting. On that first day, the major concern for everyone was to keep warm. The large empty space was unlined brick, roofed with corrugated iron, and the raw Melbourne wind swept through in icy gusts, making us all shiver. Some of the American singers who were used to central heating began to complain and finally, after spending a day or so in overcoats and gloves, we were rewarded with huge old carpets, tapestries and rugs, hung from the roof to the floor, which swayed in the wind but stopped the worst of the draughts. We even had some heaters installed, but my memory of those rehearsals was of constant, bone-chilling cold.

The opening opera of the season would be *Lucia di Lammermoor,* with Joan Sutherland in the title role. Each opera had two complete casts. The other Lucia was the charming young English soprano, Elizabeth Harwood. The tenor, John Alexander, who shared the first night with Sutherland, was unknown to most Australian singers and music lovers at that time. He was one of the New York Metropolitan's greatest stars, and we were incredibly fortunate to have him come to sing Edgardo in this country at the height of his career. He was always a consistent performer, with a beautiful warm tone and great musicality. The other singers were the baritone Cornelis Opthof, singing Enrico, and my friend from Covent Garden, the bass Joseph Rouleau, singing Raimondo. Alisa was sung by the large American mezzo, Dorothy Cole. I was to take over this small role later in the season, so was present at many of the rehearsals, watching carefully with my score and pencil, in order to learn the moves. Once this production was 'on', there would be little or no time for the second cast to have production calls. The conductor was, of course, Richard Bonynge.

The opening night was unforgettable. For those who heard Joan on that Saturday night, there will never be another Lucia. The rich creamy voice poured forth its roulades in a completely effortless way, singing as freely as birds carol, seemingly without care or preparation. The last scene in this opera is often an anti-climax but in this performance, with John Alexander singing, it was unforgettable.

Every seat for all the Sutherland performances was booked within the first day. Unfortunately for J C Williamson and the box office, this was *not* the case for the other performances, with the fine alternate casts Richard Bonynge brought to this season. I can only feel sad that all the musical world did not go to hear all the singers.

Rehearsals were carefully planned and I opened in the second opera, as Olga in *Eugene Onegin,* three days later. I loved this small but important role, in which I sang opposite Alberto Remedios, an English tenor with a fine heroic voice. The role of Olga is set for a real contralto, with the dark smooth sound this voice suggests. I knew that I should have played the role with more vivacity, as Olga is a terrible flirt, and the foil for the dreamy Tatiana. But temperamentally I found it difficult to sing this music and act in a coquettish way. I suppose I lacked experience, and the intensive direction I needed then. I was always more comfortable playing roles far removed from the real person I am. When I could play a boy or a man or a mad old woman, I was more at ease, as I could not find anything of myself in these characters and didn't have the same feeling of standing on the outside, watching myself perform.

Margreta Elkins was the Tatiana, and she sang the role with her magnificent, full-bodied voice. She had always wanted to sing as a soprano and she tried to build her career in this direction during this period of her life. I never understood why this woman, who had a ravishingly beautiful mezzo voice with a good 'top', wanted to sing the higher repertoire. She eventually received rave reviews for her performances in this opera, but during the rehearsals had great difficulty with the upper limits of her voice, often 'cracking' on the top notes and making us all nervous for her success.

The conductor for *Onegin* was the talented New Zealander, John Matheson, who had worked at Glyndebourne, Covent Garden and Sadler's Wells. We worked very hard for him because of the tight rehearsal schedule; he was very demanding, but a fine coach and conductor. Sitting in the dark of the shabby old theatre as we waited to rehearse our scenes, we snuggled down into the worn red plush seats, trying to keep warm. With our coats and gloves on, we opened our scores and prepared for the wonderful music of Tchaikovsky to warm us. This was the 'sitzprobe' (literally, seated rehearsal) of *Onegin,* when the cast sings through the music with the orchestra for the first time using scores. The chorus was singing splendidly, then I sang my little pieces of dialogue and my short aria with the other women. Then we came to the great *Letter Aria*.

Seated in the theatre, we were crossing our fingers that Margreta would get her top notes. Once again she cracked, or forgot her words (I forget which), and once again John Matheson shouted at her. Richard Bonynge came storming down the aisle from the back of the stalls, to shout, "This rehearsal is cancelled. The orchestra is dismissed!" There was a tremendous row in front of everyone, and John Matheson walked out. We learned the next morning that the opening night would be conducted by Gerald Krug. Gerald had been training the chorus and he was someone we all respected, but it was really demanding a lot for him to be thrown into such a complex work as *Onegin* at such short notice. With such a tight schedule, it was devastating to the whole cast to lose a day's rehearsal and to lose John Matheson so late in the day.

I suppose two people as volatile and strong-minded as John Matheson and Richard Bonynge could never work together without argument. Margreta had fewer problems with the top of her voice when Gerald conducted. I suppose John Matheson had 'pushed her' too far, and Richard knew this. Anyway, she received glowing reviews when *Onegin* opened a few days later.

This incident set a pattern for the season. There was always some high drama going on, and the press loved every snippet of gossip, often searching out singers to 'tell tales' against their colleagues. The journalists seemed determined to try to find unsavoury stories, in particular about the Bonynges. But as Richard once said ruefully to me, "Any publicity is good publicity."

Memories of the Melbourne season blurred, as one great 'first night' succeeded another. The third opera was *L'élisir d'amore,* with the exquisite Elizabeth Harwood, my friend Robert Allman, the golden-voiced bass Spiro Malas and Luciano Pavarotti, the slim handsome boy with a God-given voice. The second cast for this opera included Andre Montal, a young tenor with a beautiful light voice, and Joseph Rouleau, with his noble bass, but when Sutherland was not singing, Melbourne stayed at home. What treasures they missed.

Then Joan Sutherland opened in *La traviata,* partnered this time by Pavarotti. We were all stunned by this performance and remembered it all our lives.

During the intervening week I had been sitting in the cold, watching Monica Sinclair rehearse the role of Arsace in *Semiramide* with Joan. This piece was a magnificent vehicle for everyone who had the ability to sing coloratura, and I enjoyed Monica's wickedly extended cadenzas enormously. She had a great sense of theatre and capitalised at every opportunity on her ability to prance about the stage like the proud young man she was portraying. I hoped to learn as much as I could from her and to make as much of the character as she did when it came to my debut in the role. Thanks to Marie van Hove, I had no doubt I could *sing* it well, but would I remember all the moves?

Melbourne went wild when *Semiramide* opened. The

people had never seen this kind of opera before; an 'opera seria' by Rossini, sung with such style and such voices! At this time in Australia, Rossini was known only for *The Barber of Seville,* because his other works had gone out of fashion. It was Callas, and Sutherland with Richard Bonynge, who began the revival of these more unusual 'bel canto' works.

In the fourth week Sutherland opened in *La sonnambula,* again with Pavarotti as her tenor. The ability of Joan to rehearse and perform in these huge roles day after day was extraordinary, and still amazes me when I think of those weeks of one performance after another. What singer could, *or would,* do this today? Her stamina inspired us to keep going, even when the bitter winter weather made us ill with colds, and left us longing to stay in our warm beds. We would stand in the back of the darkened theatre just to hear John Alexander, Pavarotti and La Stupenda singing night after night, at the end of long days of rehearsing our own forthcoming roles.

The second casts were often just as rewarding to hear and watch! The second Violetta in *Traviata* was the Australian, Joy Mammen, and I sang in her opening performance as Annina. We were all interchanged from one cast to another, with the exception of Joan, who always sang the title role in *Semiramide.*

In the fourth week, on Saturday August 7th, I had my second major role, to sing in *Semiramide.* I felt I was in a dream, as I swaggered out to sing the opening words, "Eccomi alfine in Babylonia." ("Here I am at last in Babylon.") It seemed that the stage was an unknown space I had never seen before. Indeed, I might as well have really *been* in Babylon for all I felt at the moment. I had had no stage rehearsal, and just hoped I would retain some memory of all the sideline watching I had done in the past few weeks. The supreme moment came for me as Joan and I sang the great duets, ascending in thirds through cadenzas without hesitation, our voices responding and tingling in my ears as they sang together, gliding up and down the phrases and trills.

It was a huge role to sing, and every now and then Joan would hiss a stage direction at me out of the side of her mouth. By the end of the opera that night I had no memory at all of the moves where Arsace kills his mother, but Joan somehow managed to impale herself on my dagger and fall down dead on cue, to my joyful surprise. The audience loved it. And for the first time in opera in Australia I got a standing ovation *of my own.*

At some time during this period Richard asked me to consider the possibility of going to England to record two early operas with him and Joan for DECCA.

"I'm already going to England with Graeme at the end of the year," I said. "I'd love to sing with you again." So I came to record the title roles in *Montezuma* by Graun, and *Griselda* by Bononcini, in January of 1966, in London.

The fifth and final week of the season saw the opening of

Faust, again with Joan singing in this opera as Marguerite. Her tenor was John Alexander. Joan's ability to sing all these varied roles was amazing, in the tradition of the divas of the Victorian era. As I sang the role of Teresa in *Sonnambula,* I was on stage for the final night of the Melbourne season, when the city's establishment stood on its head. Streamers arched from balcony to stage in a wall of colour, and for the first time there was a 'stage-managed' display of enthusiasm in an opera theatre, as certain members of the cast and audience were given rolls of coiled paper to throw. This has become so common on special occasions now that it is strange to remember the wonder we felt on stage that night, as the coloured ribbons of paper seemed to become almost solid, linking stage to dress circle. But there was no doubt the enthusiasm was genuine.

The cheering went on for thirty-five minutes, and finally an upright piano was pushed on to the stage, and Richard sat down and played *Home Sweet Home* while Joan sang. The plaintive notes died away, and the audience went out into the winter's night with their eyes full of tears, and her voice still ringing in their hearts and ears.

The next day we were off to Adelaide for a two weeks season in Her Majesty's there. I sang my last role for the first time, Marthe in *Faust,* one Saturday afternoon with Georg Tintner conducting and Doris Yarick as Marguerite. Now that all the operas were 'on', we were able to get to know each other. The company began to have the feeling of a loosely knit extended family. There were the good and the wicked, and there was time to cook wonderful meals and drink wine, to entertain, to gossip and rest a little from such hard work in mounting and appearing in seven operas in five weeks. Love affairs began, some to lead to future marriages, others to end with broken hearts. Friendships of all kinds were deep and real for these few weeks and it seemed we would always share this warm camaraderie. Spiro and Marlena Malas' first baby was conceived in the white block of flats on the opposite side of the park across from South Terrace. I shared a flat with the American Dorothy Cole and I loved her sense of fun, her generous personality and her great voice. She always wore caftans because of her larger-than-life size. We swore to be friends for life, but have never seen each other since. Who knows why we never kept up our friendship - we were lazy. I didn't write, nor did she.

We opened in Sydney at Her Majesty's, on Tuesday August 31st, 1965, with *Lucia.* I was home again with my loves, Graeme, Deb and Auntie Lorna who stayed in our house during the tour. But I was no longer part of 'the tour'. My close relationship with the company dissipated and I was back in my role of housewife and mother. Most of my colleagues were still living out of suitcases, but I was HOME.

However I was *not* amused when, the morning after my triumphant opening as Arsace in *Semiramide,* a story about me appeared in *The Sydney Morning Herald,* headed "Housewife's success story as an opera singer." Once again I had been given a standing ovation opposite Joan, singing the role of the boy-general in Babylon. Why did Australia always regard its singers and artists in general as part-time amateurs? Was my role as "Chatswood housewife" to always take precedence for the journalists?

The old Her Majesty's in Sydney was managed by Don McPhee, who became a friend to all the company. He was a storehouse of stories and theatre history and a great fan of Gladys Moncrieff, whom he adored. He stayed in the theatre for every performance.

I also became aware of a charming boy who was stage manager. He always seemed to be standing admiringly in the wings when Joan was singing, hiding behind the 'blacks'. One night the fireman on duty, standing next to this boy, said, "You must be very proud of your mother."

As he held the curtain back for Joan to pass into the wings the boy smiled. "Oh, *she's* not my mother!" he said.

The boy was Moffatt Oxenbould.

The managing director of J C Williamson at this time was the distinguished Australian actor, John McCallum. Williamson's and he had shown great courage in presenting this tour and already there seemed to be financial problems. We were only halfway into the Sydney season, but the box office looked bad. Adelaide had been a severe loss financially, and Melbourne and Sydney houses were poor on the nights Sutherland did not sing.

Williamson's Sir Frank Tait had been in poor health for some time and he died during the tour. The management and McCallum must have been worried, but were unfailingly charming and supportive. McCallum and his wife, Googie Withers, had a house up at Palm Beach and at the end of the Sydney season asked the entire cast and their partners to a Sunday lunch there. I think it may have been G's and my first time visiting this fabulous part of the Sydney coastline. We all had a day of such pleasure. Watching Pavarotti and Bonynge play on the sand and Dorry Cole struggle into her vast costume and into the surf, I realised that the operatic family we had become stood in awe and respect before the immense talent of Joan Sutherland. The black Norfolk Island pines laid their shifting shadows along the sand and, to her colleagues on that day, she was the Queen and we the 'worker bees' who would always stay in her shadow.

It was a time of great reward for me, and for Australia, because of the courage and hard work of Richard Bonynge, Joan Sutherland, Norman Ayrton, John McCallum and J C Williamson. That season laid the foundations for the popularity of opera in

Australia today. In 1964, the Elizabethan Theatre had been in some financial difficulty, and when J C Williamson and Richard Bonynge proposed an international company tour, the Elizabethan was happy to provide information, some administrative staff and the chorus, and not have to stage a full season of opera themselves. So the Elizabethan had some financial respite and benefited from the audience base of new young opera lovers drawn to the Sutherland-Williamson tour. A whole group of young people who had never enjoyed this form of theatre was hooked.

The company went on to complete the tour with a short season in Brisbane, where we all sadly said goodbye to each other.

My husband, flying out of Australia at this time on his overseas study trip to visit International Houses around the world, was astounded to find Dorry Cole, sitting like a large mound in her generous caftan, on the tarmac of the airport in Fiji, rocking to and fro and sobbing, "I'm not leaving. I never want to leave Australia."

12. World Trip and Recording

Graeme's study tour took him through the United States, where he visited the four Rockefeller-established International Houses in Berkeley, Chicago, New York and Paris, to gain information about the running of these Halls of Residence around the world. Deborah, Lorna and I would travel separately and join him in the UK, where he would visit other University residences. This journey was an odyssey for him, for the International House concept of building greater understanding between peoples of different cultures and races fulfilled all my young husband's ideals.

With the help of Lorna, I had completed my last engagement for the year in Christchurch, New Zealand, then packed up and arranged for our friends the Carr-Greggs to look after our house, and flown to London with Deb and Lorna, where we met up with G.

We stayed at first in a rabbit-warren of a bed-and-breakfast place, a succession of separate terrace houses joined by connecting corridors and held together by wallpaper and dusty red carpet runners. We found the alterations in floor levels and the slight deviations of angle from one corridor to another hilariously funny, as we strove to find our way between bathrooms, bedrooms and dining rooms. London seemed so drab and *tatty* after my years away.

The first requirement was a house we could rent for three months, and we finally found one which suited us perfectly in The Vale, Golders Green. While I rehearsed with Richard Bonynge and then worked on the recordings, G travelled around England looking at some of the new halls of residence then springing up in the English Universities.

My first priority was to visit the Modestis in Paris and have some lessons. It was strange to visit the city I still felt was my second home, knowing that I now had no home there. My dear old Mme Daïan had died some years earlier and we now stayed in a little hotel on Avenue Junot. The quaint continental custom of infrequent bathing was reinforced by locking the bathroom door at the end of a passage some way from our bedrooms, and the necessity of asking for a key *and a towel,* and paying a large levy each time you wanted a bath.

Paris near Christmas-time is a secret place of contrasts: of warmth and intense cold, of chestnuts roasting in the streets and beggars seeking warmth in the Metro, playing their accordions with scarves throttled around their throats, fabulous looking breads, sweets and cakes in the little shops near the Madeleine, and beautiful jewellery and window decorations in the shops of the Place de l'Opéra.

We saw and heard Albert Lance sing *Faust* at the Opéra in a grand version, with the entire Walpurgisnacht scene danced magnificently by the Ballet de l'Opéra. Then we saw him sing *The Tales of Hoffmann* at the Opéra-Comique, and he gave us his recent recordings of *Madama Butterfly,* and *Operatic Arias,* recorded in French by Columbia, with Albert Wolff conducting. And most of all I enjoyed spending time with the Modestis, who opened their warm hearts to my little family.

While I had singing lessons, G went out to look at the Cité Universitaire, the Halls of Residence and the International Houses of the Left Bank. The Department of Foreign Affairs arranged for a delightful woman to drive him around. She amused him by trying to beat the rush hour. In French, this is called 'les heures d'affluence'. Her English was excellent, but she referred to this busy time on the roads as 'the rushing hour', an expression we have used ever since.

We had arranged to spend Christmas in Tours with our friends Jim and Wilva Andon, so it was time leave Paris. I was upstairs packing when G went downstairs to pay the account. When he saw it, he felt he was being grossly overcharged. As he didn't speak French, he was having great difficulty with the 'patronne'. At last it was sorted out, and G got his wallet out. With Deb standing gazing up at him, dressed in her tiny school blazer, the 'patronne' suddenly said, in perfect English, "I see your little girl goes to Roseville College. I taught there for two years, when I was living in Sydney!!"

We left Paris in a hired car, driving down to show Chartres Cathedral and the chateaux of the Loire to Lorna and Deb. The winter countryside wore a ghostly transparency, as if it were all photographed in daguerreotype. The towns and chateaux were outlined in black and silver pen strokes. The lines of poplars along the Loire pointed black fingers into the cloudy grey skies. After ringing the bell at the door of some great castle, we waited in the cold for the distant concierge to appear. With his great bunches of huge key rings suspended from arthritic fingers, he was a source of fascination to Deb.

We arrived in Tours for Christmas. Jim and Wilva's daughter Nicola was the same age as Deb. It was wonderful to see those two children playing happily together and, without being able to speak to each other, communicating so well. By the end of the week they were swapping words of each other's languages.

We travelled back to London, and moved into the house in The Vale as soon as possible. We all needed to be settled now, as the winter deepened, and I started work on the music to be recorded. It was Deb who found friends. She was always gregarious and that twilight afternoon, as Lorna and Graeme and I made up beds, sorted and arranged kitchen drawers and did all the thousands of jobs of settling into a house, our little girl hung over the front gate, hoping to find a playmate.

Down the road came Danny, who lived next door, and within minutes this teenage son of artist and inventor Abram Games and his wife Miriam, invited Deb into the house to meet his parents. Abram fell in love with the little girl from Australia. He never tired of asking her to say the word 'toiger', teasing her about her Ozzie accent and enjoying her solemn admiration. From that day, we would find Deb next door drawing with Abram in his studio, or hearing stories of Miriam's grown-up children living in faraway Israel. These kind people were to become great friends, and we were saddened to know that Miriam was already a victim of multiple sclerosis and would become increasingly handicapped. Abram and Miriam said they would be very happy to look after Deb for a couple of hours every day, when I would be working with Richard Bonynge on *Montezuma* and *Griselda*.

Lorna and G arranged to travel to the north of England to visit University Colleges, through the Lake District and on to Glasgow and Edinburgh, to see some of the residences for students there. Lorna was thrilled to visit Scotland for the first time and I was confident that I could look after Deb while they were away. So my days passed, going for an hour or so to the large Bayswater house Joan and Richard lived in at that time, then 'home' to Golder's Green.

Working with Richard was always a pleasure and a challenge. He was a marvellous vocal coach, sometimes demanding the impossible, but always achieving a result beyond what I thought were my capabilities. The music we were to record, from the high baroque period, was deceptively simple because the vocal line was very exposed. I was to sing the title roles in both Operas, and even though each work was cut to fit on an LP, they were still quite long.

In *Montezuma* I had three great arias and a dramatic recitative, accompanied by lute, continuing *segue* (immediately following on) into a short piece which became a fabulous duet with Joan. I sang the role of the Aztec general, Monica Sinclair was the Spaniard, Cortez, and Joan Sutherland, the Aztec princess, Eupaforice. This music was some of the most beautiful I have ever sung. At last it was ready to be recorded, with the London Philharmonic Orchestra and the Ambrosian Singers. The Kingsway Hall recording venue was well known to me (and even better known to Graeme) since we had been married there in the

Little Chapel eight years earlier. We had also attended services there from time to time, when we lived in London, and now I would be *singing* from the pulpit.

As I stood high above the orchestra on that first recording morning, I looked at the two harpsichord players sitting just below me, and down into the blue eyes of a handsome young man whom Richard introduced as Geoffrey Parsons, not knowing that this Australian would become *the* greatest accompanist of his generation and a beloved friend and colleague. The other harpsichord player was another Australian, Valda Aveling. Richard always seemed to have Australians around him. All through his life, he has helped his talented compatriots.

I was not so interested by the music of *Griselda,* which was charming but very lightweight, I thought. However the two operas were a perfect foil for each other. This opera by Bononcini, who was Handel's great rival at the time, had been written in London and I was singing the role first sung by the great English 18th century contralto, Anastasia Robinson. The recordings went very well, and we were all delighted by the quality of the sound achieved by the producer John Culshaw.

During this visit to London, we caught up with friends who were still living and working in the great English opera companies. Moffatt Oxenbould, whom I had known during the Sutherland season, was now living in London where he was working as a stage manager at Sadler's Wells. A memory stays of him with Deb, impossibly doubled up, in the rear of the Morris Mini van we were lent by (future Professor) Graeme and Nancy Clarke, en route to visit the reigning prima donna at Sadler's Wells, Elizabeth Fretwell, and her husband Robert Simmons, who was singing with the Carl Rosa Opera Company. That winter I remember Deb stamping her feet, and shouting, "I'm so cold it *hurts!*"

At last we had completed all our tasks and flew back to Sydney, making a stopover in Bangkok. We had an introduction to some charming people. It was then an old Asian city with very few western-style hotels. We were staying in the new and magnificent Peninsular Hotel. From our room, high above the houses, we saw the narrow unmade back roads and streets of the city, with their private walled compounds, as they must have been for hundreds of years.

Our Thai friends had a large compound which housed an attractive bungalow, open and airy to the outside climate. It was extraordinary, coming from winter in London to the hibiscus flowers in the garden and the strangely spicy smells of the East. The children and their Ayah slept in a large dormitory on mats on the floor. Deb seemed very happy to fall into 'bed' with the other children when the time came, and we accepted our host's invitation to dinner at a fish restaurant, confident that our much-travelled small girl would be looked after by the Ayah and the other children. Lorna came with us, of course, and we set off quite late in the evening after seeing that our little girl was well and truly asleep.

We had a delicious, spicy-hot fish meal, sitting out-of-doors in the balmy night beside the river. When we returned to the house about midnight, we found everything in pandemonium. Deb had awakened and, in a panic at the strange surroundings, had set off looking for her Mum and Dad. The Ayah had seen this and, unable to speak English and explain, had bravely set off on foot after Deb. Deb had got out of the compound gate and was wandering along the dirt road outside the house when we found them both. Even now I go cold thinking what might have happened to her. Apart from this one frightening experience, I shall always be grateful to have seen Bangkok before the westernisation of the city took place.

After landing at Sydney and going through Customs, we drove from the airport and stopped at the corner of City Road and Cleveland Street. Graeme was already able to walk over the building site and see the Round House on the corner of City Road emerge from the rubble and steel and concrete, and the tall residential building growing behind it. The prospect of this new phase of his life made him impatient for Walter Bunning's bricks, mortar and steel to become habitable. We were also looking forward to being back in our new house after this long trip. Graeme had decided to build me a music room, to have a space of my own at last in which to work.

After my performances in the Sutherland season, Stefan Haag asked me to perform the role of Azucena in *Il trovatore* in the Elizabethan Opera's 1966 season. I had never seen this opera but knew the two pieces for my voice that it contained: the aria, *Stride la vampa,* and the great duet and trio, *Ai nostri monti.* It surprises me, looking back, how little I knew of the repertoire I would later come to call my own. I had studied and worked on the Verdi role of Amneris in *Aïda* during my two years in Paris. The role of Ulrica in *Un ballo in maschera* is the vocal preparation for the larger Azucena, and I had made my Covent Garden debut in that role years earlier, in 1957.

I was now quite secure in my singing of Ulrica, but I wondered if I would be able to sustain the much bigger and longer role of the mad gypsy in *Trovatore.* I was thirty-three years old. If I really wanted to sing opera in my own country, here was my chance at last. I must say 'yes' to this role, but I secretly wondered if my then very slight body would support my big voice throughout the opera. The roles I had performed in the recent Sutherland season, which had brought me to the notice of the Elizabethan Opera management, were either very low in range, like Arsace in *Semiramide,* or very short, like Olga in *Onegin*. They had been easy in their physical demands. In concert singing, apart from the Verdi *Requiem,* the vocal demands are generally easy, without the powerful sustained high singing which opera requires. In concerts one needs greater concentration, but the demands are essentially musical. There was only one way to find out. To say 'yes' and hope for the best. I bought the score and began learning the notes.

The way I prepared major roles was the same all through my singing life. I went to the very best coach I could find, and repeated the same phrases over and over, then on to the next page or so, over and over, with the accompaniment providing the rhythmic and harmonic changes. The repetiteur must be firmly in control, stopping when the rhythm is incorrect or a word is mispronounced or the notes are wrong in pitch. The coach usually plays the singer's melody in the right hand, not necessarily what is printed, and puts as much of the harmony as he or she is able to manage in the left hand, with the singer singing along to get the tune right. You can see that the role of the coach, or repetiteur, could be incredibly boring, yet there are many fine pianists who choose to do this all their lives. It is the way most good operatic conductors learn their craft, as they study each vocal score in great depth with their singer. The coach is the unsung hero of all opera singers' lives.

I learned that the conductor for *Trovatore* would be Denis Vaughan, an Australian who had lived for many years in Rome, and who had studied Verdi's and Puccini's original scores there. He had been a pupil of Sir Thomas Beecham's. I was always rather nervous meeting the conductor for the first time. I wondered if I would 'get on' with him. Conductors sometimes adopt an autocratic manner which can be very intimidating.

Denis Vaughan made it clear that he knew all there was to know about *Trovatore* and how it was to be sung. I was soon totally in his thrall and believe that he inspired me to sing this music with the style and musicality which has always been my ambition in singing Italian opera since that time. He insisted on doing most of the coaching for the opera himself, taking his place at the piano in a way I have rarely seen a conductor do. He was a wonderful vocal repetiteur who worked in later years with the mezzo, Brigitte Fassbaender, in Munich. Every day he had me in the studio demanding vocal line in the tone to the end of the phrase, better Italian diction, more emotion and so on, until I felt he would never be satisfied. He was a perfectionist and drove most of the rest of the cast to distraction. He could make the most patient, good-natured singer irritable and drive the orchestra wild. But I was so starved for this kind of really demanding work that I loved these attempts to achieve the impossible and grew very fond of him.

Sometimes he would show me something on the printed score and say, "That's not in the original score. Ricordi (the publisher of Verdi's music) put that in." Or he would say, "This marking is quite the opposite from what Verdi wanted. The copyist made a mistake and it has never been corrected." It was Denis who taught me to weight the opening 'Str-r-r' of *Stride la vampa,* which was so telling in these first performances. He taught me to arch the sound through the phrases in a way that even my old teacher had not been able to show me.

At this time we were rehearsing in many different makeshift church halls and rehearsal rooms. The orchestra for the Elizabethan Opera Company was the resident ABC Symphony Orchestra in each state. This meant that the Opera Company did not have to pay orchestral costs which was of great financial help. Of course the seasons were much shorter then and the structure of the present permanent company did not exist.

We were going to begin the tour in Brisbane and then progress south through all the eastern states. The sets were imported from New Zealand and were brilliantly designed by Raymond Boyce. We were first shown a tiny model in a toy theatre and had no idea how steeply raked the stage would actually be. This is often the case. The carefully plotted moves, worked out in great detail on the floor of a large room in some studio, actually bear no relationship to the distances in the real set, because of the vertical and spatial dimensions in the theatre. However, these production rehearsals are not a waste of time. Each move in opera has to be placed in relation to the music and timed to a precise sound in the pit. But often the timing can only be really finely tuned after the opera is on the stage, in the final few days before the opening. This is when stage experience becomes so important. The newcomer will find it takes longer to work out the exact timing of a move, while an experienced artist will know instinctively how to get from A to B in so many bars of music.

The producer for the opera was Stephan Beinl, a Viennese who had great experience as a producer in the Vienna State Opera in Salzburg and in Weimar. Again I didn't know this older man and was rather in awe of him. When I began rehearsals on this set, I was always worried about slipping. The mountain-like slopes were clad in some metallic surface. The effect was marvellous, representing shining black hard mountains covered in ice. Our shoes had to be painted with a rubbery solution so that we could move without skidding on the slope.

I had never read anything about the story of the opera when I came to play Azucena, but I knew instantly that this opera was about the gypsy, her love for her mother and her love for her son. This is a wonderful role for a mezzo-contralto. Verdi himself saw the other two roles of the tenor and the soprano as rather wooden by comparison. Initially he had planned to name the opera after the gypsy. He says in his letters, "There is so little to this poor Troubadour ... that if we take away his courage, what will he have left? How could he possibly interest such a high-born lady as Leonora?"

In that 1966 season, the Leonora was the New Zealand soprano, Rosemary Gordon. Her voice had a fragile and beautiful German quality, not unlike the sound of Elisabeth Schwarzkopf. She was extremely versatile and at this time was the 'star' of most of the Elizabethan's productions, singing all the major roles from Verdi to Mozart with skill and musicality. The cool fragile sound at the top of her voice made me long for the more robust and secure singing of my friend Elizabeth Fretwell, who was then in London at the height of her career, but Rosemary Gordon sang with great passion in her heart. My wish then, as now, would always be for a more Italianate sound from my Leonora, like Tebaldi or Callas, but I admired Rosemary's ability to cope with the enormous demands of this role.

Manrico, the gypsy's son, was the Australian Donald Smith. His was one of the most remarkable tenor voices I ever heard. Possessing a ringing Italian sound, he sang with great passion and beauty of tone. He was always unpredictable in his movements on stage and could get 'carried away' if he was excited. This lent some added tension to the scenes I sang with him. He had a tendency to really throw you across the stage if he were aroused. Fortunately, this did not happen in my scenes, but Rosemary suffered bruised wrists for most of the season.

The other great singer in that early season was Alexander Major, who had recently migrated from Hungary. The Verdi roles of this period demand a strong baritone who can sustain a high tessitura. Major had a perfect voice for the role and produced a most wonderful sound. Rhythm was not always his strong point, but he was amazingly in tune and sang with a voice of an angel. In this production he had some difficulties with the set. The opera takes place at night with the stage always in semi-darkness and it was important that we sang standing in the carefully plotted pools of light, as we had meticulously rehearsed with Stephan Beinl. But Major would take a step to one side or the other of the crucial 'spot' and so stand invisibly, singing a major aria in total darkness. We would try, as discreetly as possible, to get him into position without actually pushing him into place!

In Act 3 we appear together, when the soldiers capture Azucena and drag her to the captain of the guard. Ferrando recognises her as the gypsy who stole the child of the old Duke. The scene always worried me in this production. Each night the two young chorus men playing my captors were *very* enthusiastic as they grabbed me, just out of sight below the top of the steps at the back of the set. With my hands bound, they hauled me helpless over the mountaintop at the back of the stage, and we all slid down the mountain to arrive in a breathless heap at the bottom, centre stage, just behind the prompt box. They then pretended to beat me and nearly every night one of them gave me a nasty karate chop on the back of the neck. I became a regular patient at the local chiropractor.

I was supposed to be their captive, but one night it was *I* who held *them* upright. As we hurtled down the hard metallic surface, there was a strange shudder in one of the boys and I heard something snap. At that point, I had a short scene of high singing to do, and was aware that the boy on my left was actually hanging on to *me* for dear life until I had to fall to my knees to plead for my life. At the end of the scene, I found that he had broken his leg.

One of these two was John Brady, who made a career overseas as the tenor John Sydney. In the following year, one of my captors was Ian Campbell, who later became the Administrator of the South Australian Opera Company, and then of the San Diego Opera in the USA.

The chorus was very small in those days; two other members who went on to sing as principals were Neville Wilkie and Malcolm Donnelly who had a great career in England, Europe and here in Australia. Ferrando was sung by the young Donald Shanks, possessing a glorious bass voice. Jacqueline Sylva was Inez.

We opened in August in Brisbane, at Her Majesty's Theatre, to the most astonishing reviews. From then on *Trovatore* was a major triumph and I was at last an opera star in our own Opera Company, in my own country.

In that season we toured three operas: *Trovatore, Boris Godunov,* with the legendary Neil Warren-Smith, and *The Barber of Seville,* with Rosalind Keene as Rosina. *Boris,* with its sweep and drama spanning the Tsar's life, had a chorus of twenty-six that year. After the Brisbane season we came back to Sydney and then went to Canberra, where we used the Queensland Symphony Orchestra for the short season. In the Canberra paper of the day I see that I "enjoyed a midnight dinner given by Mrs W Fairfax at the Town House Motel, to honour the first full opera season in Canberra."

After a week there, we went to Melbourne's Palais Theatre. I was able to stay with my friend Gwen Halstead and it was a joy to renew our close friendship. Gwen must be one of the most giving and generous people I have met, and we spent hours together trying out songs, and just confiding our dreams and talking about our children.

There was a close-knit family feeling on this tour. There were only five people on the administrative staff at this time, including Stefan Haag, the Executive Director, and Administrator, John Young, who also directed *Boris Godunov.* I remember sitting around dining tables talking of the future of opera in this country with these people who were shaping the plans for its future. We were being consulted, in an informal way, and were proud to be part of this new life. My dream was that wonderful singers like Keith Neilson and Morris Williams *could* make a full-time career by singing in opera in the future.

After this long period of constant work, I felt as if I were a real professional singer again. I was appreciated for the art and work I loved to do, and the anger and bitterness of my rejection by the Opera Company over the past five years began to heal. I was still singing my concerts for the ABC, and having found how rewarding this work was and how different from the operatic, I relished the difference and hoped I would always have the opportunity to combine the two worlds.

Between performances of this *Trovatore* season, I had been called in to replace the Adelaide contralto Nancy Thomas at short notice in *Elijah*, when she became ill with a cold. Mollie McGurk from Western Australia had replaced my friend Nance Grant for the same reason in this concert performance.

It must have been a nightmare for Sir Bernard Heinze, without rehearsal, to have two new soloists! It was also very exciting (and a bit stressful) to be involved in these ad hoc performances. I always liked to have plenty of notice before the work to be performed, so that, whatever it was, it was truly 'in the voice'. The longer a singer knows a work the more the brain responds to the muscular and physical demands on the vocal cords, and the intellectual demands on the emotions. When I had performed and then put a work aside, even if I knew it well, I liked to have the time to prepare it again, in my mind, as much as anything. To be 'thrown on' could give me a great charge of adrenalin, but I'm not sure if that always resulted in a good performance.

I recorded my first LP for the ABC in 1966, Dorien Le Gallienne's *Four Divine Poems of John Donne*. I have the greatest affection for this work. Le Gallienne was living in Melbourne in my earlier life there and was music critic for *The Age*. Perhaps because there was an unwritten rule that artists did not speak to critics, I never met him. He died before I knew these wonderful songs, which I believe are the finest settings of all of these great poems. The recording was a joint project of the ABC, the Australian UNESCO Music Committee and the World Record Club; part of that famous series of LPs called 'Australian Music Today'. This one, Volume Two, also included Felix Werder's String Quartet No 6 and Nigel Butterley's *Laudes*. For this recording my pianist was Marie van Hove. Marie at that time was living at home with her father and mother. She led an ensemble which broadcast light classics on Saturday evenings nationally for the ABC. She was also a fine timpanist, a superb coach and an excellent conductor. I think this recording of the Le Gallienne songs is as good as any I made in the future, from both pianist and singer.

This was also the time that I began a long association with Trinity Grammar School. I gave my first recital there with Dorothy White for Max Taylor's Society for the Arts. Max Taylor is a remarkable man who loves both painting and music. He was teaching history in the school and decided to build an art gallery to display and sell the paintings of some of the most eminent artists in Sydney. The concerts he presented were subsidised by the sale of paintings. It was a remarkable scheme, for which many people over the years have cause to thank him, not least the boys of Trinity Grammar. It must have been about this time that I started working with Dorothy White, learning some of Bach's arias, so this concert included Bach, Mahler's *Songs of a Wayfarer* and Schumann's *Frauenliebe und Leben*.

Towards the end of this momentous year I sang my first performance of Elgar's *The Dream of Gerontius* in New Zealand. This wonderful work became one of the most precious jewels in my repertoire. I loved the poem and the music, and have always felt that it was a privilege to be able to sing *The Dream* with the great orchestral and choral sounds painted in rich Victorian colours by Elgar. The other soloists were Raymond MacDonald and Grant Dickson, and the work of the choir was memorable.

The year ended with a *Messiah* in Newcastle, conducted by Ivan Rixon with the Hurlstone Choral Society, and ABC *Messiahs* in Tasmania with Rex Hobcroft.

13. Sydney

When we first came to live in Sydney, we were surprised at the differences in the climate, the terrain and soils in our new environment. The soil was hard red clay, with about one inch of topsoil. And the differences in climate between Sydney and Melbourne made a huge difference to what we grew with success. Although it was warm, the humidity made everything damp; our shoes and leather bound books went mouldy, and had to be wiped clean in the summer. But the winter was superb, with endless sunny days and crisp cold nights.

We began to discover the many different faces of this city, from the decayed elegance of Paddington to the grand homes of Rose Bay, from the shaded gardens of the North Shore to the open spaces of the beach suburbs, and the curious old flats of Bondi, Watsons Bay and King's Cross. Every now and then a house or church would surprise us with its echoes of the convict past of the old city. The Rocks, before the commercial development which has spoiled this rare glimpse into our past, showed how early settlers lived, after they stepped ashore from the sailing boats at Circular Quay, to dwell in this first city in Australia.

Living in this new city also meant a search for a new house-keeper/child-minder. Sometimes my aunt Edith Elms could come and stay while I was away for a long period, at other times mother's friend Auntie Lorna Monro. We tried several people from 'Dial-an-Angel'. Some were good, some were dreadful, and at last we found Peggy Crawford, who decided that we suited her and adopted us as a part of her family. She came whenever we asked her, and Deb and Mrs Crawford became great friends.

Summer in Sydney brings heat, humidity and lethargy. Arriving in January, we sweltered in the moist warm air and saw an escape in the winds on the blue waters of the Harbour. We bought a little Heron dinghy and trailer. After having the tow-bar fitted to the car, we decided we needed to launch the boat where we would not be a nuisance to more experienced sailors.

When he was driving to the University G had noticed that there were no sailing dinghies on the stretch of water near Iron Cove Bridge. It seemed very sheltered, so we decided we would 'put her in' there. We drove around till we found a launching ramp and backed the trailer into the water. The Heron was a very tiny boat. G and I were slimmer then than now and Deb was only six years old, but it was still a tight fit.

Clutching the Penguin book, *How to Sail Small Boats,* in one hand, G rigged the sails, and we climbed in and set off.

Oh bliss ...

We were off and away, blown along by a nice little breeze, well out into the bay, with the centreboard down and learning to sit on the windward side to keep upright. We dreaded falling in, or 'bottling', and having to cope with righting an overturned dinghy.

"At least we're all wearing life-jackets," I thought to myself, "and Deb is a good swimmer."

Suddenly we came to an abrupt stop. We were all nearly catapulted into the water and the little boat slowly turned on its side and filled. We all dived in and struck out frantically for what seemed like a distant shore. As my arm came over in the best swimming style I could manage, my hand struck something hard. The rudder was floating by. How could this be? I grabbed at it and my feet touched bottom. We were in less than a metre of water! The whole bay was so shallow that we had been fortunate to get the centreboard down at all. Now we knew why there were no dinghies sailing in Iron Cove. I walked through the shallows to retrieve the rudder as it washed up near Timbrel Park, we pulled the little boat upright and, with sheepish grins, towed her through the water back to the ramp, desperately hoping that nobody saw us.

For the rest of the lazy summer days of the vacation and on warm Saturdays after term started, we took a picnic and sailed at Balmoral Beach, from the lovely tree-shaded sands there, until we finally felt we could sail with confidence. Over the years we have sailed nearly every week and the pleasure has never diminished. To be moving over the water, with only the sound of the lapping waves, has always seemed like a miracle to me.

Our next boat was a bilge-keeled fibreglass experiment made by Paul Hamlyn, called a Bluefin. It had a minute cabin, into which we could wriggle, and with Deb sleeping head to our toes, all three of us could camp out overnight - and we did. The trailer for this craft had trays, which had to be manoeuvred under its fin-like keels. We found that wherever we put her in, the tidal differences would mean that 'retrieving' the Bluefin would become a challenge bordering on the impossible.

Deb went off for one week to the beautiful National Fitness Camp near Patonga in the January school holidays, before her last year of Primary School; her best friend wanted to go so much that Deb thought she would enjoy it too. Alas, she was desperately miserable, and begged us to visit her during the weekend. We decided to go by boat, and set off from the Church Point ramp. It was a long way for our four metre boat to go, and as we rounded West Head the most enormous swell swept us along, giant waves rising up behind us, hurling us forward where we hung for a moment, before we plunged into the trough beneath the crests and waited breathlessly, before rising again. It was agony, but we were helpless. Fortunately we were racing along, but it was terrifying to look behind and see the swells rising high above our mast. Worse, we had no grab-rails and could easily just slide off into the water. But we made the protected bay where the Camp was situated and were able to run up onto the beach. (This is one of the great advantages of the bilge-keel boats). We had lunch with Deb, but did not suggest she come home with us then and there, which I'm sure she wanted to do. I think we were in shock. We waved a cheery goodbye and set off with sinking hearts to reverse our journey. Fortunately the wind and tide had smoothed the swell and it was much easier going back. When I think of this day, I am still filled with horror at our irresponsibility. If something had happened to us, what would have happened to Deb?

We found a great sense of renewal in a few hours of sun and wind. Sailing demands total concentration on the direction and speed of the breeze and this wiped out all the daily cares.

G was finding the life of International House Director immensely rewarding, but there was always something to worry about. Some students were undisciplined or needing psychological counselling. Some carried tremendous sorrows from their old lives in distant countries and some were enjoying their first taste of real freedom. Domestic staff and cooks and chefs were coming and going all the time in those early years, and day and night the demands continued.

International House was full and the enthusiasm of the residents in this new College was contagious. The residents then were mainly post-graduates. They would not have been selected by their countries to come to Sydney unless they were very good in their fields. G tried to keep the ratio of half Australians to half overseas students, and the bulk of the latter were from Asian countries. But there was always to be a sprinkling of Americans, English, Scandinavians and Europeans, who had a particular interest in our literature or perhaps in our water management, or Africans wanting to study medicine or agriculture or dentistry. There were a few Papuans, amongst whom in that first year was a future leader of his country, Bernard Narakobe. There was even a Tibetan. They were lively and wonderful young people. Over the years, people from more than ninety countries have lived at International House.

The first students were admitted in January 1967 and the building was officially opened during a week of torrential rain in June of that year, by the Governor, Sir Roden Cutler. On March 3rd I had given the first of my annual recitals, to help the Women's Committee of International House make money for curtains, carpets and other furnishings. All through my singing life I gave at least one solo recital each year. At this time, the Wool Room at International House gave me an excellent venue in which to perform. The acoustics were good, I had a small but captive audience in the loyal members of the Women's Committee and their University husbands, and I could indulge my love of the recital repertoire. One of the sad facts about the City of Sydney is that there is no intimate recital venue in the whole central city with good acoustics where the rental is not prohibitive.

Then, as now, recitals very rarely made money. The joy of singing Lieder and Art Songs is an indulgence. It seems that no-one wants to pay money to hear the songs of Brahms, Schubert or Schumann, unless the singer has a worldwide reputation. Perhaps this is right. After all, the songs were written in another place and for another time, more than 100 years ago, to be sung for private pleasure in small salons, and most often in German or French.

"The times, they are a-changing," sang The Seekers cheerfully, and the Beatles were singing the song of *Eleanor Rigby*.

And yet the settings of songs of the great German poets deserve to be remembered and performed by fine singers. My great-aunts singing round the piano by candlelight in my childhood were passing on a musical heritage that all young singers should experience. These small and intimate songs have a place in our world, but the beauty of the melodies, swamped by the ghetto blasters of our age, may not survive. Yet they must be sung, as they express through music all the emotions of a human lifetime in exquisite detail.

Dorothy White was my accompanist in that first concert. G paid for the program printing, the girls in the office collated the pages and later tied the whole thing together with ribbons. At first someone donated a very indifferent upright piano to International House and this was not a pleasure for Dorothy to play. Later, the House bought a small grand piano, which was only just adequate for the room. The noise of traffic roaring along City Road was always a problem, later to be reduced by double-glazing. The issue of how to advertise the concerts was always contentious. The small numbers of people who came rarely covered the cost of a newspaper advertisement. We learnt the hard way.

I did not take a fee, but I always insisted that the accompanist be paid. The coaching I did with him or her was included in the fee. I wanted to contribute to the life of the House and felt I was helping by making some money for the Women's Committee. I was expanding my repertoire, and gaining valuable experience in this very specialised field of song. Perhaps it was as well that I didn't realise that the costs of the recital I was giving were greater than the money taken for tickets. G never told me, because he realised how much this kind of music-making meant to me.

The next great experience was to sing at the residential music festival run by Musica Viva at Mittagong. This was the seventh Easter Festival, which took place at Frensham School and Sturt. The buildings housing the residents for the conference were simple country houses with verandas, and this simplicity complemented the Clubbe Hall, which had just been built. It was thought to be a 'state of the art' recital venue. It was indeed a wonderful building for music-making, with an excellent acoustic, built in the style of the sixties, but with a warmth and spacious beauty created by a sweeping roof of honey-coloured timber, curving up and outward from the stage. The building won an architectural prize for its design.

G knew and loved Winifred West, the remarkable idealist who had founded Frensham School, and Phil Bryant, her lieutenant. But when Graeme, Deb and I were invited to stay there for the weekend, it was my first visit to this lovely part of New South Wales. Of course we knew many of the Musica Viva people in Melbourne, but the Manager, Regina Ridge, and the powerful members of the board, were strangers to us in Sydney. Never having bothered about the politics of music, and 'networking' (a new name for an old custom), I was interested to meet the rather formidable people who ran this great organisation. What a triumph those Easter Festivals were! The audiences were invited to sit in on rehearsals and enjoy a feeling of participation in the music making. Many of them brought their instruments with them and enjoyed playing string quartets and chamber music on the still afternoons, between the concerts given by the professional string quartets. I was invited to sing Schumann's *Frauenliebe und Leben* with Margaret Schofield. I was so pleased to have this great Australian pianist play for me again, after an interval of two or three years.

Charles Coleman was there, with his Leonine Consort, and conducted 'ad hoc' rehearsals, inviting the public to join in the singing. There was the Austral String Quartet, led by Don Hazelwood, with Ron Ryder, Ron Cragg and Gregory Elmalogolou; the Cremona Quartet from Melbourne, with Len Dommett, Sybil Copeland, Jack Glickman and Henry Wenig; the Sydney String Quartet, comprising Harry Curby, Robert Ingram, Robert Pikler and John Painter, who were all outstanding players; and the cream on the top was the visiting Smetana Quartet from Prague. We revelled in the wonderful music making and the discussions, which were both spontaneous and programmed. Deb enjoyed playing with the children of Roger Covell and the Hazelwoods, and went horse riding for the first time. I sang some Bach with Jirí Tancibudek, Claire Fox and Werner Baer, who played the organ, and to crown the weekend I sang Lennox

Berkeley's *Four Divine Poems of St Teresa,* with Robert Pikler conducting an 'ad hoc' orchestra made up of all the visiting string players.

I think my admission to this magic circle of great Australian musicians was due to Robert Pikler's interest in me and his support of my singing. It was a weekend of beautiful warm autumn weather and the Frensham grounds were a lovely place to relax and enjoy the country air. It was an unforgettable experience for all who went to those Easter Festivals.

Two weeks later I sang for the first time in Chalwin Castle, in the Sydney suburb of Cremorne. Vivian Chalwin was a champion swimmer and sportsman who had made a fortune owning and managing car parks in the city. He bought an old house with a superb view overlooking the harbour and proceeded to rebuild it, creating a Mediterranean villa, without however, pulling the old house down. The additions and decorations sat oddly upon the modest Victorian original, which could still be seen under the improvements. But beneath the house, in the soft Sydney sandstone and overlooking the swimming pool, he carved out a tiny baroque theatre, with a red plush and gilt interior, and a terrible acoustic. Each Sunday of the month he let a different organisation use his theatre for a classical music concert. The Mozart Society, the Keyboard Society and the Schubert Society presented concerts here for many years, and owe their continued survival to Vivian's generosity.

Chalwin Castle was situated in an extremely narrow winding street, lined by high brick-walled mansions belonging to powerful people. A Judge who lived there sought an injunction to prevent Vivian holding those soirees, because parking for visitors to any of the other houses in the street became impossible when these musical evenings occurred. Vivian's chain of car-parks meant that, on Sunday nights, uniformed white-gloved parking attendants showed you where to put your car, making it seem rather 'posh' to be parking in the street. The concerts were given for many years and only when Vivian died ceased to be a feature of the musical scene in Sydney.

In June and July I sang a return season of *Il trovatore* in Adelaide and Melbourne, and one performance in Sydney, for the Elizabethan Opera with Gerald Krug conducting. I then embarked on a number of recitals with Dorothy White for different Music Clubs around the city: at Ryde, Lane Cove and Pymble. I sang for the first time in the Great Hall at Sydney University for the International House Women's Committee, because Dorothy did not want to play the upright piano in International House any more! At Abbotsleigh, I did a recital with Marie van Hove, including some operatic arias (which I rarely sang with piano, because I felt that the song repertoire was more suited to piano accompaniment). I sang with Joyce Hutchinson for Musica Viva in Canberra. We performed some Schubert and I enjoyed her sensitive musicality. Each of these great women gave their own complementary insights to the songs. Dorothy as a teacher showed me how to be disciplined in my performing and to use the intellect behind the words and music. Marie coaxed the sweep and operatic style from me, and both were overshadowed by the lyrical touch of Joyce's fingers in her accompaniments.

In 1967, the ABC brought Elisabeth Schwarzkopf to Australia for a recital tour. Her accompanist was Geoffrey Parsons. This was the young man who had played harpsichord in the recordings I had made in London in the previous year. The ABC asked me if I would make a studio recording with Geoffrey and later have it released commercially by EMI. I had made many studio recordings by now, with Raymond Lambert, Henri Penn, Gwenda Halstead and Margaret Schofield in Melbourne, and Marie van Hove in Sydney. But Geoffrey was special. He was Schwarzkopf's chosen accompanist and I had made an impression sufficient for him to want to record with me.

He suggested that we record a group of Schubert songs and I asked for Duparc, and in the end we put together a group of our favourite songs, including two songs of Lizst. One of the Schubert songs was *Gretchen am spinnrade*. Geoffrey asked Schwarzkopf along to the studio to hear me sing it. She was the glamorous heroine of that generation of singers, beautiful, generous and above all intelligent about her art. She opened doors in the way she spoke of Gretchen and the very young girl's first love. Twenty years later I met her in Salzburg, and she had not forgotten me. I felt honoured that she remembered that day in Sydney, in the old stone church in Margaret Street with the shafts of sunlight slanting through the cracks in the curtained windows.

The year was over when I returned home after singing two *Messiahs* in Wellington, New Zealand, with Malcolm Rickard conducting. It was Christmas. We asked the residents who were left languishing in International House on Christmas Day to spend it with us at home. And then it was time once again to enjoy the languid summer days on the Harbour. For Graeme, especially at this time, going out on the water as often as possible was very important to his well being. Most of the overseas residents at International House stayed in Sydney during the vacation, so January was not a holiday period for us. As the days lengthened, G would come home and we would set out to sail in the evenings, often returning over the water in the dark.

14. Walking on the Moon

We began rehearsals for *Don Carlos* in January 1968. This Verdi opera was to be presented at the Adelaide Festival and again John Young was the director. Neil Warren-Smith was to sing Philip and Alan Light the Grand Inquisitor. Rosemary Gordon sang Elisabeth, while Alexander Major was the Rodrigo. Reginald Byers, singing the title role, was not 'Don Smith' and the charisma of the great Queenslander of the golden voice was sadly missed. I was scared stiff by the top note in Eboli's great aria, *O Don Fatale*. I loved the role, the music and the aria itself, but I was still struggling to obtain a free and easy top to my voice. I had mostly managed to achieve a good top B flat in *Il trovatore* (but sometimes not, as on the night of the ABC broadcast!) but here I felt absolutely unable to achieve the C flat demanded at the end of the aria. So I begged the conductor to let me sing it transposed down a tone and even then I still had a problem.

The mental approach is fundamental to a singer. Here was a good example. I knew I should be able to sing this well and could do so in practice rooms, but I always failed to do it when I was rehearsing in front of the chorus. The more I tried, the worse I sang. I knew I was tightening up and growing more and more tense as the weeks went by. Once the singer Elizabeth Allen said quietly to me, "Wait a moment before you try for the top note at the climax, at the end of the aria." This was great advice, but I was so tense I could not follow it. I had to leap up to that high note instantly, with disastrous results. I needed a Richard Bonynge or Denis Vaughan to help me pace myself for the climax. I may have been able to achieve a good performance, but I was so handicapped by my fear that I received kind but lukewarm notices and knew I deserved them. I really needed some good vocal coaching, but did not dare trust my hard-won technique away from the distant Modesti.

The little Scots lass with the big, extraordinary voice, Morag Beaton, who had migrated to Australia after the Sutherland season, was really suited vocally to sing Eboli and sang the part splendidly, but I was not yet ready. Towards the end of the season I did manage to sing the aria as I should and this was because, at last, I was able to do as Elizabeth Allen had suggested and wait what seemed an interminable moment, before hurling myself at the top note. And yet I loved this role and could have sung it splendidly later, when I had arrived at a different voice by my own efforts, trained by experience and age. And somehow, the Adelaide Festival was not then ready for a performance of an opera of this magnitude. The article by *The Age* critic, Kenneth Hince, said at the time, "Verdi's *Don Carlos* is a big opera. Its scoring is too big for Australian theatres. The sheer length of its four acts is solemnly noticed by all four Adelaide reviewers. It needs heroic singing and an ample production, and perhaps it needs an audience which is bigger in mind and spirit and responsiveness than we can give it."

This assessment of possibly the greatest of Verdi's operas may still be true today, but we have come a long way in our knowledge of opera and in our musical sophistication. The pit of Her Majesty's Theatre in Adelaide was tiny, and before the building of the Festival Theatre, which was to be a great improvement dramatically though not good acoustically, the opera seemed to take place in a strange vacuum in the wrong part of town and in the wrong town. The sound of the opera orchestra was not adequate for this great piece. The standard of instrumental and orchestral playing has improved immeasurably since that time. Without doubt, the operatic event of the Adelaide Festival of that year was Puccini's *Tosca,* with Marie Collier, Tito Gobbi and Donald Smith.

Musica Viva was becoming an important part of my life. The Manager, Regina Ridge, wanted to program more vocal chamber music. She, or perhaps Robert Pikler, asked me to suggest a program of works with some of the players living in Sydney at the time. I was becoming more and more interested in early music, under the influence of Dorothy White, and with her harpsichord playing in mind we arranged a program for a tour to Brisbane, Sydney, Melbourne (Wilson Hall) and Adelaide (Town Hall). The other players were Linda Vogt, flute; Bob Ingram, violin; Robert Pikler, viola and John Painter, cello. This program was *Jubilent Omnes* (Riccio), *Laudate Pueri* (Perti), three arias from *Montezuma* (Graun), Beethoven's *Serenade in D minor* for flute, violin and viola, and an imaginative and wonderful original arrangement of Kodaly songs by George Pikler.

Robert, looking for a song cycle to round off the concert, could not have imagined anything better. I sang these songs in Hungarian, with the help of the Pikler brothers, and the texture of the songs stays with me down the years. Alas, the work was never recorded and the music was lost; the work for solo voice, flute (Linda Vogt) viola (Robert) and cello (John Painter) has floated into the ether, never to be retrieved.

Working with such fine musicians was an inspiration. So different temperamentally from singers, instrumentalists seem another breed. If I say they seem more mature and more serious, I generalise, but many singers retain a childlike naivete in their view of music and of life in general. They are great fun to be with, but not to be taken too seriously. Life is a stage, on which everything is to be projected. As I write this, I think of opera singers of sensitivity and great intelligence, but ... they are rarer than one supposes.

I queried being obliged to join Actor's and Announcer's Equity, some years earlier. At that time, when all my work was in concert performances for the ABC, I had suggested that it would be more appropriate for me to be a member of The Musician's Union. Actor's Equity included 'hoofers' and 'strippers' from Kings Cross, as well as actors and radio announcers. I was firmly told that singers were not musicians!

Graeme tells the story of sitting in an aeroplane between Melbourne and Adelaide, when Robert Pikler walked along the narrow aisle. He stopped, leant down towards Graeme and said he had just played in a concert with me. "Lauris is a remarkable singer. She is a musician. That is very rare!" And then he continued on his way back to his seat.

But now, thanks to Musica Viva, I had the challenge of performing with the cream of Sydney's musical life. We put another program together comprising Brahms' *Two Songs op 91* for piano, voice and viola, Ravel's *Chansons madécasses* for piano and cello, a Beethoven Trio, and Schubert's *Auf dem Strom* in the cello arrangement (instead of horn), with George Pikler's arrangements of the Kodaly songs to finish. We gave concerts in Toowoomba, Canberra and in Mildura, following our Adelaide performance.

This was an adventure Linda Vogt and John Painter never let me forget. Mildura was having an arts festival and I remembered that the Opera Company had sent the *Il trovatore* principals there for a concert at the end of the previous year, when we had stayed in a very comfortable hotel with a swimming pool. This had been in December, and Rosemary Gordon and I had enjoyed cooling off in the pool at midnight after the heat of the concert-hall. I asked if we could be put into that hotel for two nights. This time it would be early winter. We were to give the harpsichord program in Adelaide, then drive by car to Mildura. (It must have been a headache working out the travel itinerary for this tour). We would then catch a small plane, via Melbourne, to Canberra where we would perform the other program.

We presented a very good concert in Adelaide Town Hall, a perfect venue for chamber music. We had supper with Edith Dubsky and the Musica Viva committee and went to bed, ready for an early start next morning. We set off first thing and it was a long hard drive. The roads were narrow and cars were not so comfortable then. I remember a long straight stretch of bitumen that never seemed to end. We finally drove into Mildura to find that the hotel had not been booked for us. We were to stay in a local guesthouse, which we had great trouble finding. I remember only a narrow room with linoleum on the floor and an old iron single bedstead over a lumpy mattress. The boarding-house owner said, "The bathroom's at the end of the passage," as he flicked the torn brown Holland blind up. I went to bed with a headache and endured a noisy group of teenagers talking outside in the passage all night.

I was angry. We had had a very hard few days, we were going to have more, and I was a star singer who was by now accustomed to a certain amount of pampering after my recent successes.

"Where," I asked imperiously, "are the rooms for us, booked by Musica Viva over two months ago?"

The festival organisers had decided that the currently running Bowls Convention had to be considered and they had given the bowlers our hotel rooms.

"I must have a quiet room today if I am to sing well. I need to have a sleep this afternoon," I exploded next morning. I lay pale and wan, while the other members of the Attic Ensemble hovered, anxiously watching in the doorway, behind the Festival Director.

"I have a headache, and will not perform if you don't put us all into the hotel where we were originally booked by Musica Viva."

I lay back exhausted, as he went off with a worried look. I winked at the others. Somehow the rooms were found for us all. We were able to move in, after the morning's rehearsal in the attractive new hall in Mildura. I had a quiet few hours to rest before the concert, which was just as well in the light of what followed.

The concert was enjoyable, we had supper and went to bed to sleep for a short time, before getting up very early to catch a little Fokker Friendship to fly to Melbourne. Seated in the small plane next to an unaccompanied and nervous child, I waited for the interminable and very bouncy flight to end. As we approached the old Essendon airport, the flight attendant announced that we were unable to land, owing to the terrifying thunderstorm which was buffeting us, even as she spoke! She announced that we would fly back to Adelaide, where we landed, refuelled and set off again for Melbourne. As we approached the runway once more, we were told that we might have to go over Bass Strait to Launceston. The pilot was as anxious as we were by now. We had been flying back and forth all day and were supposed to be going to Canberra, and it was already beginning to get dark. He swooped down low, the cloud lifted for a moment and miraculously in we came onto the tarmac. What a cheer went up! The grandparents of the unaccompanied child received her with great relief.

We were told we had to stay in Melbourne for the night. By the time we eventually got into the Southern Cross Hotel it was after 11pm and the next morning was going to be a rush. I liked to rehearse in the morning in the venue, in order to see the hall and feel the acoustic, so that any problems could be solved early and I could have a quiet afternoon. I was not going to be able to do this now. We were to catch an early flight to Canberra. There were not very many. So I think we were back at Essendon before 7am and we roared off again to be told as we came towards Canberra that we were not able to land there, and were going on to Sydney airport.

As Graeme and Deb sat down to breakfast in Chatswood, the phone rang.

"It's Loss here," I said.

"How nice to hear your voice so early in the morning. Where are you?" G asked.

"I'm in Sydney!" I cried.

"What on earth are you doing here?" I just had time to tell him before we re-embarked for the flight to Canberra. I think we took twenty-three hours to fly from Mildura to Canberra! It was a great night but we were very glad to be home in Sydney the next day.

We repeated the Musica Viva Attic Ensemble concerts in Avalon and in Bathurst, in October of that year. But when I asked Regina about Attic Ensemble concerts in the following year she said firmly, "Certainly not."

The Attic Ensemble tour ended in Springwood and I came home to prepare a piece written for the Sydney Wind Ensemble and me, by my friend Nigel Butterley. He was inspired by the texts of four Latin poems called *Carmina*. They were extremely difficult for me to learn and vocally lay in the low middle of the voice, where the winds often covered my rather soft-grained sound. But it was a pleasure to sing in the old Cell Block Theatre. The work took on another meaning, the words of antiquity enclosed within the hunting horns heard in spring, inside the warmth of the sandstone building with the rounded ends. Later I sang the songs with piano, with Nigel accompanying me, for the Beecroft Music Club which he created. Nigel revised these songs twenty-five years later and I sang them in the Art Gallery of NSW. I found them much more accessible and think that Nigel's revision had made them easier to perform.

The Cell Block Theatre was a very attractive venue for intimate music making, but it was very resonant. In November I sang there again with the SSO resident conductor Moshe Atzmon, who was so young and, it seemed to me, so gentle. I performed two chamber works with a small orchestra: the *Salve Regina* of Scarlatti and Lennox Berkeley's *Four Poems of St Teresa of Avila*.

This year was the first time I sang duets with a young

soprano named Marilyn Richardson and the baritone Ronald Maconaghie, celebrating two hundred years since the birth of Couperin. The program was presented by the University of New South Wales, with a commentary by Roger Covell and Winsome Evans playing the harpsichord.

I continued the busy life of a resident singer in my own country, feted and applauded on stage, enjoying travelling around the nation, going to New Zealand at least once a year and sometimes more often. But when I came home, it always took me a day or so to adjust to domesticity. There was always the washing, ironing and cooking to bring me back to earth. And the life which had been flowing along on an even keel in the suburbs of Sydney, was such a contrast to the hotel and concert hall, or opera theatre. It always proved a shock, because I was so totally immersed in singing and studying, that to come home now always filled me with mixed feelings. I loved and longed for G and Deb, but they had been living their own experiences without me. Time had not stood still while I was away. Events had happened which I could never share and sometimes it seemed I was being shut out of their lives. G thought I was being selfish in not realising that he found my return a bit difficult, too. He was as equally engrossed in his university life as I was in my world of music. I'm sure all married couples who spend time apart in separate careers have these difficulties in adjustment to each other's experiences.

For a symphony concert or recital I was usually only away for two or three days, but opera performances always meant a long period away, rehearsing the production and preparing the music. Three days after my Cell Block concerts with Atzmon, I went on an extensive ABC tour with one of this country's great accompanists, Joyce Hutchinson and the oboist Guy Henderson. We performed in Broken Hill, Mt Gambier, Albury, Wagga Wagga, Goulburn and Tamworth. Guy was a wonderful player. I don't know what the audience thought of these ABC country tours. Perhaps they thought the music too difficult. Generally we played to less than half-filled halls, with the committee making apologies like, "Its a shame the local Show starts tomorrow," or "The weather is so cold at this time of the year." The programs were excellent, with top artists, but the country people did not come. The recitals were hard work, requiring concentration and stamina from us, and the ABC Concert Officer who accompanied us also managed the box office, looked after the artists and the concert management on the night - a huge job. I made good friends with many of these people who worked so hard for the promotion of music and for the ABC, often for miserable salaries, given the amount of work involved. Bless them all.

This tour was to establish a long relationship with Joyce Hutchinson and I sang for many more years with her, always feeling secure and safe, wrapped in the warm and liquid singing sound she made on the piano. And over the years, I listened for Guy Henderson's individual and ravishing oboe whenever the orchestra played.

There was one devastating occasion when he failed me. Years later, I was singing in one of the countless *Messiahs,* looking forward to *He was despised.* I forgot that it was a new version. I think it might have been the Mozart, which substituted an oboe obbligato for the solo violin, introducing the theme of the great solo. To my horror, Guy played the haunting descending minor passage in the major key. I was so stricken that it took me several moments to begin to produce any sound at all. It took away both my breath and concentration to hear this changed cadence. Worse still, I don't think Guy ever knew what he had done!

When Sydney briefly experienced its three weeks of winter cold, Geoffrey Parsons arrived in Sydney on his annual pilgrimage to visit his mother and to delight the ABC audiences with his piano playing. That year, 1969, he was accompanying the Polish violinist, Wanda Wilkomirska, in an extensive tour. He asked the ABC to make a recording with me and I chose two works, one for each side of a disc, which were put out on an LP record later. This meant being precise about the timing of the items. I prepared and learnt the Debussy cycle *Proses lyriques* with Dorothy White, and also the *Six Gellert Songs* of Beethoven, set to verses by a German Pastor, Christian Furchtegott Gellert. The simple hymn-like songs begin with straightforward chordal harmonies, which gradually build in strength, and in the last song become a dazzling contrapuntal fugue. One of the songs is well known and I had often sung it as *The Creation's Hymn.* This poem describes the Creator making the sun and the moon and setting the stars in their ordained courses, and builds to a mighty climax of praise to the Almighty.

I prepared the rest of the cycle of six songs with Dorothy White and when Geoffrey arrived in Sydney I was ready to begin rehearsing, before 'putting the songs down'. We were making this recording in the Arcadia, an old cinema in Chatswood, which the ABC had turned into the home of the Sydney Symphony Orchestra. It was now used as an orchestral studio for rehearsals, broadcasts, recording and occasionally as a TV studio. The little stone churches in the centre of old Sydney and the funny Woolworths' building were not needed any more for recording. However, there were lots of problems with the revamped old building. The small foyer did not exclude the noise of passing motorbikes. The roof was corrugated iron so whenever it rained, which was not often but always torrential, the noise of the rain drowned out the music. Worst of all, the previous residents remained, not paying rent, but cooing languorously in their hiding places under the roof on warm sunny afternoons. Pigeons sometimes actually flew into the rehearsals, to be chased back into the dark areas of the upper circle by frantic orchestral managers.

Geoffrey was alternately startled, amused or annoyed by these problems. He was accustomed to play with the great artists of Europe, in the best working conditions available at the time. Recording for Decca or EMI with superb technicians made his Australian experiences seem a return to a frontier mentality. Later, as the ABC drifted into the managerial torpor of the '70s, he once told me how he would love to return permanently to live here, but could not abide the ad hoc attitude of its civil-service bureaucracy. There was never any money to properly convert or rebuild the old tin shed that the Arcadia was.

We rehearsed the *Gellert Songs* on a wet and cold Sunday, when the Arcadia was not required for SSO rehearsals. The recording technicians were in their control booth. For days the world had been watching and talking about the conquest of space by the Americans. Three men were travelling into the sky, sent out to land and to walk on the moon. We were loaned a TV set and, as we recorded the *Creation's Hymn,* we saw Neil Armstrong and Buzz Aldrin step into the cloudy TV picture of the moon's surface. We were moved beyond words as we stood for some minutes and watched man's footprints appear in the grey dust of the moon.

What would Beethoven, or especially Gellert, have thought? He who wrote: "Who holds the numberless stars in their courses, and who bids the sun his light diffuse." These men would not have been able to begin to imagine that the old silver moon could become part of man's new domain.

In the middle of the year I was asked to sing Ottavia in Monteverdi's *The Coronation of Poppea.* It is a marvellous opera and the cast was remarkable. Roger Covell, just beginning to build his self-constructed music department at the University of NSW, showed great courage in presenting this masterpiece. He chose the tenor John Main, soprano Marilyn Richardson and bass John Brosnan of the beautiful voice, as Seneca. The sets were horrid to behold, as the corruption of Rome was represented on the shallow stage by canker-covered pillars. A tenor named Richard Divall took one of the minor roles! I believe this was my first meeting with him.

One of the important events which took me away from home for three weeks late in 1969 was my first *Orpheus* for the Victorian Opera Company. I had studied this Gluck opera when I was a student in Paris and, with *Samson and Delilah,* it was one of two I had always wanted to sing. The VOC, struggling financially and hoping to improve its situation, put on several performances of this great work in the Union Theatre in Melbourne. I was living in Sydney and did not really know much

18. Graeme de Graaff with grandson Christopher Nelson.

19. Mother and daughter about 1965.

20. 'Young Opera' put on Handel's *Julius Caesar*.
This splendid costume was a good way to solve the problem
of a travesty role, and people still talk of this great production.

21. Lauris Elms as Julius Caesar with Marilyn Richardson as Cleopatra.

. A fearful Bradamante,
th John Wegner's
elisso in Handel's
cina. Photographs by
anco Gaica, courtesy
Opera Australia.

23. Lucretia is raped by
John Pringle, in 1971 …

24. … and consoled by
Alan Light. Photographs by
Branco Gaica, courtesy
of Opera Australia.

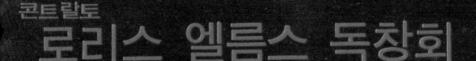

콘트랄토
로리스 엘름스 독창회

LAURIS ELMS CONTRALTO RECITAL

협연 : 시립교향악단(서울)
지휘 : 정 재 동
피아노 : 도로시 화이트

3. 19. 밤 7시　서울 - 이화여자대학 대강당
3. 21. 밤 7시　부산 - 동 주 여 상 강 당
3. 24. 밤 7시　광주 - 시 민 회 관
3. 26. 밤 7시　대구 - 효성여자대학 강 당

東亞日報・東亞放送
후원 : 주 한 호 주 대 사 관

25. This poster for the Korean tour for Foreign Affairs, in 1974, shows me wearing one
of the beautiful costumes from *The Rape of Lucretia*, designed by Desmond Digby.

26. *Un ballo in maschera,* 1971: Elizabeth Fretwell, Amelia; Lauris Elms, Ulrica; Donald Smith, Gustavus. Photograph courtesy of Opera Australia.

27. In my studio at home in 197 dressed in the gown I wore for t opening of the Sydney Ope House, on October 20th.

28. The opening concert in the Sydney Opera House was a performance of Beethoven's 9th Symphony. L toR: Charles Buttrose, John Hopkins, Her Majesty Queen Elizabeth, Willem van Otterloo, Nance Grant, Lauris Elms, Ronald Dowd and Raymond Myers.

29. The Queen Mother talks to Janice Chapman and Lauris at the Captain Cook Celebration Concert, in the Royal Festival Hall performance of Verdi's *Requiem,* conducted by Sir Charles Mackerras.

30. George Goller with Lauris Elms.

31. George Pikler's arrangements of Folk Songs were wonderful.

32. Lauris, Robert and George.

33. Recording in the new Willoughby Town Hall clockwise from left: Robert Pikler, John Har Brecon Carter, George Pikler, Lauris Elms and Ge Goller.

about the problems this small Opera Company was having at the time.

Margaret Haggart, who was on the Board, told me about this many years later. The Victorian Opera Company had grown out of a group who first sang musicals and Gilbert and Sullivan. As there was no opera company in Melbourne at the time, they decided to fill this gap, under the leadership of Kenneth and Val Taylor. With Maggie (Margaret Haggart) singing the leading soprano roles, they did some very ambitious works, like *La traviata* and *Nabucco*. Then they found out that no 'books' had been kept by the management and there was no record of how much money was owed. They wrote to every creditor and found the funds had been so badly administered that they owed $1200, a huge sum to them at the time. Without a hope of repaying the debt, they asked their creditors to wait, then went off to the Australia Council with an ambitious proposal. They asked Jean Battersby if the Council would pay my fee to sing in an opera of my choice. By doing this, they hoped that my 'name' would attract an audience. They then approached me and I asked to sing *Orpheus*.

I had always thought that this story had a special meaning in the subconscious of the myths of man and the music had a wonderful, spacious beauty.

The opera would be sung in English. I was nervous about the prospect of singing with a freelance orchestra and about the lack of professional costumes and sets, and yet my memory of the production of Brian Crossley and of the playing of the small orchestra and chorus, is that it was very good. My Euridice was Margot Cory and Amour was Margaret Haggart. The conductor was to be Peter Rourke, who unfortunately caused a great deal of trouble. He was unwell and only came to one or two rehearsals, which were taken by Ken Taylor and producer Brian Crossley. John Cargher was also involved and was often to be seen darkly hovering in the background. On the day before the opening, when temperaments are always sensitive and everyone's nerves are frayed, Peter Rourke decided to pull out.

Disaster! In the event, Ken Taylor stepped in, and thanks to him the nucleus of this company did survive, repay their debt and eventually become the Victorian State Opera. The critic Felix Werder said, "It is difficult for me to offer an objective review of one of my great loves, for Gluck at any price is worth having, and just to hear Lauris Elms as Orpheus is worth any price." I wonder what the admission price was?

After this, the end of the year brought a 21st anniversary concert in Christchurch, with Robert Field-Dodgson and Royal Christchurch Musical Society performing the Dvořák *Requiem*. I felt honoured to be invited to fly across the Tasman once more for this special occasion.

As my career developed, I found that the period around

Christmas became a kind of bookmark in my life. There were fewer engagements after the hectic period of around-Australia *Messiahs* leading up to December 25th. There were rarely many concerts in early January and these few weeks marked a rest period when we three could be quietly together. It was often a period of reflection, of planning my programs for the future. But this year it was time to begin work on repertoire for 1970. The prospects looked less than good. I was in the state of mind that arrives often in a freelance artist's life. The lack of firm engagements meant that there was little incentive to prepare a big work. At least I always had my International House recital to work up. The prospect of choosing new songs and working with Dorothy White on them was always ahead, and this was a joy.

While I was on tour in Adelaide in 1969 singing *Il trovatore,* the administrator of the Elizabethan Opera, Stephen Hall, had bemoaned the fact that there were so few good mezzo-sopranos living in Australia.

"Rosina Raisbeck is working as a saleswoman at Cornelius Furs to support herself. She is a wonderful singer and should be singing full-time for you," I said. Rosina had come back from Europe and after her excellent Marina in *Boris Godunov* had, surprisingly, not been asked to sing again for the company. The following year she was invited to come back and made her great contribution to opera in this country from that time on. This reinforced my opinion that 'out of sight' often meant 'out of mind' in this profession.

About this time I was asked to become a member of the Elizabethan Opera Company. I loved singing opera, but was aware that I might be required to sing the many minor roles that are written for mezzos. "Boys or bitches," someone once said of the mezzo repertoire, neglecting to mention the dozens of small parts for raddled old servant-ladies. But most of all, I would probably be unable to accept engagements for my beloved ABC concerts, because I would be contracted to the opera. To forgo the joy of singing Mahler, or the choral repertoire with a great symphony orchestra, was unthinkable. After years 'out' of singing opera, I had now a passion for all kinds of song, because I had learnt so much music of great beauty which I would have never experienced if I had stayed exclusively an opera singer, as in my first three years at Covent Garden.

By free-lancing, I also thought I was saving the company a salary payment. Coming in as a guest meant that I was only paid for the works I wanted to sing, leaving me free to pick and choose the number and dates of my performances. During Opera Company tours, especially in Adelaide, I would spend evenings with the young Moffatt Oxenbould and Rosemary Gordon talking about the future of opera and singing and music in Australia, and our eyes would light up as our ideas and ideals were tossed backwards and forwards. I wanted to promote and encourage the wonderful young singers this country produced, so they would have the opportunity of permanent employment. I thought that we older, more experienced singers might be called upon from time to time to give professional advice. In fact, the company being as small as it was then, meant that we did have a direct and personal contact with management and were often consulted in an informal way. I wanted to leave behind forever the old days, when singing was regarded as an amateur activity to be done in one's spare time. But the reverse side of free-lancing was the lack of regular work.

At the beginning of 1970, things looked dismal. One morning I was standing at the sink washing up, feeling blue, when the phone rang.

A voice at the other end of the phone said, "Would you be free to fly to London to sing the Verdi *Requiem* with Charles Mackerras on Monday 13th April?"

"I'd love to," I laughed. "Is it Bob (Allman) or John (Shaw) pulling my leg?"

"No, really," said the voice, "It's Ron Dowd, ringing from London. We want you to sing in this concert to celebrate the landing of Captain Cook at Botany Bay in 1770."

I shouted a shaky "YES", and so another dream of my life was fulfilled - to sing Verdi's *Requiem* in the Festival Hall.

It was the beloved and irrascible Ronald Dowd who set up the beginnings of a lifelong friendship with Charles Mackerras and his wife Judy, which has survived the years. I had never heard Mackerras conduct, except on records, and it was this concert which opened the work of this remarkable man to me. He is a wonderful singer's conductor because he breathes with the singer.

I flew to London a week before the concert, was met by someone from Australia House and booked into a hotel in Bayswater. As soon as I had recovered from the flight, I went to see my friends Vivian and Gordon Signey and they said "Come and stay." (It was on the top floor of their Cannonbury house that G and I had lived when we were first married). So I moved into their house for a few days. 'Our' old flat had been turned into a flat for their two boys and I was given the room on the floor below. On my first night there, I had to go to the bathroom in the night and, remembering where I was, I decided not to turn the light on as I might wake the sleeping Signeys. The toilet was on the narrow landing, in the bend at the end of the flight of stairs. As I came out of the door, closing it silently behind me, I forgot the one inch step up into the little room and fell, twisting my ankle. I lay there for a moment, knowing from previous experience that it was going to be a bad sprain. O hell! I limped back to bed and lay in aspro-less agony until daylight, when I told Vivian what had happened. Gordon bandaged the ankle up tightly. I had a week to recover.

I discovered with dismay that there would be no rehearsal until the day of the concert. Ronald Dowd was singing in far distant Dublin. The soprano was not my old friend Margreta Elkins as advertised (she had lost her voice) but Janice Chapman, who was scheduled to sing in Rossini's *The Barber of Seville* at Sadler's Wells that night, but was released by 'The Wells' from that performance. Geoffrey Chard would be coming from Wales, where he was singing, on the day of the concert.

I was most unhappy at the thought of singing the Verdi *Requiem* through twice, with choir, orchestra and conductor meeting for the first time, on the afternoon of the concert, with the performance following after a two-hour break. This would be just long enough to have the voice relax after being 'warmed up' and yet not long enough to be rested and refreshed. However, there was nothing to be done except to grin and bear it.

I had never sung in the Festival Hall and went off to rehearse in the afternoon taking my evening dress with me. After the exciting rehearsal, which I sang in full voice, it seemed a long wait until 8pm for the concert to begin. From time to time, people came in from the Australia House's Australian Musical Association committee to say that the hall was filling up and what a great night it was going to be. The Queen Mother arrived. The concert began.

Waiting in the dressing room, time seemed to stand still.

One of the critics said, "I must confess my heart dropped when I saw the huge audience that had turned up for the occasion, for most of them were obviously there principally to gaze at the Queen Mother. The latter's arrival was heralded by a new fanfare, incorporating a choral version of *The National Anthem,* by Australian-born Don Banks."

The critic Meirion Bowen in London commented that it was a pity that Banks, "... as an Australian, had not been asked to contribute a full-scale work." (This may be so. But I would then probably not have been invited to sing!)

At the end of the concert, the packed hall rang with applause and afterwards the excitement grew and simmered on and on. Friends from the past crowded into my dressing room and at midnight I was standing out in the street, talking to Faye and John Bailey. It was icy-cold. My throat was warm and my voice well 'warmed up', after singing two Verdi *Requiems* in the one day. The Baileys and I were so excited to see each other again and on a 'high' after the great concert. I forgot one of the most important lessons for a singer and stood talking in the cold for about half an hour. The next day I was voiceless.

Later in the week all the soloists were invited to a dinner at the home of Frank Boyle, the Executive Officer of Australia House, who had arranged the concert. I had never met Geoffrey Chard before the concert, so I looked forward to getting to know him and his wife and to spending time with my other colleagues, especially Ronald Dowd and his wife Elsie.

The Boyles had a stylish terrace house and, after removing our coats, we went into the drawing room for drinks. My laryngitis was at the stage when I could only whisper, but by nodding and smiling I hoped to survive the evening. We soon went in to dinner and the first course was warm grapefruit laced with liqueur. I took one sip of the delicious liquid and immediately was overcome by a coughing fit. As tears streamed from my eyes, I hurriedly left the table and abandoned the first course. I was able to return and finish the meal at last, after coughing in the bathroom for what seemed an eternity. The evening was one of those embarrassing experiences that stay indelibly in one's memory.

15. Ordeal by Fire

"The grand old lady burns," screamed the headlines in *The Daily Mirror* on Friday 31st of July 1970. "Her Majesty's Theatre gutted."

"One by one, the lights are going out all over Sydney," said the journalist, Frank Harris. "Where do we go from here now, before the Opera House opens in its promised glory ..."

Sydney was mourning the loss of many of its live theatres at the time, and on that night, after a magnificent performance of Verdi's *Otello* by the Australian Opera, the blaze of fire illuminated the final night of the theatre. I remember the shock we all felt as the news filtered round to the singers who had been in the theatre on that night, or were due to sing there subsequently. The article added that some of the "world's great artists trod the boards and condemned and praised the old theatre," and included comments from Dame Margot Fonteyn, Dame Joan Sutherland and Hayes Gordon.

Most of the old theatres we played in at that time were terrible old dumps, often filthy, but being built of wood they almost always had a better acoustic than the later concrete buildings. The romance of their history made them nostalgic shrines for the older generation. But I longed for a dressing room where you could put on your make-up and walk about with bare feet while changing costumes, without imagining the possibility of catching some horrible contagious disease from the dirty old carpets and broken washbasins!

I felt sorry for J C Williamson and my friend Don McPhee and the Opera Company who coped with this disaster, but I could not regret the old theatre. A year later, I did deeply regret the ugly new theatre which Williamsons built in its place. In dark brick, cheerless and indestructible, it glowered gloomily down the years, from my memory of what was once a place of dulled gilt and worn red plush where the patrons had enjoyed "a night of good entertainment."

In the year 2000 it was demolished and replaced by a block of units.

Life for me went on, with a television opera. Conducted by Walter Stiasny, the production of Weinberger's *Schwanda the bagpiper* was a pleasure to watch, and working with soprano Rosalind Keene was a delight. But when I came to sing my role of the Ice Queen, I found the tessitura uncomfortably high. Like most people, I often blamed other people or external things, for my own dissatisfaction with my performance. My memory of singing in *Schwanda* is clouded by these difficulties so that I cannot remember anything good about my own performance. I was glad when it ended.

Surprisingly the Hurlstone Choral Society was fifty years old! When I first came to sing in Sydney many of the members seemed to me to have been there since the formation of the choir or even, perhaps, the colony! But in this year, celebrating the bicentenary of Captain Cook's landing, the enthusiastic young tenor-turned-conductor, Peter Seymour, swept away the cobwebs from the choir, gave it a new name and directed a performance of Haydn's *Nelson Mass* with the young soprano, Joan Carden, singing ravishingly for the first time in Sydney. This historic concert was the first time I sang with Joan Carden. The Sydney Philharmonia has now become an institution, with a wonderful reputation for fine choral singing and the old Hurlstone Choral Society is only a memory.

That year saw the 18th International Dairy Congress taking place in Sydney. ABC Director of Music, John Hopkins, had booked me for their concert as the Sydney Symphony Orchestra's soloist two years earlier, on the understanding that we would be performing in the new Opera House. But Bennelong Point was still covered with scaffolding and it was at the Sydney Town Hall that I sang my first *Sea Pictures* by Elgar, with János Ferencsik conducting and my friend Donald Hazelwood leading the SSO. These songs were to become part of my favourite repertoire. I later recorded them in the Town Hall with John Hopkins conducting for the ABC. It was released by RCA on an LP record.

This year, celebrating the history of Australia's discovery, saw Moshe Atzmon conducting Beethoven's *Missa Solemnis* for the bicentenary of the composer's birth. This event had also been planned for the new Opera House Concert Hall, but had to be performed in the old Town Hall. The critic Roger Covell wrote in *The Sydney Morning Herald,* "Almost everything that is reflective and lyrical in Beethoven's *Mass in D* was eloquently convincing in the performance of this tremendous work."

The late David Ahern reminded us once more that this work was then very rarely performed in Australia. He said, "Once every second groundhog's day, the cobwebs are dusted from the parts to Beethoven's *Missa Solemnis* ... Written towards the end of the latter part of his life, the work's spirituality (and hence Beethoven's) deeply impressed me."

Why was this work so rarely performed then, I wonder? Perhaps its deeply serious quality was not appreciated, but I suspect its difficult choral writing made it a daunting task to conductors without the great choir it demanded. Now, at last, under Peter Seymour, the Philharmonia was ready to accept the challenge, and to sing this great work with the power and fervour it demanded. With soloists Mary O'Brien, Raymond MacDonald and William Coombes, we gave five performances.

The Victorian Opera Company called me to ask if I would do another opera, this time in the title role in Britten's *The Rape of Lucretia*. The conductor was the eminent Melbourne musician, Keith Humble, and the producer was once more Brian Crossley. The four performances were staged in St Martin's Theatre. They were well produced in and for the intimate venue, with an excellent conductor and orchestra and a cast headed by Margaret Haggart and Ian Stapleton as the two Choruses, John Rickard as Tarquinius, Trevor Reed as Collatinus, Brian Harris as Junius and Junwyn Jones and Anna Nagle as the other two women in the cast. I enjoyed singing in this *Lucretia* more than any other I subsequently did, even though it was a work I found difficult to like. The aria where Lucretia goes mad, with its descending laugh, was hard to make convincing. The piece is very 'wordy' and the vocal writing lacked the legato 'line' I found rewarding. The range lay in an awkward part of my voice and I thought Britten, with his usually unerring sense of the dramatic, somehow missed the centre of the story here. Yet I think this simple production in Melbourne had the freshness of something new and living which was lacking in the subsequent productions in which I took part.

In November 1970, Handel's great opera *Julius Caesar* was given three performances in the Science Theatre of the University of NSW. 'Young Opera' was founded by the very young Richard Divall and the future QC and judge, Brian Donovan, as Director. Richard prepared the music and worked with the singers on the opera, together with Winsome Evans. I think Richard was working at the ABC at the time and he rang me one day to ask if I would sing the contralto role of Cornelia. I did not know the opera, but knew Caesar could be sung as a travesty role. At that time it was often sung by a baritone or even a tenor. The time of the counter tenor had not yet arrived.

"Please let me sing Caesar?" I asked.

And so I did, opposite Marilyn Richardson as Cleopatra. It was here that our long friendship began and she remains one of my most beloved colleagues.

The small orchestra, made up of some of the best players in Sydney, was led by Carl Pini with Winsome Evans playing continuo. There were some wonderful moments on those four nights, and one was the duet with the horn played by Robert Johnson, surely one of the most inspired moments in music theatre, when Caesar confides to the audience his wish to entrap his enemy. The beautiful duet with violin was another moment to treasure, but my duets with Marilyn had all the fun and excitement I felt when I sang with Sutherland, as we tried to sing each other off the stage, inventing our own cadenzas as we went along. In fact, because I was less in awe and more at ease with Marilyn, I could enjoy this opera to the full. People remember the inspired designs of Colin Williams who put me into a baroque wig and costume, setting the opera in Handel's time rather than in ancient Egypt. Marilyn, surely the most beautiful Australian singer of her generation, was also dressed magnificently. Twenty-five years later, people still remember those performances.

At the end of the year the New Sydney Woodwind Quintet (Neville Amadio, Guy Henderson, Donald Westlake, John Cran and Clarence Mellor) gave a remarkable concert for Musica Viva at the new Macquarie University. These players are all legends in their own lifetime in Sydney and the concert ended with a first performance of a song-cycle written by Ian Cugley for the group, and for Marilyn Richardson and myself, called *The Six Days of Creation*, to the poem of James Macauley.

As Australians, we were beginning to think that we were maturing musically. In *The Bulletin* at the end of that year Kenneth Robbins notes that, "when the 'celebrity' season is over, we are no longer left with a musical desert, and we are often in for some of the most delightful concerts of the year by resident performers."

How wonderful it was to read this. It was true. The concert and music scene was more adventurous and experimental in the '70s than it is now, I think. There was a pioneering spirit in the city's music making which is lacking today. People wanting to make music did not expect a government grant and often put on concerts funded from their own resources. Indeed, sometimes one was not paid for work done, even after the exchange of contracts. The other side of the coin was the lack of certainty about the finances of the entrepreneur.

Summers for us meant a short trip to Victoria to spend the Christmas week with both our mothers and fathers in Melbourne, then home to the glory of sailing in the long summer days, as often as we could. As a college principal, G had to handle the admissions and interview all the Australian applicants for places at International House before the academic year began, making it impossible to go away on holiday, but we used the long summer evenings, after he came home from work, to get out on the water and breathe the soupy breath of summer.

G was always tired at this time. A shadow began to appear in our relationship as he came home looking strained at the end of each day. It now seemed better not to ask, as he now always said brightly, "I'm all right," when I asked if was he feeling tired, or perhaps, ill? He began to be short-tempered and irritable, he who was always so kind and generous. Then finally he confessed that he was having sudden unexplained flashes of searing pain in his face and head. Days or weeks would pass without an incident and then another slash of the pain would strike him and leave him sweating and momentarily helpless. These episodes were so short and far apart that initially he had thought they were unimportant, but now he had to seek medical advice.

His GP sent him to see several specialists and he was finally diagnosed as having trigeminal neuralgia (tic doloureux), a disorder of the large nerve travelling around the side of the head and down the face.

At first he was treated with a drug (Tegratol) which had horrible side effects, making him vague, sleepy and nauseous. Life for the three of us entered a grey zone. Our days were coloured by anxiety. G was terrified of what was happening to him and of what the outcome would be. Deb and I were also afraid for him and silently watched as he went from Tegratol to one drug after another. Because G's disability was not visible, it was hard to explain to outsiders that he was not well. Often now he, who had come to every concert I did in Sydney, chose to stay home and try to sleep the pain away. Pale of face, he struggled to maintain the life of International House as it had been and to maintain his personality as if life was normal.

At last he went to the neurosurgeon, John Grant, who advised a small operation to sever the nerve in the eyelid fold, above the eye. This would render the cut almost invisible, so G happily agreed. Miraculously the pain was gone and for a time he got relief, but then the trigeminal nerve would regenerate and the stabbing pain would begin again. The faintest touch of a breeze, or a feather stoke on the side of his face would render him almost unconscious. It seemed that when G was stressed by a problem at International House, the pain was more frequent and worse. So John Grant repeated the procedure, this time with the addition of the drug Tegratol which was so unpleasant. After a few months, again the pain would return.

In all, over the next two or three years G had this operation done about five times, with various periods of relief, but with the anticipation of the recurrence always present, he dreaded the pain so much that he was always tense and anxious, waiting for it to begin again. It was a terrible time, lasting well over four years which, looking back now, seems to be clouded in a dismal despair.

Often I had been contracted to sing one or two years earlier and so I was torn between a commitment to go on with my career, while knowing Graeme needed me so much at this time. Deb was now a great strength to him, and they became very close to each other. My own memories of this period are blurred by the guilt of leaving my husband for a day or so, to discover him recovering from yet another bout of terrible pain or even from another spell in hospital.

Mrs Crawford was a great help. She came and 'lived in'

whenever I was away singing and was great friends with Deb by this time. Her interest was breeding Pekinese dogs. Deb became enamoured of the pretty things and once Peggy Crawford actually brought her bitch to stay with us, while it gave birth to several pups all through a long and wakeful night. Deb was entranced. (I was glad to be absent and G was sorry he was at home). Eventually she gave one of these lovely little dogs to Deb, and we were 'into' Pekinese for quite a few years!

One terrible morning G collapsed. I heard a crash and found him slumped in the bathroom, unconscious. I rang Harold and Molly Maze, who lived nearby, to come and help me lift him and take him to hospital. Dr Grant said he could perform a dangerous operation, severing the nerves in the cortex behind the brain. This would render one side of G's face permanently insensitive to touch and feeling. It also might damage the facial muscles, causing the face to drop on that side, or might even paralyse the speech muscles like a stroke. He would need to be wary of getting anything in that eye as it would be numb to all feeling.

We agonised over this, but there could be no real debate, because he was now so desperate with the pain he was beginning to contemplate suicide. He went to the Adventist Hospital and I watched him sleeping in intensive care after the operation, then came and went as he recovered in the following days. Would he be cured we silently wondered?

It was a long recovery period, but at last G came home and the three of us held our breaths, silently watching and hoping. There was no damage to his face, nor to his ability to talk and slowly we realised the operation was a success. How wonderful to know that the cure would last this time. He now had to adjust to the dead feeling spreading over half his head and face, and his tongue. He could not bear the lightest touch. The operation also destroyed his ability to recognise hot food when he ate, so he often burnt the inside of his mouth. It was sad, to watch him now grapple with another disabling sensation, but at least his pain was banished, hopefully forever. I have always wondered if the intense cold on his face that he had suffered during those two years of motor-scooter journeys from Oxford to London had contributed to this terrible condition. Gradually, after what seemed a long time, his spirit returned to its old quirky good humour. His fear of the pain faded, and he grew accustomed to the numbness of his face and tongue, and to the vertigo he experienced. We would be all right, Graeme, Deb and I.

My life as a singer, separate from the grey worry of these four or five years, was satisfyingly busy. I found relief in the music I was always learning. It seemed that I would never sing the same work twice and that each new one was more splendid than the last. One of these concerts was *Semele* with Charles Mackerras, in the Sydney Town Hall. As the music of Handel wound and cascaded through the galleried building, I felt grateful to be performing. I have never forgotten this concert.

What a contrast with that other great English composer, Elgar. *The Dream of Gerontius* was now a work I knew well and felt I could really get inside, to reveal what it meant to me. The difficulty with singing a new work was that I often came out after a performance with the knowledge that, even if I knew the notes and words well, there was a deeply-felt underlying music I had only begun to explore. Now I began to feel *The Dream* in my bones, to experience the strength of Elgar's faith and Newman's poetry as I sang. I loved this work. This was an especially poignant *Dream* in 1971.

Saturday February 13th was Election Day and, as I had a rehearsal in the Sydney Town Hall in the morning, G decided to drive me in; we would vote on the way. We all bundled out to the car in a great hurry, got in and as G reversed up the drive, there was a terrible scream from beneath the car.

Deb gasped, "Ricky!"

The beautiful white Pekinese with the soulful eyes had somehow got out from the back yard and had been sitting under the wheels of the car. We lifted the poor little shuddering form into Deb's outstretched arms and went straight to the vet, only five minutes away. As we drove, my beautiful brave little girl whispered, "He's gone. I felt him shudder. He's gone."

We carried him in to the vet, and it was true. Nothing could be done. Deb was numb with shock and so were we. G decided to drive me in to the rehearsal, then take Deb to see Mrs Crawford, who had given her this very valuable small dog, to explain what had happened. It was with extra emotion that I sang that morning. Can the small soul of a pure white Pekinese be carried over the waters by the Angel, I wondered as I sang with a lump in my throat?

When I got home from the rehearsal that morning, *my* small angel was clasping a tan-coloured ball of fluff in her arms. Mrs Crawford had a new litter of puppies and this one had a bent tail, so was not suitable for 'showing'. Deb was ecstatic, with a naughty little puppy to look after. It almost made up for Ricky's tragic death. We had this wicked little dog for many years. He was our punishment for not looking after his father properly!

During these years, every six or eight weeks, I went to see my dentist. From my teeth the fillings dropped out with monotonous regularity, always on the morning of a rehearsal and sometimes on the day of a concert. I had now had most of my lower teeth crowned, a lengthy and expensive process. I was wearing a bridge on which I had four front teeth and gradually one or two back teeth were added. Sensitive to acid, the dentine on the teeth was slowly wearing away. It became a sort of game, wondering how long before I went to the dentist again and always having to be fitted in at short notice. I was addicted to eating 'Anticol' cough lollies, which the dentist said was very bad for my teeth, as they contained Vitamin C. But, like all singers, I was terrified of getting a cold and I discovered these sweets were helpful to my voice. I dreaded the day when I had to have my teeth out, but knew it was only a matter of time.

In this year the Australian Opera's Melbourne season included *Un ballo in maschera*. I was singing my old role of Ulrica again. After the season, some of the Opera Company went to Tasmania for a few performances of *Ballo* in Hobart, playing in the oldest theatre in Australia, the Theatre Royal. We then took the last train ever to go from Hobart to Launceston. The small company and orchestra, singers Donald Smith, Elizabeth Fretwell, at her peak as a great spinto soprano, tenor Reginald Byers, Cynthia Johnson (singing Oscar), Robert Allman, Alexander Major and conductor Geoffrey Arnold travelled on the slow little train through the beautiful green island for hours. Here I met Max Oldaker, a famous singer from an earlier generation, who had returned to live in Launceston and was now the local music critic.

We gave two performances of *Ballo* in Launceston. The principals arrived in the theatre about mid-day for the Saturday matinee, to begin getting ready for the performance due to start at 1pm. I loved playing that old fraud, Ulrica, and Bernd Benthaak's production was clever and satisfying. The old theatre's tiny dressing rooms were separated from each other by walls held together by wallpaper and one heard the conversations on the other side without even trying. As I sat quietly putting on my grey-brown 'face' and drawing in the exaggerated lines for the old hag, I was suddenly riveted by the twangy sounds of Donald Smith's speaking voice, possessing as it did great carrying power.

"I will not go on this afternoon!" he shouted. "I refuse to sing!"

Elizabeth Fretwell shared the wall on the other side of my room. I raced in to her and whispered, "Come and listen to this."

Together we pressed our ears to the thin wall and heard Stephen Hall desperately trying to persuade Don to perform. It was already twelve-thirty. We heard Stephen using all his considerable powers, but to no avail. The management would have to find Reginald Byers, the alternative Gustavus, in time to get him into his costume for 'curtain up'. Someone went off and searched the town, and eventually Reg was discovered in a cafe, eating his lunch. He was rushed in to the theatre to be 'put on stage' in record time. With Caroline Lill in the prompt box, there was never a moment's nervousness about the singers being well looked after, and Reg gave a fine performance. He did some excellent work with the company in those years but did not have a very long career.

It must have been a great strain to be thrown on like that. I always needed a time of self-imposed quiet before a performance. Although I never practised any formal method of meditation on the day I was to sing, I retreated into myself, trying to find 'the still centre'. If something disturbed me, I was liable to blow up in a temper and pick a fight with the cause of the problem. My ego at such moments was exceptionally fragile and I think most performers are similarly prone to react to small events when a performance is approaching.

Don Smith began to cancel performances. His wonderful voice, one of the greatest of the century in my opinion, was to become less and less frequently heard in opera in the coming years. Was it a lack of confidence? His health was then becoming a problem and he was eventually diagnosed as suffering diverticulitis. It was a tragedy for him, for us his colleagues, and for the opera lovers of Australia, to no longer hear him sing.

1972 was another busy year for me. I received glowing reviews for the annual recital I gave in the Great Hall of Sydney University for International House. I took great care in choosing the programs and working on the songs. With Joyce Hutchinson as my pianist I was splendidly secure, knowing I could attempt any effect and she would be beside me to carry me into the music's inner meaning. Both reviews in the Sydney papers lamented the small audience, saying how well we presented the wonderful cycle of Berlioz' *Les nuits d'été,* and Debussy's *Proses lyriques.* The interior of the Great Hall, while being beautiful to look at, is a disaster for a singer with a large voice as it is very 'boomy'. You have to wait for the sound to 'come to rest' after it rotates a few times across the vaulted spaces. I was learning at last that I could get 'mileage' out of the same music and I now used this program a few times, instead of trying to learn something new for my next recital. This was a very well designed program, with some Mozart songs to begin and the great concert aria *Ch'io mi scordi di te,* with its showy piano obbligato, to end the first half, after the Berlioz. I got great pleasure from the shape of the music as it rolled out through the evening. I often felt like this as I sang my songs; here was a journey on a magic carpet that the audience and I were undertaking together.

In August Nigel Butterley asked me to give my first master class at the Beecroft District Music Club. For the first time I experienced the pleasure, and sometimes the pain, of trying to explain the essence of the performer's art to young performers. What makes one singer more enjoyable to listen to than another? Certainly a beautiful voice, well produced and polished, is the most important thing. But style and sensitivity to the words and to the composer's intention are also important. It was a revelation to me how differently voices can respond to the same advice.

Edward Downes came out to give three 'concert' performances of *Il trovatore* in the Elizabethan Theatre in Newtown. The critic Roger Covell took issue with the opera not being staged or in costume, saying that the company should have saved Downes' debut for the following year, when he would take up his position as the new Resident Conductor of the Opera Company when it opened in the almost completed Opera House.

We leading singers were now asked to perform trial concerts in the concrete shell of the Opera House, as the interior began to take shape. I remember standing on the area which would later become the stage of the concert hall, with daylight filtering in through the edges of the shell-shapes, singing to hard-hat-helmeted workmen who were sitting on the grey risers of the concrete steps. After the controversy and 'politicking', it was almost miraculous to know that, very soon now, the opening would take place.

There had been so many false dates set that when John Hopkins rang me one day to ask me to sing at the opening ceremony before the Queen, on October 20th 1973, I wailed, "But that's my birthday. I certainly don't want to sing Beethoven 9 on my birthday!"

I think I have expressed my thoughts on this work! The other three soloists all have difficult and demanding music to sing, especially the bass, who opens the vocal music in an echo of the great cello cadenza. But the poor old mezzo might as well stay at home, as far as I could see, and I had decided I had sung it enough. But John, good friend that he was, boomed down the phone in his North Country accent, "Now Lauris, don't you be a silly girl! This is a great occasion, perhaps the most important of your whole career. You must sing on this day. Van Otterloo will conduct and the world will be there to see the building and to see the beginning of a new era in Australian music."

So I agreed to perform 'the 9th' on that day and wrote it in my diary for 1973. I shall always be grateful to John. He gave me the best birthday present of my whole life.

'Marietta' in her column in early October said that I was getting star treatment. I was engaged to open the Adelaide Festival Theatre in June of '73 and to sing in the new Christchurch Hall in November of that year. What a year of celebration of music and of new concert halls in abundance at last. (But oh dear, all those Beethoven 9ths! What a bore for me!)

But there were still a few things to do in 1972. The Beecroft Music Club and Nigel Butterley had commissioned Larry Sitsky to write me a song cycle. Larry chose five magnificent poems of Walt Whitman, which he set to very thickly textured piano writing. Being a magnificent pianist himself, I suppose

Larry saw no problems in making the piano part complex. My friend Gwen Halstead came up from Melbourne to play this recital with me. She had the ability to help coach me through the labyrinth of Larry's music, while playing her own part with assurance.

Roger Covell said at the time that the songs were of an "angular astringency, sometimes declamatory, sometimes yearning for a lyricism just beyond its reach." I found myself struggling to make my way through the thickness of Larry's writing, in the very low part of my voice, so rarely used by composers, but which I relished as my home territory. In these songs I often thought I could not be heard at all. We were to record the songs in the ABC Studios in Melbourne, with Larry sitting in the control-booth.

In a day of searing heat. I had gone out to North Balwyn to rehearse the songs at Gwen's house. We had a sandwich, feeling ill with nerves, and set off to drive back to the ABC recording studios at Waverley. At noon we drove down the long hill along a deserted tramline, to see, gradually appearing in the shimmering heat, a tall angular old woman walking rigidly along the footpath. As we approached, she seemed to slowly slide stiffly sideways over the low brick front fence of a suburban house, ending upside-down in the flowers over the little wall. It was one of the most amazing and frightening things I have ever seen!

A chemist's shop was almost opposite. I ran in, and breathlessly explained the frightening sight we had witnessed. Would they please call an ambulance immediately? They assured me they would, and we sped on. I'm sure Larry has no idea how nervous we were that day. To have the composer listening to us perform these difficult songs made us aware of how much work we still needed to do on them, and we both went off to be sick after the nervous strain of this recording. Some years later, Larry arranged these songs for voice and orchestra, and when they were recorded they were much easier for me to sing, as the sustained sound of the strings suited the songs and my temperament better.

Chatswood has changed a great deal since 1965 when we first arrived to live in Sydney. Of all the varied areas of Sydney, I have always thought that the North Shore most resembled Melbourne. This was one of the things we liked about living there when we found we could not afford a harbour view. It was like Caulfield or East Malvern and we felt at home. Near Chatswood station were single-fronted two-storeyed little shops, except for the large new emporium of Grace Brothers, trying hard to look like a shopping complex. Where the Willoughby Town Hall now stands was a row of what looked like private houses that had become shops, where I once bought dresses or visited the dentist and optician. These buildings were torn down and a fence was erected around a large hole in the ground, in the time honoured Sydney tradition. At last a bulldozer arrived and began the building of the Town Hall and Council Chambers. The character of the rather humble shopping centre changed and Chatswood began to grow. The developers were here at last and the sleepy suburb became a busy metropolis. The Willoughby Town Hall was at last completed and opened by Roger Woodward in 1972.

About this time my father suggested I make a recording. Like all of our generation, he loved the voice of Kathleen Ferrier and said he would pay for me to make a disc of folk songs such as hers. Having admired the wonderful settings of Kodaly's *Folk Songs* that George Pikler had made for Musica Viva, I went to his house and sat with him for hours, working through collections of songs from many countries. At last we had fourteen songs and then we carefully chose appropriate keys for them. I suggested he write the arrangements for a string quartet. I was dismayed when he expanded the number of instrumentalists to nine! That meant his brother Robert would have to conduct the songs, as we now had too many players to perform like chamber musicians, but I believed that the added colour would suit the songs very well. The new Willoughby Town Hall - only completed a few weeks before - would be an ideal place to record the disc, and Robert Pikler assembled the most splendid group of players. John Harding and Brecon Carter (violins), Nathan Waks (cello), Linda Vogt (flute), Claire Fox (oboe), Winifred Durie (viola), Beryl Potter (piano), George Golla (guitar) and George Pikler himself on clarinet made a wonderful sound as we played the traditional folk songs in their new arrangements. Ross Sheard was the recording engineer, and I was thrilled with the result.

The ABC broadcast the tape and the World Record Club took it up. It was issued in February 1975. The Melbourne critic, Kenneth Hince of *The Age,* headed his review of the LP "Elms with a real yorker." Not being a cricketing expert, I wasn't sure if that was praise or pan, until I read on to find that Kenneth Hince thought that I would have been signed up by a major recording company if I had lived in Europe or America. He loved it. But a pitifully small number of copies sold.

My father was disappointed with the arrangements, which made the Negro Spirituals sound like soulful Slavic laments. His ears were outraged in particular by the dissonances of *Nobody Knows de Trouble I've Seen*. However, the dear man paid all the artists a small fee for their time and work, as always indulging me in spite of himself.

The Willoughby Town Hall has a special place in my heart because of the memory of those days spent with George and Robert Pikler, and the plangent sounds of cello and guitar, string quartet and piano. Looking at the building now, it seems dated architecturally and too lively acoustically, but the Major Concert Hall, as it was called at that time, was much needed then and is still in constant use by the North Shore community.

December 1972 saw the first concert performance in the Opera House Concert Hall. Roger Covell, reviewing the year's music, said, "The Sydney Opera House took all the public honours with a test concert, given by the SSO under Sir Bernard Heinze's direction, that raised very high hopes for the way in which orchestral music will be experienced in the main hall.

"Such was the sense of occasion generated by this Sunday afternoon performance, in fact, that everyone who attended it will remain convinced that he was present at the real opening of the Concert Hall, whatever official functions may be registered in the calendar in future."

I was not there on that day, but the excitement amongst musicians and music lovers was now at fever pitch. All Sydney waited for the day when music in this city would have a fitting home. Around the world, the press and musicians were also interested in what the building held beneath the arching white sails which advanced into the blue water from the end of Bennelong point.

16. The Opera House Opens

The dreamy summer slipped away into the new year and another 'bookmark' was placed in the pages of my life. I knew this would be a momentous year for Sydney, with the opening of the Opera House, and for me personally, with a tremendously busy year of singing. But this year would have resonances for me which I did not anticipate.

In February I sang Beatrice in Berlioz' *Beatrice and Benedick* in the Sydney Town Hall. In this first Australian performance, the SSO under John Hopkins played like angels and Ronald Dowd sang like one. My passion for the music of Berlioz was rewarded with glowing reviews from *The Sydney Morning Herald*, except for Roger Covell's regret that the acoustics of the old Town Hall swallowed up a good deal of the "needlepoint detail of the orchestral writing." I had been nervous about the high tessitura of the role, but Ron Dowd persuaded me that I could do it

Deb went this year to PLC Pymble. We decided that, instead of the hassle of trying to find a nanny or housekeeper when I was away, we would see if Janette Buckham, the principal, would allow Deb to be a weekly boarder when I was on tour. Miss Buckham as a young woman had taught me at PLC Melbourne. She agreed to our request and we gratefully thought our domestic worries in this matter were over.

Early in March, as the first soloist under a cultural exchange program, I went to Korea for the Department of Foreign Affairs to give master classes and recitals in Seoul, Pusan and Degu. It was difficult to decide what to sing and Foreign Affairs could not give me any guidelines, except to say that Australian music should be performed where possible. I decided to do the kind of works I would sing at home, since music students should be given the opportunity to hear good music in recital. Dorothy White would go with me, and having tried my recital program out at International House, I set out with a rather esoteric solo recital including *The Six Poems of Judith Wright* by Margaret Sutherland, which have great beauty although they are difficult to sing, never sitting easily in the voice and having a really unforgiving vocal line, like most of the Australian vocal music then being written. It seems strange that a nation that has produced so many great singers should have so few great songwriters. I think all composers should have a year's singing lessons before they attempt writing songs!

Dorothy and I set off eagerly on this journey. She was an intrepid traveller, having camped out in much of outback Australia and travelled the world before the Second World War, when she was a young woman. She seemed brusque and severe when we first met, but now after several years we were close friends and she would be a wonderful companion on this adventure. I knew that I was going into a new world and, at the end of the Korean War, this ancient society was changing incredibly fast. There were always one or two Korean students at International House at this time, and they were intelligent post-graduates, often married and very ambitious.

When we arrived in Seoul after an overnight stop in Tokyo, I felt I had stepped back hundreds of years. Seoul is encircled by seven high mountains in a most spectacular setting. The Cultural Attaché was an old friend, Adrian Buzo, who had been a student in the first years of International House. He was a mine of information about the customs and the changing world of Korea. Leaning from my hotel window in the early morning on that first day, I could see a twisting dirt road crowded with grey-clad people. Riding bicycles and ringing their bells, they wove between hundreds of pedestrians. Low-pitched, red-tiled and thatched roofs, topping stone walls, lined the steep, narrow streets and the strangest clicking sound accompanied by a strangled cry intrigued me with its rhythmic percussion. When I asked Adrian what it was, he told me it was the 'scissors man' touting for business, sharpening knives and scissors. Other vendors cried their wares. I thought that this must have been what the noisy London of Henry Fielding and Hogarth was like.

There were then fifteen universities in Seoul alone and Dorothy and I took our recitals to three of them. We were treated as distinguished visitors and were amazed at the standard of the music. I took master classes, hearing some outstanding singers, in particular several fine tenors. Many of the singing teachers had studied in Germany or France, and to have the experience of hearing young people from another culture singing Bach, Brahms and Bartók so well was a humbling experience for this young woman, who thought, in her ignorance at that time, that the West was where musical excellence began.

In Seoul I sang in an orchestral concert with the Seoul City Symphony Orchestra. I had sent off a list of works so that the Embassy in Seoul could obtain the necessary orchestral parts. As a contralto, I sang Berlioz' *Les nuits d'été* in the low setting. The ABC had apparently sent the parts, but in the original keys. I had not stipulated the key for the work! As the orchestra began to play on the first rehearsal and I began to sing, I realised that something was seriously wrong. Originally this song cycle was written for soprano, alto, tenor and bass, so some of the songs are for low voice, while some others are very high. There was no way I could get new parts sent to Seoul in time for the concert, so I muddled through, enjoying the low and beautiful *Spectre de la rose* and *Sur les lagunes,* and dreading the first song and *Au Cimitiere* in particular. This lesson taught me to always carefully check the keys and the orchestral arrangements of the works I would sing in the future.

But the enthusiasm of the audiences everywhere was exciting. Having sung a solo recital to an audience of one hundred or less, year after year for International House, it was amazing to have two thousand people standing to cheer me at the end of a night of lieder singing. To be mobbed by autograph hunters and feted after the concert like a pop singer was unbelievable! At last all the work I had put into my solo recitals over the years was rewarded. The program was Beethoven's *Six Gellert Songs,* Schumann's *Frauenliebe und Leben,* the five Debussy *Proses lyriques,* one of Sutherland's Judith Wright settings and some showy Handel and operatic arias to finish the night. The operatic arias were, as always, the most popular part of the program.

After our recital in Pusan we set off by car to drive north and east, back into the hills. We were in the charge of a former resident of Sydney International House, who had become one of the Directors of Education in that area of Korea. A plump pleasant man, he was horrified when Dorothy insisted that we must make a detour to see a Buddhist shrine near Deagu and climb up to the cave containing the statue of the Buddha.

"It's too far to travel, and we wouldn't have time to climb up," he insisted.

Dorothy was not to be put off. She hadn't come all this way just for the music! She took out her own map and showed the doubtful Mr Dangman-Yi that we had plenty of time to do this detour and still get to Deagu by evening. He finally gave up and sat silently while we drove for a couple of hours through beautiful mountainous country. At last we arrived at a monastery, where we stood high above the plain and heard the gongs ring out the time for the prayer. We then went on some distance to a steep narrow bush path and what looked like a small hill rising vertically above it. Dorothy grinned. "I'm off," she said. "Anyone coming?" I stepped out of the car. It was a warm day and we were fortunately wearing high boots, which happened to be fashionable at the time.

Mr Dangman-Yi gazed despairingly around then said, "I cannot let you go alone. I come too!" So off we went. The track went up over rocks and we had to hold back branches, through lovely pines soughing in the cool air. As we got warmer, we shed our coats, tying them around us, Dorothy striding ahead, leaving Mr Dangman-Yi and me panting in the rear.

He turned to me, grinning. "How can that old woman walk so fast?"

But I was having too much difficulty keeping up to even reply.

After about an hour we at last arrived at the cave, just below the summit of the mountain. The mouth of the cave opened high above us and there in the gloom sat the Buddha, serene and golden, smiling at us from his five hundred years of contemplation.

Mr Dangman-Yi's eyes filled with tears. He sighed and sat down on the earthen floor. We left him there for a time as he lit a candle and wiped his eyes. It was a moment for all of us to review our lives in the serene calm of the space.

Climbing down later, Mr Dangman-Yi said to me, "I have not been there since I was a small child. When she suggested seeing the temple, I thought I could not let that old lady (Dorothy!) beat me, climbing up that path. Then I thought I would never get there! But I'm so glad I went."

Willem van Otterloo, taking up his Chief Conductor's appointment with the SSO, conducted a superb Mahler 3rd Symphony, in which I sang the alto solo. This was to be the beginning of a long and wonderful time for the Sydney Symphony as it grew in stature and authority under van Otterloo's benevolent dictatorship.

In May the SSO and van Otterloo gave a special concert in the nearly completed Opera House and at last I was able to hear what our city would enjoy in its new Concert Hall. After the rather soupy resonances of the Town Hall, it was miraculous.

On June 2nd I was in Adelaide singing Beethoven 9 for the opening of the Adelaide Festival Theatre by the Hon E G Whitlam, QC, MP, Prime Minister of Australia. Under Gough Whitlam, all artists in Australia felt they had at last been accorded a recognised place in the work force and that the arts were a legitimate activity. No longer were musicians and painters to be asked what they did for a living. What Menzies did for Education in our country in the fifties, Whitlam was to bring to the Arts in the early seventies. And Don Dunstan, the remarkable Premier of South Australia, gave that city a brighter, broader view of the world.

The Festival Theatre was a multi-purpose hall, a compromise between a live theatre and a concert hall. I believe the concept was excellent for a city of the size of Adelaide at that time. But alas the acoustic was pretty dead, dampened by the interior's heavy-looking carpet. I was amazed at the clear, resonant sound the stagehands heard backstage, in comparison to what the audience heard seated out front. Why, oh why did the engineers never ask musicians what was needed in their search to find the right 'ambiance'? My old friend Denis Vaughan, becoming a burden to all his friends and a joke to his enemies, deluged the newspapers with letters of advice, advocating the use of wood to build the interiors of the best concert halls. He cited the great halls of the world, the Concertgebouw in Amsterdam and Edinburgh's Usher Hall, saying that their shape, an elongated horseshoe, was another requirement in building this perfect sound-space. He believed that the under-structure of a hall had to have a space below the floor, shaped rather like the belly of a great drum, to create resonance, and that great concert halls should be equipped with sprung floors. I am convinced he was right. The beautiful appearance of the Sydney Opera House concert hall is not the only benefit of the building. The wooden interior and its shape are of immense value in giving the lovely sound we singers enjoy when performing there.

The Adelaide opening demonstrated the uses to which the hall could be put. After the speeches, a fanfare by Richard Meale was played, before a staged performance of Act 2 Scene 1 of *Fidelio,* with singers Rosemary Gordon, Ronald Dowd, Raymond Myers, Neil Warren-Smith, Lyn Clayton and the SASO under Georg Tinter. This was a triumph. After the interval, the stage was arranged in a conventional concert set-up and the Adelaide Festival Chorus were seated on stage behind the orchestra, to launch into Beethoven 9, under Ladislav Slovák. As a demonstration of the adaptability of the theatre, it was all very successful.

On July 22nd there was a free concert given by the SSO, conducted by Vanco Cavdarski, at which I sang the deeply romantic work of Chausson, *Poème de l'amour et de la mer.* I was always looking for orchestral works in my vocal range and suggested this piece for an ABC tour with the orchestra to Bathurst, Orange and Dubbo, with Vanco conducting. We set off by train and, as I had many friends in the orchestra, I had time to enjoy their company. This time it was good to have the Civic Halls two thirds full for the orchestral concerts. It was cold out in the west of NSW at that time of the year, but the wonderful program being given made me sorry that the whole town did not turn out! They played Mendelssohn's Symphony no. 4, *The Italian,* then the Chausson and Beethoven's 7th Symphony.

In each place we visited, the day after the evening performance the orchestra always gave a schools' concert, which was a different program entirely, so the players worked very hard. On the other hand many of them regarded the trip as a holiday, and a good deal of celebratory drinking took place. Quite often, the second desk players were sent on these tours, to give their fellows a rest, so the concerts were as variable in standard as in venue.

Later that month, with van Otterloo conducting, I sang Mahler's glorious *Lieder eines fahrenden Gesellen (Songs of a*

Wayfarer) in German, for the World Dental Congress. This concert had been booked two or three years earlier, in the expectation of the Concert Hall being fully operational before 1973. No one then would have known that the building would not yet be finally completed. So it was with a sense of wonder that I stood on the stage of the Opera House Concert Hall for the first time, looking out into the vast cathedral shapes of the golden auditorium, which was absolutely packed with people. It was an honour to stand on the stage of this building and a wonderful place in which to sing.

Composer Nigel Butterley at this time of his life was working two days a week as a teacher in Newcastle, in order to support himself in his real metier as a composer. In another of his capacities, that of running the Beecroft Music Club, Nigel asked me to conduct a master class in which I heard four young singers, amongst whom were Susan Kessler singing Bach and Yvonne Kenny singing *Piangero* from Handel's *Julius Caesar.* Both unknown then, they went on to work with Eric Vietheer and Geoffrey Parsons in London. Sue died at a tragically early age, but Yvonne Kenny is now bringing glory to the world's stage.

As my birthday approached, the plans for the Opera House opening began to excite the whole city. Rehearsals for the Australian Opera's season were also taking place in different venues all over the city and the major interest was in Prokofiev's *War and Peace,* which would be the first opera staged in the Opera Theatre. Edward Downes was now installed as the new Musical Director, with John Winther the General Manager and Stephen Hall the Artistic Director. Downes was galvanising the chorus and orchestra with his dynamic conducting style and scorching vocabulary. I rehearsed a demanding recital program to sing with John Winther, a wonderful accompanist, for Musica Viva, in the Opera House Music Room at the end of October.

The month we had all been living for was here. I was contracted to eventually sing all three mezzo roles in Puccini's *Il trittico,* but the opening night was to have Rosina Raisbeck singing Frugola in *Il tabarro* and Zita in *Gianni Schicchi,* with my role for the opening night being La Principessa in *Suor Angelica.* These short roles are wonderfully contrasted, and I was happy to think that Rosina and I were both singing in these operas on this occasion. She did not rehearse the Principessa, but concentrated on her other two short roles, whilst I occasionally went to watch her rehearsing, when I was free. I knew that soon I would sing the other two parts and was spending every available moment learning the involved inter-woven ensemble lines in *Gianni Scicchi,* one of the most difficult operas I have sung.

"Thank goodness it's short," I thought. "Thank goodness all three operas are short."

The dress rehearsal came and the company and their friends crowded into the new black-painted opera theatre. It seemed so small, after the old theatres of the past. The stage was extremely deep, but the wings were non-existent. You had to be careful that you were out of the sight lines when you were waiting to go on stage, as you pressed close into the ropes in the wings.

As *Il tabarro* that morning ended and the curtain dropped, Moffatt Oxenbould came on to the set, placing little pot-plants in a border along the steps. Moffatt was the personal Assistant to the General Manager at this time and the producer of *Il trittico*. I was disappointed that Desmond Digby's design for the second act, the cloisters of *Suor Angelica* seemed rather unimaginative. I walked carefully over the set in my huge and bejewelled costume for the first time, estimating the timing it took to drag the train of the dress over the steps, and along the front of the stage, on my way to my declaiming and complaining exit.

"Clear the set!" shouted the stage manager, and we all went to our tiny wing space to wait for the second act to begin.

My good friend Rosemary Gordon followed 'the young nuns' on to the stage as Puccini's music wound its sinuous thread. My entry music came, and soon the rehearsal happily concluded with poor Sister Angelica vanishing in clouds of light-filled smoke which made us all cough, as she gathered the pretty child, her supposedly dead son, into her dying arms. "This story is pretty awful stuff, actually," I thought, "But great music, and very good singing from Rosemary, given it is not really her *fach*." Climbing out of the costume, the largest and grandest I ever wore, I reflected the rehearsal had been quite easy considering it was the first time we'd ever been on the set.

Next evening we were all at the theatre in good time. After the curtain fell on *Il tabarro,* I was on the side of the stage, waiting in the wings and trying to sqeeze my huge skirt into the small space between the blacks. I watched with amazement as Moffatt trotted out with dozens more little plastic pot-plants and began arranging serried banks of tiny cyprus and Mediterranean-looking herbs into a vastly enlarged garden, for the poor little nuns to wander about in. It all looked incredibly crowded on the narrow stage, but the order came to clear the set, the nuns began their pretty warbling, and *Suor Angelica* had commenced.

I swept on, enjoying my power over the snivelling soprano at my feet. For the first time I had a soprano where I wanted her, even if she was my friend Rosemary!

The audience tittered.

"Squirm, you snivelling sinner." I sang, in Italian. "Never shall your guilt leave you for one moment."

The audience gave a howl of laughter.

"How could they laugh?" I thought. "I'm acting to the best of my ability."

My eyes flashed and I snarled at the audience, and at poor Rosemary, crouched at my feet.

"Sign this!"

The audience were hysterical with mirth.

I gathered my train and my cane, and with all the hauteur I could muster, I stormed off.

"What on earth was all that about?" I demanded as soon as I got off-stage.

The Stage Manager explained that as I swept over the stairs on to the stage, I swept up one of the largest of Moffatt's many plastic pots. As I turned and moved, it righted itself and rode majestically behind me on my train, following each move I made like a small dog. When I went up the steps to exit, it rolled sedately over and righted itself, as I regally left the scene. No wonder the audience laughed. I was the talk of the town.

I shall always blame my colleagues. Not *one* of those sopranos, nor *even* the contraltos, dressed as nuns, lifted a Christian finger to set the pot plant to its proper place. With friends like that, who needs enemies! Rosemary, the one who might have helped me, was on her knees to me pleading in her most ardent tones, and was probably not even able to see or be aware of what had happened. As I struggled out of my costume on that night, I cursed its enormous size and weight. It was so vast and heavy that I never even felt the extra presence on my 'train'. It was really very funny, but I smarted under the giggles of amusement.

Worse was in store that season.

Because I was not a member of the company, I had my contract with the Australian Opera altered to state that when I sang, my name would appear on each relevant newspaper advertisement. It was then the practice for the Opera Company to list only the name of the opera and the dates, and as a member of the public I found it appalling that the artist singing in any performance should not be named. As an opera-goer, I wanted to know if I would hear Robert Allman or John Shaw, and to know which of the tenors, Reginald Byers or Donald Smith, were singing. These two often alternated the same role within the season. I felt the public was entitled to know whom they would hear at any given performance, and maybe my contract would persuade other singers to make the same conditions.

I had been so busy that I had never even looked at the newspaper advertisements that season. On the Sunday morning, a friend rang to say she had enjoyed my discomforting experience in the theatre at the opening night enormously. "It was so funny," she cooed.

She was also ringing to say that my name had not been listed in the paper on the appropriate day. "When will you be singing again?" she asked.

I told her the dates of the following performances I would be singing, and hung up. I began to seethe with rage.

Graeme and I discussed the fact that the Opera Company had not honoured a clause in my contract which I considered important enough to have had 'written in' as a matter of principle. I rang Moffatt at his home that Sunday morning and apologised for disturbing him, explaining that I did not have John Winther's telephone number. I told him my problem, and said that I wanted to be assured that my name would appear in subsequent advertisements, and that I wished to speak to John Winther about this matter on that Sunday morning.

"If I don't hear from him by midday today, I will not sing on Monday night."

The morning dragged by, and my anger grew.

The day passed and there was no further word, so on Monday morning I rang the Company office to say I would not be singing. I was told that it was against company policy to name any singer, as it would encourage a 'star' system. I thought it was a bit too late to have a company without 'stars' when we already had singers of the calibre of Donald Smith, Neil Warren-Smith, John Shaw and Robert Allman. I was determined not to back down.

I never even thought of the effect my action would have on my colleague, Rosina Raisbeck.

We had begun the season on the premise that she would sing four or so performances of the *Tabarro* and the *Schicchi,* with me singing the *Angelica.* Then I would take over all three roles, and later she would sing all three. This meant that we were both eased gradually into the three operas. With rehearsal schedules rather tight, neither of us had been pressured into the production calls of each other's operas, allowing plenty of time to learn the extra music and moves as the season progressed. Now Rosina was flung into the short but absolutely crucial role of La Principessa. She was furious, and the other singers in the company believed that I was a prima donna who only wanted my name in the paper.

Meanwhile, at home I was utterly miserable at letting down the Opera and the other singers, and the thought of the lost performances and the work I had done being wasted. It never occurred to me to back down, or that I could have sued the Company for breach of contract. I could not have afforded the legal costs, anyway. The newspapers had a field day, making me out to be very difficult, but a woman of principle. Not a word did I receive from the General Manager or from Moffatt. However, the stage manager rang and said that my name would be listed in the newspapers on the third performance, and that was the end of the matter.

I sang seven of the eight contracted performances, and

enjoyed playing and singing the roles of Frugola and Zita enormously when the time came for me to sing them. Rosina Raisbeck never spoke to me for many years!

I always felt that there were faults on both sides in this dispute. Someone from the management should have had the courtesy to return my call on the day I rang, or first thing on the Monday morning, and apologise. By leaving me alone I was unable to climb down and I was so upset that I could not have done so anyway. I felt betrayed and never recovered my old easy friendship with either Moffatt or the Company.

I enjoyed the lively acoustic of the small Opera Theatre and the intimacy that the size of the house gave to the performances. It was always an easy house to 'fill' as you sang. I quickly learned that it was best to be down front-stage as far as possible, a fact often forgotten by present-day directors with their elaborate demands on the new generation of singers, making them sing far back on the deep stage, at the expense of the music and of their voices.

We rehearsed the Beethoven 9 with van Otterloo and were thrilled with the sound of the orchestra and choir in the Concert Hall, after the cloudy acoustic in the old Town Hall. The orchestra were still coming to terms with the sound of the new venue. The Concert Hall's clarity made each player's ability to play in tune and judge the crispness of his attack an extra challenge.

Finally it was the 20th October. This would be a birthday to remember all my life.

The Queen was to open the building at three in the afternoon and we watched this event on television. The enormous crowd was massed like hundreds and thousands on a cake, in carefully arranged groups around the white swan. The wind tore at the trees and tried to blow the Queen's hat off her head, as she made the performative utterance. At last, the building that the city, the country and the world had found so remarkable, beautiful and controversial, was opened.

G and Deb were to be part of the audience for the concert that evening and thirteen-year-old Deb was to wear her first long dress. During the wait before the concert, they and all the other members of the audience were able to see the fireworks that cascaded over Sydney and illuminated the Harbour. Meanwhile the artists were gradually becoming accustomed to the new building which would soon become a regular work place.

The Beethoven finally began and I was lifted into that special space I called 'performance in progress'. This was a kind of no-man's-land of the mind, where I had no real idea of how it was sounding 'out there', but was totally immersed in the music surrounding me on the stage. Apart from something dreadful happening during the music, this was an attitude of mind, a place where I would stay until the end of the performance. However, I always waited with some apprehension for the bass soloist's opening, "O Freunde," hoping for a great sound. So often in this work, the poor bass soloist sounded as if he had lost his voice the instant he opened his mouth and that he would never ever recover to sing again. However, Raymond Myers sang the opening as if he had invented it especially to celebrate the occasion and the performance ended in a blaze of sound, as Beethoven intended. As the applause thundered, I followed my silver-voiced colleague Nance Grant off the stage and took my place between her and Ronald Dowd in the line-up to be presented to the Queen by Charles Buttrose, long-time Assistant General Manager of the ABC. It was my third Royal Performance and the most momentous for me because of the occasion. I gave a special smile to John Hopkins, thanking him with all my heart for telling me the previous year that I had to be part of this day.

I have always been surprised that no-one has ever realised that the photograph of the Queen which was taken at this moment and which has been reprinted in many different publications over the years, is printed in reverse, so that the Queen wears the Order of the Garter over the wrong shoulder and we are apparently standing on the wrong side of the stage.

On October 31st, Musica Viva presented an inaugural concert in the Music Room in the Opera House. Accompanied by John Winther, I presented a program comprising the Beethoven *Six Gellert songs,* four Wolf songs, (I recorded both these works with Geoffrey Parsons that year for the ABC), the four Debussy *Proses lyriques* and Sutherland's Judith Wright songs. The Music Room had a tiny sliver of a stage with a rather dry acoustic, owing to carpet pasted on to the cement interior. I always had the feeling that I was singing in a cupboard under the stairs, as I pictured the glories of the Concert Hall above. But the intention had been to create a small theatre for chamber music and this was it! Listening to music here was a pleasure for the audience, even if it was hard for the performer, for the size of the space was perfect for small-scale works.

One of my life's most memorable experiences was a performance of the Verdi *Requiem* conducted by Edward Downes in November of this year, 1973. Downes trained the Australian Opera chorus to give its absolute all in this most remarkable performance. As we soloists stood in rehearsal on the Concert Hall stage, Downes harangued the Opera chorus, screaming that Verdi's *Dies irae* was so terrifying that they were to recreate this terror in the souls of the audience.

"I want you to shit your pants," he snarled. "This is hell you are singing about, and you are standing in it!"

It was a remarkable rehearsal, as he drove us all to perform beyond our capacities and everyone who attended that performance will always remember it.

This remarkable year in my life, and in the life of opera and music in Sydney, was drawing to a close. There was a Sydney Town Hall *Messiah* with Sir Bernard Heinze to perform, and then our usual dash to Melbourne for Christmas to see our parents. We were dreading the drive south in the hot weather and had seriously thought of not going, until we had installed air conditioning in the car. But the time of year made us sentimental and we longed to see our families. We missed them.

Isanern, G's parents, always came to stay for a couple of weeks in the May holiday period, as they drove up to Port Macquarie to avoid winter in Melbourne, and on their return they stopped off again. My parents also travelled north in winter, to fish and camp in the warmth of Queensland, but they did not often come through Sydney. Towing a caravan through the suburbs filled my father with understandable horror and he always travelled via the Newell Highway.

This year I carried a secret, a gift which I thought would please my father, but which I decided I could not yet tell him. I had been offered the OBE, to be announced in the New Year's Honours. There were few women at that time offered this award and I knew that Mother, bursting with pride, would not be able to keep it a secret, so I did as I was bid and only discussed it with G, who was positive that I should accept.

We were back in Sydney when, the evening before the published announcement, I rang Ti (my nickname for Mother) to tell her.

"Good gracious," she gasped, as I shyly told her to look in the paper next day, "The OBE? Whatever *for?*"

Dad was terribly pleased, and I was too that he, who had helped me financially in those early years, should see his faith in his daughter recognised in this way.

17. Medieval Music: Early to High Baroque

The 12th century miracle plays, *The Play of Herod* and *The Slaughter of the Innocents,* were extraordinary pieces for Young Opera to present, as far in distance as in time from the Benedictine Monastery in Fleury, where the manuscript for this 12th century pop musical was discovered. But Winsome Evans, Director Frederick May and stage manager Brian Donovan let their considerable imaginations range back in time, to transport the performers and singers into another world. We sang in the original Latin and the Bible stories regained their power from Professor May's English commentary. The Magi and the Shepherds moved down the aisles of the Conservatorium as Winsome's Renaissance Players processed onto the stage as if they were residents of another era.

Apart from the usual worry I always had about amateur theatre going awry because of lack of adequate production rehearsal, I remember the difficulty of the music. Winsome had written out a most beautiful decorated manuscript, which she had arranged from the 12th century notation. The notation at that time indicated pitch, but not rhythm, and by studying the metrical rhythm of the words Winsome had evolved the time values and written out the music in modern notation. All this required great scholarship on her part and hours of dedication. Although the new manuscript was beautiful to behold, it was hard for everyone to read but, on reflection, the results were so memorable this seems a small price to have paid.

The lovely Beatrice of Berlioz took me into a different France in the Melbourne Proms of 1974, when John Hopkins conducted this Berlioz opera once more, with Ronald Dowd my Benedick again. It was always inspiring to sing with Ron, not least because of the adrenaline charge he gave me. He had a gift of saying the very thing to spark a flicker of anger in me, at the moment when I was most vulnerable. His needling always managed to arouse me to fury, yet I loved the old so-and-so for his artistry, generosity and his wonderful voice.

I had foolishly mentioned to him the fear I had of the high tessitura of some of the writing. It was always a mistake to confide in anyone about difficulties during a performance. But his support and praise of my performance was enough to carry me through with flying colours and I really enjoyed the role of the feisty Beatrice against his taunting Benedick.

In Canberra I sang a Handel Cantata, *Ah crudel, nel pianto mio* for the first time, with Ernest Llewellyn conducting the Canberra Symphony Orchestra. This long piece sat very high for me. I chose it because it was so dramatic, but it stretched me to my limits and I never really felt it was mine, although I loved singing it. And the orchestra, although led by some of Australia's finest players, was then an ad hoc affair, under-rehearsed by Ernie, whom I felt did not understand Baroque style. I think many people do not realise that the music of this, and of the classical period, is more difficult to bring to a satisfying standard than the romantic music of a later century. Early music is much more exposed, and faults of intonation and rhythm show up immediately. But most of all, style is the most important factor in presenting this elegant music.

Five days later, very early one autumn morning, at San Remo in Victoria, alone and putting his boat into the water to go fishing, my Father died. They said he had a heart attack and died instantly.

I'm sorry I never said 'goodbye' and 'thank you' to him.

His breath went out of his body at the turn of the low tide, as he looked out over the stilled waters he loved so much ...

We three flew down to Melbourne and on a cold day of showers and puddles, paced the paths of the Springvale Crematorium between the banks of camellia trees. I was strangely calm. I wondered how my mother would manage. I regretted all my unspoken words of gratitude to my father, for his wonderfully generous and grumbling support of my improbable life. I was especially glad we had had those few weeks together in Europe in 1956. He had loved the whole trip and that journey had changed and broadened his view of the world forever. His farming and his great financial ambitions had left him frustrated, but he had made two very successful and different business careers, in spite of living through the Depression and the war years. And he had died as he would have wished, doing what he loved most in all the world, quickly and cleanly.

Mother, alas, had not said 'Goodbye' to him. She was dissuaded from seeing her Harry after his death by the local doctor, who thought the sight of the body would distress her too much. Although she never mentioned it, I think she always felt regret and a great loss at not saying a final farewell on that day.

The funeral was a bitter-sweet affair, meeting long-lost friends and relatives. Graeme's mother Isabel (Issie) had arranged for an afternoon tea to be provided by the ladies at the Dandenong Bowling Club. Many of these women were lifelong friends of both Mother and Dad. I thought again how an old country town, as Dandenong was when we were living in the district, had such a sense of community, so different from the big impersonal city where we now lived.

My sister and her husband helped sort through the details of mother's needs and finances. She decided to continue living at San Remo for the present. And then we all said goodbye and left her, to resume our different lives. I had lived so far removed from him for so many years, but the loss of my father changed my view of the stages of my life.

My father was a powerful unseen presence when, on Friday May 3rd, I was invested with the Most Excellent Order of the British Empire (OBE) by the Governor, Sir Roden Cutler, at Sydney's Government House. My mother was there to see me receive the medal. I was more nervous about the stage management of this event than of any of my operatic roles, forgetting to curtsey properly and stumbling on my way to the dais.

Another piece of early music took up all my attention for several weeks. To make something of Vivaldi's *Juditha Triumphans* was, frankly, difficult. Vivaldi had written this lovely music to be performed by the young women of the foundling school in Venice. All of the five principal roles are written for either mezzo or contralto and many of the arias are performed at similar tempos. The music, when heard complete over two hours, takes on a repetitiveness that could only be described as boring. Yet it is all very beautiful. Richard Gill, a young man of great charisma and talent, had conceived the idea of a Venetian Festival to take place over five days in the Sydney Conservatorium. He had found some rare and wonderful music, but the performance of *Juditha* was doomed by its bland texture. And the orchestra, led by some of the top players in the city, was not helped by the intonation of some of the back-desk student string players. But for me singing the principal male character, Holofones, it was an introduction to yet another style of early music. I enjoyed it hugely and have never forgotten Graham Powning's beautiful oboe obbligato to my main aria.

Gordon Watson performed some Horace Keats songs with me in a concert at the Conservatorium, at which I also sang the Ravel *Chansons madécasses* for the first time. These songs have remained part of my repertoire ever since.

Over in Christchurch, New Zealand, that year a musical battle raged. In July, when I stepped off the plane to sing Mahler's *Songs of a Wayfarer* with Vanco Cavdarski, the city was filled with excitement. The project to fund a nucleus of twelve full-time professional players and a resident conductor to provide a basis for a permanent orchestra had gathered momentum. A series of ten concerts was planned for the year. This city of great choral singers, with its two great choirs, felt they must build their own orchestra in order to be independent of the Wellington-based NZBC National Orchestra. I could only wholeheartedly agree. But, as in my own country, funding an orchestra is always difficult. To justify the cost against the demands of education and health care is politically and socially dangerous.

I approved the aims, as spelled out when appealing for subscribers to help fund the project: "To make music a habit in the lives of young and old alike, by taking concerts to primary and secondary schools, hospitals, homes for the aged and mentally and physically handicapped, to factories, institutions and so on.

"To continue the services of a full-time conductor [who was Vanco Cavdarski at that time] ... To increase our contribution to the Christchurch Harmonic and Royal Musical Society Choirs, as well as ballet and opera companies. To provide employment right here in our own city for the many excellent young musicians who graduate from the Christchurch School of Music ..."

I wished very much that the same aims could be applied to building orchestras in all our larger rural cities. I had proposed a similar idea to Ken Tribe. He was conducting a report into the establishment of small regional orchestras in our major rural cities, starting with Newcastle. However, Ken said I was hopelessly unrealistic, and that there would never be the funds for such a thing in a country as sparsely populated as Australia.

The concert with Vanco was a success, but Christchurch music politics were heavily partisan, with factions for and against Vanco, and the whole plan was obviously a football to be kicked about from one team to another. I loved my dear friends in the RCMS, but could see the writing on the wall, as they became embroiled in legal battles with the council and the Mayor, eventually taking the problems all the way to their Supreme Court.

Although I was not singing with The Australian Opera, the Victorian State Opera, re-grouped and renamed the Victorian Opera Company, asked me to sing Handel's opera *Julius Caesar* again. My friend Marilyn Richardson would sing Cleopatra and the conductor would be the young Richard Divall. Richard, the VOC's Musical Director, remembered the huge success of this opera in Sydney and hoped it would rescue the always-ailing finances of the Melbourne company.

If I had thought Christchurch in winter was icy, I really had no conception of cold until rehearsing in the crypt of St Paul's Cathedral that winter. There was no heating at all, and the cast wore overcoats, hats, gloves and scarves, to try to survive. As it was, we passed our head colds from one to another during the rehearsals. But this was nothing to the pioneering experience of finally opening in the dilapidated Palais Theatre in St Kilda. One of the biggest theatres in Australia at the time, it was very cheap for the VOC to rent. I suppose the Company thought they might fill the auditorium with the well-known singers at their disposal. Not so, however. The half-empty theatre sighed as draughts of icy air swept through it and Melbourne stayed away, supposedly because of the weather. During the first of the three performances, the heavens opened and buckets had to be placed strategically under the drips coming from the roof, which we only now discovered was being repaired. The roof was actually half off the stage area which was open to the clouds over the Esplanade in St Kilda. The noise made by the raindrops made an interesting percussion sound in the gentle legato of Handel's music. As always, singing with Marilyn was great fun, outdoing each other with our improvised cadenzas and rolling out our perfectly matched thirds in our duets.

Musically it was a pleasure, physically an ordeal, like most of my VOC experiences! One of the critics, commenting on our short Roman tunic costumes in this production, said, "Anyone for tennis?"

In September I was back in Melbourne for a concert in the Camberwell Civic Centre. Given by the Melbourne Symphony Orchestra with Robert Rosen conducting, it was a popular program of operatic arias. I flew down on a morning flight to begin rehearsing at 2pm in the ABC's Waverley studios. The weather was rather unpleasant, with Melbourne's hot north wind blowing, which always made me feel very 'prickly'. But the program I had chosen was easy, I was to sing all my old 'war-horses'.

Pandemonium reigned when I arrived in the rehearsal room. Brass players were reading their newspapers and exchanging betting tips, string players were talking amongst themselves, and Robert Rosen was trying to make himself heard above the din. They were obviously giving him a bad time. As I stood in front of the conductor tapping his baton, but achieving nothing, I let fly. After all, these people had once been close colleagues when I had lived in Melbourne.

"Ladies and gentlemen," I boomed out over the racket, "I have just come from Sydney to rehearse with you. I've no intention of singing with such an undisciplined bunch of musicians. I'm going to leave this rehearsal and cancel my concert, after I've been to wash my face and cool off."

A dreadful hush settled over the room as I strode out, across the foyer and into the old-fashioned ladies' toilet, where I splashed cold water on my face. I was really angry, as much for Robert Rosen as myself.

After a moment, the door of the toilet opened and a hesitant man's voice whispered, "Lauris, can I come in for a moment?" In came the leader of the orchestra, looking very crestfallen.

"Please don't leave," he said, "You were quite right to complain about our behaviour. I'm truly sorry we upset you. We're so pleased to have you back singing in Melbourne and we hope you'll accept our apology and come back to rehearse. We promise to behave," he added with a grin. (I should remind the reader that it is the duty of the orchestra leader to maintain discipline).

After such a speech, I went back in to sing *Softly awakes my heart* with passion. I felt like the schoolmistress I had once been. The rehearsal went smoothly without further problems and the concert in the evening went very well. Afterwards, I was presented with a great sheaf of beautiful flowers from the orchestra with their apologies and their thanks.

I was back in Melbourne again in November, when Richard Divall asked me to sing Gluck's *Orpheus,* in English, in the Great Hall of the State Gallery of Victoria, for the VOC. The critics said it was a great occasion. John Sinclair wrote in *The Age* that "Every seat in the hall was occupied last night, and to be a member of such a large and responsive audience is, for any Melbourne critic, among the rarest of pleasures." It was wonderful to sing this music, but the magnificent, and very resonant Great Hall is not ideal for music making. Nance Grant was the Euridice with Rhonda Bruce as Amor (Cupid) in this performance.

For the rest of that week Richard Divall recorded this work for the ABC, with the aim of producing an LP record. Alas, owing to some mistake with the technicians involved, it was recorded in mono instead of stereo and the master was declared unplayable for permanent use. Perhaps the fact that the work was recorded in English also made it unattractive for commercial release, but what a tragic waste of all that work! At this time the ABC was guilty of unprofessional gaffes such as this and was always struggling to make ends meet.

By the time the Opera House opened, with the Whitlam Government promising wonderful advances and additional funding in the arts, there was euphoria amongst artists. But with hindsight, perhaps the Whitlam decision to discontinue the Radio and Television Licence Fee was a mistake. By raising revenue for the ABC in this way at least the National Broadcaster had an independent income. Subsequently it would depend on a government handout and each successive government has always tried to reduce the value of this most wonderful asset. Those of us who have lived in other countries have only to compare the quality of our national radio and TV stations to know that we possess a treasure here which *must* survive as an independent organisation.

18. Amneris, Carmen and Other Feisty Ladies

We decided to buy a bigger boat.

We owned an 18-foot swing-keel boat, called a 'Matilda'. The cabin was tiny, and we made extra space outside by erecting a tent over the cockpit. If we went into the cabin, we had to bend down low and then sit on the bunks, as it only had sitting head room, but we were warm and dry at night and often slept overnight in Towlers Bay on Pittwater.

The first time we stayed overnight in this sheltered bay, the stars began to appear in the twilight and a memorable sight astonished us. As the reflections of the trees slowly began to tremble on the grey water, a huge cabin cruiser drifted in to anchor near us. The ripples widened and dispersed and from the three-story deck high above us there appeared men and women in formal evening dress, who quietly and slowly dropped fishing lines into the still water. It was like a scene from a surreal ballet. Who were these beautiful silent people, we wondered?

For all three of us, sailing had become very important. Life seemed a lot less stressful if we were able to get out on the water for a few hours each Sunday. We went winter and summer, our only worry being that if we had a gale-force wind we might 'bottle' (tip over) in our swing-keel boat. Now we decided we needed a boat with a fixed keel, so we placed an order for a Space Sailer 24. We would have to be patient while it was being built and were not able to sail for several months that summer.

In the January summer season of 1975, I sang my first Amneris in Verdi's *Aïda* for the Australian Opera. I had longed to sing this role from the moment I began to learn it in Paris at the end of 1955. Modesti said then that it would take ten years for me to be capable of sustaining this greatest of the dramatic Verdi mezzo roles, and now at last I was given the opportunity. When I started to learn singing, my operatic heroine was Ebe Stignani and I played her Verdi *Requiem* solos over and over on my LP record player. I longed to replace the soft-grained quality of my own voice with the powerful 'bite' of her tone, but I was grateful for my own softer sound when it came to singing lieder and Mahler. What I loved about Stignani was the rough conviction and power with which she sang her Verdi villains. So when the Australian Opera asked me at last to sing this role, I was overjoyed. By 1975 I felt in my bones that the power of the Princess was at last mine. It was twenty years since I first looked at this score.

I was disappointed not to be singing on the first night of the season, when the role would be performed by the dramatic mezzo-soprano Elizabeth Connell. There were to be two different casts and I was thrilled to have the big, warm performance of the *Aïda* by Elizabeth Fretwell to sing with and to act against. The tenor was Reginald Byers and Raymond Myers was Amonasro.

The sets of designer Tom Lingwood were the most thrilling thing about this summer season. For the first time the Australian Opera performed in the Opera House Concert Hall and the effect was dazzling in its immensity. The critic Maria Prerauer said in her review, "By making his towering fixed set a continuation of the hall architecture, Lingwood somehow succeeded in turning the entire auditorium into the forecourt of an Egyptian palace."

The beginning of the Nile Scene was always full of suspense for me in this production. Here a boat was supposed to glide on to the set. In the concert hall, this was suggested by a cleverly designed boat which came on below the stage level and behind the orchestra. As there were no 'wings' on this stage, the boat 'unfolded' piece by piece and I had to carefully judge the time to step on the deck. Sometimes it was still a little 'crumpled' as I stepped aboard and, as it unwound, Maestro Carlo Cillario would give me a wicked grin as I jerked my way towards the centre of the stage, ready to step out on to the 'dry land' of the concert hall stage.

Carlo was always a wonderful conductor of Italian repertoire and of Verdi in particular. He drew from the orchestra the singing legato that most of his colleagues in the pit seemed unable to achieve. However, as he grew older he often expressed his opinion of a singer's performance in very straightforward terms. Once he shouted at a soprano who was singing away up on the stage above him, "Why you sing so 'orrible?" On another occasion, he bellowed in rage and, holding his nose, pulled an imaginary WC chain.

From the pit he would shout indiscriminate directions to the players in the orchestra, or to the singers on the stage. If he were enjoying himself he would often sing loudly along with whoever had the tune. At one rehearsal his performance bid fair to upstage my own. I stopped singing and strode down to the footlights.

"Maestro!" I shouted over the racket, "You're making so much noise that I find it impossible to hear the orchestra." He always treated me with great respect and affection after this.

The Bulletin's Brian Hoad said, "… it is mostly a matter of just sitting back and enjoying a brilliant score unleashed from the orchestra by Cillario with often stunning immediacy, an involving, enveloping and often totally overwhelming experience for the audience, and also at times for some of the singers too." The reviews for my performances were very complimentary. Comparisons between the two casts were inevitable, but all the critiques said of my performance that it "almost stole the show."

These performances were amongst the operatic highlights of my life. It was so wonderful to sing this role at a time when I was vocally at my peak and when many of my own technical problems had been resolved by time and experience. It had taken me more than the ten years to have the stamina and technique to sustain the role, as M Modesti had predicted. At last I felt that I really knew how to sing.

My next engagement was a disaster. Hungarians Erzsebet Hazy and George Melis were famous in Eastern Europe and compatriots of theirs brought them out to give operatic concerts and recitals in the major Town Halls and Concert Halls around the country. The people who ran Rhapsody Promotions were obviously inexperienced in concert management. They felt that the local Eastern Europeans would flock to hear the voices of these two famous singers and that the local singers of high quality partnering them would encourage the Australian opera fans. They asked me to suggest a tenor for the tour so we could sing duets, trios and quartets in the concerts. They proposed a concert of lieder and song and one of operatic excerpts in Sydney and Melbourne, and one concert only in Adelaide and Brisbane. I asked my colleague Raymond MacDonald to do the opera concerts and for the song and lieder program I suggested Robert Gard. The fees were agreed on and we three local artists worked on our programs separately, awaiting the arrival of the 'stars' with whom we would sing.

The 'stars' arrived and we rehearsed and found they were indeed wonderful. In particular, George Melis was a great bass, who sang with authority and experience. The soprano had a very light, rather bright voice which was not so much to my taste, but she was gorgeous to look at, glamorous and in every sense a 'prima donna'. The tour should have been a sell-out, but there was no pre-publicity and one small notice in *The Sydney Morning Herald* was the only advertising for the first concert, the lieder recital at the Sydney Town Hall. As we each walked out on to the stage for the first time, our hearts sank at the sight of the rows of empty seats. The voices of the visiting artists were huge and echoed into the spaces of the empty hall. The critics were enraptured by the singing and by the playing of John Champ, who was also our excellent and polished MC, but it was a disaster financially.

We were flown to Melbourne, where there was also a large Hungarian community, and the audience was even worse. On returning to Sydney we were told that the tour was cancelled.

185

We waited for a week or so, then began to ask the Rhapsody management if they had forgotten to pay our fees for the concerts we had done. Suddenly they were no longer answering the telephone and finally Actors' Equity wrote to say that they had absconded and we would never get our money. Apparently they *did* pay the visitors, but we local artists felt 'hardly done by'! It was a shameful thing that two great overseas artists should have come all this way to be treated so poorly.

This unfortunate story showed how difficult it is for artists to negotiate engagements for themselves. Up till now I had handled my own singing career, with help and advice from Graeme. With the opening of the Opera House, Australia's musical horizons were expanding. In 1975 experiments in concert-giving were happening every day in Sydney and elsewhere in the country. With the return of many expatriate performers and the development of international air travel, it was timely to be greeted by Jenifer Eddy when I went to Melbourne to sing. In March of that year she returned from London to live in Australia and in April she began her Artists' Management.

The possessor of a very beautiful high coloratura with astonishing technique and agility, she went to London just before I returned to live in Australia. Ronald Dowd and his wife gave a party there to welcome her, and to farewell G and me. Jenifer was quickly engaged at Covent Garden and, after making her debut in London, began making appearances in some of the major opera houses in Europe and signing contracts with some of the record companies. She was on the brink of a major international career when a strange illness struck her. For the next few years she was in a terrible situation. From having had an absolutely secure top E or F in *alt* in her range, so that Zerbinetta in Strauss' *Ariadne auf Naxos* was a favourite role, she found that sometimes she was able to sing but at other times her voice would not respond and she would be unable to produce these high floating sounds which were her unique gift. In despair, she began to cancel engagements and at length decided to withdraw from a singing career and to return to Australia.

Her London agent, Lies Askonas, suggested that the gifted and intelligent Jenifer become an agent, handling singers living and working in Australia and also managing Askonas' international artists here. Her husband, David Beamish, was a successful engineer. They returned to Australia and shortly after their return I became one of the first artists on her books.

Before Jenifer Eddy Artists' Management there had been no fee scale for singers. Every singer was assessed by the ABC or by the Opera Company on the Management's terms. For a private engagement each artist demanded their own price, which was usually modest, in order to get the work. Now my fees increased dramatically and I had some idea of my 'worth' on the market. I also had someone else to govern my availability. Jenifer's arrival

186

was a tremendous asset to singers in Australia at that time. The kind of messy negotiations preceding my appearance in the Sutherland-Williamson Opera Season would never arise again. Alas, neither would an opera season sponsored by a private entrepreneur.

In September I took part in a real 'highlight' in my career, a solo recital with Geoffrey Parsons in the Main Hall (Verbrugghen) at the Conservatorium. This handsome and self-composed young man was loved by all who knew him. I believe that all artists who worked with him thought that they had a special relationship with him. He had the gift of making every artist feel as if they alone were his favoured performer and inspired supreme self-confidence. If he ever felt the nervous tension all performers experience as they begin a performance, I never knew it. From the moment he began to play, there was no doubt that *this* was the tempo and the mood of the song. I never needed to discuss the work before going into the performance. He sat behind the opened lid of the piano, touching the keys with such surety that I could sing on forever, supported and transported by his playing. Sometimes I would be so involved in the beautiful sounds he was producing that I would forget to sing, as I listened to him.

Until this time, I had recorded each year in the ABC studios with this great Australian, but had never given a public concert with him. A Lieder Society had been formed in Sydney and I was to sing in the inaugural concert. We presented a beautiful program where I sang for the first time Haydn's *Arianna a Naxos,* Wagner's *Wesendonk-Lieder,* Debussy's *Baudelaire songs,* and Dorien Le Gallienne's great setting of the John Donne sonnets. The object of the Society was to promote the love and performance of song, but as Fred Blanks said in *The Sydney Morning Herald,* we were preaching to the converted. Lindsey Browne pointed out that I "... placarded the absurd and snobbistic (sic) narrowness of the new song-society's name by choosing to sing practically no lieder at all!"

Unfortunately for us in Sydney, some Melbourne singers had decided to start the Lieder Society of Victoria at exactly the same time and my friends of many years in that city were gravely affronted by the title of the new Sydney society, which we unwittingly called the National Lieder Society of Australia. I was horrified to discover the *fury* the title of our new venture invoked and no amount of explanation that we did not know that the other group in Melbourne was starting up was able to smooth the troubled waters.

This year I adjudicated an Eisteddfod for the first time. The 28th Hartwell Eisteddfod was held at the end of October that year and I returned to the Hartwell Presbyterian Church where, as a teenager, I had sat like a wallflower and watched my sister and my friend Faye Mishael with their boys, dancing to the songs of Irving Berlin and Gershwin, Frank Sinatra and Judy Garland.

In that old church hall I gave the prize to a singer called Robin Bugg, who was called up on stage to receive her award. The compere remarked that she should change her name if she wanted to have a successful career. She was very firm in her rebuttal, angrily saying that she was proud of her father's name and would always continue to sing with it!

In October I was asked to think about recording an LP disc of operatic arias for the ABC. "Whom would you like to conduct?" the voice on the telephone said. I knew that the Chorus Master at the Opera, Geoffrey Arnold, was a very good accompanist and conductor, so together we began to plan the items and time the arias for recording the following year.

On November 11th the Whitlam Government was brought down and the reforms and changes of the three year-old regime were halted. We, who had grown up in Australia for twenty-three years under the benign voice and beetling eyebrows of Robert Menzies, had never doubted that 'one day a Prince would come' to release Australia from its unchanging dream and old-fashioned security under a Conservative government. When that time came, great reforms were rushed through too soon and the conservatives did not like it. As a performer who had admired the style of the new Labor Government's financial support for music and the arts, I was angry about the methods used to bring down that reforming government, and could only regret the swift passing of the new era. With Malcolm Fraser we were back to conservative times again

In November that year, tragedy struck one of the most influential women in Australian music. Regina Ridge had been the manager of Musica Viva for many years. It was her interest in singing which had first led to lieder being introduced into Musica Viva programs. She expanded chamber music repertoire in Australia and her imaginative programming had taken Musica Viva into a new direction. On an overseas trip to Czechoslovakia to see her beloved Smetana Quartet, she was knocked down in traffic and killed. A requiem for Regina showed how great was her sphere of influence. William Hennessy, who was still a student, led the Conservatorium Chamber Orchestra in a splendid performance conducted by Robert Pikler, and with Pikler and Joyce Hutchinson, I sang the evocative Brahms opus 91 songs with viola.

In her critique in *The Australian*, Maria Prerauer said that "the exceptionally gifted William Hennessy was in the springtime of his career, Lauris Elms was in high summer of magnificence, and Robert Pikler in the mature and fruitful autumn of a long professional career." What a lovely tribute this concert was, to one of Australia's first great women administrators. But what a tragedy that Australian music was deprived of her energy at that time.

After receiving good press for my Amneris performances last January, the Australian Opera only offered me a few performances for the end of the season of *Aïda* planned for 1976, at a reduced fee. I felt I was justified in saying "No," and then chose to explain my reasons in a letter to *The Sydney Morning Herald*.

" ... I can only regret my infrequent opportunities to perform in opera, in view of the fact that I trained as an opera singer ... I wish to express my thanks to those members of the public who have voiced their disappointment at my infrequent opera appearances."

An intimation of mortality came with the death of my dear colleague and friend, Dorothy White. It was Dorothy who once said that I had become the singer I was because of my marriage to my wise and clever Graeme. I had become so used to her presence, her shrewd guidance in all musical matters and her diffident criticism when it was necessary to pull me into line. I was still selfishly young and self-interested. To contemplate working without 'Doh' was a frightening prospect. I had not seen her so regularly in recent months because I was singing in so many orchestral concerts, and travelling a good deal. I usually prepared all my early and baroque music with her and had learnt so much from her about baroque ornamentation. I did not take much notice when she said she had to have an operation in the previous January of 1975 and so could not teach Deb piano. We agreed that Deb's lessons would be resumed when Doh felt better. She managed to suggest that the operation was a minor matter. Beyond that I did not wish to invade her privacy, so I asked no more.

When she did ring some months later, I said that for the present Deb would not resume piano lessons, because at the age of twelve it was a real effort to get her to practise. Deb was always absorbed in something and now she had discovered the clarinet. The morning or evening battle to get her to do half an hour on the piano ceased. When she began to practise the clarinet, I saw that Deb was really absorbed. Dorothy said she would rather cut down on the number of pupils anyway, so it suited us both. But I realised now that I did not see Dorothy and her mother nearly so often, during that year. At last, in mid July, she rang to say that she would have another operation and I went up to see her. She always had dark shadows under her eyes and now they were starkly obvious. I knew suddenly that she was afraid, this woman whom I knew was so courageous. I did not know what to say. As a colleague, I had regarded her as being of my own generation. Now I suddenly knew that she was much older.

She went into the 'San' (Adventist Hospital), was operated on and never left the hospital. Visiting her, I was for the first time aware how life can hang on a knife-edge. When you are young and healthy, it is inconceivable, incomprehensible to imagine how you can suffer if your health is impaired.

Dorothy White left a considerable library of music, two harpsichords and a sum of money to establish a trust at Sydney University Music Department. This remarkable woman had spent much of her life training and teaching the young and quietly aiding those musicians who needed financial assistance to achieve their ambitions. A concert was held in the Great Hall in December to honour her memory.

In September of that year I went down to Hobart to sing my first and only performances of Bizet's *Carmen* in the historic Theatre Royal. Early in the year I had sung the *Habañera* in an outdoor concert in Melbourne at the Myer Music Bowl. An enthusiastic young man pushed his way into the dressing room at interval.

"You're the most wonderful voice to sing Carmen this century, in this country! The sound of your voice is perfect for this great role. I'll put on the opera for you in Hobart. We'll make the whole *nation* listen to a new opera company in the tiny state of Tasmania, built with the enthusiasm of the local people, and around your voice."

I was amused by his enthusiasm, but did not believe it would ever happen. It seemed too improbable that this young man could start yet another opera company, when so many were dying around him. Months later the offer came.

I was to stay with Michael Lanchbery, the young man, and his wife Greta in their home at Kingston Beach for the rehearsal and performance period, as they could not afford to pay hotel accommodation in Hobart. The opera would be sung in English and directed by Michael. Don José would be sung by John Main, who was an excellent tenor. Lyal Bevan would sing Escamillo and his wife, Mavis Brinckman, Micaela.

I went down to Tasmania in early September, having forgotten how very cold it can be. Kingston Beach was glorious, an easy twenty minutes drive from the theatre, sparkling water and empty sand stretching to the horizon. I understood why Greta loved it so, and enjoyed her strong quiet nature and her gentle company.

Michael was another matter. I discovered he was the nephew of John Lanchbery and that he found the theatre irresistible. Like many producers, he used sarcasm as a method to achieve his results and by the end of the first week of rehearsal

I was afraid that one or other of the principal men were ready to punch him on the nose. It seemed to me that he 'played favourites' with the cast and chorus, which is never helpful.

I was unhappy with the orchestra, the Tasmanian Symphony, under my old friend Vanco Cavdarski. It was soon obvious that the players hated working with Vanco as much as the singers disliked Michael, and were going to play as badly as they could manage without having a serious complaint made against them.

The exquisite little Theatre Royal is the oldest theatre in Australia. However, an opera like *Carmen* needs a stage area of some size and a fairly big chorus, and the charm and intimacy of the Royal was working against Bizet's rather ambitious demands. As time went on and performances approached, I was covered with bruises from John Main's enthusiastic manhandling and asked him to tone it down a bit. This made the action much tamer and when the local critic, 'Pleiades', said "Carmen's fire, venom is missing," I could only sadly agree. I knew I was not temperamentally suited for this opera. And yet I sang it so well. With a wonderful director and better orchestra, I might have been inspired to the achievements of my Amneris and Azucena.

In November I went across the Tasman to sing Amneris in a concert performance of *Aïda* for Robert Field-Dodgson. The conductor was again Vanco Cavdarski, who was in fine form, and the Christchurch Town Hall was sold out, to the delight of the Royal Christchurch Musical Society. It is strange to remember that all their concerts were unfunded and operated as commercial events without government assistance.

Then I went to Perth to sing for a week with Geoffrey Arnold and the West Australian Symphony Orchestra, to make the LP record for the ABC. We put down the entire record in four days, the first day being spent in rehearsing and checking the music for the enormous program of operatic arias I had chosen to sing. I sang all my 'war-horses' and managed to achieve a good result in two or three 'takes'. I decided that the recording of *Una voce poco fa* was not up to my wishes, and when we had to drop out one item, this should be the one to go.

The ABC re-issued this on a CD in 1995, without asking my permission or even notifying me of its intentions. I did not receive any additional money for this CD as I had signed the original contract in 1975, giving full rights to the ABC. It included *Una voce poco fa!*

As we often did at this time of the year, we drove down the Hume Highway, through the golden grass of the sheep country and over the Cullerin Range to Victoria, with its dryer heat and constantly changing temperatures.

On December 28th, we went to the ceremony to commemorate the settlement of Western Port and the declaration of formal possession of Victoria, on December 3rd, 1826 at Rhyll,

191

and at Settlement Point on December 12th, 1826. This very old part of Gippsland was a beloved part of all my family memories and it was wonderful that the small local community could rally support to celebrate this important event. At 5pm on a still hot summer's day, we gathered near the water's edge at Corinella on the edge of Western Port to hear Manning Clark and the Premier, Sir Richard Hamer, speak of the first Englishman to set foot on this quiet and forgotten shore. The Wonthaggi Citizens' Band played and the Wonthaggi Theatrical Group re-enacted the landing.

We looked across the water into the western sun, to the two islands, French and Phillip, listened to the words of the Thanksgiving Speech and I thought of the tall timber that had once clothed these bare golden hills which rose like domes behind us; all the great trees, destroyed to make small dairy farms on those bald hills. The dense rainforests of Gippsland rolling down to the seas of the wild Bass Strait became the bare hills of Kilcunda and Wonthaggi, home to the coal miners and their grim struggles. No mention was given to the shadowy Aboriginal inhabitants, who had disappeared into the vanishing trees.

On that hot afternoon, it seemed a lot of labour and heartbreak for such a short history of white settlement and endeavour, in this now quiet and dreaming landscape. I silently saluted my own settler ancestors, the Elms, the Halfords and the Bonwicks, whose courage and backbreaking work in this part of Gippsland seemed to have gone for nothing. The bush and forests are now beginning to reclaim the felled timber and the ravaged brown hills are returning to their green-grey gums.

19. The ABC's and Other Orchestras

I wonder if we do learn anything from history? Looking back to January 1977, I find that ABC funding was then, as it seems to have been ever since, a very live issue. The Fraser Government wanted to cut ABC funding and the orchestras were the prime target.

I took part in a splendid concert in the Sydney Town Hall. Sir Bernard Heinze, John Lanchbery and the past ABC Director of Music, John Hopkins (who had come from the Victorian College of the Arts), were all happy to work together to 'Keep Music Alive'. Having three conductors for one program was surely an unusual event for an SSO concert. Gladly donating my contribution, I sang the *Habañera* from *Carmen, Mon coeur s'ouvre a ta voix* from *Samson et Dalila,* and *O mio Fernando* from *La Favorite.*

An inquiry into the orchestras under the Fraser government had concluded: "Subsidising symphony orchestras is now a largely anachronistic and inappropriate activity for the ABC as the National Broadcasting Service. If the Government intends that such subsidies should be made, they should be properly administered through some other body, such as the Australia Council, which already subsidises the Elizabethan Trust and Western Australian Arts Orchestra to the extent of about $1.7 million a year, as well as giving ad hoc grants to amateur orchestras."

The Town Hall was filled with irate supporters of the ABC orchestras, who showed by their presence that they were grateful for the more than forty years of concert giving. From its very beginnings in 1932 the ABC had promoted live music performed by local players, and the many thousands of people around Australia who attended Symphony concerts showed that there was a real appreciation of the work of the various state music departments.

The ABC at that time was a real public service bureaucracy. There were some lazy and complacent people in it, who had started as office boys and held their jobs for many years, finally becoming departmental heads simply by seniority. But most of the people working in the music department were very dedicated and, over the years, had developed a great knowledge and expertise in orchestral management, program building and concert presentation. The ABC had become one of the largest concert managements in the world, bringing out international artists for extensive tours covering the whole vast continent from Perth to Hobart. But the paternalistic attitude to programming, emanating from Sydney, enraged the small states like South Australia and Tasmania who felt they should have some say in the choice of artists and music.

Many fine musicians in the SSO found the conditions governing their daily life intolerably restricting. For petty reasons players were often refused the opportunity to play as soloists and to tour, when there were other musicians available and, worst of all, the standard of pay for these people of great talent and many years of study was abysmally low.

I find, looking back, that the historian has a hard task to sift the truth from the myths. Some of my musician friends from the SSO tell me now that they were in total agreement with the Boyer report. However, I sang at this concert firmly believing that the aim of the concert was to demonstrate that there was enormous public support for the ABC's management of the Symphony Orchestras!

In this summer I repeated my Amneris in the Concert Hall production of Tom Lingwood's *Aïda*. Accustomed to receiving rapturous reviews, I was upset to find that all the critics thought I was less in command this season.

I was feeling less able to maintain the feeling of living inside the skin of the woman whom I was portraying. It was important to me to have the power of full concentration during the performance and I no longer had the sensation of sinking into and living another's life. Until now I had always felt, when singing opera, that I was singing as if there were no tomorrow, as if only the present mattered, and that I would live and sing forever. I think that I was turning a corner in my professional life. I had always believed that I should take risks with my voice, but sometimes now The Voice, that other 'me', began to say, "No." Although I did not know it then, my concert and recital work was growing in stature and this was where I would now develop. Perhaps I was beginning to feel that the days of my life were in their solstice. I was in my forty-sixth year.

I was always worried about my teeth. The slightest pain seemed to indicate a new cavity and I spent many hours in the dentist's chair, being drilled in every remaining tooth. Sometimes as I lay there it seemed as if the days were passing and I would never have the time to sing all the great works I still longed to learn. I looked up and out of the surgery window at the days with their blue skies, viewed aslant as I reclined in the chair of the gentle torturer in his white uniform.

In April I did a regional ABC tour with Marilyn Richardson. She asked the Adelaide accompanist, Noreen Stokes, to accompany us. This kind of touring was a feature of ABC concert promotion in the early years, but in 1977 there was a noticeable fall in ticket sales and eventually the recitals would be discontinued in country centres altogether. We sang a wonderful program of duets and solos in Wagga Wagga, Goulburn and Wollongong, and as always I loved singing with Marilyn. Temperamentally we set each other off on exciting paths of exploration, competing, yet complementing each other as we sang. We both found it rewarding to be able to bring live music to the people of rural Australia.

Another important event for me had been the establishment of the Hunter Symphony Orchestra back in 1975. I thought it was necessary to expand the number of orchestras in regional areas. I realised that if I had been obliged to live in the country I would be deprived of one of my own greatest pleasures, that of listening to live music. When Ulric Burstein had asked me to help by addressing the council and the Mayor, I was very happy to drive up to Newcastle several times to 'lobby' for funding. Now the orchestra had a grant and Ulric conducted the Verdi *Requiem* in the University of Newcastle Great Hall as a fund-raising concert. The other soloists were Pearl Berridge, Raymond Macdonald and John Brosnan.

Over the next few years the fortunes of the Hunter Orchestra went up and down, largely owing to Ulric's difficult personality. In spite of his vision, he was always prone to take offence and to give it, at the slightest opportunity. He was an adequate but not inspiring conductor, and as I came to know him better I suspected his real aim in establishing this orchestra was to provide himself with a group of musicians to conduct. I wished he would agree to allow a really first-rate conductor to take over the concerts after he had done the preparation with the 'band'. However this was never a possibility. Nevertheless, he had made a real attempt to change the face of the cultural life of the Hunter region, which owes him a considerable debt.

Eventually the prospect, for me, of performing with the Hunter Orchestra became truly agonising. The committee of management changed, after some bitter rows, and then I was no longer asked up to Newcastle to sing with Ulric. We lost touch. Later I was appalled to hear of his tragic early death. The Hunter Orchestra survived almost until the end of the century.

Later in this year I met the visiting pianist Jorge Bolet. He played a wonderful performance of the Rachmaninoff 3rd Piano Concerto, with Willem van Otterloo, when we shared an ABC concert. I fell in love with the playing of this musical giant, and Graeme and I took him and his manager-partner sailing on Pittwater one idyllic Sunday. He came to be one of my idols in the playing of the more showy romantic repertoire. He admitted on that day that the thing he most regretted in life was that he was always known as a performer of the later, wildly romantic works and he would have sometimes liked to play the great classics. Giant as he was, he was the most gentle and kind of companions.

These years of working with van Otterloo made me very aware of the lesser ability of the other conductors around at the time. He towered above them all. He was so sensitive, carrying the sound of Mahler on velvet wings and raging storms and raising the SSO to magnificent heights in their performances of the classics, which are the most difficult works to bring off because they demand such clarity and precision. He seemed remote and severe to me then, but I enjoyed a complete trust in his judgement. I knew every semi-quaver was locked into an integral plan in the shape of the whole, behind his domed forehead.

In September Bartók's wonderful opera *Bluebeard's Castle* shook me once more with its passion and strange, symbolic story. John Hopkins conducted a staged production by Robin Lovejoy in the National Gallery in Melbourne, for the Victorian State Opera. Lovejoy achieved magical effects, with lights shining through the ceiling of the Great Hall and down into the darkened room. My huge Bluebeard was Noel Mangin. This magnificent New Zealand bass had now been a colleague over a long period and his performance as the sadistic husband seemed perfectly right.

His was a strangely lonely personality, jovial and supremely and maddeningly egotistical on the surface, but I knew that underneath he was tortured with self-pity, loneliness and self-doubt. His voice was remarkable, with its power and sonorous weight, and listening to its sound rolling down the Gallery, it seemed to come from the heart of some far distant and unattainable country.

Poor Noel and Robert Bouffler and Ulric, all died so young! And Dorothy White and Jorge Bolet and van Otterloo. Strange to think that all of these talented people are now dead, taking their music and some of their unattained dreams with them.

I enjoyed a recital in the Opera House for the Lieder Society in early December with John Winther playing superbly for me, and in January I had a less rewarding experience when Stephen Hall, the director of the Sydney Festival, failed to advertise a concert of Australian contemporary music to be performed for the Fellowship of Australian Composers, under the umbrella of the Festival. I had asked Sharon Raschke, a fine Newcastle pianist, to play for me. I was still looking for a permanent partner after Dorothy's death. Sharon was a very good accompanist. We really enjoyed working together and perfecting the songs over many weeks.

We arrived in the Town Hall a little after 7pm on the night of the concert to check the piano's stage position, make sure the piano stool was in place and 'warm up the voice', as I always did before a concert. We found Stephen Hall in a great panic. There were no sales for the concert. Would we cancel the performance? The year before Stephen had asked me to do a Verdi *Requiem* and I had accepted the engagement. Later he called me to say the concert was off, as he had left it too late to book either a tenor or an orchestra!

I had refused other work in order to sing the Verdi *Requiem* in the Festival of 1976. I was not paid a cancellation fee and now, because he had not done his job in publicising this concert in 1977, Sharon and I risked losing money yet again for the work we had done and the time we had spent. I was furious. Sharon had some friends who were driving down from Newcastle to be there at eight o'clock. I said we were going to perform and I would sing for the twenty people who had come to hear the music. "The show must go on." So we presented Malcolm Williamson's *English Lyrics,* Margaret Sutherland's *Six Poems of Judith Wright* and Dorien Le Gallienne's *John Donne Sonnets,* to a very select audience who had, like the 'wise men' travelled from afar to hear the good news.

We *were* paid by the Festival!

This year was the two-hundredth anniversary of Schubert's birth. Musica Viva presented a series of Lieder concerts in his honour. I loved singing with John Winther and we began this tour in historic *Rippon Lea* in Melbourne. This property had been acquired by the National Trust and was a lovely venue for this kind of chamber music. We brought the program to Sydney, where we performed in the intimacy of the Queen Street Galleries. Alas, the acoustic in this large room was extremely resonant. Anne Schofield and G hung carpets around the walls to try to dampen the sound, so that we could hear ourselves in the lively echo. I tried standing in every place on the small dais-stage and at last said I would sing standing behind the piano. I fear the people who came to the concert thought this very peculiar, but it was the only place I could hear 'the voice' as I wished.

Schubert was becoming a passion of mine; the boy who wrote music describing such emotions as could not be expressed in words, and who enhanced the written words of the great poets of his time with the inexpressible depth of his music. I sang songs that were well known and found some, which filled me with longing and sadness, which were comparatively obscure. I loved constructing this program and sang it many times with different pianists over the years. It was Winther who suggested I sing the great *Ave Maria.* It was the one song in the whole program I was worried about memorising. I sang many, many recitals over my life, but this song was strophic and I was terrified of forgetting the verses, so I always held the words for it.

I was now searching for an accompanist who was a splendid pianist and who would have the kind of quiet sustaining strength of Geoffrey Parsons. I had enjoyed working with many other excellent Sydney pianists in concerts and David Andrews, the charming John Champ and Sharon Raschke from Newcastle were all great accompanists. I was also trying all avenues to find a good repetiteur who was not tied up with the opera company, as I always needed coaching in my concert and recital work. I found a friend in Kath Fowles, with whom I worked for a year or so, but Kath also died of cancer. An important person in my life at this time was John Winther. As a pianist and accompanist he ranked with Geoffrey Parsons but, to me, filled with doubt about his role in my troubles with the AO, he was not a 'friend' in the way I needed when travelling and singing.

Now I turned to Joyce Hutchinson. As well as accompanying my recitals, I began to use her as my repetiteur, going to her at least once weekly and sometimes more frequently. She was a truly wonderful teacher and coach. She was the regular pianist for the SSO concerts and loved her orchestral playing. Employed on a casual basis, she was terrified of being supplanted, as she had no 'tenure'. To me this situation seemed grossly unfair, as the long years of her work in this area had made her so competent and she knew all the orchestral repertoire so well. Of course, she was not always available for my rehearsals and recitals. I decided I needed another regular person who would fit me temperamentally and as a pianist, for the times when Joyce was busy with the orchestra.

A young man arrived from out of nowhere. A telephone enquiry put us in touch and David Miller arranged to come out to my home to meet me, play for me and rehearse with me. I was really 'auditioning' him, although he did not know this at the time. At ten thirty one morning he rang the door bell. I opened the door to see a shy young man, very tall and good looking, with a satchel in one hand and a baby in a cane carry-basket in the other. He smiled nervously and explained that he had to mind the baby, as his wife was working. At this time of my life I was at the top of my career and was accustomed to think of the hours I spent paying for and working with my coach as precious. I had a young daughter who had also needed to be 'minded' but I always tried to arrange for this to be done away from my work. I explained to David that I really needed to give my undivided attention to my music for the hour and a half I demanded. I had discovered that this was a good length for a coaching session for me; one hour was not enough, and two hours straight singing were too tiring vocally. I probably came across as a temperamental 'prima donna'. David explained that he had not been used to working with a professional singer. So, leaving the angelic baby sleeping in the dining room downstairs, we worked together and I knew that he was the answer to my needs. Serious and conscientious, he had a superb technique and a love and understanding of vocal music. I felt great warmth towards him and thus began my long and close working relationship.

Born in Victoria, David had graduated from Queensland University and travelled to England with his young wife Fran. He had worked as a music teacher in a Public School, trying to find his niche as a musician. In London he had spent five years studying with Paul Hamburger, specialising in vocal and instrumental repertoire, and this made him committed to playing as an accompanist. He was totally dedicated to this idea when he came back to Sydney as a young father of three. It must have been hard to establish himself in this field, which has always been and is still little rewarded or recognised. I am grateful that our paths crossed in his early career. At last I had found my favourite pianist and perhaps I was able to help him a little to become established as one of Australia's great musicians.

The year contained many treasured memories: singing the Mahler *Des Knaben Wunderhorn* with conductor Elyakum Shapirra and baritone Brian Hansford in Melbourne, and the greatest of all Mahler's vocal works, *Das Lied von der Erde,* with the tenor Anthony Roden and Charles Mackerras, who was growing in stature and reputation as a conductor, especially of vocal and operatic repertoire.

Towards the end of the year, my old friend Werner Baer asked me to sing at a concert in aid of the Ku-ring-gai Old People's Association.

This remarkable man had a profound effect on music in Australia. He had come as a refugee from Berlin at the beginning of the war. Having studied music there, he came to Sydney to find that his gifts as an organist, musicologist and pianist were often not realised, but with his feisty character and remarkable personality he elbowed his way into the narrow world of music in Sydney. I first met him when he was a music programmer for the ABC, but by the time I came to live in Sydney he was also busy teaching, coaching singers and playing as an organist and accompanist. As I grew to know him I learned to love the old fighter. His knowledge of German opera was encyclopaedic, with a special interest in Wagner, so that I learned Fricka with him before the aborted MSO *Valkyrie* performances. I also learned some Wolf songs with him, always finding new insights into these remarkable pieces. Whenever I wanted to know more about some facet of the German repertoire, I went to Werner. I miss him still.

Werner offered a fee of $200 for the old people's concert, saying that he would like me to sing two brackets of songs. At this time, through my agent Jenifer, I was commanding a fee of at least $1000 and often more for a similar 'spot' in a program. I explained that it would be unfair to sing for such a fee, when other entrepreneurs would have to pay so much more. "I'll sing for you for nothing as it's such a worthy cause," I said.

Ten years later I was amazed to hear from Philip Woods, the organiser of the Federated Music Clubs of NSW, of which Werner was also a committee member. "We have a sum of money which has been set aside in your name by Werner Baer and wish to offer a prize for a Contralto in the City of Sydney Eisteddfod." So the Lauris Elms Award for Contralto Voice was really a gift of Werner's. By putting the rejected $200 dollars into the investment funds of the Music Clubs and by their good management, the prize was and is still able to be offered on an annual basis, and I am very grateful to him for thinking of this award, which he named in my honour.

During the year I made a recording for the ABC, later issued by RCA. With John Hopkins conducting the SSO in the Sydney Town Hall, I recorded the Elgar *Sea Pictures* and, a few weeks later, the Chausson *Poème de l'amour et de la mer* with Robert Pikler. I am very proud of both these recordings.

This year was the end of secondary schooling for Deborah. She had decided she wanted to be a musician, to our dismay, as we knew how difficult the world of music making can be. That she was extremely musical we did not doubt, and we sympathised with her search to find a suitable teacher and tertiary institution - in that order. She was studying with John St George, who had been a pupil of Donald Westlake. Don had left the SSO to head the Wind Department in Canberra and start the Canberra Wind Soloists. G drove her down to Canberra for her audition and she heard that she was accepted, which was very pleasing to us all. But she had also applied for the Sydney Conservatorium and would have to wait until her HSC results were out to know if she would be accepted there. She had an agonising wait of three or four weeks before she could make her choice.

I decided to take her to Europe in January 1979, during this 'no-man's-land'. I knew this might be the last time she and I would have time to spend together and in fact it proved to be so. As my beautiful daughter stood at the threshold of her life, we might share a special experience, travelling together before she took a new direction. During the year, the visit of Robert Bouffler had resulted in an invitation to sing a Schubert recital with him in London and also in Heidelberg, Germany. Robert was hoping to have a career as an accompanist. He was able to entrepreneur several engagements, which gave me a goal in planning my trip with Deb.

G stayed at home, to cope with the admissions to International House for the coming year, and we left Sydney in its warm humidity for a wintry London. We stayed with G's cousin Margaret and her husband Terry, who was a Minister in the Labour Government. They lived in a town house on the Isle of Dogs, on the banks of the Thames in the East End of London. Sometimes when the tide was out a mud bank appeared below the window of the sitting room, but mostly water lapped at the wall at bottom of the house.

Robert Bouffler was a shy boy who had grown up in Bathurst before coming to study in Sydney, at the Conservatorium and at the University with Dorothy White. He wanted to be a composer as well as a pianist. He assured me that we had met when he was a student, but I had no memory of him then. Now he was truly memorable as he rode a powerful motorbike, dressed in leather and winkle-picker shoes and affected side-burns with long fine hair brushed across a premature balding spot, so that he resembled a dishevelled Lisztian Teddy boy.

He was a sensitive and gifted pianist and I enjoyed preparing the lunchtime recital he had organised for us in St John's, Smith Square. There was a splendidly large audience of mainly expatriate Australians at the concert and a glowing review in *The Financial Times*, which filled me with gratitude to Robert for arranging this concert.

We presented another program in the Wigmore Hall at which I sang Britten's *Charm of Lullabies*, Dorien Le Gallienne's *Four Divine Poems of John Donne*, Ravel's *Histoires naturelles*, Brahms' *Songs op 105* and some little Spanish songs by Obradors.

As always on a day of performance I think I was rather bad-tempered, needing to be very quiet and alone, not wanting to talk. Margaret, our hostess, was very understanding and Deb knew to keep well out of the way. We went into the hall early to have a little warm-up. I was surprised how small the auditorium was and how humble the backstage area seemed. After the years I had spent singing in other places and other times and countries, there was a feeling of returning to the Edwardian era. As I waited in the brown-timbered backstage rooms, I looked at the photos and portraits of the greatest singers of the twentieth century and of earlier times. My heart was filled with gratitude for the great singers and musicians who had given the world such pleasure.

"And now," I thought, "It is my moment to tread on this stage and sing in this historic place."

It was one of the few times when I was not so much nervous as excited. In the evening after the concert I was greeted by dozens of Australian and English friends from the past. In arranging this concert, Robert had been a splendid ambassador for the music of Australia.

Deb bought her first pair of professional clarinets whilst we were in London and she was longing to try them out. She was accepted by the Sydney Conservatorium and decided to stay at home rather than go to Canberra. She threw herself into her new life and began to live for her new friends and most of all, her music.

I came back to G and to my singing, taking part in Mark Elder's performance of *Das Rheingold* in concert with the SSO at the Opera House. This was my first Wagner role since Covent

Garden and I sang Erda, a perfect role for me. The very young Mark Elder conducted a great performance, which heralded the international career he would achieve. The Australian Opera, like the MSO earlier, spoke of putting on *The Ring,* and every five years one or other of the major Australian companies has toyed with plans to put on all the four operas. In 1998, Adelaide at last mounted the great cycle in Australia for the first time since 1913.

In June I achieved one of my own dreams when I sang a full recital of lied and art song to a packed Sydney Opera House Concert Hall, in the ABC Recital Series. The ABC asked me to choose my accompanist and I unhesitatingly selected David Miller. Twenty years later I am still amazed that the concert hall was full to hear a local singer, in song with piano. I walked out to begin the program with Britten's *A Charm of Lullabies,* to see every seat in the vast space occupied. I nearly wept with surprise. So often I had sung to tiny audiences of devoted fans and friends. This love of lied was an indulgence, to be fostered and nurtured because of the lovely marriage of poetry, piano and melody, but definitely not to be encouraged by serious entrepreneurs who could never hope to make enough money to recover their expenses. I felt as if I were flying that night as I sang the same program I had recently presented to a tiny audience in the Wigmore Hall. This time more than two thousand people heard me singing the songs I had chosen with such love and care. Best of all I was singing music of great beauty in my beloved Sydney Opera House. It was then that I knew that I was accepted at last as a local singer. My own career was recognised as a success, a big fish in a small pond, but an Australian fish, singing in the fishpond of Sydney Harbour! I believe I am the first local resident singer to have been honoured by the ABC to give a solo lieder recital in the Sydney Concert Hall. I am very proud of that.

David and I were on such a high that we wrote our names on the 'white board' in the soloist's spacious dressing room. David had played as superbly as only he could. We were so excited that when we saw a huge glow across the harbour, lighting the midnight sky with rosy flames and sparkles, we felt that our performances had lit the whole of the city with joy. Only later did we find that the 'celebratory bonfire' was a major and terrible tragedy. Luna Park had gone, taking the lives of seven people, on the same night as the greatest solo recital of my life.

A month later I was in Melbourne, where I sang in the first staged performance in Australia of Mozart's opera, *La clemenza di Tito,* for the MSO. Kenneth Hince's critique said, "Lauris Elms memorable and exciting." It was a memorable and exciting series of performances as I had Anthony Besch as my director and the sets designed by John Stoddart were really beautiful. Richard Divall did a splendid job conducting the orchestra which was led by my old friend, Mary Nemet. There was a first-rate cast. Margaret Haggart, recently returned from

202

Europe, sang Vitellia and Gerald English brought great experience to the role of Titus.

Before beginning the plotting of a scene, Anthony Besch marked out every person's position with chalk on the floor and the principal's feet were also placed on the stage by a mark. Then each person had to hold to that position absolutely and woe betide the slightest deviation. The lighting was absolutely wonderful and the rather static opera, especially the chorus scenes, made a picture which looked as if it were richly lit and composed by Rembrandt. As Sextus, I was dressed in a classical Greek tunic with draped cloak, and I gather the effect solved the problem for those people who found women in pants parts, a difficulty. The role of Sextus was the only Mozart opera role I have ever sung. He did not write for my heavy contralto and I found the other mezzo roles of this most wonderful of all composers beyond my range.

In this year, one of the moments I treasured was performing for Graeme Murphy. This slightly built star of Australian dance was involved in a ballet festival in October-November and I was thrilled to be not dancing, but singing, in the Australian Dance Festival season in the great work of Ravel, *Shéhérazade*. It was a work I loved dearly, although it was written for soprano. When I was called in to the stage rehearsal, I discovered with dismay that I was built several sizes larger in all directions than the tiny dancers who were grouped around me. Graeme placed me high upon a dais and I, looking like a giant, towered immobile over the little people with their lissom bodies. 1979 made me realise, not for the first time, that singers are generally built like tanks and dancers are like moving reeds, blown about by the rhythm of the music they dance to.

20. Obsession, Ambition

1980 began with a memorable performance in the Adelaide Festival. I was asked to sing Rossini's *Petite messe solonnelle* for the first time. This large choral work for four soloists and full chorus is 'small' only in that it uses no orchestra, but employs two pianos and a harmonium. For the singers, the earlier Rossini *Stabat mater* ranks with the Verdi *Requiem* in difficulty and drama. This late work stands apart as a more intimate expression of Rossini's faith, in his old age.

The performance was made remarkable for two reasons. I heard the lovely soprano voice of Rosamund Illing for the first time and my old friend Robert Allman was the baritone. Bob and I did not often have the chance to sing together during our long careers.

I flew to Adelaide, arriving on a breathlessly hot day, and was met by Colleen Beinl, the widow of the producer of my first *Trovatore*, Stephan Beinl. She had remained a dear friend through the years. She drove me to her flat in North Adelaide where I would stay for two nights. We had a most extraordinary sandwich for lunch which had a filling of banana, cheese and Lebanese cucumber! This sandwich has become a favourite when we have picnics and is known as 'Colleen's Sandwich'! Then she took me down to St Peter's Cathedral where we had a piano rehearsal.

There were two performances under conductor Myer Fredman, the second of which took place on a hot Sunday afternoon when I, and no doubt many in the audience, felt more like having a sleep. I knew it was going to be difficult to concentrate.

There was no artists' room in the Cathedral, so we assembled in our positions on the low platform well before the 3pm start. I was seated and I dreamily watched the Cathedral fill completely, noticing that people were standing even right at the back. Finally Myer appeared and raised his baton to begin the concert. As he did so, a shabbily dressed woman glided forward from the aisle and sat down on the edge of the low dais behind him, smiling rather sweetly to herself. There was very little room on the dais. Myer was standing squarely in the centre of it, conducting with his characteristic broad sweeps of the arm, quite unaware that about two feet behind him, his every gesture was being reproduced by this middle-aged woman. He was the only person in the whole cathedral who could not see her.

I was no longer feeling sleepy!

As the performance warmed into the opening choral *Kyrie,* the seated woman rose to her feet, still conducting, and continued while we four soloists wondered what would happen. It was most disconcerting to have two pairs of arms waving about in front of us, ever so slightly out of 'sync'. Thomas Edmonds rose to his feet to begin the first tenor solo of the mass and my heart stopped. How could he sing, with that strange double image waving in front of his eyes?

As Myer began conducting for the soloist, two people tip-toed down the aisle behind him and, gently laying a hand on each arm of the woman, walked her silently to the side door of the cathedral. There had been no interruption to the performance and I doubt that Myer even knew it happened.

On June 10th, Sir Bernard Heinze died. He had played an incredibly important part in the musical life of this country and in my own career. I owed him a great debt of gratitude. Scoffed at by many of my musical colleagues, he had performed and encouraged unjustly neglected works of all kinds, introduced many innovations into the narrow provincial world he returned to before the Second World War and helped found the ABC Symphony Orchestras. He was truly a 'prophet in his own country'. He had a vision for what our musical life could become.

Later in the year I sang *Six Songs of Walt Whitman* by Larry Sitsky, in Brisbane at the Ferry Road Studios, in a concert conducted by Vanco Cavdarski. I always enjoyed singing with Vanco, but Larry's songs were a difficult work to bring off. The composer wrote much of the work for the low, and best, part of my voice, but also filled the orchestral texture with thick sound which I knew would be impossible for my voice to cut through to reach the audience. I also knew that my voice was subtly changing. It felt different as I sang now. Very gradually, as I sang more and more mezzo roles, the deep rich low part of my voice was losing its power.

There was a physical reason for this. Years earlier, Joan Sutherland had said to me, "Be careful about having anything done to your teeth." Well, she was proven right. During the past two or three years my life had been a misery as I spent hours having fillings done at short notice, often on the day of a performance. My dentist said that the dentine coating of the teeth was wearing quickly and my teeth were being ground away making my 'bite' narrower, and that I was developing overclosure of the jaw. The final straw came when I ate a grapefruit for breakfast one morning in 1979 and my mouth suddenly filled with fiery pain. The acidic fruit had demolished the last protection on the surface of my teeth.

In despair, my own dentist sent me off to a specialist who crowned all my lower teeth, an incredibly long and expensive process. He decided to give me a denture on the upper, and by placing the denture on top of my existing stumpy back teeth, open the 'bite', thus increasing the length of the upper teeth and the jaw opening. Suddenly I looked years younger. A rumour went through the opera company that I had had a face-lift.

The effect of having my 'bite' altered rapidly and radically was disastrous for my voice. The small muscles controlling the relationship between the opening of the jaw, the root of the big tongue muscle which has such an important role in the production of the tone, and the muscles connecting down to the diaphragm, all combined over the next nine months to begin a real breakdown in my breath-control and ultimately in my vocal technique and power.

I was fortunately not singing major operatic roles at this time. But I was trying to fulfil a busy schedule of concerts and recitals.

I had no idea what was going on, so subtle was the change. At first I felt only the loss of breath-control and the power of my voice. But gradually the truth dawned that my new denture was the problem. By this time the damage was done. I, who had always sung with a firm and strong tone and technique given me by Modesti all those years ago, found that I had to learn to sing again with a new technique, because my poor tongue was now displaced and had no 'home'. Tired and longing for a place to rest, it rolled about in my mouth day and night and I found at last that I had to learn to force it to lie up on the roof of my palate as its 'home'.

The worst was at night as I lay down to sleep, to will my tongue to stay there away from its real and former resting place, behind the lower front teeth. I know that each person has a different anatomy and physiology, and what I describe may not be so for all people, but for me, whose world had been bound by the joy of singing, it was an agonising process of discovery. I knew my voice was still as healthy and beautiful as ever but that I could no longer make the sounds as I had previously. Then the worst thing of all happened. After singing for any length of time I felt as if I was suffering from a 'stitch' in the side of my ribs, as if I had been running for half an hour. My whole breathing apparatus was out of kilter. What was happening to me?

I got the dentist to reduce the height of the teeth he had built on the denture. I worried and fretted until my teeth and my singing became an obsession. After all, it was my whole life, and had always been so easy and comfortable for me. By working with books such as *Freeing the Natural Voice,* by Kristin Linklater, and having lessons in the Alexander Technique, I finally realised how drastic were the changes which had occurred to the small and invisible muscles and tendons in the throat, chest and rib-cage. There was no one who could advise me as I had no teacher, and I think that only a dental expert who sang could have helped. My own dentist was a dear man but had no idea what I was talking about.

It was difficult to convey the feeling to anyone who has not experienced the weird sensation of the tongue being displaced and having no resting-place in which to lie. I began to suffer torments of doubt about my singing so that each performance had me anxious. I would ask Graeme how I sounded after each performance. He who knew my voice so well for so long was often brutally frank but I knew I could trust his opinion.

Deb began offering me advice about how to sing. She had become a superb clarinettist. We did several recitals together, most memorably when she played the clarinet obbligato in Mozart's *Parto, Parto* from *La clemenza di Tito* in a wonderful recital given by Rita Hunter in the Sydney Town Hall, in which I appeared as Rita's associate artist. Alas, I could not follow the good advice of my daughter, because of the changes to my vocal instrument. I was in despair and from now on I was never to sing with the pleasure, freedom and ease of my former years. My dentist said it was my age and he was probably right, in part. It was now very difficult to retrain the voice. As it grows older there are major changes in quality, so it was probably a combination of factors, but I knew that my voice was still there inside, as good as ever. So I began my own program of learning to sing again. I did not want to tell anyone else of my problems. I was still continuing my busy concert life and apart from Deb and G, few knew of my mental anguish and physical problems when I was singing.

In the following year I sang in two splendid concerts of Wagner's *Die Walküre* and *Götterdämmerung,* in which I heard the superb voice of Rita Hunter ringing out as Brünnhilde. What a tragedy that Australia did not hear her magnificent voice more often! The concerts were in the Melbourne Town Hall, conducted by Sir Charles Mackerras. Both the Australian Opera and the Victorian State Opera hoped to gradually mount *The Ring* on the operatic stage. These big Wagner concerts were repeated in the Sydney Opera House in October that year.

In September I sang in a concert performance of Handel's *Semele,* with soprano Joan Carden making a great impact in the title role. Peter Seymour was the conductor of this memorable night in the Concert Hall.

In the 1982 Australia Day Honours, I was awarded the AM for

services to music. This Australian honour meant a great deal to me. Over the years I had gradually been shifting in my political loyalties. From being apolitical as a performer, I was becoming a committed republican. To the honour of the OBE which I had received when I was forty, I was now being honoured ten years later for a different career, achieved within my own country. I thought seriously about the change in my ideals over the years and whether I should perhaps return the earlier honour. I had sung on four occasions before the Queen, three times when she was a very young woman. I was then also young and like most of my generation, loved her for her personal integrity and courage. Now in my own middle years, I sang for music and for my own country. And as a woman, at that time when very few women were so honoured, I felt a statement was being made about the work a woman singer could achieve in her own land. I was grateful that I had two different honours, received at different times in my career and in different stages of my own life.

Perhaps I have not explained that usually I was engaged to perform a year, and sometimes two, ahead. My diary at this time covered a two or three year period. Of course, some engagements came immediately and unexpectedly out of the blue, like the great Verdi *Requiem* I sang with Mackerras in London, but I generally had a long time to prepare and, if necessary, learn a work, or, as in this case, re-learn it.

I was now deeply worried about my voice, but Graeme said it sounded fine; that it only felt different to me at this stage. But during the past few years I had become prone to bilious attacks and headaches if I ate food which was very rich or not well prepared. I blamed the sumptuous food of the dear departed Agathe in my two years in Paris for this growing problem, remembering the groaning table and wonderful, rich and enormous repasts of those days. Now the attacks suddenly increased in ferocity and frequency. I was suffering crippling abdominal pain once or twice a month and my GP said I had gallstones and must have an operation immediately.

In August that year I once more faced the challenge of Gluck's *Orfeo,* singing it in French with the Philharmonia and under the baton of Peter Seymour. I loved this work so much and so much wanted to sing it that I did not tell Peter Seymour and David Garret how ill I was. I think David Miller knew how much pain I suffered that week, as I sang through the role in a piano rehearsal with him at the keyboard one afternoon in a rehearsal room at the Opera House. The room was so small that David Garret, pencil and score in his hand, sat on the floor curled up with his back against the wall beside the piano, making notes for Peter who stood conducting, following my singing with David

Miller's accompaniment. At the end of the 'sing-through' I felt so ill I just wanted to join David Garret on the floor, curled up in a foetal ball. But I went on to rehearse with the Sydney Philharmonia Motet Choir and the Australian Youth Orchestra, of which Peter was conductor. He was also Chorus Master of the Australian Opera at the time. Rhonda Bruce sang Euridice and Romola Tyrrell was Amour.

On the night of the concert, the Opera House Concert Hall was packed. The performance washed past me with the wonderful score of Gluck carrying me over waves of pain into a place above ordinary experience.

"Elms unlocks the gates of heaven and hell," said one of the critics the next day and it was true for me. I had no recollection of how well I sang, only a deep gratitude that I got through the concert.

"It is one of the great mezzo roles, and Elms was sheer bliss to listen to, as the velvety torrents of beautiful sound poured out in response to its every subtlety." (David Gyger)

"Lauris combines noble dignity with warmest human feelings; she is unfailingly guided by the right instincts, and her intellectual penetration will always remain in evidence." (Hans Forst)

I was on autopilot. It must indeed have been true that my instincts guided me. The next day I entered hospital and had my gallstone removed. I also had the varicose veins in my left leg done at the same time. Alas, the surgeon also took out my appendix and made the most enormous incision, cutting across the muscle of the diaphragm. I was horrified to see the size of the scar and worried about how soon I would manage to get back to singing. I had allowed time to sit around resting with my leg up as much as possible. What I did not know was how quickly my 'muscle tone' would come back, after a prolonged break from singing. I felt that at my age I would never get my breathing back, as I tried to fill my lungs in the old way. I began to do some physical exercises with the help of a physiotherapist who had come out from Scotland with the '56 Olympic Games team, and had remained in Australia. He developed a program which suited me well. I was trying desperately to get some kind of system to aid my recovery. Singers in general do not take much exercise and are generally resistant to hard physical activity.

And at last, after a seven-year wait, I was invited back to sing and perform for the Australian Opera. What a joy! I had served out my sentence of banishment, and Patrick Veitch, the new manager, welcomed me back with a warm note. Poor man! He little knew what a viper he was harbouring in his bosom when he wrote:
"Dear Lauris,
I am enormously pleased that your return to the company

is in one of my favourite roles in opera and that 1983 will be a banner year for us because of your major commitments to the season. All my best wishes are with you tonight. P.V."

So in 1982 I sang my first Mistress Quickly in Verdi's *Falstaff*.

As a young singer in 1958, when I was in Israel, I had asked Rafael Kubelik what roles would suit my then very deep voice. One of the roles he had mentioned was this one. It was an opera of which I knew nothing, never having seen it nor heard it. Now Stuart Challender, the young, handsome and charismatic Australian conductor with the AO, asked me to sing this role. I was also to sing La Principessa in Puccini's *Suor Angelica* that season. I was back in opera again!

As I began work on *Falstaff*, I realised what a true masterpiece this work is. The last of Verdi's operas, it has the musical difficulty of a great symphonic work. The intricate ensemble and dialogues between the voices are unlike any other Verdi opera, in that the voice parts are part of the whole orchestral texture, quite unlike the usually tuneful arias, with their clear melodic outlines accompanied by the orchestra, in the earlier works. As I listened to it on the LP recording I bought, I felt Verdi was creating the music that Puccini, with its separated but integrated melodic line, would soon write in the next generation of opera composers. The colouring of the symphonic texture was so subtle, expressing the bawdy fun and tender sweetness, the drunkenness and the wisdom of the old scoundrel Falstaff

Then there was the fun of putting the production together. There is so much going on during the scenes where the four merry wives trick the old soldier that often we were falling over each other giggling, as we pushed the huge basket around and folded washing and tried to keep singing together musically in time. It was the most fun of any opera I ever sang. But it was so low in the voice.

At the time, before the building of the car park beneath the Opera House, the singers were allowed to park their cars in the area below the Botanic Gardens. One day, as we walked back together around the curve of the fence outside the Gardens to collect our cars, Stuart Challender said to me that he had heard one of the greatest German contraltos say that singing Quickly had wrecked her voice, because it was so low. To get the necessary power to cut through the orchestra in the low middle register, it was often necessary to sing in 'chest', the dangerous low register of the voice. I looked at Stuart with horror, as I had indeed felt the temptation to sing on this big 'chest voice' in rehearsal. I knew I must only use the chest voice for performances, or I would soon develop a big 'break' in my voice. I was also upset that he had told me this story. I have always been superstitiously suggestive and it was bad psychology at that moment to put doubts in my already insecure mind about my technique. He did not know of my vocal troubles or the problem caused by my teeth, so could not know how worried I was about my singing.

This role was the most challenging of my career. I loved the fun and games of the production but was very disappointed with the appearance of the set, which was made to look like a two-dimensional cardboard cutout. But singing the mad little aria to Falstaff (Ron Maconaghie) about the midnight hour was great fun, and I loved trying to scare him and the audience into believing in the magic of midnight in Shakespeare's *Merry Wives*. I am not a comic actress like my great colleague Heather Begg, but I loved the challenge of this role.

At the end of 1982 Deborah graduated with high distinction from the Conservatorium.

Our beautiful daughter was launched into her chosen career as a clarinet player of exceptional ability and we were both so proud of this twenty-two-year-old, who had become an adult without our noticing. She had removed herself from the threesome we had been to become her own person.

In the early part of this year, she moved into a little flat above a shop in Roseville and began to teach at Ravenswood School. One morning in the early part of that year, she rang to say she would be coming in to see us. Graeme was at home in the worst stage of a severe bout of 'flu, suffering high temperatures and feeling terrible.

"Don't come today," I said, "G is really ill."

"I must come," said Deb, "I'm bringing my friend Bruce to see you." And she hung up.

G got into a dressing gown and, complaining, I set the table for lunch.

When Bruce arrived, he was *wearing a tie* ... G and I looked at each other!

They were married in May.

A week before her wedding Deb won the Instrumental Section of the ABC Concerto and Vocal Competition. She chose to play a showy and technically fiendish Concerto by Jean Françaix. Playing runs at dazzling speed, she had worked for hours to achieve the facility and technique she displayed on that night. She never confessed the terrible price she was paying or the pain she endured in her hands and arms, until she had won at the final orchestral concert which took place in Perth. She was diagnosed as having Repetitive Strain Injury. This was a cruel blow, as she had been selected to represent Australia in a major overseas competition in Munich. She decided to travel to Europe with her new husband, Bruce Nelson, and making the trip a honeymoon, attend the Congress as an observer. They travelled extensively, finding out about treatment for her RSI in Budapest, Hungary, where a doctor attached to the Liszt Academy was very helpful. She was beginning the long five-year journey it took her to complete recovery. G and I could only stand on the sidelines and watch as she struggled with her ambition and with her obstinate desire to play, aided by her patience. I salute my brave and beautiful daughter and her devoted husband.

In 1983 I sang my largest number of operatic roles in Australia since returning from Covent Garden all those years before.

Handel's *Alcina* began the year, with the beautiful sets of John Pascoe and the production of Sir Robert Helpmann, with Dame Joan Sutherland in the title role. I had been asked by Richard Bonynge to look at *Alcina* in 1979, and had assumed I would be singing Ruggiero. Imagine my surprise to find Margreta was to sing the leading male and I was to sing Bradamante, the female who dresses as a boy for a little time. It was a real challenge and I worked very hard to get the low part of my voice 'running', to achieve the very low and difficult coloratura this role demands. I was rewarded, as it was just the most perfect vocal exercise I could have had at this time. I was proud of my performance in this ungrateful role in what the critics saw as a dull opera. I believe these performances were magnificent examples of this type of baroque singing and both the opera and its production were triumphs of the AO. Lacking in drama, it was probably at once too esoteric and too stylistic for the local critics. 'Panned' for being boring, I imagine that the splendid singing was probably very close to a performance in Handel's day.

I began to rehearse *Trovatore* in a new production, with Dame Joan Sutherland as Leonora. Most memorable were the sets by Sir Sidney Nolan, the production by Elijah Moshinsky and the wonderful costumes by Luciana Arrighi. Set in 19th century Italy, the direction was aimed at reinforcing the role Verdi played as a patriot and as a hero of the revolutionary 'Risorgimento Movement'. The soldiers were dressed in the uniforms of the Hapsburg army. Azucena and Leonora were dressed in what we, in Australia, would call 'Victorian dress'. Most interesting of all, in some scenes the backcloth was a painting by Nolan representing two faces in profile, like the Janus of Roman legend. The story of two brothers who hate each other is as old as human history, appearing in the Bible in the story of Cain and Abel and in Greek mythology. Verdi himself wrote at least two other operas based on this idea (*I Masnadieri* and *La Forza del Destino).*

I was called to my first rehearsal in the main rehearsal room at the Opera House to meet Elijah Moshinsky. He was seriously ill at the time, which made him tire easily, and he looked deathly pale. On that first morning I was surprised at the lack of any discussion about the direction the production would take. I was introduced to the tenor, who was a tall handsome Spaniard named Francisco Ortiz, and we plunged straight into the rehearsal of our big scene together. As the poor man spoke no English, we found conversation difficult and Ortiz was very ill at ease and miserable. I doubt that he had ever worked with a director like Elijah, who gave very subtle indications of his ideas.

A huge chair was dragged into the centre of the rehearsal room in the Opera House, which has an unpleasantly boomy acoustic making it difficult to hear oneself when singing. I was told to sit in the chair and begin singing "Stride la vampa." The morning wore on and I longed to rise from the chair and begin to move around, but every time I tried to lever myself out, Elijah, smiling, indicated with his hand that I was to stay seated.

The poor tenor was obviously unable to sing. He was thrown into rehearsal the day after he had arrived in Australia and, like many European singers, had no idea of the effects jet lag would have on his voice. Whether he did not know the role and thought he could learn it in the three weeks before we opened, or whether he was ill (he certainly seemed to have a cold) I don't know. Anyway, he persisted in singing out of tune and driving the cast and the staff in the Opera Company wild. So I came home that evening to my husband in despair and anger. Almost in tears, I told him about my day.

"I can't just sit and sing that great aria and the whole scene seated. I'm not used to singing sitting down!"

My wise husband laughed and said, "It's going to be just wonderful for you. The director is making you take centre stage and you'll be the focus of the whole opera!"

He was right. Elijah followed Verdi's original concept of having this opera centred on the old gypsy. It is unusual for the contralto/mezzo to have the main role. It had never occurred to me that anyone would see the opera in this way. Elijah made the gypsy into an obsessed woman. He wanted me to imagine her with an agonised and aching heart and a terribly aching head, and made me see the vision of the fire in which the child burnt.

Azucena never appears nor sings with Leonora, except at the end of the opera when she sings the great trio in her sleep. I did not see any of the rehearsals of the scenes with Dame Joan, but I think she was very unhappy with Elijah's direction. She never seemed to enjoy the season and was certainly unhappy about the tenor. In the last four days before the opening, a new tenor appeared in the rehearsals and for the first time I heard the wonderful voice of Kenneth Collins, who had flown out from London to replace Ortiz. Scheduled to sing later in the season, Ken sang like an angel and like the true professional he is, stepped in at the last moment to do the opening without any problems.

For those of you who have only seen this production on TV or video, I must tell you that this is only a poor shadow of the original performance, as it was so dark, that on the small screen it was difficult to see the full scale of the marvellous Nolan sets with their two faces of the brothers. The sound on the video was not always faithful to the voices or to the orchestra. Manrico's brother was, of course, the wonderful expatriate baritone Jonathan Summers, and the splendidly noble voice of Donald Shanks rolled out as the bass, Ferrando.

During this *Trovatore* period we continued to sail regularly on Pittwater. I had learned that when I had to sing, breathing in the cold winter air was a disaster. If I had a Monday performance I now avoided going sailing on winter Sundays, but I loved it so much that I would still go out if I only had rehearsals on the following day. I knitted myself a woolly Balaclava which covered my mouth and throat. On the cold winter days, rugged up in a thick sailing jacket, all I revealed to the breezes was a slit opening for my eyes.

One afternoon I was standing alone at the tiller looking down the sparkling bay towards Lion Island, heavily disguised as a bank-robber. Graeme was down below when suddenly a small motorboat came fussing alongside and a voice I knew well shouted over the noise of the motor, "Hi, Lauris! Good to see you out on this splendid winter's day." It appeared that Don Shanks liked to go out fishing on Pittwater in his run-about. Don said at rehearsal one morning that he would keep an eye out for us in our boat on the water, but how he managed to recognise me when he knew neither the colour nor the name of our boat remained a mystery. "How did you know it was me?" I asked.

Don laughed. "No-one but a singer would ever wear the gear you had on," he said with a grin.

As Azucena, I had a triumph. People who had not seen me sing in opera for seven years were amazed that I could still 'deliver the goods' in this way. I was amazed at the success of my performance and secretly thought a lot of it had to do with Elijah keeping me seated, instead of the usual rushing about of most Azucenas. It is wonderful to have a fine director in whom one can trust. It is not enough to sing a role splendidly. The director needs to know the dramatic strengths and weaknesses of his cast and build around the different personalities he has available, if he has the time and if the cast is amenable to his ideas.

The next opera in this wonderful year of work was Rossini's *Semiramide*. As soon as *Trov* was 'on', we began rehearsals for this big Rossini opera seria. It was originally advertised as a semi-staged production, but in the event was staged very effectively by Moffatt Oxenbould, using sets and costumes from older productions in store within the company.

One morning, as we came into the Green Room to rehearse after a *Trovatore* performance the night before, Dame Joan and I agreed despairingly that we could not have found two less compatible works to perform 'back to back'. With hindsight

I think we were wrong! Nothing Rossini wrote ever caused harm and the wonderful vocalising of Arsace was a perfect antidote for me to the dramatic singing I had done in Azucena.

"Feast of great singing in Rossini opera," was how one critic headed his review.

This production brought Dame Joan and me together again as a team in the opera which had signalled my operatic career's beginning in Australia. Again Richard Bonynge had the baton and this opera was directed as a 'Stand and Deliver' production from the last century. And maybe that was the very best way to present it.

In my heart of hearts I knew that the vocal beauty of Joan's voice was no longer what it had been in the wonderful Sutherland-Williamson season and certainly my own voice did not take wings inside me and *fly* as it had in those earlier days. Twenty years had passed and gone.

There is a legend that when you sing, for every high note which is sent out into the air, those notes come off the total of your measured span and are debited at the end of your life.

The year went on, with an opera conducted by Cillario. He has always been a truly great conductor of Verdi and the Italian repertoire and I was a firm admirer of his ability. But this time he was to conduct Wagner's *Walküre!* Wagner was not a great admirer of Verdi and vice versa. There was a world of difference in those contemporary composers. Bruce Martin was a wonderful Wotan. Rita Hunter's radiant voice rolled through the Opera Theatre, unfortunately unsupported by the violins in the orchestra which sounded as if they were mosquitoes humming along under the clarion ride of the horns. The voices in the Valkyrie riders were amplified around the back of the tiny auditorium, as if they were calling across from a hamburger stall. It was terrible.

I was singing Fricka. It says in the score that she arrives on stage in a chariot drawn by a golden ram. So I did. The ram looked exactly like the symbol for Golden Fleece at a petrol station. The audience fell about laughing. I think standards of theatrical production have changed in the hundred years since Wagner wrote that direction.

The performance was splendid as far as the singing was concerned, but the orchestral sound was so appalling that the opera company began work on enlarging and rebuilding the pit which has now achieved an acceptable sound.

The Melbourne Concert Hall was also being criticised for its acoustics. The MSO's wonderful resident conductor, Hiroyuki Iwaki, was trying to improve the quality of the orchestral sound. I remember that from the time the hall was first built, I always felt when I was singing there that I was desperately striving to cut through the orchestra. It seemed as if I was singing into the warm soft wrapping of Yarra mud which actually surrounded the outside walls of the building. If only the acoustic advice of Denis Vaughan had been followed when he first offered it, a lot of trouble and expense would have been avoided!

My friend Geoffrey Arnold died in August. He had been chorus master of the AO for nearly a decade and conducted a number of operas. A wonderful coach with a great sense of style, he would be sorely missed as the chorus tried to find its voice over the next few years. At my request he had conducted my ABC LP record with the West Australian Symphony Orchestra and I was grateful that this marvellous recording was a kind of memorial from me to him.

21. Touring in China and Australia

From time to time my career would be placed 'on hold', as months would pass when no future engagements seemed to be forthcoming. At these times I would feel depressed and abandoned. So when the Department of Foreign Affairs offered a tour to China, I felt honoured and excited.

My 1984 recital with David Miller at International House gave us a chance to try out a concert program we would give in China in early April, in Shanghai and Beijing. I wanted to show as many facets as I could of operatic and concert repertoire to the singers of these cities.

On arrival in Beijing we were met by two charming ladies who were our 'minders' for the next week or so. They spoke excellent English and took us to our hotel where they immediately ordered in advance breakfast, lunch and dinner for us for the five days we were to stay in the city. Beijing, with its enormous population, was then dominated by the walled Forbidden City, which rose above the rest of the buildings. Most of the dwellings in the city at that time were single storey compounds, with occasionally a two or three storey building standing above the surrounding red-tiled roofs. The entire vast population seemed to be out on pushbikes, riding home through the twilight to their evening meals. It was the end of winter in this far northern city and there was a shortage of food. Whenever we went out in the daytime there were long queues of people waiting to buy cabbages. Muffled against the cold, many of them covered their mouths against the bitter wind and I did the same, making sure that I did not speak when I was outside. I wanted to sing well on this tour.

The hotel in which we were billeted was at some distance from the centre and especially built to accommodate people from 'the Ethnic Minorities regions'. We were amused to think we performers were put into this hotel. It seemed to me appropriate to accord us the low social status which our Victorian grandparents accorded opera singers, actors and other undesirable entertainers. From our rooms we overlooked the humble compounds, rectangular stone-walled communities where several families lived side by side, sharing outside toilets at the end of the block of houses which were bounded on all four sides by high walls abutting the narrow streets.

On the third floor of our hotel we each had a small suite, with a tiny sitting room in which stood a piano, where we were obviously expected to rehearse. I was touched at this thoughtful arrangement, but we had such a busy schedule that I don't think either David or I ever had time to rehearse separately in our rooms.

The morning after our arrival, I conducted a master class at the Conservatorium, beginning at 8.30. The air was so cold that I could not imagine how the poor young singers were able to sing so early. I have always thought it unwise to start rehearsing before 10am, when the vocal chords can begin to be 'warmed' by the body's movement and the action of the tiny muscles in the throat, when speaking. The drab fog outside drifted into the studio through the open windows and as it lifted, the day seemed to get colder. There was a fine dust everywhere, blown from the Gobi Desert on a breeze which was present for the whole time we stayed in Beijing. I heard some splendid voices that morning. Trained by Chinese teachers in the Western operatic tradition, it seemed to me that the young singers had little future in this land of great poverty and hardship, in a tradition which was totally alien. On television we saw Western-style talent shows, and here there were opportunities for these young singers to sing their operatic arias in Italian and German and perhaps win a prize, but the thought of their career paths filled me with despair. Few Western opera companies would employ these young Asians, unless they were phenomenal. I gave them my comments about their songs and voices and thought how brave and devoted their teachers were, these men and woman who had all studied in the West and survived the Cultural Revolution at tremendous cost.

The next day Australian Ambassador, Hugh Dunn, and his wife Margaret, gave a party for us at which David and I performed. I sang some of my favourite songs in their drawing room, for the expatriate Europeans in Beijing. On the following morning I went to the shabby Conservatoire studio to see a performance by the students of an opera written by a local composer in Western style. It was a tale of wronged love set against a background of Communist ideology. The music was terrible. The story resembled *Cavalleria Rusticana* with an overlay of starvation, and hunger was an ever-present image in the form of a large cooking pot in the centre of the room. Again the singing was good with some fine young sopranos and a truly memorable mezzo.

We went on a tour of the Royal Palace (the Forbidden City) in the afternoon. Our little lady guides were amused to see us struggle with chopsticks and showed us that it is possible to pick up and eat a whole unpeeled apple, with the greatest delicacy.

"Is it delicious?" they asked with a smile. I felt like a

Western barbarian as I struggled to eat the apple.

On the morning of the recital, we four Westerners were driven by car through the bicycles to the shabby concert hall. I always checked the position of the piano, the stool and the acoustics, having learned early in my career to leave nothing to chance. With our guides, we arrived to find a battered grand piano standing in the centre of the stage. The hall could have been any country Town Hall of the fifties in Australia, uncompromisingly functional, ugly and with a hard acoustic. But there was something strangely different about the piano, I thought. As David and I stood looking at it, a man came on to the stage, clutching what looked like a small harp. Bowing to us first, he proceeded to place a chock of wood on the floor under the centre of the piano and, using this as a prop, placed the pedal mechanism upon this and attached the lyre of the piano to the underside of the piano case. It was explained that the piano was so precious, being the only one in Beijing after the Cultural Revolution, that this was the way the instrument was preserved from damage. By disconnecting the lyre from the piano, no one could play it.

David was apprehensive, but the piano, while not being good, coped with the great demands he placed on it that day. The evening came and we were warned to allow one hour to get to the concert. Our car and driver arrived and we sat in the densest traffic of bicycles I have ever seen, crawling along in the dark at snail's pace to cover the one kilometre distance to the hall. I have never seen such crowds and the three-thousand-seat hall was packed to capacity.

Looking back, I think my program was too highbrow. I had thought I should show a cross-section of vocal music from the time of Handel to Wagner but, as in Korea ten years before, the audience only wanted to hear popular songs and arias. The most popular items were the arias such as *Mon coeur s'ouvre a ta voix,* the *Habañera* from *Carmen* and *Danny Boy.* I ended up singing all my 'pot-boilers' to a huge ovation.

The next day we flew to Shanghai. The two cities were as different as London is from Rome. The air was warm and moist, the banks of the Whangpoo River were lined with warehouses and the buildings were not unlike those you would see in great European shipping centres. Indeed, from the river, this city could have been any Mediterranean city in Europe.

The area where our hotel was located was comfortably European and there seemed to be no shortage of food. We were three hours flight to the south from Beijing and the warmer climate no doubt made the growing of crops and general living conditions easier. The Conservatorium was a very much more pleasant building for the students than the stark conditions in Beijing.

The Director, Xu Ping, was an attractive woman who had

been studying singing in Paris at the outbreak of the war, so had remained in France until the end of the Second World War. She found on her return that conditions were harsh. Many of the people we met were understandably unwilling to discuss their years during the Cultural Revolution. She said, with a rueful smile, "I dug potatoes for ten years in a remote village in the West of China." This sophisticated woman showed us no sign of bitterness at the life she had been forced to lead and wanted only to talk about music. David and I gave joint master classes, he assessing the pianist-accompanists and I the singers. We found there were some good performers here, as in Beijing, and again I wondered how our visit could possibly help them, in a culture so different from our own.

At the end of our visit to each city we left behind all the photocopied music I had brought. I always travelled with second copies of each song I sang, in case of loss, but also so that I could study the music while on tour. The greatest need these teachers and students had was for printed music. Much of it was in hand-copied manuscript, in which there are always mistakes. I also remember how paper was treasured. Every piece of paper had writing on both sides, and every inch would be covered before being used as wrapping paper as the last resort. It reminded me of the way we saved everything during the war: bottle-tops, pieces of string, paper bags and bottles were never thrown away, but carefully recycled.

Both China and Korea have changed since I was there! The West has dragged them into the new century and the social fabric of both countries must be also very different. We all have to make some steps toward understanding other cultures and try not to make judgements that our ways are always for the best. I am grateful that I saw these countries at the time I did and can appreciate the tremendous step they have made in trying to reach a higher living standard. For China in particular, it will be a long journey to democracy. Back in Sydney it seemed the buildings were so far-flung and spread out along the empty streets, after China's poverty and crowded thoroughfares.

In June I sang another Wagner role for the first time, in a concert performance of *Siegfried*. In Israel in 1958, Rafael Kubelik had written in the vocal score of Beethoven's 9th that one of the roles I would one day sing in opera was Erda. Nearly 30 years later I now sang this short but important role in Melbourne, with Charles Mackerras conducting Rita Hunter and Alberto Remedios, in a concert version. Alberto gave a memorable performance, not so much for its vocal prowess, but rather for his histrionic ability. It was announced that he was suffering from a throat complaint. His voice sounded very dry as he sang in the first Act, but at the start of the second Act he came on with a jug of water and a glass and before every entry, it seemed, he began to drink and then, still holding his glass, gesture with it until the stage around his chair was wet with the splashed water he was flinging about. It was dangerous to be seated near him as the tidal waves rose in the dark forest of Wagner's legend. I remembered the young, ardent Lensky of Alberto, playing lover to my youthful Olga in the *Onegin* of the '65 Sutherland season, and decided a lot of water had flown (or been thrown) under the bridge!

It is horrid to have to sing when you are ill and the decision about whether to perform or not is always difficult, but drinking water on stage is never going to resolve laryngitis. There was no other Siegfried in the country so the concert would have been cancelled if Remedios had not appeared.

With Charles Mackerras to guide me, I now stepped into the golden sandals of Dido in Carthage. Troy was a long way from the city of Sydney in the 20th century, but perhaps not so far from Beijing or Shanghai in time. I had loved *The Trojans* music since the days of my debut at Covent Garden, when I heard and sang the music of Berlioz for the first time. Now at last I was ready to sing the greatest role of my career, even if the opera was not to be staged but to be performed in concert.

My Aeneas was the English tenor Philip Langridge, whom I did not know and had only heard on record. When we began to rehearse, I agreed with *The Sydney Morning Herald* critic, Fred Blanks, who said on the night of the concert that "Philip Langridge sang with luminous ardour." It was a thrill to have such a colleague, and to know that he would leave for a distant country at the end of each performance made this Dido weep each night. It was the first time I ever did allow real tears to come to my eyes in my whole career, as I sang my "Adieu." The cycle is in two parts: *The Taking of Troy* and *The Trojans at Carthage,* which were presented on subsequent nights. The rest of the cast comprised the fine Anna of Elizabeth Campbell, and the wonderful singers Margreta Elkins as Cassandra in Part One, Geoffrey Chard, Grant Dickson, Jeffrey Black, Noel Mangin, Beverly Bergen, Thomas Edmonds and Narelle Tapping.

One month later I was singing with Zubin Mehta in an Australian tour given by the Israel Philharmonic Orchestra for the ABC. It was another privilege to sing with the charismatic, youthful and handsome Mehta. The Israel Philharmonic was also a step back into my distant past, as I had performed so long ago with this legendary orchestra in its infancy. And the work was to be one of my favourites, Mahler's Third Symphony.

I flew to Perth to begin the tour, singing one of my few performances in the Perth Concert Hall. To sing with Mehta was the beginning of a one-sided love affair as I watched him coaxing luscious sounds from the violins and commanding strength and huge climaxes from the brass. It is amazing to contemplate the differing techniques of conductors and to consider their different personalities. Mehta was a charmer. I loved watching him conduct when I was not singing, as I sat for the long half-hour before my entry, and then seeing his face light up when at last I began to sing, looking to him for my entries.

We went on to perform in Sydney and ended the tour in Melbourne. Security was very tight as there was a real possibility of bombs. Threats had been made against the great Jewish orchestra and I travelled separately from the players, who had their own plane. The ABC did a superb job in arranging the flights and screening the rehearsals. G and I had decided we would drive down to Melbourne and then on to Adelaide after the final Mahler concert, in order to have a few days together before my next engagement, a season of two operas with the State Opera of South Australia. I would have my VW Golf in Adelaide for the two months I would be there. For the two nights in Melbourne we would stay with my mother in her retirement village unit in Ivanhoe, a suburb of Melbourne.

Our friends Louis and Lily Kahan would be at the Melbourne concert and they asked us to 'brunch' on the Sunday following the concert. We had two days to make the journey to Adelaide before I had to start rehearsals there. I went off to the Concert Hall to rehearse, to find that security here was the tightest of any city we had yet visited. I would be coming back later in my car at about 7pm, so I was given a 'pass' for the Concert Hall car park for that night.

The Melbourne Concert Hall, which had then not been improved, did not respond to the rich warmth of the great orchestra in the same way as the concert halls of Perth and Sydney. It seemed as if the sound stopped in the front stalls, but it probably travelled up the domed sides into the second gallery. The vibrant string sound of the violins in particular seemed to suffer. But the audience loved the concert and the applause lasted for many minutes.

After the concert we were invited to a reception for the orchestra in a private home in Toorak, so we made our way to the car park, being almost the last to leave the concert hall. I said good-bye to the Stage Door man, who had to open the automatic gates on the parking area. We went down the steps and I got in. G switched on the ignition and dense black smoke leapt out of the dashboard. We jumped out of the car, wondering if a bomb had been planted. We ran back to the Stage Door, where the doorman was going off duty, and begged him to call the RACV. This he obligingly did and the RACV said they would be there within the hour.

"Oh well, that's the end of the farewell party," I said, and rang our hosts from the stage door to say we were not coming. I never did say goodbye to Zubin Mehta or the Concert Master, violinist Shlomo Minsk, who had been a member of this orchestra when I sang in Israel in 1958!

We waited and waited. The street darkened and grew silent. All creatures slept, except for the ghostly seagulls which eternally circle the floodlit phallic tower built over the Arts Centre. It was *cold*. We sat on the stone steps in the street, waiting in the dark. When a man finally came, he said there was an electrical fault in the dashboard and we would have to be towed away for the night and get it fixed by an auto-electrician. We sat and waited for a tow-truck.

At 2.30am we were towed away, having driven the little car up on to a car transport, and went clanking through the streets of Melbourne in the dead of night.

"Heavens! What will the old folk think when we arrive in the sleeping Retirement Village?" we asked each other. "They'll all wake up, thinking they are being attacked!"

It was amazing to drive through the deserted streets in my wonderful evening gown on top of the world. The cabin of the tow-truck was so high that we looked down on the empty streets as if we were drifting above them. It seemed that the world had come to an end, we were so tired and cold and 'let down' after the excitement of the concert. Arriving at last at the narrow street where mother lived, the RACV man let down the metal plate on the back of the tow-truck with an earth-shattering crash. He let go the chain around the little car and it slid to rest by the kerb. We slunk off to bed and mother never even knew till next day what time we had come in. I thought all the old folk in the village must have been stone deaf!

We woke about 9am and immediately rang Lily Kahan. We thought if there were any person in Melbourne who would know the whereabouts of an auto-electrician on a Sunday morning, she would.

She was terribly sorry to hear we wouldn't be coming to 'brunch' and yes, she would ring her *butcher,* who would know an auto-electrician who would help us!

Ten minutes later she rang back to tell us that, if we could get the car out to Blackburn, a man would fix the problem so we could get on the road for Adelaide. Lily had saved the day.

We rang the towing company and the same man arrived to load the little car. We said goodbye for a few months to Mother, climbed into the high cabin of the transport and processed through the quiet Sunday morning streets. In another hour we were on our way to Adelaide, after having several wires permanently disconnected in the dashboard.

Because we had not had 'brunch' with Lily and Louis, we were now running a little ahead of our travel schedule and decided we could go up through Victoria to look at the Little Desert, which had just been declared a National Park.

We drove through the winter afternoon into the beauty

and hills of Ballarat and on to the more open country of Horsham, where we stayed the night. Next morning we set off to Dimboola, the play of this name having recently made an impact on theatre in Australia. The morning was grey and a fine misty rain clouded the landscape, but we had never visited this part of the state, so we drove off the highway at the signpost to the Little Desert and began looking for the little numbat, the animal which prompted the creation of this Park. The bush was low, and stunted trees and mulga grew densely on the sides of the sandy-looking track. G noticed it was rather wet and skiddy after the rain, so was travelling very slowly. We had driven about four kilometers, when suddenly the car made a ninety degree turn and slid to a stop, saved from hitting a tree by the steeply-embanked side of the track. We both opened our doors to get out and, on putting our feet to the ground, found a surface as slippery as ice and yet incredibly soft. As we withdrew our feet, four inches of soft mud were attached to the soles of our shoes, so that we were elevated as if on platform soles. It was like walking in deep but slithery snowdrifts, but the snow was a soft metallic grey in colour.

We had planned to arrive in Adelaide that day and G had a plane booking to fly home to Sydney in the late afternoon.

He gallantly said, "Stay with the car. I'm going to walk into Dimboola."

It was only about six kilometres, so I said, "OK," and off he went, walking on the long grass on the side of the road, as it was impossible to stand up on the track itself.

The bush seemed very quiet when he had gone and I decided it was best to sit in the car, as I didn't want to slip over.

I settled down for a long wait.

After a surprisingly short time, I heard the sound of a motor and around the bend came a tractor. With a farmer driving up and the sight of G tramping back through the bush, things looked more cheerful. The farmer told us the track we had driven along was impassable in wet weather and that there was a notice to this effect at the junction of the road. We should never have driven in, he grumbled at us. We said how sorry we were to trouble him and he cheerfully pulled us out, and along the waterlogged road to the bitumen. This journey was proving to be a light-hearted nightmare. Bowling along the road to Adelaide, we wondered what else could go wrong.

We drove straight to the Adelaide airport, to find G's plane on the tarmac and boarding passes being issued. With relieved giggles at our eventful holiday, we said a touching farewell and G boarded the plane and flew off into the winter sky. I drove on into Adelaide and found the flat my agent Jenifer Eddy had arranged and booked for me. A one-bedroom unit, it was convenient, and would be very comfortable except for the curtains, to which I took an instant dislike. In huge diagonal acid-green stripes, they drew a headache across the end of the room and over the large windows. I discovered they were lined with a neutral-toned backing cloth, so re-hung them in reverse, with the stripes facing out to the passing traffic.

The next day I began intensive rehearsals for the first of the operas in Adelaide. The Handel opera *Julius Caesar* was to be produced in a set designed by Tom Lingwood. In these exquisitely beautiful sets, Beverly Bergen, my Cleopatra, looked as seductive as the legend and sang with panache and great beauty. It was always a pleasure to come back to singing Handel.

On August 13 that year Beverly and I gave a concert of excerpts from *Julius Caesar* in the charming Adelaide Town Hall, with Brenton Langbein conducting the ACO. This concert was a taste for the general public of the music they would hear in the staged version and the reviews said we all "made magic in the Town Hall." It was the second time I sang with the wonderfully talented expatriate Brenton Langbein and I regret I did not get to know him well. He was such a charming person, it would have been good to know and work with him more often, but his birth in Adelaide and career in Switzerland meant that our paths rarely crossed. He died tragically young a few years later.

The opera opened on August 25 and there were only three performances. My old friend Denis Vaughan was the conductor. He was appointed as the Musical Director of the State Opera of South Australia in 1981 and by the time we were to work on the Handel together, he would have conducted sixteen operas in Adelaide. In an article written at this time, he said his goal in returning to his home city was to create an ensemble company in which young singers could gain experience in performing. His tremendous ability in coaching singers was not appreciated in Adelaide and many people found him arrogant, pedantic and hard to please. I thought that all singers had something to learn from him, but I was, by now, the only person to praise him. I had not worked with him since 1967, when he had brought forth the Azucena which was in me, and I could not be anything but grateful. I was sad to see that the administration of the Opera Company and the music establishment in Adelaide made a laughing stock of him.

But what was truly awful was the treatment the ABC gave to a broadcast of the wonderful singing and the excellent playing of this *Julius Caesar*. Some bright young thing in the production side of the Adelaide Music Department decided that they would liven up the supposedly 'dull' music of Handel by making a spoof of the opera. The radio production was meant to sound as if people in a box in a theatre of Handel's time were watching and talking and gossiping, as indeed they did in the 18th century, while the singing and playing was going on. So what we heard on radio was dialogue, with singing in the background. All the music, the voices of Beverly Bergen, Claire Primrose and myself, and the sweet violin playing of the strings, was lost. When the broadcast went to air, weeks after the performances were over, it was billed as a broadcast of the opera, so that I settled back to listen to a repeat of the music we had performed. I was so disappointed that an opportunity to have this historic performance recorded was ruined. It would have been a rich source of wonderful music from the period and from the end of Denis' era as Musical Director of the State Opera of South Australia. I wondered if the recording was ruined in this way because Denis had so many enemies. The company was riven with faction fighting and the atmosphere was of intrigue and political manoeuvring. Anyway, the performances went well, the production was enchanting and it was a joy to work with the director Tom Lingwood once more.

The Victorian State Opera 'bought' the production from South Australia and the cast went over to Melbourne to give seven performances in the beautiful new State Theatre. Richard Divall conducted and of course had different ideas about the cuts and the style. We only had one rehearsal, as we had done so many performances in Adelaide. As always, I found Richard's lack of consultation with the principals irritating. He often seemed to expect us to know what he wanted without telling us. On the one and only dress rehearsal, I walked out to sing an aria and got to the middle section when I was stopped and told that the recitative and second part of the aria I had been singing in Adelaide was cut.

Because I was upset at the rehearsal being interrupted and being made to look a fool in front of everyone, I said something rude from the stage about "Richard doing things in an amateurish way, *as usual*, and *why* was I not consulted?" There was a gasp of astonishment that I should dare to speak to the Director like that. Because of our long relationship, I still regarded Richard as a youngster who was learning his profession.

I think the impact of the gorgeous Tom Lingwood sets was muted in Melbourne's much larger theatre; and the much bigger proscenium opening made the 'picture' from the front less beautiful. But the performances were a success and I was sad to say goodbye to G F Handel at the end of that September. It was like saying goodbye to a beloved friend that one may not see again. My years of singing were becoming more limited now and I might never sing that role again.

During the previous months, I had been talking to Rodney Wetherell of the ABC and, with the aid of a tape-recorder, making a documentary about my life as a singer. Rodney would ask me a leading question and then sit back whilst I reminisced about the past. As my life unrolled, he would edit his questions out of the tape and my eventual monologue went to air as a two hour 'Radio Helicon' program. My dear Aunt Edith, after listening lovingly to the whole evening on radio, said in a puzzled voice,

"But you only got up to 1965!" G said I was beginning to talk too much!

Going back to Adelaide, rehearsals now began for *Il trovatore*, with Denis Vaughan conducting his farewell performances with the State Opera of South Australia. Kenneth Collins was the heroic tenor, Manrico. Margaret Haggart made a splendidly strong Leonora and I heard David Brennan singing his first Di Luna. I enjoyed the fresh input Denis gave me in coaching the new production and was sorry that many people around me were not prepared to listen to his advice.

There were eleven performances, a lot for such a small city with a very limited number of opera-goers. I do not know if the season was a success financially. James Christiansen's direction seemed rather old-fashioned after the recent Moshinsky production in Sydney, but worked well. We received rave reviews from the critics, who said our singing was the finest ever heard in Adelaide. However it seemed a small scale *Trovatore* in the tiny Adelaide theatre, remodelled from the old Her Majesty's Theatre. The acoustic had no ring, and the small part-time chorus, the tiny pit and the thin-sounding orchestra seemed to produce only a shadow of the full-bodied sound required by this big Verdi opera. I felt that my own performances were being reduced in scale, that I had taken a step backward in time, to the semi-professional standards of my youth.

But in December in Melbourne again, the wonder of Berlioz' *The Trojans* returned for me, singing this time with Richard Divall. He conducted in the Melbourne Concert Hall as if he were a member of the elite maestros of his generation. Coaxing beautiful playing from the MSO, he gave a splendid reading of the marathon score, and never one to hold grudges, conducted me with loving care. My Aeneas this time was Alberto Remedios. Lacking Philip Langridge's musicality and fine tuned style, I was disappointed to hear Alberto shouting when lyrical singing was required. At the end of each of the three performances, Dido's *Farewell* to love and life was a little death for me, as I said goodbye to another beloved role. I will always remember the standing ovation I received.

In January 1985 I had an unexpected letter from Richard Davis, who had written to me some years before asking for details about the singer Anna Bishop. I knew she was the wife of Sir Henry Bishop and the sister of my great-great-grandmother. An opera singer and a woman who travelled the world with a man not her husband, she was rarely mentioned in the Presbyterian manse of my grandparents. But Richard Davis wrote to say he had completed the writing of a book about her remarkable life and was sending me a copy.

After reading the manuscript, I was amazed at her courage and determination, in a world where Victorian values made a woman her husband's property. It was an amazing saga of adventure and I, who had known nothing about her life, became instantly very proud to acknowledge Anna Bishop as my own great-great aunt. I determined to help Richard get the book published if I could, and telephoned and wrote to many publishers. The book was finally issued by Currency Press in 1997.

The operatic year began for me in January with some more performances of *Trovatore* with a new Italian conductor, the young and talented Evelino Pido, who achieved a real Verdi sound from the small Sydney opera pit. In Melbourne in March 1985 the conductor was Stuart Challender and there were splendid reviews for the orchestra in the great pit of the new State Theatre. There was no doubt in my mind that this was now the best operatic venue in Australia. Joan Carden sang her exquisite Leonora for the first time and the young baritone Michael Lewis came back to Australia to sing a splendid Di Luna. Kenneth Collins was once again Manrico.

The reviews were curiously mixed regarding the production and looking back now I think I understand why. Moshinksy's use of the chair in Azucena's scenes worked very well within the small proscenium of the Sydney theatre, but when the action was transferred to the much larger stage in Melbourne, the intimacy was dissipated and the poor old gypsy's staring eyes were lost in the vast space. So it was the same with the other scenes and the sets, which were all designed for the smaller venue. The production should have been enlarged in all directions. The opera theatre in Sydney is wonderful for its intimacy and the audience can always see the small detail, like some of the great old Continental opera houses. It is certainly much easier to sing and 'fill' than the State Theatre. I enjoyed the Moshinsky-Nolan production very much, with its emphasis on the mad gypsy. I now felt more at home in it than in a traditional production like the one in Adelaide.

From Melbourne and *Trovatore,* we returned to Sydney and began preparing another great Verdi opera, this time with Cillario taking the company to Melbourne for a season and giving three performances in Adelaide. The Aïda was a stunning, big-voiced singer from Eastern Europe, named Maria Slatinaru. I always wondered why she was not immediately re-engaged for more of the big Verdi repertoire. I know she wanted to return to Australia. Perhaps her larger-than-life voice and personality were intimidating for the local management at that time.

Whilst we singers were very busily engaged in touring and singing, taking *Aïda* around the country, the Management of the opera company in Sydney were engaged in some difficult decisions. In June it was announced that the Company was in bad financial shape and would probably have to be reduced to part-time status. The singers were appalled. We were the people who carried and delivered the operas and this decision was being made by Board Members without consultation or advice, and by people whose large incomes and whose employment were in no way dependent on singing. All wealthy businessmen and socially prominent women, only the music critic and lecturer, Elizabeth Silsbury, was a professional musician. It had always and still does astonish me that there has seldom been a singer on the Board, nor in the top administration of the AO. What did these people know of the uncertainties of a profession where physical health and regular employment were the most important aspects of the development of a great talent? As for the gentle nurturing of young artists, it seemed to me that I saw, and still see, too many singers of great promise exploited from the moment they are engaged, singing roles too big and demanding for their age and experience, before being passed over and forgotten, as the next 'young hopeful' is discovered.

It filled me with rage that not only the principals were to be left to moulder from month to month, as in the beginnings of my career, but the chorus, who were now full-time salaried employees, were to be thrown onto the scrap-heap and then picked up when the opera decided there would be a six-month season. Was this what the profession had come to? It would be back to the bad old days, when everyone had to have another job and sing in their spare time!

I told my friends in the chorus and the salaried principals that I would happily be a spokesperson for them, if it came to a fight. After all, I had a good deal of concert work with the ABC and other organisations, I had had a long career and if it came to the worst, I could survive again without singing opera. We would wait and see.

Actors' Equity secretary, Marion Jacka, began talks with the singers and we began to plan our fight with the Management. It seemed to many of us that the General Manager, Patrick Veitch, was to blame for the breakdown of relations between the Board and the singers.

The early management style of the Elizabethan Opera Company was very different. When it was founded, Robert Quentin was appointed to run it with Joseph Post as the first Musical Director. Within a short time he was supplanted by Stefan Haag. Stefan was a brilliant and eccentric theatre-person, who was an artist rather than an administrator.

As a child, Stefan came on tour to Australia, as a member of the Vienna Boys' Choir in 1939, a few months before Hitler invaded Poland. The members of the Vienna Boys' Choir spent their childhood and youth here in Australia, and some of them chose to remain here. Stefan joined the National Theatre Opera

Company in 1947 and sang as a baritone principal, as well as producing many operas. I remember best his staggering production of *The Consul* by Menotti. The Royal Performance for the young Queen Elizabeth's visit in 1954, of Offenbach's *The Tales of Hoffman,* was also a triumph.

Then John Young, with his background as a singer, came to run the company and he was the person whom I first knew in this position. The Opera then was a small, closely-knit family, giving short seasons in the year, with a very small company of chorus singers. Most of the singers within the group had known each other for years as fellow-students and rivals in competitions, and had 'grown up' together within a very small profession.

We, who had come through Gertrude Johnson's National Theatre in Melbourne and Mrs Lorenz' company in Sydney, remember our early struggles to establish a career as singers. The setting up of a company on a permanent basis was the fulfilment of our dreams. In those early years, it looked as if the Elizabethan Theatre would be a viable beginning.

John Young was very successful in building the opera within the Elizabethan Theatre, and singer and actor, Stephen Hall, came into the management, first as Secretary then, in a sideways move, became General Manager. All of these people were easily approached and talked to, in those far-off days, because we were so close in age, experience and ideals.

Within a year, Donald McDonald was Stephen Hall's successor. Financial troubles began as the successful company grew and the length of the seasons extended. The growth and development in artistic sophistication of the productions meant more expense. Over the next few years, the company began inviting many Australian expatriate singers to come back for guest appearances and now these people were persuaded to return to live here. My friend Elizabeth Fretwell remembers a letter from John Young asking her to return and join the company. Like all Australians, she longed to come back and live in the sun and, with John Shaw, Robert Allman and Donald Smith, was delighted to finally accept the offer of permanent work in Australia. So the company now began to develop a wonderful nucleus of singers with great overseas stage experience.

But the Board fought amongst themselves and with the arts funding bodies. Governments never took seriously the problem of proper arts funding for this most expensive art form. Donald McDonald resigned in 1972 and we singers were sorry to see him go. He was the last of the 'approachable' General Managers to talk to us as people. From now on the successive General Managers were remote, separated by more staff, secretaries and status.

The next General Manager, John Winther, was a fine musician but held himself aloof and rarely addressed the company. His wife, the excellent dramatic soprano Lone Koppel-

Winther, became a regular performer and this led to some feeling against John amongst the other principal singers. He was eventually replaced by Peter Hemmings, for a very short time.

The singers complained about the need for a Musical Director, and it was certainly a serious lack. My old friend Moffatt Oxenbould had risen through the ranks and, from being Stage Manager in the first ten years, now held a great deal of power. Edward Downes was appointed Musical Director for the Opera House opening seasons, but he did not renew his contract because of family pressure to return to England, and because he objected to the increasing artistic involvement of Richard Bonynge, who became the next Musical Director.

Finally, Patrick Veitch was appointed General Manager by Charles Berg and the Board. This young man was able to attract private and corporate sponsorship and to raise it from $632,427 in 1980 to $2,073,548 in 1986. Great news, but we singers were not told this, nor were we consulted when the Company bought an abandoned factory about this time, for a 'song' of about $2,000,000, to become the Company's headquarters. What we were now told, but not by Patrick who kept a very low profile, was that we *were* 'going part-time'. I don't know what he was paid at that time, but the salaried principals and chorus were disgusted at this move to maintain the administration and to sacrifice the singers. After all, it takes many years and great talent to make a good singer and the salary of chorus singers was always low.

With hindsight, buying the Opera Centre was a great decision, and the move to attract private sponsorship was good. However, the amount of Government funding went down in those years, from 42.6% in 1969 to 29% in 1986. The Arts have always been the last priority for every Government. Looking back, the sad fact is that simple communication and consultation with the singers would have prevented the trouble within the Board and possibly the nasty manoeuvrings and scandalous behaviour of some of the Board members.

My next concert was a performance of Handel's *Saul,* with Peter Seymour and the Philharmonia, to celebrate the three-hundredth anniversary of the birth of the composer. It was good to sing the wonderful role of David, away from the stresses of gossip and the intrigues of the seemingly doomed Opera Company. I had coffee with Peter in the Opera House Green Room one morning before going off to our rehearsals. At this time he was the Chorus Master of the Opera as well as the conductor of the Philharmonia, and I noticed he was looking pale and tired. When I asked him if he was feeling all right, he said wistfully, "I'm always tired these days."

I told him he was doing too much and should cut back

and try to get more rest. He said he was going to have a check-up. Together later, as we rehearsed the *Saul*, I found myself wondering if he had been to the doctor. He seemed so pale and thin. But the performance in the Concert Hall had the old spark and the choir he had built sang with all its joy and vigour. Raymond Myers delivered a truly great performance as the Saul on that night.

The magazine *Opera Australia* said of this performance, "*Saul* rises above time limit."

A week after the *Saul* performance, I opened in a production of *Un ballo in maschera,* conducted by David Agler from America. Because I was used to the sweep and surge of Cillario when he conducted Verdi, David Agler seemed to conduct a tame, foursquare performance. I hated this production, for Ulrica, the palm-reading fortune-teller, had been turned into a blind woman. The production of my scene became a farce and I enjoyed sending it up as much as I could. It was ridiculous to have a blind palm-reader, but I always enjoyed playing these mad parts. The American Carol Vaness was the splendid soprano, Amelia, and Kenneth Collins sang Gustavus once more as a great Verdi tenor.

I sang again with Peter Seymour in November when the Philharmonia gave a great performance of the Verdi *Requiem* in the Concert Hall. I always enjoyed singing this work so much that I was less aware of Peter's health at this concert and was not to know that this was, in fact, my last concert with my old friend. He had worked tirelessly to promote music in this city all his life. He had been a singer himself, worked at Sydney Grammar as a music teacher, conducted and founded student orchestras, conducted the chorus and operas for the Australian Opera and raised the dying Hurlstone Choral Society to create the Sydney Philharmonia. I had seen almost the whole of his life's work and been a part of many of these facets of his enormous spread of energy and talent. Yet I was not aware how ill he was until I heard that he was in hospital. A few months later, in 1986, I went into his quiet room and held his hand for a brief moment, as he smiled to see me. He died a few days later and I was filled with the sense of loss at his cruel early death.

22. The War of 1985

For months the singers had been unhappy with the direction the Australian Opera was taking. The Press now reported that the company was to go 'part-time' and that the Administration would stay in place, but the chorus and the principal singers on full-time contract would only be employed five months of the year, thus saving the Company a large sum. This would mean that they would lose their future superannuation and long-service leave entitlements. Management remained silent.

In a letter to *The Sydney Morning Herald,* baritone Robert Eddie said that the Administration, numbering fifty-nine and geared to finance, funding and promotion, had not been able to stop a decline in subscriptions from 79% in 1980 to 53% in 1985. The State and Federal Governments were all contributing to the funding of the Australian Opera, which was supervised by the Australia Council.

At this time, I was asked by the Australian Opera to do an interview with Jill Sykes, for the magazine *Opera Australia.* She asked me my opinions on the AO management and I did not hesitate to say that I thought that management was top-heavy and that there were too many people being imported from overseas in management, musical staff and singers. I also said that there should be fewer new productions and that sets and costumes could be re-used more and for longer periods, in order to save money. "Above all," I said, "... the company must take care of its greatest strength, its singers. The choristers have been working for salaries that are just above the poverty line all their lives. They haven't been able to save money. To expect these people to go and find other work for five months of the year is ridiculous. Where does a forty-year-old tenor get an alternative job?"(And maintain his expertise while he does something else for a living?)

"... Lauris Elms would hate to see the Australian Opera change its composition from a full-time ensemble company, yet she feels that if it can't manage on the money it gets, it should simply become a State Company with completely different guidelines and operations. If that happened, the Australia Council's opera funding should be divided equally between all the States, she says. But she hopes that the 'disastrous policy being pursued by the company will be halted in time' ... "

This article understandably brought the wrath of AO management down on my head.

Patrick Veitch wrote, in a letter to *The Sydney Morning Herald:*

"… We do not believe Miss Elms' views are based on an adequate knowledge of the facts, since this distinguished singer has never been and is not now significantly involved in arts administration. Since Miss Elms is currently appearing with the company, we don't consider it appropriate to further comment about her statements."

The small circulation *Opera Australia* magazine was withdrawn from sale in the Opera House Shop, which gave the article and my views more publicity than they would ever otherwise have received.

And then another disaster loomed in which the singers were not involved.

Ever since the building of the Opera House, before the Opera House car park was constructed, the staff, stagehands and musicians were allowed free parking in the grounds adjoining the foot of the Botanic Gardens, where a bitumen roadway had been provided. One was given a pass entitling one to park there for a nominated period. Feeling was high at the proposal to end this privilege, in order to re-design the forecourt. For the stagehands, actors and singers it was unpleasant and dangerous to leave the deserted Opera House around midnight after a show, and for the musicians carrying heavy and valuable instruments, public transport would be impossible. So the Musicians' Union and Actors' Equity mounted a series of protests that month, in the form of a letter outlining these grievances which was read at ABC concerts and before other shows at the Opera House. Several performances' starting times were delayed as a result.

We were well into the run of *Un ballo in maschera* and the night for an ABC TV simulcast came around. It is required that the cast be in the theatre half an hour before 'curtain-up'. As is usual on the night of a performance, the cast came into the building one by one, some going into the cafeteria to have a snack, while others went into their dressing rooms and began to 'warm-up' the voice or to put on makeup. I went straight into my room as usual and began the slow process of getting into character. For me, this meant a kind of self-hypnosis, where I became quiet and introspective. I hated interruptions at this time, as I dreamily undressed, climbed into my robe and began applying the sticks of colour to my face. People began to drop in to say that there might be trouble from the back-stage crew. Finally the 'curtain up' time came and went and we still were not 'called'. Then at last an announcement was made, the letter of explanation was read in front of the curtain and the performance began. The opening scene went splendidly. Kenneth Collins was in great voice. Glenys Fowles as Oscar and Jonathan Summers as Anckarstroem were splendid. My scene began, and the exploding chair and the other effects went well, visiting soprano Carol Vaness was in great voice as Amelia and we finished Act 1. Leaving the set, I went down to the dressing room and got out of my costume, deciding to watch some of Act 2 on the monitor in the Green Room. As the curtain went up on the TV screen, the set suddenly blacked out and then we heard that one of the backstage crew had pulled out the plug to the outside ABC television van.

The singers that night were really upset. This was not done by anyone in the Opera Company, but to the general public it looked as if it were all part of the simmering discontent. The two issues of the parking and the great worry about the AO's future were not related, but as the TV blacked out, it seemed our future as a great opera company was ended.

"Goodwill went down the drain when the plug was pulled," said Ava Hubble in *Opera Australia* magazine. Robert Eddie, Gregory Yurisich and Brian Messner had formed the Australian Opera Singers' Action Committee and moved a unanimous vote of 'no confidence' in the Board of the AO.

I was very hurt when some of my best friends, including Robert Allman and my agent Jenifer Eddy, criticised my action in defending the singers against the Board. I suppose the fact that I was a guest artist with the Company did put me in the wrong. I always regarded myself as a member of the company because I had sung with it for over twenty years. My greatest desire was for the opera to succeed as a full-time company. It had seemed the dream was realised and the battles were won. Now, suddenly, there was a threat of harking back to the dark days of the '50s, when my old friends Morris Williams and Keith Neilson had to choose between the security of a profession, and the uncertainties of a stage career.

In November, the Australia Council commissioned an independent study into the funding requirements of the AO. At the same time, Actors' Equity and the singers' representatives commissioned an independent study, criticising the Board's decisions. Finally the three parties involved helped develop a new method of direct funding, seemingly resolving the present crisis. It had been a terrible time, for the things which were said and printed in newspapers could never be undone and some singers suffered in their careers, as their work with the Opera ceased.

In January 1986 *Opera Australia* magazine said the new season's revival of *Un ballo in maschera* was an excellent reason for the Company's survival. The cast had completely changed except for myself. Marilyn Richardson was Amelia, Anckarstroem was sung by Robert Allman, Lamberto Furlan sang Gustavus,

Rosamund Illing was the excellent Oscar and the conspirators were the basses, Clifford Grant and Arend Baumann. Elke Neidhardt worked some magic with John Cox's mannered production and Vlado Kamirski put such vitality into the pit that the whole *Ball* danced along as Verdi would have wished. It was fun and I could enjoy it. I think the whole company of singers sang with their grateful hearts that season. It seemed we were reprieved!

On Wednesday February 12th, I was sitting on the stage of the Sidney Myer Music Bowl in Melbourne, looking at the daylight fading in the sky and praying that the weather would be kind, "Not too hot, not too cool, but just right." Over the years I had developed a healthy hatred of outdoor performances. Ever since the time I had seen a moth fly in and then out of Marie Collier's opened mouth, I had had a nervous respect for all who perform outdoors!

The Myer Music Bowl, scene of my very first public concert, had been positioned to be a perfect wind tunnel, funnelling the west wind into one's open mouth with a fine exactitude. And the players in the orchestra always seemed distracted and sloppy in these outdoor conditions. They were always worried about their music blowing away! I think it is impossible to hear the 'balance' properly outdoors and for fine orchestral players there is no sense of ensemble possible. The sound is dispersed into the dark blue sky and floats away into eternity.

That great bass Noel Mangin and I were to sing *Bluebeard's Castle* together again. We both loved the opera and singing it together, but Noel was incredibly self-centred and badly behaved on stage. While I was singing he would do terrible things like taking out his handkerchief to blow his nose, or moving his chair during an emotional moment. It was always a challenge to prevent him upstaging me.

Singing beside him, looking out into the starlit dark and thinking of the strange Bluebeard legend with its hidden meanings was a profoundly moving experience. The repeated "Judith, Judith," rolled out with such pathos. I never knew what made him the artist he undoubtedly was, a huge ego encased in a huge frame, and yet Noel had a sweet, sad side to his nature. He suffered a long illness in a terrible end to his life. Singing this wonderful music in English altered the accents and weight of the music greatly and I regretted once again that I had not taken the trouble to ever learn it in Hungarian. Well, it was getting late in my life to learn new things. I found it increasingly difficult to memorise a new work and the prospect of putting the Bartók into a new language was not demanded of me at this stage, for which I could only be grateful. Early in my life, singing opera in English was the rule, and singing it with John Hopkins had made it seem to belong to me in my own language. The critic Kenneth Hince said I "... sang superbly, with a noble combination of splendid timbre, dramatic intensity and almost literal fidelity to her part." (What did this mean? I wondered).

In February Charles Berg resigned as chairman of the AO Board. I was sad that perhaps I had contributed to his resignation and to his ill health. He had served on the Board of Musica Viva for many years and I had known him slightly for all that time. I believe he always had the future of music in this country at heart, but the Board's arrogant attitude to its principal employees had been his downfall. The troubles in the AO were still simmering. The singers held a meeting calling for the resignation of Patrick Veitch.

"Singers with the AO, through their union Actors' Equity, yesterday dismissed as inadequate reforms announced by the company, saying they were no substitute for big changes at board level. The new chairman, Sydney banker Mr David Clarke, addressed his first news conference yesterday, outlining his confidence in the national opera. Last Friday, his first day in the job, Mr Clarke unveiled changes to close the rift between the singers and the board, and to tighten spending.

"The singers had long wanted a liaison committee with management, which Mr Clarke has announced. But Actors' Equity said yesterday it was a token gesture, and that talks it had had with management had not allayed their concerns ... The singers want half the board to have direct experience in the performing arts or music. At present there is none." *(The Sydney Morning Herald).*

I was, for the first time in my life, beginning to have less than glowing reviews. I was constantly worried about my teeth and the strain imposed on my technique by the dental work which had so altered my mouth, my instrument. I was getting tired of struggling against the forces of nature, and growing tired meant a different kind of emotional stress which I had never suffered before. After the first glowing notices of *Ballo* at the beginning of the year, the critics one by one began to criticise my later performances in Melbourne.

Similarly, in *Aïda* in July with Leona Mitchell, I was aware even as I sang and before the notices appeared, that the fire had gone. I was not able to deliver the rage and the torment of Amneris. I was too tired. At the last performance, I knew I was saying goodbye to this most beloved of all my 'wicked women'. My throat closed and I tried to gulp down tears as I sang the end of the Judgement Scene. It was time for me to let Verdi go. I had no news of future engagements with the AO, and as one who had generally been engaged a year or two in advance, I knew without being told this meant that my work in opera was near to or at an end.

A holiday seemed a good idea, so I went to Salzburg with music critic Eva Wagner. It was wonderful to hear the great singers of the day in concert and in opera, in wonderful productions and in the sublime setting of Salzburg. Eva was a wonderfully generous companion and we were joined for a few days by my dearest friend, Gwen Brooker Halstead from Chicago, and her friend Dorothy Arvidisian, a funny, witty and warm American. This contact was to have further results, as you will hear. I went to hear Elisabeth Schwarzkopf conduct her Opera class and she recognised me and greeted me warmly, after all those years, remembering me as a young woman singing with Geoffrey Parsons, in an ABC studio in Sydney! Singing 'the Countess' for her in her class that year was a young Australian, Louise Camens.

Eva and I parted after ten days of wonderful music, I to visit my 'professeur', Maitre Dominique Modesti, at Ampus in the south of France. It was a journey to recover myself and I had done just that. And yet I knew when I began to sing, that I was not able now to do what I had once been capable of.

I asked Geoffrey Parsons how I would know when it was the right time to retire.

He said to me with a rueful smile, "People will stop asking for you to sing. Go on till then." I was still being asked to sing concerts, but the number of opera performances was diminishing.

In October David Miller and I made an LP recording of Liszt songs for 2MBS FM. It was possibly one of the very last records in Sydney pressed in vinyl. It sold out, but by this time everyone was buying compact discs, so it has never had the success that it should have had.

On Christmas Day that year Stefan Haag died, after a long illness. It was ironic that he died in the same year that the AO was talking of extinguishing the full-time Opera Company which he had helped create.

1987 was to be a year for G and me to review our lives together and separately. After twenty-one years of being the head of International House, G had decided he could no longer take the restrictions and irritations of the University of Sydney's administration. The changing laws about unfair dismissals had made these last few years of his life as an employer of staff a torment. He struggled to run the college as an example of service and harmony to the residents, but it was becoming impossible for him to sleep at night as he worried about the well-being of his students. He decided to retire. He was tired.

I had two wonderful engagements in the early part of this

year. The Australian Ballet was planning to perform a new ballet based on Mahler's *The Song of the Earth*. Opportunities to perform this work were not frequent, and I loved singing it so much, but was really daunted by the prospect of doing it nine times each week for three weeks. I asked if they would consider a second singer to do the two matinees, but they were adamant. They were not able to pay another singer, they said. I was upset that my agents left me to do this kind of bargaining, when they should have put my interests first. I then said I would only do it if the Ballet would allow a pupil of mine to 'cover' me, for a very nominal amount, to give her some experience, in the event that I got ill. I was feeling really tired and was prone now to frequent colds, a sure sign I was not well. After a great deal of delay, the Ballet reluctantly agreed. I was also thrilled to know that I would get a regular salary. I knew my performing days were nearing an end.

G and I decided that after his retirement, and at the end of the Ballet run, we would have an overseas trip and visit his good friends Howard and Diane Cook in the USA. Howard had been President of International House, New York, when G had first visited the great Mother House on Riverside Drive, and he had been a wonderful friend for more than twenty years. And at this time Gwen Halstead's friend, Dorothy Arvidisian, invited me to take part in the Tenth Anniversary of the Lake Geneva Opera Festival, Wisconsin. Dorothy was a fine landscape painter and a good singer in her own right. Each year she ran the gala to raise money to give funds for cultural projects in the Milwaukee and Wisconsin area. The Board of this committee included Ardis Krainik, Director of the Chicago Opera, and was impressively loaded with wealthy and musical patrons. Gwen would be the accompanist on this occasion and the performance would take place on the Lake, in a cruise which included dinner and the concert. We began planning the trip as a rewarding end to G's work as Director of International House, but first I had to complete my ballet engagements.

Early in the year I had a concert to sing in the Opera House, and as I sat on the stage waiting for the solo in Mahler's great 3rd Symphony I felt so tired, I thought to myself, "I've never felt like this in all my life. I simply cannot stand up to sing!" My cue came, and with a huge effort I stood and sang my solo. What was the matter with me?

That week I gave my regular Red Cross blood donation, and a few days later received a note from the Blood Bank saying that I had an exceptionally high cholesterol reading and that I should see my local doctor immediately. The mystery was solved. With very high blood pressure too, I had to be very careful, take tablets and watch my diet. I realised that I was the same age as my father had been when he had had his first major heart attack. I was even more pleased I had arranged to be 'covered' during

239

the forthcoming performances for the Ballet.

Then a letter came, asking for me to present myself for Jury Service during the same days as the Ballet performances. I begged my agents to pull strings to get me off. If I were to be able to complete these performances, I knew I needed to rest all day in bed, to get me through the nights. I got a letter from my Doctor. There was no way the Jury Service could be waived. I finally said I would not be able to sing for the Ballet. I was by now so stressed that I was not able to do anything but rest. I added to my health problems a nervous breakdown. At last, the doctor managed to have the Jury Service waived, because I was really too ill to go to court.

My relief was immense. I was able to accept with gratitude that Margreta Elkins should sing my beloved Song of the Earth. However, it did rankle when I discovered that she was not having to sing all the performances each week, but that my agents had arranged for a second singer to do the matinees, after the battle I had fought on my own for this condition.

I sang my last concert for Sheelah Hidden and the 'Music and Heritage' Series, in the tiny historic church of St Mary's in Waverley, with the Australia Ensemble. The *Chansons madécasses* of Ravel were a temporary farewell to Sydney.

It had been a very hard time emotionally for Graeme. He had finished his life's work in establishing the wonderful institution of International House at Sydney University. We should have left on this trip as soon as he retired, to make a break in his life, so that he could re-define his world when he came home later. Retirement is very like walking a tight-rope, alternating between depression at having to do nothing, and the joy of not having to do anything after a lifetime of obligation.

23. America and the Belgians

The experience of travelling across the States was a revelation, in its variety and huge contrasts. Each city we saw was completely different in style and character. The clean, modern, surreally empty, 21st century sweeps of superhighway in LA on the May Day holiday of our arrival, the garish lights of Las Vegas at the Casino at midnight, the dignified grandeur of the central Chicago architecture, the gracious suburban mansions of Hinsdale and the dirty slums and busy canyons of the sky-scrapers of New York, all revealed contrasts on a larger scale than we see in Australia. And to the beauty of the up-state New York birch forests, we added the wonderful West in all its savage glory.

At the end of our stay in Chicago, I fulfilled my engagement with Dorothy Arvidisian. Gwen arranged a couple of rehearsals in her home with the other three singers who were to take part in the Lake Geneva Opera Gala. The program for the concert was a typical list of popular arias and duets, beginning with the quartet from *Rigoletto*. I sang, for the only time in my life, the Champagne song from *Fledermaus* at the end of the night. It was two months since I had sung. The rest had been good for me and I was in great form.

The night was a big success as a fundraiser for the Charity. The list of patrons was a list of 'Who's Who' in the world of business and power in this part of the United States. The wealthy in this country seemed anxious to have their patronage of the arts acknowledged and the prestige generated by being a large donor was greatly prized. That night I met Ardis Krainik. She asked me to contact my agent in Australia immediately, as she would like me to sing in Chicago in the coming season. As soon as we got back to Gwen's the next day, I put through an excited call to my agents to ask them to arrange an engagement immediately with Chicago Lyric Opera. This had to be done quickly, as the planning for their forthcoming season was almost finished. The next day G and I said goodbye to the Brookers and set off on the rest of our great journey. I was now beginning to feel really well. With the medication I was taking, every day I felt stronger and more like my old self. I was excited at the prospect of returning to sing in America.

An audition had been arranged for me at the vast San Francisco Opera House. As I stood on the stage of the vast auditorium, I knew this audition was happening twenty years too late in my life. My voice was not the 'glowing knife' it had been, to cut through the huge theatre. Nice noises were made by somebody in the dark and I smiled back, thinking, "Well, I have at least sung on this stage."

I was astonished when I got home to find that my agents had done nothing about arranging a possible engagement in Chicago. As their business had developed from handling a very few singers to become the biggest and best of the local agents, it became obvious that I was just another mezzo on their books.

The Victorian State Opera planned its first season of Wagner. I was thrilled to be offered the role of Fricka in *Walküre*. I had looked at the short scene in Paris with Modesti, but now began to commit the few pages to memory, and loved this frosty woman for her honesty. In those early days of feminism, she spoke to me, and for many women. "Clever old Wagner," I thought. I spent some money on learning and coaching with the best people in Sydney, especially Werner Baer, and looked forward to the period of rehearsal in Melbourne when I would see my mother and other friends. Opening the September edition of *Opera Australia* magazine, I was amazed to read that the VSO had cancelled all plans for their future *Ring Cycle* and the first projected *Walküre* performances for the following month. Instead, they would put on some performances of *Aïda* with Margreta Elkins as Amneris!

I was stunned. I had sung for Richard Divall many times and regarded him as a friend. I had sung the role of Amneris to much acclaim in the recent production of *Aïda*. If the *Walküre* was to be cancelled, surely the first people to be told should be the already engaged cast, and why was I not then offered the wonderful role of Amneris as compensation? Finding out about this in a magazine added insult to injury. Why had my agents not told me and asked for the role to be given to me? When I rang them to ask about this, I said I should receive some financial compensation for the broken contract and the work I had done in learning the role. The response was that there was no point, as the Victorian State Opera was in such poor financial shape they could not pay anything. This contributed to a lack of faith in my agent which eventually led to the parting of our ways.

Geoffrey Parsons' prediction of a falling number of engagements as my career slowed down was beginning to happen. But I still had some great concert work, and in September I sang in the first Australian performance of Schoenberg's *Gurrelieder* with Rita Hunter, Alberto Remedios, Thomas Edmonds, Gerald English and Gregory Yurisich. Conducted by Hiroyuki Iwaki in the Melbourne Concert Hall, this work was a revelation for me. I was to hear the two great English Wagnerians singing this late romantic music as if it had been written for them alone. Alberto's huge role was sung with beauty

34. Sir Herman Black makes me a Doctor of Medicine.

35. Another special day. I receive the AM. Taken at Government House, Sydney with Graeme.

36. La Principessa with Leona
Mitchell as Suor Angelica.
Photograph by Branco Gaica,
courtesy of Opera Australia.

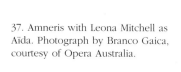

37. Amneris with Leona Mitchell as
Aïda. Photograph by Branco Gaica,
courtesy of Opera Australia.

38. Azucena for the Australian Opera with Kenneth Collins as Manrico. Photograph Branco Gaica, courtesy Opera Australia.

39. Azucena for the State Opera of South Australia. Photo by Grant Hancock, courtesy SOSA.

40-42. It was always fun singing with Marilyn Richardson, and here we are singing *What can we poor females do?* by Purcell, with Geoffrey Parsons and Dennis Condon. Photographs courtesy of Mrs Gordon Clarke.

43. Brahms Opus 91 was the recital work I performed most in my career, here with Irena Morosova.

. L to R: Lauris, Hiruyuki Iwaki, Alberto Remedios, Rita Hunter and Gerald English after the Melbourne Concert Hall performance of Schoenberg's *Gurrelieder*.

45. My daughter, the clarinettist Deborah de Graaff.

46. The next two generations of musicians. Christopher, Deborah, and Oliver on Bruce's knee.

Two beloved men in my life.

47. With Geoffrey Parsons on a cold we[?] day, recording in the Chatswood studio of the ABC, about 1985.

48. ... and with Dominique Modesti on a warm day in Provence, about 1993.

and conviction and soared over the orchestra in a way I found new and exciting. My own smaller solo part of the Wood-dove was wonderfully rewarding, and my notices said I was magnificent. I was no longer sure if this was indeed the case and could only be grateful that the critics thought it was so. By now I was so lacking in confidence in my performances that I was unable to judge how well or ill I sang.

I realise now that every concert I ever sang with Iwaki had been a memorable and rewarding experience. This tiny, inarticulate and self-effacing maestro, with whom I had rarely exchanged more than one or two words, wove magic every time he conducted the MSO. I had been privileged to sing with him over many years, both in the Robert Blackwood Hall at Monash and the Melbourne Concert Hall. He always had something important to say to his audience and to me as a performer.

I still seemed to have plenty of recitals to do for local music clubs and I sang at Springwood and Wahroonga that November with David Miller, my reliable and accomplished accompanist. I was still trying to add new works to my repertoire and found it stimulating to build a recital program of contrast. I was still finding songs of beauty and interest, and now I regretfully knew that my singing life would never be long enough to sing all the music I wanted to.

There was one thing I really wanted to do. I had never found it easy to ask to perform a work and I think all the opera and concert engagements I ever had were of works chosen by other people. Recitals were different and I almost always chose my own programs. In the early part of my life the ABC had engaged me to record recitals of their choice, but now Malcolm Batty, the beloved ABC live-music recording manager, always agreed if I asked to make a recording for the ABC. The national broadcaster had dozens of splendid tapes of mine, ranging over more than thirty years, mostly with Geoffrey Parsons and Joyce Hutchinson. Now I began to do some interesting works with David Miller for them.

For some time the composer Derek Strahan had been coming to my concerts and asking me to commission a work of his. As the 1988 Bicentenary of white settlement approached, I wanted to sing of my love for Sydney and to the beauty of this city I had come to call home. Derek said he would write such a piece for clarinet, piano and contralto, for the trio combination with David Miller and my daughter Deborah.

I said a piece about fifteen or twenty minutes in length would be useful for our trio. Derek said he would write the words himself. I was doubtful about this, but G looked at the first poem, and said "That's fine." So the project began. Derek sent me a new poem each week and then the music began to arrive. The final work was forty-eight minutes long! The manuscript was difficult to read. The music was often splendid and interesting but sometimes repetitious. I applied for funding for the commission of this piece, but it was refused. I paid Derek a pitifully small sum for such a large composition from my own pocket.

I had asked the Opera House if I could present the work in the Recording Hall, which we did in November 1987. We also recorded it on CD at Derek's expense. My daughter played with her own great style and panache and the piano part, which was extremely difficult, was marvellously played by David Miller. When we did it at the Opera House we called the program 'To Sydney with Love'.

On November 30th, G and I were invited to a State luncheon given by the Government of NSW in honour of the King and Queen of the Belgians. We accepted. It was lovely to be able to go out during the day together now that G was retired.

When I was singing in full career, I never wanted to travel anywhere by train because of the gritty winds and acrid smell that tore along the underground tunnels at Wynyard and Town Hall and got down my throat! But G did not want to have to park a car in the city, so we went in by train from Chatswood. It was a breathlessly hot and humid day. The walk from the station took us up through the Strand Arcade, where G bought a Panama hat. I was wearing one of my own very rare creations, a dress made from a beautiful blue-grey silk which I had cobbled together in my slap-dash way. I knew that the sleeves were not finished off properly. I had left the selvage edge, instead of putting facings into the sleeves. The dress was beautifully cool and I knew that the colour suited me and that I looked good in it. However, by the time we had walked up the hill to the State Office Block, I was red faced and sweating, and there were large patches of perspiration under my arms.

We were very early, and when we walked through the door of the State Reception Rooms, the 'flunkeys' were only too glad to welcome us as the first of the arrivals. I went off to the bathroom to comb my hair and splash cold water on my beetroot-red face. I cooled down in the air-conditioning and began to feel comfortable, having held my arms above my head for a few minutes to dry out my armpits.

When I got back to the doorway G said, "Let's find our table and look for our places." The ushers watched as we explored the far reaches at the back of the second room, where we were usually allocated to sit at Royal Functions. (We had been to several of these over the years). Finally someone came over and asked our names. His expression changed as G told him and we were shown to our table. In the centre of the room, near the dais and microphone, G was seated next to the King and I next to the Queen, with the Dutch Ambassador on one side and the Government minister for the Arts, Barry Cohen, and Barry Unsworth, the then Premier, in between. After gazing open-mouthed at the place cards, we both went off to the bathroom again to do some more titivating. Then we were ushered into a small room where we were soon joined by the Premier's assistants and the Royal Party and, with drinks in our hands, chatted for a little time before being taken in to the luncheon.

The Premier, Barry Unsworth, was still not present but as we took our places he sidled into his seat on the other side of the Queen. We looked at him with immense interest. It was the day when there was going to be a struggle for the leadership of the Labour Party. The papers and TV media had rarely had a better story. I had never met, let alone spoken to the Premier before, but felt sorry for him as he stared unseeing into his entree plate of Tasmanian filleted trout. How he must have longed to be anywhere else, rather than to have to talk politely to his official guests.

I was having a wonderful time. The Queen, it appeared, was intensely interested in singing and opera and soon we were exchanging ideas and enjoying talking together so much that we had to be reminded to stop, to allow the official speeches to begin. Barry Unsworth, poor man, made some rather vague and tactless noises about NSW being larger in area than France and then sat down still looking stunned. The King of the Belgians made a short and charming speech. We went on with the meal.

Suddenly, out of the blue, Mr Unsworth leant across the Queen, and in a soft voice asked me, "Miss Carden?"

It was my turn to be stunned, but I smiled back and said firmly, "Miss Elms!"

And that was the extent of my conversation with the Premier.

G had as enjoyable a time as I had, talking with the King. He asked how it was that the title of that ruler was 'the King of the Belgians' and not 'the King of Belgium'?

The King told him that the country of Belgium had only existed for a hundred and fifty years or so and was created at a time when there were lots of 'out of work' Royal Princes and members of noble families without kingdoms. The people of the newly created country of Belgium decided they wanted a King and chose the great-grandfather of the present king, a European nobleman, inviting him to the position. So he was really the chosen King of the people, hence the 'King of the Belgians'. We thought that was a charming way to have begun a royal dynasty.

The Queen was a beautiful woman, a member of the Spanish royal family. She had grown up speaking English as her first language and spent some of her childhood in England and some in Switzerland. We had the most wonderful lunch and G and I felt we had made two friends.

Mr Unsworth was deposed from the leadership that afternoon. No wonder he was so distracted.

245

24. Celebrations

As the year crossed over into 1988, I knew the days of our white Anglo-Celtic beginnings in Australia were to be celebrated from two differing viewpoints. While some of us rejoiced that Captain Cook came to Botany Bay and that we had been in this wonderful country for two hundred years, the original inhabitants, who had been here for many thousands of years, could not celebrate an act which involved the usurping of their country by stealth and the systematic destruction of their heritage.

On January 1st 1988, I was engaged to sing in a performance of Beethoven's 9th Symphony to dedicate the opening of the Federation Pavilion, Centennial Park. In 1901 there had been a splendid pavilion built in Centennial Park to mark the 'swearing in' of the first governor-general, Lord Hopetoun. A crowd of sixty thousand watched the inauguration, which took place in a very pretty Edwardian structure made of plaster of Paris! A temporary affair, it was removed three years later when it began to disintegrate. The new building was erected on the granite base of the earlier building.

I was very conscious of the honour of singing on such a special day, in this, my least favourite work. The conductor would be John Hopkins with the SSO; and soloists Joan Carden, Kenneth Collins, Grant Dickson and the Sydney Philharmonia Choir.

Security was very tight and we soloists were told we would have to be taken in by Commonwealth car as the area was closed to all traffic for the day. The day began with circus acts, jazz and Punch and Judy shows. The official opening of the Pavilion was to be at 3pm and the Beethoven 9th Symphony would be played at the conclusion, at 5.30. And it would be out-of-doors!

The day dawned to fierce sun, dazzling blue skies and a tearing westerly wind, the kind of 'mistral' that sometimes bedevils Sydney. It is a horrid wind that 'gets under your fingernails'.

On the morning of the concert we were collected from our various homes at 11am for our rehearsal on the marquee'd stage erected in the Park, which housed the several hundred performers taking part in the concert that afternoon. Already the audience was taking its place on the grass before the concert area. We soloists were shown to our 'dressing rooms', two small 'on-site' caravans. The area behind the stage was a maze of tubular steel scaffolding holding up the very large stage on which we would all sing and play. The wind tore at my hair and the orchestra tried in vain to secure their pages of music to the music stands with clothes pegs. Somehow we did a 'balance' for the broadcast, which was to go out nationally. John Hopkins, who was usually very relaxed, was worried.

"There's a big storm forecast for the late afternoon," he said. "If we can keep things moving, we might just get the Symphony over before it comes."

We were driven back to our suburban homes and told we would be collected about 3.30pm. We arrived back at the caravans behind the stage on that terrible afternoon to find the fierce wind almost unbearable. A curtain of jet-coloured cloud from the south was gradually dividing the radiantly blue sky. It looked most dramatic. A famous Sydney southerly-buster was imminent.

John Hopkins had to make the decision, should he start the Ninth Symphony now, or wait and see? He decided to wait a few minutes and hope the wind would drop, which it did, abruptly, after twenty minutes. The sky was now completely overcast and the concert began.

John had suggested we soloists wait in our caravans while the first three movements were played. The enormous choir was seated already, awaiting the time to sing in the final movement. The clouds darkened and lowered. The first tension-filled movement went by, with dramatic additions from the screaming microphones. The Scherzo was illuminated by flashing lightning and screeching galahs accompanied the coda. Beethoven would have loved the drama of it!

Joan Carden, Ken Collins, Grant Dickson and I prepared to climb up the steep stairs at the back of the scaffolding to be in our places for the final movement. I listened with pleasure, as I always did, to the beautiful third movement beginning to wind and unwind in its circles.

After a few moments, the first huge drops of rain began to spatter on to the canvas roof of the stage. Suddenly the few drops became a sheet of rain and we were swept back to our caravan by a stampede of orchestral players, hurrying down the stairs to save their precious instruments from the deluge. The huge audience on the grass in front of the stage was now a sea of umbrellas. The performance was abandoned. We never even got on to stage to sing the *Ode to Joy*. A bedraggled crowd shambled home through the torrents.

The Festival of Sydney, still in the charge of Stephen Hall, asked me again to give a recital in the Vestibule of the Sydney Town Hall. My Chicago friend, Gwen Brooker, decided to make a visit to see her family in Melbourne and I invited her to be my pianist. She came to spend a week in Sydney and we rehearsed and enjoyed our time together. Gwen always found the humidity in midsummer here an appalling trial. We had installed air conditioning and I think it was one of the best improvements we ever made to our house.

The ABC recorded the program we gave in the Vestibule. This pretty building had been the Sydney Town Hall before the Centennial Hall addition was made in 1888. It has a very high and beautifully decorated ceiling, and is an acoustic disaster for a voice like mine. The sound rang around the gilt cornices and made it difficult for me to hear the piano or my own singing. A vocalist uses such feedback to mould the sound he or she makes, in a very subtle blending of aural and oral craftsmanship, which develops with experience. It seems a general rule that the people who put on concerts never care to ask advice about the kind of sound-structure you need to sing within. Anyway, this venue looks lovely and was horrible to perform in.

"Glorious voice in ravishing form," and "Romance not lost in Vestibule swamp," were two headlines I find in the 'crits' from this concert. Fred Blanks in *The Sydney Morning Herald* took me to task for not including 'Australian content' in this recital. I sang Schumann's *Frauenliebe,* Mahler's *Rückert Songs,* Herbert Hughes' arrangements of Irish songs, as well as some wonderful Castilian songs Gwen Halstead had found, by Spanish composer Jesu Guridi.

In February Charles Berg died. He had been a very important figure in the growth of Musica Viva and in the development of the Opera Company. It was a shame that the end of his Chairmanship of the Board of the AO was clouded by an autocratic style of business management, instead of the conciliation processes beginning to be used in other industries. I was sorry that his final years with the opera were a subject of criticism.

In March that year Charles Farncombe conducted Mahler's 8th, the so-called *Symphony of a Thousand,* with the Malcolm Sargent Festival Choir, the boys of the Melbourne Philharmonic and the MSO in the Melbourne Concert Hall. Each time I sang there the acoustic had been improved, by the use of hanging plastic 'dough-nuts', amongst other things. Shaped like the interior of a cavern, the Concert Hall had always swallowed the sound, but now it began to be possible to 'hear' the sound I was producing, as it fell out into the vast dome-like space. However the critics said once again that the choral sopranos and the boy sopranos were inaudible. Mahler's 8th is difficult to sing and to learn and requires very good musicianship. It was perhaps the most demanding of all the concert works I have ever performed, in both concentration and commitment. Like many major vocal/choral works, I think it is probably more fun to perform than to listen to. The soloists were Nance Grant, Ghillian Sullivan, Irene Waugh, myself, Alberto Remedios, David Wilson-Johnson and Noel Mangin of the wonderful voice, who waved his handkerchief around like Pavarotti when other people were singing.

On May 7th, a warm Saturday morning, G drove Deb and me in to the carpark at International House and parked the car. I had been there a thousand times, but on this May visit we walked from there over the grass to the Great Hall of Sydney University with a certain lightness in our step. I, who had only completed my Intermediate Certificate at school, was to become a Doctor of Music at the oldest University in Australia. I felt nervous as I was taken upstairs to the Senate Room to don my borrowed academic gown. I would 'process' with some of the great teachers and thinkers of this city, down the aisle between the stone walls of this building in which I had so often sung, and take my place on the dais with the *real* Academics.

The Chancellor, Sir Herman Black, was the portentous voice I had listened to as a child when he was H D Black on ABC radio, giving his 'Notes on the News'. Now this wonderful old man read the list of distinguished recipients of honorary awards, and at last it was time for me to rise. I was called to step forward and Sir Herman said, "In the name of the Senate, and by virtue of my authority as Chancellor, I admit you to the degree Doctor of Medicine, honoris causa."

Out of the corner of my eye, I saw the figure of a startled Lady Black rise a little from her seat in the front row in surprise, but Sir Herman's beautiful voice rolled on, intoning the great deeds, and worthy recipients of the other honours of this University. G and I exchanged a secret glance, with a grin. My great-grandfather, Professor Halford, was the founder of the medical school in Melbourne. Would I now be the least qualified MD from Sydney University? We were relieved to find that the parchment scroll I received from Sir Herman's hand stated firmly that Music was my discipline.

On 29th July, Dolly Modesti died in Ampus. A week or so later, I received a card from her family, saying: "Madame Dorothy Modesti née Smith, survenu brutalement le 29 Juillet 1988 a Ampus."

This gallant and generous woman had been a profound influence on my life and on the lives of a dozen or more Australian singers. How fortunate we were who knew her, this strong, vigorous and beautiful woman who gave herself wholeheartedly to whatever she did.

How lonely her husband Dominique would be now! She had not suffered. Standing up to open a window on a hot summer day, her life had closed forever. But he, who had loved her for so many years, now had to live on alone. In Shelley's poem set by Respighi, *Il tramonto,* I sang of a lover, he "died not, nor grew wild, but year by year lived on." Modesti died ten years later, ten days before his one hundredth birthday.

September brought a joyful concert with my colleagues Marilyn Richardson and Geoffrey Parsons. The series 'Geoffrey Parsons and Friends' had been in the planning for two years. Since she had married Jim Christiansen and moved interstate, Marilyn and I did not meet often enough and our chances to perform together were rare, so we began to plan our program of duets together with great pleasure. We started the concert with a group of three Purcell songs, including *What shall we poor females do?* (A good question!) Then I sang two Schubert Suleika songs, and Marilyn sang four songs by Rachmaninov. A group of Schumann and Brahms duets followed and after interval I sang the two Brahms songs, opus 91, with viola player Irena Morosova. Marilyn sang Poulenc, and we finished with the great Rossini duets *Serate musicale.*

We decided that we wanted something really amusing to sing at the end of the program, so we asked the composer Peter Sculthorpe if he had anything for two old friends, soprano and alto, to sing together. He said he was too busy to write anything new for us (!) and sent us a simple song he had written for the Bicentennial, which was an arrangement of a solo written for Joan Carden. This seemed too serious, so eventually we sang an amazing version of *La Cucaracha* written for us by George Pikler, with some additional original lyrics by the talented M Richardson. The song brought the house down at the end of a night of the greatest fun for me, Geoffrey and Marilyn. As always, it was wonderful to have Geoffrey back in his Sydney Town Hall, the scene of his earliest beginnings as the world-famous pianist he became.

After the performance of Elgar's *The Dream Of Gerontius* later in the month, Thomas Edmonds, Grant Dickson and I went through the backstage labyrinth to the Northern Foyer of the Opera House, where a reception was held for the conductor Sir David Willcocks, the three soloists and guests of the Philharmonia Choir. I was presented as the Choir's new Patron. I was very honoured to be given this position by the distinguished choir, with which I had sung for over thirty years.

Elgar said of his work, *The Dream,* "This is the best of me," and now I was at the stage of my life when the best of me was beginning to come to an end. Each concert now made me grateful to have the chance to once again sing with orchestra or piano and present music I loved to people who still wanted to hear me! I was aware that there were young singers of great talent who were waiting to have the chances I was still being given.

Across the Tasman, in Christchurch, my old friend Robert Field-Dodgson was coming to the end of his career as a great choral conductor. From Australia, Christa Leahman and I were going to sing with New Zealanders Anson Austin and Noel Mangin. Robert conducted Verdi's *Requiem* as his lasting tribute to the music he had made over forty years. It was a great occasion, and the audience rose at the end to pay tribute to Bob and his leadership of the RCMS.

December brought *Messiah* into my repertoire once again, but this time in a form I had never heard. The version arranged by Sir Eugene Goossens was given a splendid performance by Richard Divall and the MSO in the Melbourne Concert Hall. The soloists were the wonderful young soprano and tenor Deborah Riedel and Glenn Winslade, with Noel Mangin and me making up the 'heavies'.

Kenneth Hince noticed for the first time, "... I have heard that masterly contralto Elms in better form than she was on Friday."

I knew he was right. I too had been thinking this for a long time. When I got home I asked Glenn to give me some advice about my singing, but I also knew that the problem was not of my making, nor even of my age. It was the strain put on my vocal mechanism by the change to my dental shape and oral muscles. Glenn was charming and kind, but nothing seemed to help. My dentist did not understand and I knew I was beginning to sing noticeably less well. Now it was always an effort to sing.

At the end of the year, for the second year in a row, I organised a Carol Singing Fundraiser for Community Aid Abroad. I asked Eric Clapham to conduct some of the best voices in the country, as on the previous occasion, in the Queen Victoria Building on Christmas Eve, and once more my generous colleagues gave of their skill and time to sing for charity.

As we sang praises to the baby Jesus, I wondered how my daughter was. She gave birth to our first grandson, Christopher Graeme Nelson that afternoon, as we sang of the birth of the Christ-child.

"Unto us a child is born."

On Friday 30th of December 1988, I sang in recital with Rachel Valler for the first time, in the new Powerhouse Museum, in a little theatre the perfect size for chamber music. Unfortunately the theatre in the Powerhouse was not a success acoustically, as it was geared to presenting films and discussions. Sydney still needed an intimate chamber music venue. Rachel was a beautiful pianist who could make the piano sing; I also enjoyed the viola playing of Alexandru Todicescu when we performed the Brahms op 91 songs. *The Cradle-song of the Virgin* was full of memories, as I thought of my daughter and her new baby, and the time we heard that carol in the snow in Munich together, almost ten years earlier.

25. In Search of Times Past

Werner Baer had been part of Sydney's music scene for the whole of my time in this city. It was inconceivable that he should have suddenly left us, almost in mid-sentence. He had often spent time in hospital with a chronic heart complaint. Short tempered and hard working, he drove himself and all who worked with him. But his knowledge of music was encyclopaedic, and to think that he had left us was a great loss. The memorial service held for him in the Great Synagogue was a fine tribute to his memory. I would sing two wonderful songs of Mahler.

As Graeme dropped me off in front of the Great Synagogue on that pouring wet March night, he groaned through clenched teeth, "Trust Werner to choose this night for his memorial." G was wearing a new suit for the first time that night. It was ruined!

I could not help smiling, thinking how Werner would have enjoyed the sight of all the dripping umbrellas and sodden coats of the mourners. I listened to the Sydney Jewish Choral Society and with Rachel Valler playing for me, sang for Werner's memory.

I was planning a little holiday to go to see my dear Dominique Modesti, now living in Aix-en Provence with his son and family. I felt I must talk to my old teacher and thank him again for all he had done for me. He was in his nineties and I could not leave it much longer.

I told Rachel Valler and her mouth opened in surprise. "But I'm going to Europe with Don Hazelwood and Anne (Menzies); the Hazelwood Trio are doing a tour. Why don't you come along and join us for part of the time?"

So I would fly to Rome and go to Florence before meeting up with Don, Anne, Rachel and her husband, Walter, in a tiny village called Gargonza, where Australian expatriate Vivienne Pittendrigh ran a music festival. I began my trip in Monte Carlo, before travelling by train to the old city of Aix. I spent five lovely days there, enjoying the wide clean outer boulevards and the narrow cobbled centre of this southern French city. The old town has great charm and the mountains beyond reminded me of those in the film *Jean de Florette*. Monsieur Modesti was great fun - stimulating and still interested in painting and vocal teaching. We had many enjoyable hours together. At ninety-four he still had some singing pupils and we talked about the teaching of singing.

One of the high points of my stay in Aix was the visit of Lance Ingram and his wife to M Modesti while I was there. In the years that had intervened, Lance (or Albert Lance, as he now was) had become the darling of the audiences of the '60s and '70s, personally decorated with the Legion d'honneur by De Gaulle. He was by this time teaching singing in the Conservatoire de Nice. Still handsome and slim, he seemed completely happy in his life. We had last met on stage at Covent Garden in 1958 when we sang in *Rigoletto* with John Shaw and Joan Sutherland. He wanted to know how things were now in Australian music, singing and opera, since he had left 38 years before. His wife was also a singer and we had lots to talk about during our three hours in the sunshine of the beautiful garden of the Modesti house in Aix.

I left Modesti to go to Monte Carlo and then on to Siena where I spent five days looking at the wonderful paintings and churches of that remarkable city and the great black and white Cathedral - not beautiful, I think, but astonishing.

I wrote to my family in Sydney, "Here in Siena, I feel I am caught in a time-warp. As I heard someone say, while walking around the extraordinary gallery here called the Pinacotheca Nazionale, 'You can OD on these Madonnas'."

On the last day I accidentally met the Australian baritone Russell Smith. He was in Siena studying an intensive Italian language course. We spent a wonderful day together in San Gimignano talking non-stop about singing, music and living in Italy. I had been very lonely in these few days. The strangeness of Siena had reminded me of the first lonely weeks of my time in Paris, when the communication and understanding of a different society was so difficult and one seemed to step back into a different time zone. Russell helped me feel a return to my normal self after five days in a solitary state.

I went by bus across country through the Tuscan hills to Monte San Sevino, to be picked up by Vivienne Pittendrigh. Vivienne ran a series of music festivals in Europe for people who wanted to play chamber music themselves, as well as to listen to fine professional musicians making music.

This particular festival was situated in a medieval castle which the present owner, Count Roberto Guicciardini, had converted into attractive individual apartments inside the castle walls. Sydney's Hazelwood Trio was in residence and it was time for me to get back into practice and get my voice in shape. It was thrilling to live in this fairy-tale place for five days, hearing gifted amateurs play string quartets and trios from dawn to dusk and then enjoying professional performances in the evening. My recital with Rachel Valler included Le Gallienne's setting of the John Donne Divine Sonnets, the Brahms *Songs with viola,* opus 91, and the Mahler *Songs of a Wayfarer.* Don Hazelwood, Anne Menzies, Rachel Valler and I also gave a lecture on Australian music and illustrated our words with examples of some of our composers' music.

In Rome, my host Margaret Baker-Genovesi, her husband Vittorio and I went to a concert performed in the Rome Embassy by the Hazelwood Trio. They played superbly and were congratulated by some of Rome's most eminent musicians, including players from I Musici and the Leader of the Santa Cecilia Orchestra. I met expatriates pianist Margaret Barton, cellist Anthea Scott-Mitchell and artist Justin O'Brien. And then I had to leave this exciting city and fly home to Sydney, after a fantastic journey of discoveries, contrasts and pleasures, both visual and aural. I felt a renewal in my spirits as I contemplated the work awaiting me.

Len Vorster arranged for me to go to Melbourne to sing in the George Fairfax Studio one Sunday afternoon in July. I had now contracted the 'flu. Perhaps I had caught it from Deb. I did not make an explanatory announcement but sang, and horrified myself once or twice when some ugly noises issued from my dry and croaky throat. This year was the anniversary of the poet Shelley's death and Len wanted to have a program based on his poems. But living in different cities made consultation difficult, so we opted instead for a program of works I had sung before, with a new work from composer and oboist Graham Powning, to which I fitted some of Shelley's poems. Deb had been going to play these songs but because she was ill, Grania Burke was the third member of the trio. I was also singing some Verdi songs I had brought home from Ricordi's in Rome. We hear so few Italian songs that I was keen to show how this wonderful operatic composer could also write for the 'salon'. But the trauma of singing when I was not well was a horrible strain.

Recovered, and in the middle of winter, G and I set off to drive to Orange. This beautiful part of central NSW had become the home of John Gould. John was a fine viola player who had played in some of the top string quartets and orchestras in Sydney. He had become disillusioned with city life and had set up a music school in this attractive rural city. He invited me to go 'out west' to give a recital of songs there, and of course we included the Brahms songs opus 91, with viola. A fine local pianist, Anne Stevens, would be our accompanist and the concert would be held in the Orange Regional Gallery.

When we arrived, feeling that we were on holiday, we

found the Gallery to be a charming venue for music with a lively but rich acoustic. The exhibition on show was of works of Ken Done, based on a Japanese theme in glorious reds and greens, and I loved being surrounded by these colours. The concert was a delight to me as much as to the audience.

On 24th August I heard of the death of my violin teacher, Stella Nemet. I think she had opened doors to a young girl who would not otherwise have seen the first glimpses of another life, growing up on the outskirts of suburban Melbourne. I did not achieve the expertise I needed to become a really excellent violinist, but her musical judgement and keen ear helped to mould the singer I later became. Her teaching of the technique of bowing helped me to develop my own vision of a legato line in song. Her daughter Mary says her mother's advice to any artist was "A cool head and a warm heart is the ideal combination."

In Port Fairy again that October I was engaged to sing a program of duets with Margaret Haggart. Maggie had been a friend for many years, from the time of the founding of the Victorian Opera Company in the '70s. She had a terrific sense of humour and was a great friend of Michael Easton and Len Vorster. Together Michael and she were hysterically funny and Len, with his serious face and grave manner, was the straight man to their comedy. This year was again a lot of fun, the hard work overlaid with lovely surroundings and amusing companions. As well as the duo recital, Margaret and I sang a couple of Mozart and Handel duets with the orchestra in the old bluestone church.

Sometime in the latter part of the year, Belinda Webster produced a CD recording for 2MBS-FM. A potpourri of Victoriana and ballads, it was a flop. It was meant to replicate the kind of parlour-music which I had sung for the Glee Club on ABC radio in 1953-54. David Miller played piano and Eric Clapham provided the occasional Hammond organ. Because the recording was done in the tiny studio and on the old piano at 2MBS-FM, the balance was not very good. But there was a good deal of nostalgia on my part for the old ballads!

26. Exit on Cue

1993 and an empty diary. It seemed as if I had no engagements. It meant that G and I could spend time sailing and enjoying other people's music making. In summer in Sydney there was always a feeling of lethargy, as the warm humid days and sultry nights rolled by. We had visits from English and American friends and lots of entertaining in this holiday time. But I felt bereft. As the days grew cooler I felt the old stirrings of desire to sing, but it was hard to practise without the incentive of work in progress. So I went to see Barry Benson at the Opera House. He promised me a recital in the Concert Hall where we could perform in 'reverse mode', the audience seated in the choir stalls and the artist singing with her back to the large hall. I was thrilled. A date was agreed on, and I rang David Miller to start work on the recital. We selected a program and commenced rehearsals. But as the date approached I became nervous. There was no mention of the concert in any of the Opera House publicity. At last, ten days before the concert date, I rang the organiser to be told that nothing had been noted about my conversation or engagement and there was no time now to advertise the concert at such short notice.

I was devastated.

Then the phone rang. Would I go to Bermagui to sing with 'The Four Winds Festival' run by Michael Brimer and his wife Judith? I had met them a few months earlier in Port Fairy and they had mentioned that they would like me to sing for them sometime. I had laughingly said that they had better hurry up and ask me as I would soon be retiring. This invitation came suddenly out of the blue because a singer whom they had booked for the Festival was in England and wanted to remain in London. Michael suggested the Mussorgsky *Songs and Dances of Death* as a possible song cycle. I was thrilled, as long as I could sing it in English. At this stage of my life I was finding it increasingly difficult to memorise new music. I knew these wonderful songs would have sounded so much better in the richness of the original language, but I felt it was too late for me to learn them in Russian. However, Michael and I put together a splendid program.

We drove down to the South Coast on a glorious sunny

Thursday before Good Friday. We were billeted with a delightful couple whom G had known in his Queen's College days. The weather was exceptionally hot for the time of year. The festival was to take place in the open air in a beautifully green field on the slopes of which the audience would sit on rugs, looking across a pond of water dotted with water-lilies at a sound-shell especially erected for the occasion. We had a sound balance on stage in the morning and I realised with horror that the sun was shining directly on the decorative sheet of water in front of the stage and on to my face. I would be on stage for at least one hour and a half, looking directly into blinding sunlight. The effect of the sun shining both directly on my face and reflected up from the water was like a doubled spotlight. My eyes watered and tears poured down my face as I sang. I decided I would have to wear sunglasses for the afternoon on stage. I sang the Mussorgsky and also the Elgar *Sea Pictures* with piano, without eye contact with my audience. The grand piano felt hot to my touch as I put my hand on it. I wondered about the terrible effect the sun would have on the instruments of the other musicians.

The wind blew and music had to be pegged down. The audience came and, sitting on the slope above the pretty little music bowl with their backs to the warm sun enjoying the picnic atmosphere, probably had no idea of the difficulties we artists were experiencing. The program was recorded for a broadcast and I was horrified later to hear a constant flutter, caused by the breeze blowing across the microphone. My voice sounded ghastly. But the beauty of the place and meeting friends from long ago meant that we came home feeling we had had a holiday.

In September 1993 I was asked to go to Canberra with Geoffrey Parsons to give joint master classes in Lieder singing and vocal accompaniment. This was a great honour for me and to have the pleasure of his companionship was wonderful. His knowledge of singing was as great as mine, I think, after his lifetime spent working with great performers. He showed ability in directing the young pianists in their choice of colours and timbre, in the different styles of music we heard that day. He talked at length about the use of the pedal in colouring the sound and I think this was the secret of his own performing art.

In July I made a sad journey to Adelaide to sing in a memorial service in honour of Brenton Langbein, whom I only met and sang with once or twice, and who had lived most of his life in Switzerland. I sang with the pianist Lance Dosser and violinist Beryl Kimber, whom I had admired all my life and never had the opportunity to perform with before. I sang the Brahms song from the *Four Serious Songs, Tho' I speak with the tongue of men and of angels and have not love I am as nothing* (1 Corinthians 13:1), and the great aria from the *St Matthew Passion, Erbarme dich,* with Beryl filling the vaulted arches of St Peter's

Cathedral with the music that this great Australian musician had loved.

In January I went to Albury for John Ross, the Director of the Conservatorium there, to sing a program based on old Victorian ballads. It was fun singing these old songs from my childhood again and I enjoyed the ease of not having to remember foreign texts. This would be my last year as a singer I decided. The news filled Len Vorster with sadness and he asked if I would give a farewell with him at Mietta's Restaurant in Melbourne. I sang a group of Schubert songs.

Back in Sydney, the old church on the crest of the hill opposite the corner of Telegraph Road on the Pacific Highway at Pymble, which we had driven past countless times, was now the Ku-ring-gai Town Hall. The Catholic Church had decided to part with this building. The noise of the traffic going up the hill as road-trains changed gear outside no doubt made it difficult for the inmates to hear themselves meditate during the religious service. This highly unsuitable venue had somehow been acquired for the council to use as a concert hall.

Deborah very much wanted to display her ability as a virtuoso soloist. This year she joined with Michael Brimer in a concert series called Ku-ring-gai Virtuosi. All the halls in the city were far too expensive, often costing more than a thousand dollars to hire, without the cost of a good piano, staff and advertising, and the artists' fees. As residents of Ku-ring-gai, they could have the use of the Ku-ring-gai Town Hall with the blessing of the local Council and a small grant besides. So with G as Treasurer, Deborah, and Bruce Nelson as Artistic Adviser, and a dream in my mind that we might have vocal chamber music as part of the program, we planned a season of five concerts in the funny old Spanish Mission Church.

Dark and gloomy inside, the noise of the traffic was bearable if the audience sat close enough to the stage, but anyone who chose to go to the back of the hall was to find the subtle soft tones of my daughter's clarinet drowned by motor noise. The acoustic was 'boomy' and the heating and lighting erratic. However Bruce felt he could keep the lighting sufficiently subdued to hide the shabby interior. At this exciting stage in the group's beginnings, it seemed important to find the best possible combination of players. We knew from experience that it was not enough to have technical ability, but that people had to be attuned temperamentally.

Michael would be both soloist and take part in the chamber music. The first couple of concerts were well patronised, proving the desire of the upper North Shore to have another really good quality music series. By adding my presence to the series, we thought it might lend some support to the new venture and encourage more subscribers. I announced these performances as my Sydney farewell season of recitals. And so in June I gave my last Sydney recital in the Ku-ring-gai Town Hall, with Michael Brimer and Deborah de Graaff. It seemed a funny little place in which to have ended my career. As a freelance artist, there was no organisation in whom I could confide my desire to give a farewell and I hoped that the fact that I sang in the Ku-ring-gai Series that year would perhaps give these concerts a certain cachet. And so it proved, as old friends from near and far came to celebrate the end of my career and the beginning of the series of concerts which might help Deborah become really established in her own right.

The series has become a success and we found that after a short time we needed to find a better venue. The Turramurra Uniting Church was built just that year and in the following year the concerts moved into this lovely building, with its sense of space and peace and beautiful acoustic. Michael Brimer found that he did not have the time to rehearse the chamber music section of the program as he wanted to devote his free time when he was not teaching to his own performing as a soloist.

After that year it was decided to ask David Miller who agreed to play in the chamber music as well as being the accompanist. It made me realise again that David Miller was a treasure, who was prepared to rehearse with the other people in the group.

A new and exciting opportunity came for me when I was asked to adjudicate the City of Sydney McDonald's Performing Arts Challenge. I had had very little experience in adjudicating, but thought that I would have as good an idea of what was required in a young singer as anyone else. I remembered my own difficult and stumbling beginnings and hoped I could repay my debt to the people who had helped me to become established in a career, in my turn.

That year was a remarkable flowering of talent and, with Ronald Maconaghie as my partner on the panel, we heard some splendid young singers. As an adjudicator, I found that it is a delicate tightrope to walk between the likes and subjective choices of two people. My first choices were not always ranked in the way that Ron chose, but we agreed unanimously on the finalists and they were outstanding. We agreed that any one of the splendid sopranos we heard that year would certainly have careers. When we were joined by Myer Fredman as the third adjudicator, the prize went to a young tenor who showed great potential, whose name is Stuart Skelton. The long process of selection over four nights from nearly 100 singers, then two quarter-finals of thirty-two, then sixteen in a different hall and finally the eight finalists, meant that we had heard these young people each presenting five arias in different situations on different nights, and surely this was as big a test of their skills as anyone could imagine. I knew from my lifetime of singing how hard it is to 'deliver the goods' on cue all the time. We knew that most of those young people would succeed. Listening with a critical ear to different kinds of voices is very demanding, and there is always the subjective liking of one sound as compared to another by two or more judges to take into consideration. It was a fascinating experience.

The end of my operatic career was great fun and I enjoyed performing with Margaret Haggart, Joanna Cole, Geoffrey Chard, Jeannie Marsh and Gregory Brown in Port Fairy. I sang in an opera by Sir Lennox Berkeley, *A Dinner Engagement,* directed with great wit by Grahame Murphy and conducted by Brian Stacey, who was killed in a motorbike accident shortly afterwards.

The following afternoon I gave my last performance with the Victorian College of the Arts Chamber Orchestra conducted by the distinguished cellist, Phillip Green. Lennox Berkeley's *Four Poems of St Teresa of Avila* were written for my idol, Kathleen Ferrier. The last five words are, "For He is God Omnipotent."

My faith is founded on the music that I love. For me, it is *music* which is omnipotent.

The Lieder Society in Melbourne had asked me to give a farewell concert for them in St John's on Southbank. I asked Angela Dahr, who had played for me in my earliest concerts in Dandenong, to accompany me.

St John's has a wonderful acoustic and I felt my voice travel into the space and fill it. Through my ageing eyes I looked out over an audience which spanned my forty years of singing. To my surprise, I recognised people from all the phases of my early life: those who had attended the church fellowship with me when I was a young teenager, from Swinburne Art School, old students and teachers from Methodist Ladies College, from Madame Wielaert's singing studio, from the National Theatre Opera School and from the later period when I lived as a young mother on campus in Queen's College.

At the end of the recital Linda Phillips, the 'good fairy' who had arranged a meeting with the Modestis all those years before, now a frail little lady in her nineties, came on stage and made a moving speech.

What a rich life I had led! How fortunate I had been with the gifts I had received at my birth. I was overwhelmed by gratitude for great good fortune. The recital was a kind of thanksgiving for the gift of my voice, the gift of all my singing and the happiness of my life, as I sang to all my friends on that night.

AN DIE MUSIK
(Franz von Schrober)

Du holdé Kunst, in viefiel grauen Stunden,
Wo mich des Lebens wilder Kreis umstrickt
Hast du mein Herz zu warmer Lieb entzunden,
Hast mich in eine bessre Welt entruckt!

Oft hat ein Seufzer, deiner Harf entflossen,
Ein susser, heiliger Akkord von dir
Den Himmel bessrer Zeiten mir erschlossen,
Du holde Kunst, ich danke dir dafur!

TO MUSIC
(my own translation)

O fairest art,
So often in life's grey hours
You have warmed my heart with love
And carried me to a better world.

From your harp strings
Sweeter, holier harmonies have floated
And opened a heavenly vista to me.
O fairest art, for this I thank you!

Discography

1959
• *Peter Grimes,* Benjamin Britten (Mrs Sedley). ROH, conductor Britten.
Decca SXL 2150-2. CD426 191-2 CD414 577-2.

1965
• *Australian Music Today; Vol.11.*
Four Divine Poems of John Donne Dorian Le Gallienne; piano Marie Van Hove.
World Record Club AA 602.

1967
• *Montezuma,* Graun. LPO, conductor Bonynge, with Sutherland, Ward,
Woodland, Harwood, Sinclair.
Decca Stereo Set 351, reissued WRC R 046691, Decca CD 448977-2 London OS.
• *Griselda,* Bononcini. LPO, conductor Bonynge, with Sutherland, Sinclair,
Elkins, Malas.
Decca Stereo Set 352 Seranata 411 7199-1, reissued WRC Decca CD 448 977-2.
• *A Festival of Baroque Operas: Griselda and Montezuma.* LPO, Bonynge
London OSA 1270 Stereo.

1968
• *Recital of Schubert, Liszt and Duparc Songs.* Piano Geoffrey Parsons.
EMI Stereo OASD 7537, reissued WRC Stereo RO2224 1975.

1969
• *Musicians of Australia Vol. 1.* Lauris Elms Geoffrey Parsons. *Proses Lyriques*
by Claude Debussy, *Six Gellert Songs op 48* and other songs of Beethoven.
WRC -R 02420 also in ABC RRCS1287 Stereo.

1975
• *Lauris Elms: Songs and Ballads.* Arr George Pikler, conductor Robert Pikler.
WRC RR 01874 (S-5758) reissued 1997 as *I know where I'm going,* Chartreuse
CRCR 1393.

1978
• *Stars of the Australian Opera sing Verdi.* Conductor, Eric Clapham, SSO.
(Condotta elliera in ceppi from *Trovatore,* and *Canzone nel Velo* from *Don
Carlos).*
ABC AA95059 Stereo, reissue EMI YPRX 2364-1, and ABC 442 368-2.
• Elgar. *Sea Pictures,* Chausson: *Poème de l'amour et de la mer.*
SSO, conductors John Hopkins and Robert Pikler.
RCA GL 40749, also cassette GK 40749.
• *Poème de l'amour et de la mer:* Chausson. SSO, Robert Pikler.
ABC Classics CD 446 279-2.

1981
• *Lauris Elms mezzo-soprano: Operatic Arias.* West Australian Symphony
Orchestra, conductor Geoffrey Arnold.
ABCL 8102, reissued ABC Classics CD 442369-2. ABC Encore (5 Boxed CD5 438
196-2 (SET 438 191-2), (only *Una voce poco fa); and French and Italian Opera
Arias.* ABC Classics CD 442 33711-22 & 442 373-2. Reissued ABC Eloquence 465
650-2.

1982
• *Country Gardens,* Percy Grainger. Sydney Symphony Orchestra, conductor John Hopkins. (Under En Bro). EMI EMD 5514.

1984
• *The Apocalypse,* Eugene Goosens, Sydney Symphony Orchestra, conductor Myer Fredman. With Grant Dickson, Gregory Yurisich, Ronald Dowd, Narelle Tapping, Raymond McDonald.
ABC L 70225/6 Cassette C 70225/6.
• *Arianna a Naxos,* Haydn. Piano Geoffrey Parsons.
ABC Transcription Service Australian Artists, LP Stereo YPRX 21187BB. ABC AA 91112B.

1985
• *Lauris Elms Lieder:* Brahms, Berg, Le Gallienne. Piano, Geoffrey Parsons.
ABC LP Polygram 426 191-1 CD426 191-2.

1987
• *Liszt Songs:* Lauris Elms & David Miller. Including *Three Petraque Sonnets, The Lorelei, Mignon's Song, O Quand je dors, Es muss ein wunderbares sein, Du bist wie eine Blume, Es war ein Konig in Thule, Freudvoll und Leidvoll,* & *Die drei Zigeuner.*
MBS 17.
• *Rose of the Bay,* Derek Strahan. Clarinet, Deborah de Graaff, piano, David Miller.
CD REVOLVE RDS-003.

1992
• *Bless This House: Ballads and Songs:* Piano, David Miller, organ, Eric Clapham.
MBS 29 CD.

1993
• *A Schubert Lieder Recital.* Piano, Len Vorster. SCREENTHEMES ST5003.

1995
• *Lauris Elms: Schubert Lieder.* Piano John Winther.
Reissue *French and Italian Opera Arias.* WASO, conductor, Geoffrey Arnold.
ABC CD 2 Compact Discs 442 371-2.

1999
• *Schubert: 17 Favorite Lieder.* Piano, John Winther.
ABC CD Eloquence 464 190-2.
• *Lauris Elms: French and Italian arias.* WASO, conductor, Geoffrey Arnold.
ABC CD Eloquence 465 650-2.

Private recordings:
• 29th Intervarsity Choral Festival Melbourne. *Stabat Mater,* Rossini; *Te Deum,* Berlioz.
BONN BRE-025B.
1984
• 2MBS FM. *The First Ten Years:* clarinet Deborah de Graaff. *Three Songs of William Blake by,* Graham Powning; *Laughing Song ,* Anthony Legge.
• *Stars of the Australian Opera.* LP issued by the Australian Opera Benevolent Fund, about 1987.
• *Requiem Verdi.* Australian Youth Orchestra, conductor Peter Seymour. BRE-017D

Forthcoming release
• A double CD of Lauris Elms' most memorable performances is to be released later in 2001 in the ABC Classics Australian Heritage Series: cat. no. 461 879-2.

Catalogue of Performances

• This list of performances has been compiled primarily from Lauris Elms's own scrapbooks of press clippings and programs, which are located in the archives of the State Library of NSW.
• Printed programs were often undated. In some cases research into Lauris's appointment diaries filled in the dates. In other cases information has been left out rather than guessed at.
• Broadcast recitals are not for the most part listed.
• Recital items are not necessarily listed in the order in which they were presented.
• Orchestras in Australian capital cities were normally the local ABC Symphony orchestras.
GF de Graaff, February 2001

Abbreviations
b. - baritone; cl. - clarinet; c. – conductor; fl. – flute; o. – organ; ob. – oboe; p. – piano; s. - soprano; t. – tenor; v. - violin; va. – viola.
ABC – Australian Broadcasting Commission
MSO – Melbourne Symphony Orchestra
SOCH – Sydney Opera House Concert Hall
SOH – Sydney Opera House, Opera Theatre, Recording Hall, or Music Room
SSO – Sydney Symphony Orchestra
SUIH – Sydney University International House
TH – Town Hall
VSO - Victorian Symphony Orchestra

1952
Recital. p. Ingram; Dandenong: 27 Jan. *Salaam* (Lang); *My Ain Folk* (Lemon); *A Summer Night / Knowest Thou The Land* (Thomas).
Carols by Candlelight. Melb. Myer Music Bowl; 21, 24 Dec.
Recital. p. Elms; Mt Beauty: *Down in the forest*; *My dear Soul* (Sanderson); *Mon coeur s'ouvre à ta voix* (Saint-Saëns).

1953
The Consul – Menotti - Vera Boronel. Simmons R (Sorel), Collier (Magda), Rettick (The Mother), Shaw (Secret Agent), Deagan (Secretary), Allman (Kofner), Simmons J (Foreign woman), Fretwell (Anna), Nolan (Magician), Haag (Assan); c. Post, Melb. Princess Theatre; March.
Merrie England – German - Queen Elizabeth. c. Curnow; Melb. TH: 28 May; c. Logie-Smith; Ballarat: 3 Jun.
Elizabeth of England – Elizabeth. South Melb. TH: 2 Jun.
Solos with Hermann Schildberger's Choirs. c. Schildberger, Canterbury: 14 May; Melb. TH 21 Aug; Malvern: 18 Oct; Horsham: 7 Oct.: *My Ain Folk* (Lemon); *Sink Red Sun*; *Softly Awakes My* Heart (Saint-Saëns); *Caro Mio Ben* (Giordani); *Morgen hymne* (Henschel); *Largo* (Handel); *Che farò* (Gluck); *Elégie* (Massenet).
Pilgrimage of the Rose – Schumann. c. Schildberger, Brighton: 13 Apr.
Messiah - Handel. c. Douglas; Melb. TH: 1 Dec.
Messiah – Handel. c. Logie-Smith; Ballarat: 9 Dec; Geelong: 10 Dec.
Messiah - Handel. c. Stewart: Bendigo; 23 Dec.

1954
Merrie England - German - Queen Elizabeth. c. Curnow, Melb. TH: 13 Feb.
Concert p. Sisely; Wangaratta: 5 Apr. *A Summer Night* (Thomas); *Mon coeur s'ouvre à ta voix* (Saint-Saëns).
Concert. p. Meadows; Sandringham: 11 May. *The Swan* (Grieg); *Ombra mai fu* (Handel); *At night* (Rakhmaninov); *O Don Fatale* (Verdi).
Faust – Gounod - Martha c. Susskind; Melb. TH: 12 June.
A Tale of Old Japan - Coleridge-Taylor. c. Hardy; Wangaratta: 5 Apr; Bendigo: 17 July; Melb.: 28 July.
Concert. p. Clark; Broken Hill: 30 Oct. *Homing* (duet with b. Keith Neilson) (Del Riego); *O lovely night* (duet with b.) (Ronald); *Like to the Damask Rose / Shepherd's Song* (Elgar); *Che farò* (Gluck).
Farewell Recital. p. Stott; Dandenong TH: 25 Nov. *Che farò* (Gluck); *Ombra mai fu* (Handel); *At night* (Rakhmaninov); *Knowest thou the land* (Thomas); *To the forest* (Tchaikovsky).
Messiah - Handel. c. Logie-Smith; Ballarat: 1 Dec; Geelong: 2 Dec.
Messiah – Handel. c. Davis; Melb. TH: 11 Dec.
Tales of Hoffmann – Offenbach -Voice of the Mother. c. Post; Princess Theatre Melb.
La traviata – Verdi - Annina. c. Post; Princess Theatre Melb.

1957
A Masked Ball – Verdi – Ulrica. c. Downes; Cardiff: 4, 6 Mar.; Manchester: 26, 28 Mar.; Southampton: 9, 11 April; Covent Garden: 27, 29 Apr; 15, 18 May; 7, 9, 13, 17, 20 Dec and 13 Jan '58.
The Trojans – Berlioz – Anna. c. Kubelik; Covent Garden: 6, 11, 14, 20, 29 June; 2, 8, 11 July.
Tales of Hoffmann – Offenbach - Voice of the Mother. c. Downes; Covent Garden: 9, 13, 16, 19 July; 30 Oct; 5, 7, 13, 21 Nov; 2, 5, 11, 18 Dec.
Elektra – R Strauss - First Maid. c. Kempe; Covent Garden: 16, 19, 22, 26 Nov.

1958
The Dialogues of the Carmelites – Poulenc - Mère Jeanne. c. Kubelik; Covent Garden: 16, 18, 21, 24, 27 Jan.; 7, 24, 26 Feb; Manchester 10 Mar.; Oxford: 24 Mar.
Rigoletto – Verdi – Giovanna. c. Downes; Covent Garden: 5, 8, 10, 13, 18, 21 Feb; 5, 25, 29 Apr; 27 May; Oxford: 26, 29 Mar; Manchester: 12, 15 Mar.
Symphony no 9 – Beethoven. Israel Philharmonic Orch., c. Kubelik; Israel: seven performances in Haifa and one in each of Jerusalem and Haifa, during April.
Peter Grimes – Britten - Mrs Sedley. c. Kubelik; Covent Garden: 29 Jan; 1, 3, 6, 12, Feb; 11, 15 April. Scene for Covent Garden Centenary Gala 10 Jun.
Elektra – R Strauss - First Maid. c. Kempe; Covent Garden: 14, 16, 29, 31 May
The Trojans - Berlioz – Anna. c. Kubelik; Covent Garden: 16, 19 June; 10, 17, 19 July.
Die Walküre – Wagner – Grimgerde. c. Kempe; Covent Garden: 24 Sep; 7 Oct.
Samson – Handel – Micah. c. Leppard; Leeds: 16, 17, 18 Oct; Covent Garden: 15, 18 Nov; 12 Dec.

1959
Samson – Handel – Micah. c. Leppard; Covent Garden: 3 Jan; 2, 11 Mar; 8, 12 June; c. Gibson; Oxford: 28 Mar.
Lucia di Lammermoor – Donizetti – Alisa. c. Serafin; Covent Garden: 20, 23, 25 Feb; 12, 19, 25 Mar.; c. Balkwill; Oxford: 1, 4, 7, 10 Apr.
Parsifal – Wagner - Second Esquire. c. Kempe; Covent Garden: 15, 28 May; 1, 4, 16, 19 June; 1 July.
The Dialogues of the Carmelites – Poulenc - Mère Jeanne. c. Kubelik; Covent Garden: 23, 26, 29 June; 8 July.
Recital. p. Kimber; Dandenong TH: 27 Oct. *Botschaft / Vergebliches Ständchen / Wie bist du, meine Königen* (Brahms); *Joys that are pure / Then long eternity*

shall greet thy bliss (Handel); *Biblical Songs* (Dvorák); *Mon coeur s'ouvre a ta voix* (Saint-Saëns); *Un certo non so che* (Vivaldi).
Concert Solos. c. Douglas; VSO; Melb. Festival Hall: 29 Oct. *Gypsy Songs* (Dvorák), *Träume* (Wagner), *Bel Raggio* (Rossini).
Recital. p. Clapham; Berwick Community Hall: 8 Nov. *Five Biblical Songs* (Dvorák); *Botschaft / Vergebliches Ständchen / Wie bist du, meine Königen (Brahms); Return O God of Hosts* (Handel); *Les lettres (Werther)* (Massenet); *Un Certo non so che* (Vivaldi); *Se Florindo* è *fedele* (Scarlatti).
Samson – Handel – Micah. c. Schildberger, concert performance; Melb. Assembly Hall: 1 Dec.
Messiah – Handel. c. Morgan; Korrumburra Picture Theatre: 3 Dec.
Messiah – Handel. Tasmanian Symphony; Hobart: 17 Dec.
Messiah – Handel. c. Heinze; Melb. TH: 22, 23 Dec.

1960
Recital. p. Scott; Balwyn: Jan. *Five Biblical Songs* (Dvorák); *At the cradle* (Greig); *Plaisir d'amour* (Martini); *Roundelay / Music for a while / She flies me everywhere* (Purcell); *Amour viens aider* (Saint-Saëns); *None but the lonely heart* (Tchaikovsky).
Concert. c. Crawford; Melb. Myer Music Bowl. 6 Mar. *Amour, viens aider ma faiblesse* (Saint-Saëns).
St Matthew Passion – Bach. c. Krips; Melb. TH: 9 Apr.
Recital. p. Halstead; Toorak: 28 Apr.; *Les nuits d'été* (Berlioz); *Gypsy Songs* (Dvorák); *Che farò* (Gluck); *O mio Fernando* (Donizetti).
Missa Solemnis – Beethoven. c. Heinze; Melb. TH: 8 Oct.
Jephtha – Handel - Storge. c. Schildberger; Melb.: 30 Nov.
Das Lied von der Erde – Mahler. c. Krips, t. Neate; Melb. TH: 3 Dec.
Messiah – Handel. c. Heinze; Melb. TH: 20, 21 Dec.

1961
Concert. c. Hopkins; SSO; Syd. TH: date uncertain: *Les nuits d'été* (Berlioz).
Concert. c. Douglas; VSO; Melb.: date uncertain: *Sea Pictures* (Elgar), *Lieder eines fahrenden Gesellen* (Mahler).
Concert. c. Crawford; Melb. Myer Music Bowl: 4 Mar.
Broadcast. p. Lambert; ABC Melb.: 16 Mar; *Frauenliebe und leben* (Schumann).
Recital. p. Halstead; Bendigo: 18 Mar; *Les nuits d'été* (Berlioz); *Gypsy Songs* (Dvorák); *Ah mio cor, schernito sei* (Handel); *Plaisir d'amour* (Martini); *Un certo no so que* (Vivaldi); *Se Florindo* è *fedele* (Scarlatti).
Elijah – Mendelssohn. c. Hopkins; Wellington NZ: 28 June.
Recital. p. Neilson; Wanganui: 6 July; *Canzone* from *Linda di Chamounix* (Donizetti); *Chanson triste / L'invitation au voyage / La vague et la cloche / La vie antérieure* (Duparc); *Gypsy Songs* (Dvorák); *Che farò* (Gluck); *Ah, mio cor, schernito sei / Ombra mai fu / Then long eternity* (Handel); *He was a funny fellow* (Head); *Ces lettres* (Massenet); *Amour viens aider ma faiblesse* (Saint-Saëns); *Frauenliebe und leben* (Schumann).
Recitals. same program as above in Wellington, Nelson, Timaru, Hamilton, New Plymout, Napier, Dunedin and Christchurch during July.
Stabat mater – Dvorák. c. Ancerl; Adelaide TH: 16 Aug.
Broadcast. p. van Hove; va. Pikler; ABC Syd.: 12 Nov; *Gestillte Sehnsucht / Geistliches Wiegenlied* (op 91 Brahms).
Samson and Delilah – Saint-Saëns – Delilah. c. Post; ABC Syd.; live Telecast.
Messiah – Handel. c. Martin; Geelong: 2 Dec.
Messiah – Handel. c. Heinze; Melb. TH: 22, 23 Dec.

1962
El Amor Brujo – Falla. c. Pritchard, London Philharmonic; Brisbane: 15 Mar; Adelaide: 20 Mar; Melbourne: 26, 27 Mar.
St Matthew Passion - Bach. c. Krips; Melb. TH: 14 Apr.
Elijah – Mendelssohn. c. Wilkie; Melb. TH: 11 May.
Concert. p. Meirs; Northcote: 6 June. *Mon coeur s'ouvre à ta voix* (Saint-Saëns).

268

Das Lied von der Erde – Mahler. c. Hopkins; Wellington NZ: 28 June.
Recital. p. Nielsen; Hamilton NZ: 2 July; *Botschaft / Vergebliches ständchen / Wie bist du, meine Königin* (Brahms); *Chanson triste / L'invitation au voyage / La vague et la cloche / La vie antérieure* (Duparc); *Biblical Songs* (Dvorák); *Ombra mai fu / Joys that are pure / Then long eternity shall greet thy bliss* (Handel).
Recital. p. Nielsen; Lower Hutt: 3 July; same program as Hamilton 2 July.
Recital. p. Nielsen; Wellington: 4 July; same program as Hamilton 2 July.
Recital. p. Nielsen; New Plymouth: 5 July; same program as Hamilton 2 July.
Recital. p. Nielsen; Timaru: 7 July; same program as Hamilton 2 July.
Recital. p. Nielsen; Hastings: 9 July; same program as Hamilton 2 July.
Das Lied von der Erde – Mahler. c. Hopkins; Christchurch NZ: 10 July.
Joan of Arc at the stake – Honegger. c. Tzipine; Melb. TH.: 3 Aug.
Recital. p. Schofield; Melb. Assembly Hall; *Lieder eines fahrenden Gesellen* (Mahler)
St John Passion – Bach. c. Krips; Adelaide Town Hall: 5 Oct.
Concert. Broken Hill: 27 Oct; *Gypsy Songs* (Dvorák); *Lieder eines fahrenden Gesellen (Mahler).*
Recital. p. Morcom; Ballarat: 3 Nov; *Gypsy Songs* (Dvorák); *Lieder eines fahrenden Gesellen* (Mahler); *Frauenliebe und leben* (Schumann); *English Art Songs* (Head).
Messiah - Handel. c. Heinze; Syd. TH: 6, 7, 8 Dec.; Melb. TH: 21, 22 Dec.
Concert. c. Dixon; SSO; Syd. TH: 12 Dec; *Ombra felice / Per pietà, ben mio* (Mozart).

1963
Royal Tour Concert. c. Heinze; VSO; Melb. Myer Music Bowl: 24 Feb.; *Land of Hope and Glory* (Elgar).
Recital. p. Halstead, fl. Chugg; Wangaratta: 29 Mar.; *Les nuits d'été* (Berlioz); *Ombra felice / Per pietà, ben mio* (Mozart); *Gestillte sehnsucht* (op 91 Brahms); *Softest Sounds* (Handel).
Bluebeard's Castle - Bartók – Judith. c. Hopkins; SSO; Syd. TH: 11, 13, 14 May.
Requiem – Verdi. c. Hopkins; Auckland NZ: 2 June.
Concert. cl. and va.; Melb. Assembly Hall: 7 June: *O men from the fields* (Gilfedder).
Concert. c. Freccia; Brisbane CH: 14, 15 June; *Wesendonk-Lieder* (Wagner).
Concert. c. Tzipine; Hobart: 9 July; *Les nuits d'été* (Berlioz).
Concert. c. Tzipine; Hobart: 12 July; *Il segreto per esser felice* (Donizetti); *Bel raggio* (Rossini); *Amour, viens aider ma faiblesse* (Saint-Saëns); *Habañera* from Carmen (Bizet).
Broadcast. p. Halstead; ABC Melb.: 24 July; *Barbara Allen / Charlie is my darling / Danny Boy / Drink to me only / My ain folk / Over the mountains* (folk songs arr. Quilter)
Concert. c. Cosma; Melb. TH: 13, 14 Aug.; *Ombra felice / Per pietà, ben mio* (Mozart).
Requiem – Verdi. c. Tzipine; Melb. TH: 31 Aug.
Four Poems of St Teresa of Avila – Berkeley. c. Clare, Victorian Chamber Orchestra inaug. conc.; Melb. Assembly Hall: 24 Sep.
Spring Symphony – Britten. c. Matthews; Melb. TH: 23 Nov.
Messiah - Handel. c. Logie-Smith; Melb.: 4 Dec.
Messiah - Handel. c. Keck; Ballarat: 18 Dec.

1964
Peter Grimes - Britten. Mrs Sedley c. Clapham; Melb.: ABC telecast.
Messiah – Handel. c. Logie-Smith; Melb. Myer Music Bowl: 1 Mar.
St John Passion – Bach. c. Heinze; Syd. TH: 25 Mar.
Elijah - Mendelssohn. c. Heinze; Melb. TH: 23 May.
Concerts. c. Tzipine; Geelong: 11 June; Warrnambool: 12 June; *Habañera* (Bizet); *Bel raggio* (Rossini); *Amour, viens aider ma faiblesse* (Saint-Saëns).
Recital. p. Schofield; Bendigo: 24 June; *Gelobet sei der herr / Murre nicht, lieber*

Christ (Bach); *Habañera* (Bizet); *Gypsy Songs* (Brahms); *Barbara Allen / Charlie is my darling /Drink to me only /* (folk songs arr. Quilter); *Bel raggio* (Rossini); *Amour, viens aider ma faiblesse* (Saint-Saëns).
Concert. p. Meirs; Ballarat: 3 July; *Habañera* (Bizet); *Bel raggio* (Rossini); *Amour, viens aider ma faiblesse* (Saint-Saëns).
Recital. p. Schofield; 'cello Veit; Melb. Assembly Hall: 28 Oct.; *Gelobet sei der herr / Murre nicht, lieber Christ* (Bach); *Gypsy Songs* (Dvorák); *Chanson triste / L'invitation au voyage / La vague et la cloche / La vie antérieure* (Duparc).
Solos. p. Grieger; Melb. Lutheran Ch.:1 Nov: *All praises to the Lord / Murmer not Christian soul* (Bach); *O thou that tellest* (Handel).
Das Lied von der Erde – Mahler. c. Paul; Syd. TH: 11, 12 Dec.
Recital. NZBC; 16 Nov.; *Aufenthalt / Die Allmacht / Die junge Nonne / Frühlingsglaube / Frülingstraum* (Schubert).
Requiem - Dvorák. c. Dodgson; Christchurch NZ: 21 Nov.
Messiah - Handel. c. Callaway; Perth: 11, 12 Dec.
Messiah - Handel. c. Keck; Ballarat: 16 Dec.
Messiah - Handel. c. Warne; Bendigo: 19 Dec.

1965
Elijah – Mendelssohn. Adelaide TH: April.
St Matthew Passion – Bach. c. Johnson; Syd. TH: 16 Apr.
St Matthew Passion – Bach. c. Logie-Smith; Melb.: 17 Apr.
Eugene Onegin – Tchaikovsky – Olga. c. Krug; Melb. Her Majesty's Theatre: 13, 16, 21, 23, 31 July; 2 Aug; Adelaide Her Majesty's Theatre: 17 Aug; Syd. Her Majesty's Theatre: 2, 4, 7, 14, 30 Sep.
La traviata – Verdi – Annina. c. Bonynge; Melb. Her Majesty's Theatre: 28 July; 6, 13 Aug; Syd. Her Majesty's Theatre: 16, 18, 20 Sep.
Semiramide – Rossini – Arsace. c. Bonynge; Melb. Her Majesty's Theatre: 7 Aug; Syd. Her Majesty's Theatre: 22 Sep.
Lucia di Lammermoor – Donizetti – Alisa. c. Bonynge; Syd. Her Majesty's Theatre: 25 Sep.
La sonnambula – Bellini – Teresa. c. Bonynge; Melb. Her Majesty's Theatre: 11, 14 Aug; Syd. Her Majesty's Theatre: 7 Oct.
Faust – Gounod – Martha. c. Bonynge; Syd. Her Majesty's Theatre: 9, 28 Sep.
Dream of Gerontius – Elgar. c. Field-Dodgson; Christchurch NZ: 3,5 Nov.
Messiah - Handel. c. Johnston; Syd. Cell Block: 27 Nov.
Messiah - Handel. c. Heinze; Adelaide TH: 2, 3, 4 Dec.
Messiah - Handel. c. Heinze; Syd. TH: 9, 11 Dec.

1966
Elijah – Mendelssohn. c. Heinze; Adelaide TH: 18 June.
Concert. p. White; Syd. Trinity Grammar School: 29 July; *Du Herr, du kronst allein / Gelobet se der Herr / Murre nicht, lieber Christ* (Bach).
Il trovatore – Verdi - Azucena c. Vaughan; Brisbane Her Majesty's Theatre: 19, 25, 27 Aug.; Syd. Her Majesty's Theatre: 9 Sep et al.; Melb. Palais Theatre: 29, 31 Oct.; 2 Nov.; c. Rosen 9, 12 Nov.; c. Krug 16, 18 Nov.
Lieder eines fahrenden Gesellen – Mahler. c. Hopkins; Newcastle: 23 Aug.
Messiah - Handel. c. Rixon; Newcastle: 3 Dec.; c. Heinze; Syd. TH: 9, 10 Dec.; Melb. TH: 23, 24 Dec.; c. Hobcroft; Hobart: 14 Dec.

1967
Nelson Mass – Haydn. c. Hopkins; Syd. TH: date uncertain.
Recital. p. White; SUIH: 3 Mar.; *Chanson triste / L'invitation au voyage / La vague et la cloche / La vie antérieure* (Duparc); *Ah mio cor, schernito sei / Then long eternity* (Handel); *Das irdische Leben / Frühlingsmorgen / Ich ging mit Lust / Rheinlegendchen* (Mahler); *Cruda Sorte* (Rossini); *Mon coeur s'ouvre à ta voix* (Saint-Saëns); *Frauenliebe und leben* (Schumann).
Stabat mater – Dvorák. c. Hawkey; Christchurch NZ: 18 Mar.
Concert. p. Schofield; Mittagong: 23 Mar.; *Frauenliebe und leben* (Schumann).
Concert. p. Baer; Mittagong: 24 Mar.; *All praises to the Lord / Chains of bondage*

(Bach).

Concert. c. Pikler; Mittagong: 26 Mar.; *Four Poems of St Teresa of Avila* (Berkeley).

Recital. p. White; Syd. Chalwin Castle: 9 Apr.; same program as SUIH 3 Mar.

Requiem – Verdi. c. Robinson; Adelaide TH: 29 Apr.

Stabat mater – Dvořák. c. Dixon; Syd. TH: 2, 13 May.

Recital. p. White; Roseville: 31 May; same program as SUIH 3 Mar.

Recital. p. Schofield; Killara: 6 June; same program as SUIH 3 Mar.

Recital. p. White; Syd. Chalwin Castle: 18 June; *Come raggio di sol* (Caldara); *Amour, viens rendre a mon ame* (Gluck); *Del mio destin tiranno / Non sapri curare il vanto / Se il dovere in quest'addio* (Graun); *Ah, mio cor* (Handel); *Ombra felice / Per pietà* (Mozart); *O nuit* (Piccinni); *Se florindo e fidele* (Scarlatti); *Un certo non so che* (Vivaldi).

Il trovatore – Verdi – Azucena. c. Krug; Adelaide: 27, 30 June; Melb.: 3, 6, 8, 12, 15 July; 5 Aug.

Concert. p. White; North Syd.: 23 Aug.; *Montezuma (three arias)* (Graun); *An evening hymn / The Blessed Virgin's expostulation / We sing to Him* (Purcell).

Broadcast Recital. p. Parsons; Syd. ABC: 24 Aug.; *Gretchen / Frühlingsglaube / Die junge Nonne / Ständchen / Aufenthalt / Die Allmacht.* (Schubert).

Recital. p. White; Ryde Music Club: 11 Sep.; Lane Cove Music Club: 16 Oct.; *Gretchen am Spinnrade / Frühlingsglaube / Die junge Nonne / Ständchen / Aufenthalt / Die Allmacht.* (Schubert); *Waly Waly / The Ash Grove* (Britten); *Les lettres (Werther)* (Massenet); *Ombra felice* (Mozart); *O nuit* (Piccinni); *Drink to me only / Over the mountains* (Quilter); *Cruda Sorte* (Rossini); *Un certo non so che* (Vivaldi).

Recital. p. White: Syd. University Great Hall: 14 Sep; *Chanson triste / L'invitation au voyage / La vague et la cloche / La vie antérieure* (Duparc); *Ombra felice* (Mozart); *Gretchen am Spinnrade / Frühlingsglaube / Ständchen / Die Allmacht.* (Schubert).

Il trovatore – Verdi – Azucena. c. Krug; Syd. Tivoli Theatre: 16 Sep.

Concert. p. Hutchinson; Canberra Musica Viva; 2 Oct.; *Gretchen am Spinnrade / Frühlingsglaube / Ständchen / Die Allmacht.* (Schubert).

Recital. p. van Hove; Syd. Abbotsleigh School: 9 Nov.; *Che faro* (Gluck); *Charlie is my darling / Drink to me only / O Waly Waly / Over the mountains / Since first I saw your face / The Ash grove* (Quilter); *Habañera* (Bizet); *O don fatale* (Verdi).

Concert. p. White; Pymble: 29 Nov.; *Three arias* from *Montezuma* (Graun); *An evening hymn / The Blessed Virgin's expostulation / We sing to Him* (Purcell).

Messiah - Handel. c. Rickard; Wellington NZ: 9, 11 Dec.

1968

A Masked Ball – Verdi - Ulrica c. Downes; Melb. Princess Theatre; Launceston: performances dates unknown.

Recital. p. Schofield; Swan Hill: date unknown; Syd. International House: 10 June; Strathfield: 11 June; Bendigo: 15 Nov.; Dandenong 21 Nov.; *Vier ernste Gesänge* (Brahms); *A Song of Autumn / Like to the Damask Rose / Queen Mary's Song / Rondel / Shepherd's Song* (Elgar); *O nuit,* (Piccinni); *Ah, prends pitié* (Rossi); *Gretchen am Spinnrade / Frühlingsglaube / Ständchen / Aufenthalt /* (Schubert).

Sea Pictures – Elgar. c. Hopkins; Syd. TH: 17 Feb.

Don Carlos – Verdi – Eboli. c. Feist; Adelaide Her Majesty's Theatre: 8, 11, 13, 16, 19, 21, 23, 29 Mar.; Melb. Princess Theatre: 18 Apr. et al.; Syd. Her Majesty's Theatre 13, 28 June, 6, 13, 20 July.

St John Passion – Bach. c. Johnston; Syd. TH: 12 Apr.

Lieder eines fahrenden Gesellen – Mahler. c. Heinze; Syd. TH: 30 Apr., 1, 2, May.

Concert. The Attic Ensemble, Musica Viva; Melb. Wilson Hall: 6 May; Adelaide TH: 7 May; Mildura: 9 May; Canberra: 11 May; Syd. TH: 27 June; Wollongong: 11 Oct.; *Gestillte Sehnsucht / Geistliches Wiegenlied* (op 91 Brahms); *Three arias* from *Montezuma* (Graun); *Five Hungarian folk songs* (arr George Pikler);

Laudate Pueri (Perti); *Jubilent Omnes* (Riccio).
Concert. The Attic Ensemble, Musica Viva; Toowoomba and Avalon, dates unknown; Bathurst: 26 Oct.; Springwood: 31 Oct., *Air sérieux* (Couperin); *An evening hymn / The Blessed Virgin's expostulation / We sing to Him* (Purcell); *Five Hungarian folk songs* (arr George Pikler); *Gestillte Sehnsucht / Geistliches Wiegenlied* (op 91 Brahms); *Chansons madécasses* (Ravel); *Air* from *Mitrane* (Rossi); *Auf dem Strom* (Schubert).
Concert. The Attic Ensemble, Musica Viva; Newcastle: 18 Oct.; *Five Hugarian Folk Songs* (arr George Pikler); *Gestillte Sehnsucht / Geistliches Wiegenlied* (op 91 Brahms) – Va.: Robert Pikler; *Chansons madécasses* (Ravel); *Auf dem Strom* (Schubert).
Recital. p. White; Syd. St. Stephen's: 2 Aug; *Vier ernste Gesänge* (Brahms); *Auf dem See / Gruppe aus dem Tartarus / Klärchen's Lied / Schlummerlied* (Schubert).
Kindertotenlieder – Mahler. c. Llewellyn; Canberra: 7, 8 Aug.
Recital. p. White; Syd. Chalwin Castle: 11 Aug.; *Vier ernste Gesänge* (Brahms); *Lieder eines fahrenden Gesellen* (Mahler); *Gretchen am Spinnrade / Frühlingsglaube / Ständchen / Aufenthalt / Die Allmacht / Auf dem See / Gruppe aus dem Tartarus / Klärchen's Lied / Schlummerlied* (Schubert).
Concert. p. Hutchinson; Mosman. 17 Aug.; *Vier ernste Gesänge* (Brahms); *Gestillte Sehnsucht / Geistliches Wiegenlied* (op 91 Brahms).
Carmina - Four Latin poems of Spring – Butterley. New Sydney Woodwind Quintet; Syd. Cell Block Theatre: 1 Nov.
Cantata 43, God goeth up – Bach. Oriana Choir; Waverley: 22 Nov.
Messiah - Handel. c. Heinze; Syd. TH: 7, 8 Dec.

1969
Coronation of Poppea – Monteverdi – Ottavia. c. Covell; Syd. Science Theatre: dates unknown.
Recital. p. White; Wahroonga Music Club: Feb; *O nuit* (Piccinni); *Ah, prends pitié* (Rossi); *Les lettres (Werther)* (Massenet); *Mon coeur s'ouvre à ta voix* (Saint-Saëns); *Let us garlands bring* (Finzi).
Symphony no 3 – Mahler. c. Hopkins; Syd. TH: 15 Feb.
Concert. Syd. Harp Society; harp – Loney, flute – Vogt; Syd.: 12 Mar.; *Cantos del Tucumán* (Ginastera); *Four Songs* (Stravinsky).
St Matthew Passion – Bach. c. Thomas; Melb. TH: 29, 30 Mar.
St Matthew Passion – Bach. c. Johnson; Syd. TH: 4 Apr.
Recital. New Syd. Woodwind Quintet; Beecroft: 12 Apr.; *Carmina* (Butterley); *A Shepherd in a shade / Flow not so fast, yee fountaines* (Dowland); *Phyllis was a fair maid* (Earle).
Recital. p. White; Syd. Chalwyn Theatre: 20 Apr.; *Six Gellert Songs* (op 48 Beethoven); *Fidelity / My mother bids me bind my hair / The Wanderer* (Haydn); *Bergerettes / Gia dagli occhi / Non più di fiori / Parto inerme, e non pavento* (Mozart).
Concert. c. Atzmon; Syd. Cell Block Theatre: 23 May; *Four Poems of St Teresa of Avila* (Berkeley); *Salve Regina* (Scarlatti).
Recital. p. Hutchinson, ob. Henderson; Mt Gambier: 28 May; Albury: 2 June; Tamworth: 12 June; *Let us garlands bring* (Finzi); *Che faro* (Gluck); *Four Divine Poems of John Donne* (Le Gallienne); *Crude sorte* (Rossini); *Aufenthalt / Frühlingsglaube / Mondnacht* (Schubert); *Widmung* (Schumann); *Was Gott tut das us wohlgetan / Ach Herr! Was ist ein Menschenkind* (Bach).
Recital. p. Hutchinson; Broken Hill: 26 May; Wagga Wagga 4 June; Goulburn 6 June; *Murre nicht, lieber Christ* (Bach); *Gypsy Songs* (Dvorák); *Fidelity / My mother bids me bind my hair / The Wanderer* (Haydn); *O nuit* (Piccinni); *Ah, prends pitié* (Rossi).
Concert. c. Johnston; Syd. Cell Block Theatre: 9 Aug.; *Salve Regina* (Scarlatti); *Serenade in F* (Schubert).
Concert. p. Schofield; Melb.: 21 Aug.; *Six Gellert Songs* – (op 48 Beethoven); *Les nuits d'été* (Berlioz); *Gia dagli occhi / Parto Inerme* (Mozart).
Orpheus and Euridice - Gluck – Orpheus. c. Taylor; Melb.Union Theatre: 26,

27, 29, 30 Aug.
Kindertotenlieder – Mahler. c. Krips; Adelaide TH: 11, 12, 13 Sep.
Recital. p. Demant; Newcastle: 20 Sep.; *Six Gellert Songs* – (op 48 Beethoven); *Vier ernste Gesänge* (Brahms); *Gypsy Songs* (Dvorák); *Lieder eines fahrenden Gesellen* (Mahler); *Frauenliebe und leben* (Schumann).
Recital. p. Demant; Newcastle: 21 Sep.; *Bergerettes; Les nuits d'été* (Berlioz); *Chanson triste / L'invitation au voyage / La vague et la cloche / La vie antérieure* (Duparc); *Les lettres (Werther)* (Massenet); *Habañera* from Carmen (Bizet).
Concert. c. Robinson; Launceston: 25 Sep.; *El amor brujo* (Falla); *Salve Regina* (Scarlatti).
Recital. p. White; Trinity Grammar School: 3 Oct.; *Les nuits d'été* (Berlioz); *Let us garlands bring* (Finzi); *Chansons madécasses* (Ravel); *Auf dem Strom* (Schubert); *Six Gellert Songs* – (op 48 Beethoven).
Recital. p. Hutchinson, ob. Henderson; Syd. Music Hall: 26 Oct.; *Murre nicht, lieber Christ / Was Gott tut, das ist wohlgetan* (Bach).; *Gypsy Songs* (Dvorák); *Let us garlands bring* (Finzi); *Ah, prends pitié* (Rossi); *Crude sorte* (Rossini).
Requiem – Dvorák. c. Field-Dodgson; Christchurch NZ: 1 Nov.
Recital. p. Till; Christchurch NZ: 3 Nov.; *Six Gellert Songs* – (op 48 Beethoven); *Gypsy Songs* (Dvorák); *Five Songs* (Elgar); *Let us garlands bring* (Finzi); *Four Divine Poems of John Donne* (Le Gallienne).
Das Lied von der Erde – Mahler. c. Llewellyn, t. MacDonald; Canberra: 26, 27 Nov.
Messiah - Handel. c. Logie-Smith; Melb.: Dec.
Christmas Oratorio – Bach. c. Seymour; Syd.: 6 Dec.

1970
Daisy Bates – Blom – Daisy. c. Blom; Syd. ABC TV live transmission: 1970 date uncertain.
Symphony no 9 – Beethoven. c. Brissenden; Wollongong: date uncertain.
Nelson Mass – Haydn. c. Seymour; Syd. TH: date uncertain.
Concert. c. Matteucci; Brisbane Festival Hall; 28 Feb.; *El amor brujo* (Falla); *Kindertotenlieder* (Mahler).
Recital. p. White; Syd. Chalwin Castle: 8 Mar.; *Andenken / Lied aus der ferne / Mignon / Six Gellert Songs* – (op 48 Beethoven); *Kindertotenlieder* (Mahler); *Am Grabe Anselmos / Die Rose / Fischerweise / Prometheus* (Schubert).
Requiem – Verdi. c. Mackerras; London Festival Hall: 13 Apr.
Missa Solemnis – Beethoven. c. Atzmon; Syd. TH: 19 May.
Schwanda the bagpiper – Weinbrger - Ice Queen. c. Stiasny; ABC Syd. Telecast: 24 May.
The Rape of Lucretia – Britten - Lucretia c. Humble; Melb. St Martin's Theatre: 30 June, 1, 3, 4 July.
Recital. p. White; SUIH: 19 July; *Six Gellert Songs* – *Wonne der Wehmut / Lied aus der Ferne / Andenken* (op 48 Beethoven); *Les nuits d'été* (Berlioz).
Recital. p. White; Ryde Eastwood Music Club: 14 Sep.; *Six Gellert Songs* (op 48 Beethoven); *Sea Pictures* (Elgar); *The Wanderer / Fidelity / My mother bids me bind my hair* (Haydn); *Music for a while /Bonvica's song / Epithalamium / 'Twas within a mile of Edinburgh town* (Purcell).
Requiem – Verdi. c. Field-Dodgson; Christchurch NZ: 25 Sep.
Recital. p. White; Syd. St Stephen's: 8 Oct.; *Six Gellert Songs* (op 48 Beethoven); *Sea Pictures* (Elgar); *Music for a while / Bonvica's song / Epithalamium / 'Twas within a mile of Edinburgh town* (Purcell).
Sea Pictures – Elgar. c. Ferencsik; Syd. TH: 12 Oct.
St Matthew Passion – Bach. c. Holland; Canberra Albert Hall: 17 Oct.
Recital. p. White; Killara Music Club: 26 Oct.; *Six Gellert Songs* (op 48 Beethoven); *Sea Pictures* (Elgar); *The Wanderer / Fidelity / My mother bids me bind my hair* (Haydn); *Irish Folk Songs* (Hughes); *Music for a while / Bonvica's song / Epithalamium / 'Twas within a mile of Edinburgh town* (Purcell).
Julius Caesar - Handel – Caesar. c. Pini; Syd. Science Theatre: 13, 14, 15 Nov.
The Six Days of Creation – Cugley. c. Colman; Syd. Macquarie Uni: 28 Nov.

1971
Wesendonk-Lieder – Wagner. c. Pini; Syd.: date uncertain.
The Dream of Gerontius – Elgar. c. Hopkins; Syd. TH: 13 Feb.
A Masked Ball – Verdi – Ulrica. c. Reid; Melb. Princess Theatre: 24, 27 Mar., 3, 6, 8, 12, 14, 16 Apr.; Syd. Elizabethan Theatre: 23, 29 June, 3, 6, 9, 13, 16, 22, 24, 29, 31 July.
St John Passion – Bach. c. Johnston; Syd. TH: 9 Apr.
Semele – Handel – Juno. c. Mackerras; Syd. TH: 22 Apr.
The Rape of Lucretia – Britten – Lucretia. c. Bacon; Syd. Elizabethan Theatre: 27 May, 2, 12, 17, 26 June.
Recital. p. Hutchinson; Mozart Society, Syd. Chalwin Castle: 20 June; *Lied aus der Ferne / Wonne der Wehmut / Freudvoll und leidvoll / Die Trommel gerühret* (Beethoven); *Abendempfindung / Als Luise / Dans un bois solitaire / Ridente la calma / Ch' io mi scordi di te* (Mozart); *Son tutta duol / Se Florindo e fedele / Se tu dell mia morte* (Scarlatti).
Il trovatore – Verdi – Azucena. c. Downes, Syd. Capitol Theatre – concert performances: 10, 12, 14 Aug.
Requiem – Verdi. c. Field-Dodgson; Syd. TH: 25, 26 Aug.
Requiem – Verdi. c. Atzmon; Syd.: 14 Sep.
Lieder eines fahrenden Gesellen – Mahler. c. Llewellyn; Canberra: 22, 23 Sep.

1972
Recital. p. White; Syd. Con.: 26 Jan.; *Habañera* (Bizet); *Three songs* (Lees); *Che faro* (Gluck); *Proses lyriques* (Debussy).
Lieder eines fahrenden Gesellen – Mahler. c. Paul; Melb. Myer Music Bowl: 12 Feb.
The Kingdom – Elgar. c. Hopkins; Syd. TH: 15 Feb.
Recital. p. Hutchinson; SUIH: 26 Feb; Abbotsleigh School: 22 Apr.: *Les nuits d'été* (Berlioz); *Proses lyriques* (Debussy); *Les lettres (Werther)* (Massenet); *Abendempfindung / Als Luise / Dans un bois solitaire / Ridente la calma / Ch'io mi scordi di te / Oiseaux, si tous les ans* (Mozart); *Crude sorte* (Rossini); *Mon coeur s'ouvre à ta voix* (Saint-Saëns).
The Rape of Lucretia – Britten – Lucretia. c. Bacon; Adelaide: 14, 16, 18 Mar.; Melb. Princess Theatre: 9, 23, 24, 30 Mar., 1, 4, 8, 10 Apr.; Canberra: 1 June; Syd. Elizabethan Theatre: 12, 17, 25 June.
Il tramonto – Respighi. Fidelio Quartet; Syd. Con. for Musica Viva: 12 May.
Recital. p. Hollier; Canberra: 5 June; *Les nuits d'été* (Berlioz); *Proses lyriques* (Debussy); *O mio Fernando* (Donizetti); *Abendempfindung / Als Luise / Dans un bois solitaire / Ridente la calma / Ch'io mi scordi di te / Oiseaux, si tous les ans* (Mozart); *Crude sorte* (Rossini); *Mon coeur s'ouvre à ta voix* (Saint-Saëns).
Mass no 3 – Bruckner. c. Rieger; Adelaide TH: 13, 14, 15 July.
B Minor Mass – Bach. c. Sutcliffe; Syd. St James Church: 26 July.
Concert. Fidelio String Quartet; Syd. Trinity Grammar School: 28 July; *Three arias* from *Montezuma* (Graun); *Four Sonnets* (Martin); *Folk Songs* (arr G.Pikler); *Il tramonto* (Respighi); *Salve Regina* (Scarlatti).
Recital. p. Hutchinson; Syd. Chalwin Castle for Mozart Society: 20 Aug.; *Three arias* from *Mass in B Minor* (Bach); *Der Kuss / Der Wachtelschlag / Ich liebe dich / Marmotte / Mit einem gemalten Band* (Beethoven); *Two Arias* (Haydn); *Two arias* (Mozart).
B Minor Mass – Bach. c. Ehrling; Syd. TH: 30 Aug.
Recital p. Schofield; Melb. Assembly Hall: 9 Sep.; *Abendempfindung / Als Luise / Dans un bois solitaire / Ridente la calma / Ch'io mi scordi di te / Oiseaux, si tous les ans* (Mozart); *Frauenliebe und leben* (Schumann); *Les nuits d'été* (Berlioz); *Proses lyriques* (Debussy).
Requiem – Verdi. c. Logie-Smith; Melb. Dallas Brooks Hall: 13 Sep.
Cantata. c. Pini; Syd. St Mary's Cathedral: 4 October; *Ah! Crudel, nel pianto mio* (Handel).
Concert. c. Gati; Victoria Symphony Orchestra, Vancouver Island, Canada: 22, 23 Oct.; *Cantata 170* (Bach); *Lieder eines fahrenden Gesellen* (Mahler).
Recital. p. Scott; Victoria, Canada: *Les nuits d'été* (Berlioz); *Proses lyriques*

274

(Debussy); *Abendempfindung / Als Luise / Dans un bois solitaire / Ridente la calma / Ch'io mi scordi di te /* Oiseaux, si tous les ans (Mozart); *Crude sorte* (Rossini); *Mon coeur s'ouvre à ta voix* (Saint-Saëns); *O mio Fernando* (Donizetti).
Recital. p. Halstead; Beecroft Music Club: 18 Nov.; *Six Gellert Songs* (op 48 Beethoven); *Proses lyriques* (Debussy); *Frauenliebe und leben* (Schumann); *Whitman Cycle* (Sitszy); *Five Songs* (Tibbits).
Dream of Gerontius – Elgar. c. Field Dodgson; Christchurch NZ: 25 Nov.

1973
Beatrice and Benedick – Berlioz – Beatrice. c. Hopkins; Syd. TH: 10 Feb.
Recital. p. White; Seoul, Korea: 19 Mar.; Taegu, Korea: 26 Mar.; *Les nuits d'été* (Berlioz); *Che faro* (Gluck); *Lieder eines fahrenden Gesellen* (Mahler); *Mon coeur s'ouvre à ta voix* (Saint-Saëns); *Frauenliebe und leben* (Schumann).
Recital. p. White; Syd. University Great Hall: Feb.; Pusan, Korea: 21 Mar.; Kwang-ju, Korea: 23 Mar., *Six Gellert Songs* (op 48 Beethoven); *Proses lyriques* (Debussy); *Iris hence away /Ombra mai fu / Where shall I fly* (Handel); *Frauenliebe und leben* (Schumann); *Six Poems of Judith Wright* (Sutherland).
Lieder eines fahrenden Gesellen – Mahler. c. Rieger; Melb. Symphony Orch.; Canberra: 10 Apr.
Alto Rhapsody – Brahms. c. Paul; Perth: 13 Apr.
St Matthew Passion – Bach. c. Callaway; Perth: 19 Apr.
Symphony no 3 – Mahler. c. van Otterloo; Syd. TH: 2, 3 May.
Symphony no 9 – Beethoven. c. Slovák; Adelaide Festival Hall – opening: 2, 3 June.
Sea Pictures – Elgar. c. Keats; Willoughby Orchestra; Willoughby Concert Hall: 14 June.
Il tramonto – Respighi. c. Pini; Syd. TH: 24 June.
Concert. with Richardson, MacDonald and Easton; p. Golding; Trinity Grammar School: 28 June; Willoughby Concert Hall: 27 Sep.; *Joys that are pure* (Handel); *Duets* from *Semiramide* (Rossini); *Il faut pour assouvir ma haine* (Saint-Saëns); *Trio* from *Il trovatore* (Verdi); *Quartet* from *Rigoletto* (Verdi).
Lieder eines fahrenden Gesellen – Mahler. c. van Otterloo; SOCH: 18 July.
Poème de l'amour et de la mer – Chausson. c. Cavdarski; SSO; Syd. TH: 22 July; Bathurst: 24 July; Orange: 25 July; Dubbo 26 July.
Concert. o. Goode, v. Nemet; Syd. Christchurch St Laurence: 11 Sep.; *Erbarme dich* (Bach); *Laudate Pueri* (Perti).
Il trittico - Puccini – Principessa / Frugola / Zita. c. Reid / Elder; SOT : 2, 4, 10, Oct., 19, 24, 29 Nov.
Symphony no 9 – Beethoven. c. van Otterloo; SOCH: 20 Oct.
The Six Days of Creation – Cugley. s. Richardson, c. Bacon; SOH Music Rm.: 23 Oct.
Recital. p. Winther; SOH Music Rm.: 31 Oct.; *Er ist's / Denk es, o Seele! / Fussreise / Verborgenheit* (Wolf); *Lied aus der Ferne / Ich liebe Dich / Andenken / Wonne der Wehmut / Mit einem gemalten band* (Beethoven); *Vier ernste Gesänge* (Brahms); *Proses lyriques* (Debussy); *Six Poems of Judith Wright* (Sutherland).
Requiem – Verdi. c. Downes; Eliz. Th. Orch.; SOCH: 15 Nov.
Messiah - Handel. c. Heinze; Syd. TH: 7, 8, 9 Dec.

1974
The Play of Herod / Slaughter of the Innocents c. Evans; Syd. Con.: Jan. date uncertain.
Concert. Syd. Baroque Ensemble, v. Nemet; SOH Music Room: 26 Feb.; *Arias* from *St Matthew Passion* (Bach); *Laudate Pueri* (Perti).
Beatrice and Benedick – Berlioz – Beatrice. c. Hopkins; Melb. Town Hall: 2 Mar.
Recital. p. White; Syd. University Great Hall: 9 Mar.; *Habañera* (Bizet); *Botschaft / Der Gang zum Liebchen / Von ewige Liebe* (Brahms); *Cari Luogi / O mio Fernando* (Donizetti); *Che faro* (Gluck); *Di Quel Bel* (Handel); *Oblivion*

Soave (Monteverdi); *Three arias* from *La clemenza di Tito* (Mozart); *Connais-tu le Pays* (Thomas); *Er ist's / Denk es, o Seele! / Fussreise / Verborgenheit* (Wolf).
Concert. c. Llewellyn; Canberra: 13, 14 Mar.; *Ah crudel nel pianto mio* (Handel).
Concert. p. Schulz, s. Richardson, t. Edmonds, b. Easton; Adelaide Festival Theatre: 18 Mar.; *Barcarolle* (Offenbach); *Semiramide duets* (Rossini); *Il faut pour assouvir ma haine / Mon coeur s'ouvre à ta voix* (Saint-Saëns); *Ai nostri monti / Quartet* from *Rigoletto* (Verdi).
St Matthew Passion – Bach. c. Seymour; Syd. Philharmonia; SOCH: 7 Apr.
St Matthew Passion – Bach. c. Johnston; Oriana Singers; Syd. TH: 12 Apr.
Concert. p.Watson, fl. Vogt, cello Waks; Syd. Con.: 19 Apr.; *Four Songs of Christopher Brennan* (Keats); *Chansons madécasses* (Ravel).
Concert. p. Potter, s. Richardson, t. MacDonald, b. Easton; Trinity Grammar School: 26 Apr.; *O nuit d'extase* (Berlioz); *O mio Fernando* (Donizetti); *Quartet* from *Faust* (Bizet); *Trio* from *Cosi fan tutte* (Mozart); *Barcarolle / Trio* from *Act III Tales of Hoffman* (Offenbach); *Semiramide duets* (Rossini).
Mass in B Minor – Bach. c. van Otterloo; SOCH: 8, 9 May.
Juditha Triumphans – Vivaldi. Holofernes c. Gill; Syd. Con.: 12 May.
Requiem – Verdi. c. Krips; Adelaide Festival Theatre: 24, 25 May.
Semele – Handel – Juno. c. Pyers; Melb. Dallas Brooks Hall: 1 June.
Saul – Handel – David. c. Schildberger; Camberwell: 10 July.
Concert. p. Duke; Chatswood: 17 July; *Che faro / O del mio dolce ador* (Gluck); *Mon coeur s'ouvre à ta voix* (Saint-Saëns).
Lieder eines fahrenden Gesellen – Mahler. c. Cavdarski; Christchurch NZ: 27 July.
Das Lied von der Erde – Mahler. c. Iwaki, t. MacDonald; Melb. TH: 6 Aug.
Julius Caesar - Handel – Caesar. c. Divall; Melb. Palais Theatre: 8, 9, 11 Aug.
Schéhérazade – Ravel. c. van Otterloo; SOCH: 24 Aug.
Bach Recital. o. Smith; Syd. St Stephens: 2 Sep. *Agnus Dei (Mass B Minor) / Du Herr, du kronst allein / Gelobet sei der Herr; Grief for Sin / If my tears be unavailing (St Matthew Passion); Prepare thyself Zion / Slumber Beloved / Keep O my spirit* (Christmas Oratorio).
Recital. p. Winther; Syd. Chalwin Theatre: 15 Sep.; *Arianna a Naxos* (Haydn);
· *Abendempfindung / Als Luise / Ridente la calma* (Mozart); *Sehnsucht / Wonne der Wehmut / Mit einem gemalten Band / An die Hoffnung* (Beethoven).
Concert. c. Rosen, MSO; Melb. Blackwood Hall: 18, 19 Sep.; *Habañera* from *Carmen* (Bizet); *O mio Fernando* (Donizetti); *Che faro* (Gluck); *Mon coeur s'ouvre à ta voix* (Saint-Saëns); *Strida la vampa* (Verdi).
Recital. p. Bacon; Syd. Con.: 27 Sep.; *Sehnsucht / Wonne der Wehmut / Mit einem gemalten Band / An die Hoffnung* (Beethoven); *Botschaft / Der Gang zum Liebchen / Von ewige Liebe / Vergebliches Ständchen* (Brahms); *Er ist's / Denk es, o Seele! / Verborgenheit* (Wolf).
Recital. p. Schofield; Mornington: 12 Oct.; *Botschaft / Der Gang zum Liebchen / Von ewige Liebe / Vergebliches Ständchen* (Brahms); *Sehnsucht / Wonne der Wehmut / Mit einem gemalten Band / An die Hoffnung* (Beethoven); *Les nuits d'été* (Berlioz); *Six Poems of Judith Wright* (Sutherland).
Orpheus and Euridice – Gluck – Orpheus. c. Divall, Victorian Opera; Melb. National Gallery: 22 Nov.
Orpheus and Euridice – Gluck – Orpheus. c. Dival; MSO studio recording made 1974; broadcast: 26 Oct. 1976 and 26 Feb. 1980.
Missa Solemnis – Beethoven. c. Logie-Smith; Melb. Dallas Brooks Hall: 5 Dec.
Messiah - Handel. c. Dommett; Melb. TH: 13, 14 Dec.

1975
Concert for relief of Darwin. Willoughby Concert Hall: 10 Jan.; *Arias* from *Aïda* (Verdi).
Aïda – Verdi – Amneri.s. c. Cillario; dir. Lingwood, staged in SOCH: 1, 6, 8, 11, 14 Feb.
Concert. p. Champ, t. MacDonald; Melb. TH: 22 Feb.; Syd. TH: 2 Mar.; SOCH: 8 Mar.; Melb. TH: 16 Mar.; *O mio Fernando* (Donizetti); *Chanson triste / L'invitation au voyage / La vague et la cloche / La vie antérieure* (Duparc); *Duets*

from *The Trojans* (Berlioz); *Duet* from *Carmen* (Bizet); *Duet* from *Il trovatore* (Verdi).
St Matthew Passion - Bach. c. Eros; Perth Concert Hall: 26, 27 Mar.
Saul – Handel – David. c. Seymour, Syd. Philharmonia; SOCH: 5 Apr.
Das Lied von der Erde – Mahler. c. Thomas; Brisbane Concert Hall: 12 Apr.
Alto Rhapsody – Brahms. c. Seymour; SOCH: 2 May.
Requiem Mass K 626 – Mozart. c. Kamu; Perth Concert Hall: 30, 31 May.
Recital. p. White; SUIH: 7 June; *Se tu m'ami* (Pergolesi); *I see she flies me everywhere / Music for a while / Secrecy's Song / Welcome, more welcome, does he come* (Purcell); *Se tu della mia morte* (Scarlatti); *The House of Life* (Vaughan Williams); *Four sacred songs* from *the Spanish Song Book* (Wolf).
Recital. o. Smith; Syd. St Stephens: 23 June; *Qui sedes ad dexteram / Agnus Dei* from Mass in B Min. (Bach); *At Midnight Hour / Primeval Light / Ah, garish world* (Mahler); *Traüme* (Wagner).
Symphony no 2 – Mahler. c. Iwaki; Melb. Dallas Brooks Hall: 25 June.
Requiem – Verdi. c. Logie-Smith; Melb. Dallas Brooks Hall: 11 July.
Mass no 3 in F Minor – Bruckner. c. van Otterloo; SOCH: 19, 21 July.
Symphony no 2 – Mahler. c. van Otterloo; 29, 30, 31 July.
Noye's Fludde - Mrs Noye c. McLaren; Pymble Ladies College: 11 Aug.
Lieder eines fahrenden Gesellen – Mahler. c. Pikler; Willoughby Symphony Orch.; Willoughby Concert Hall: 14, 17 Aug.
Requiem – Verdi. c. Seymour; SOCH: 30 Aug.
Les noces – Stravinsky. c. Hopkins; SOCH: 6 Sep.
National Lieder Society – Inaugural Recital. p. Parsons; Syd. Con.: 11 Sep.; *Arianna a Naxos* (Haydn); *Four Divine Poems of John Donne* (Le Gallienne); *Wesendonk-Lieder* (Wagner); *Proses lyriques* (Debussy).
Poème de l'amour et de la mer – Chausson. c. Cavdarski; Hobart: 16 Sep.; Launceston: 17 Sep.
Concert. c. Logie-Smith, Astra Orchestra; Melb. Dallas Brooks Hall: 24 Oct.; *Sea Pictures* (Elgar); *Cantata Nigra* (Szokolay).
Concert. p. Hutchinson, va. Pikler; SOH: 9 Nov.; *Gestillte Sehnsucht / Geistliches Wiegenlied* (op 91 Brahms).
Concert. p. Champ, s. Maughan, t. MacDonald; Trinity Grammar School: 14 Nov.; *Duet* from *Beatrice & Benedick / Duet* from *The Trojans* (Berlioz); *Barcarolle* (Offenbach); *Flower Duet* from *Madama Butterfly* (Puccini); *Una voce poco fa* (Rossini); *Strida la vampa / Trios* from *Il trovatore* and *Aïda* (Verdi).
Messiah - Handel. c. Field-Dodgson; Christchurch NZ: 13 Dec.

1976
La Vida Breve – Falla. c. Cavdarski; Melb. Blackwood Hall: 4 Nov.
Aïda – Verdi – Amneris. c. Cillario; SOCH: 1, 6, 8 Feb.
Recital. p. Powell; Syd. Hakoah Club: 11 Feb.; *Six Songs* (op 86 Brahms); *Five Hungarian folk songs* (Kodály); *Auf dem Strom* (Schubert).
Concert. c. Cavdarski; Melb. Myer Music Bowl: 14 Feb.; *Seguidilla* from *Carmen* (Bizet); *Che faro* (Gluck); *Una voce poco fa* (Rossini); *Amour, viens aider ma faiblesse* (Saint-Saëns).
Spring Symphony – Britten. c. Groves; Dunedin NZ: 22 Mar.
St Matthew Passion – Bach. c. Seymour; SOCH: 11 Apr.
Recital. p. Champ; Wahroonga Music Club: 23 Apr.; St Marys Cathedral: 7 May; Armidale: 21 July; *Six Songs* (op 86 Brahms); Six songs from *Before and after Summer* (Finzi); *Arianna a Naxos* (Haydn); *Serate Musicali* (Rossini).
Requiem – Verdi. c. Hopkins; Melb. Dallas Brooks Hall: 10 May.
Recital. p. Schofield; Geelong: 1 June; same program as Wahroonga above.
Requiem K626 – Mozart. c. Sanderling; SOCH: 7 July; stand in for Elkins.
The Dream of Gerontius – Elgar. c. Dennison; Melb. St Pauls Cathedral: 10 July.
Das Lied von der Erde – Mahler. c Shapirra, t. MacDonald; Adelaide Festival Theatre: 16, 17 July.
Concert. c. van Otterloo; SOCH: 31 July; *El amor Brujo / Psyché* (Falla).
Clarice Lorenze Testimonial Concert. p. Baer; Syd. Con.: 8 Aug.; *Aria* from

La Favorita (Donizetti).
Solomon – Handel - Solomon. c. Seymour, Syd. Philharmonia; SOCH: 4 Sep.
Carmen – Bizet – Carmen. c. Cavdarski; Hobart Theatre Royal: 25, 27, 29 Sep., 1 Oct.
Concert. p. Andrews, s. Maughan, t. MacDonald; Trinity Grammar School: 15 Oct.; *Duet* from *Beatrice & Benedick* (Berlioz); *Duet* from *Carmen* Act 2 (Bizet); *Deh per quest 'istante* (Mozart); *Flower Duet* from *Madama Butterfly* (Puccini); *Trio* from *Aïda* (Verdi); *Knowest thou the land* (Thomas).
Recital. p. Hutchinson; Sydney Chalwin Castle: 17 Oct.; *Six Songs* (op 86 Brahms); *Cavatina* from *Le judgement de Midas* / *Romance* from *L'amitié a l'épreuve* (Grétry); *Arianna a Naxos* (Haydn); *Two arias* from *La clemenza di Tito* (Mozart); *Serate Musicali* (Rossini).
Sea Pictures – Elgar. c. Berglund; Brisbane: 26 Oct.
Recital. p. Vickers; Brisbane: 29 Oct.; *Six Songs* (op 86 Brahms); Six songs from *Before and after Summer* (Finzi); *Arianna a Naxos* (Haydn); *Serate Musicali* (Rossini).
Aïda – Verdi – Amneris. c. Cavdarski, concert performance; Christchurch NZ: 20 Nov.
The Dream of Gerontius – Elgar. c. Hopkins; SOCH: 27 Nov.
Messiah - Handel. c. Seymour; SOCH: 9, 10, 11 Dec.
Keep Music Alive Concert. c. Hopkins, c. Lanchbery; Syd. TH: 16 Dec.; *Mon coeur s'ouvre à ta voix* (Saint-Saëns); *Land of Hope and Glory* (Elgar).

1977
Symphony no 3 – Mahler. c. van Otterloo; SOCH: 1977.
Aïda – Verdi – Amneris. c. Cillario; SOH: 14, 17, 21, 24 Jan.
Dorothy White Memorial Concert. p. Evans; Sydney University Gt Hall: 6 Feb.; *Ah! Crudel nel pianto mio* (Handel).
The Dream of Gerontius – Elgar. c. Hopkins; Syd. TH: 19 Feb.
Mass B minor – Bach. c. Franks; Christchurch NZ: 19 Mar.
Duet Concert. p. Stokes, s. Richardson; Wollongong: 3 Apr.; Wagga Wagga: 13 Apr.; Goulburn: 15 Apr.; *Five Songs* (op 107 Brahms); *Orfeo Act 3 duet* (Gluck); *Julius Caesar duet* – *Act 3* (Handel); *Hänsel & Gretel, duet* – *Act 1* (Humperdinck); *Four duets* (Mendelssohn); *Barcarolle* (Offenbach); *Shepherd, leave decoying* / *Lost is my quiet for ever* / *Sound the trumpet* (Purcell); *Semiramide Act 1 duet* (Rossini).
Mass in B minor – Bach. c. Logie-Smith; Melb. Dallas Brooks Hall: 5 Apr.
St Matthew Passion – Bach. c. Seymour; SOCH: 7 Apr.
Shéhérazade – Ravel. c. van Otterloo, SSO, Canberra: 20, 21 Apr.
Jeremiah - Symphony no 1 – Bernstein. c. Shapirra; Adelaide Festival Theatre: 28 Apr.
Requiem – Verdi. c. Burstein, Newcastle Symphony Orch.; Newcastle: 7 May.
Saul – Handel – David. c. Dennison; Melb. Dallas Brooks Hall: 13 May.
The Dream of Gerontius – Elgar. c. Wilson; Auckland NZ: 18 June.
Duet Concert. p. Hutchinson, s. Berridge; Willoughby Concert Hall: 8 July; *Five Songs* (op 107 Brahms); *Orfeo Act 3 duet* (Gluck); *Julius Caesar- two duets* (Handel); *Hänsel & Gretel duet* – *Act 1* (Humperdinck); *Four duets* (Mendelssohn); *Barcarolle* (Offenbach); *Shepherd, leave decoying* / *Lost is my quiet for ever* / *Sound the trumpet* (Purcell); *Semiramide Act 1 duet* (Rossini).
Oedipus rex – Stravinsky. c. Cavdarski; Melb. Blackwood Hall: 4 Aug.
Alto Rhapsody – Brahms. c. van Otterloo; Syd. TH: 20, 22, 23, 24 Aug.
Recital. p. Miller; Newcastle: 27 Aug.; *Habañera* from Carmen (Bizet); *O mio Fernando* (Donizetti); *Sea Pictures* (Elgar); *Stride la vampa* (Verdi).
Recital. p. Bouffler; Syd. Con.: 29 Sep.; *Five songs* (op 105 Brahms); *Seven classical Spanish songs* (Obradors); *Histoires naturelles* (Ravel).
Concert. c. Divall, Melb Eliz. Orch.; Melb. Dallas Brooks Hall: 14 Oct.; arias from *Rinaldo* and *Xerxes* (Handel) and *Juditha Triumphans* (Vivaldi).
Recital. p. Woodley; Christchurch NZ: 3 Nov.; *Five songs* (op 105 Brahms); *Seven classical Spanish songs* (Obradors); *Charm of Lullabies* (Britten).
Requiem – Verdi. c. Field-Dodgson; Christchurch NZ: 5 Nov.

278

Missa Solemnis – Beethoven. c. Seymour; SOCH: 25 Nov.
Recital. p. Winther; SOH: 4 Dec.; *Auf dem Kirchhofe / Immer leiser wird mein Schlummer / Klage / Verrat / Wie Melodien zieht es mir* (Brahms); *Erinnerung / Frühlingsmorgen / Hans und Grethe / Rheinlegendchen* (Mahler); *Frauenliebe und leben* (Schumann).
Messiah - Handel. c. Tintner; SOCH: 9, 10, 11 Dec.

1978
Recital. p. Raschke; Syd. TH Foyer: 3 Mar; *Four Divine Poems of John Donne* (Le Gallienne); *Six Poems of Judith Wright* (Sutherland); *English Lyrics* (Williamson); *Seven classical Spanish songs* (Obradors).
St John Passion – Bach. c. Seymour; SOCH: 19 Mar.
St Matthew Passion – Bach. c. Wilson; Auckland NZ: 22 Mar.
Recital. p. Hutchinson; Wahroonga Music Club: 21 Apr.; *Charm of Lullabies* (Britten); *Rheinlegendchen / Das irdische Leben / Des Antonius von Padua Fischpredigt* (Mahler); *Seven classical Spanish songs* (Obradors); *Histoires naturelles* (Ravel); *Suleika I & II* (Schubert).
Stabat mater. c. Hopkins; Melb.TH: 27 May.
Recital. p. Winther; Newcastle: 8 June; Melb. Ripponlea: 30 June; Syd. Queen St Gallery: 13 July; *Suleika II / Am Grabe Anselmos / An die Musik / Aufenthalt / Ave Maria / Du bist die Ruh / Ganymed / Gretchen am Spinnrade / Gruppe aus dem Tartarus / Heiss mich nicht reden / Jäger, ruhe von der Jagd! / Die junge Nonne / Kennst du das Land / Nur wer die Sehnsucht kennt / Raste, Krieger / So lasst mich scheinen / Was bedeutet die Bewegung?* (Schubert).
Duet Recital. p. Miller, s. Berridge; Trinity Grammar School: 23 June; *Duets* from *Orfeo, Julius Caesar,* and *Semiramide.*
Sea Pictures – Elgar. c. Gill, Sydney Youth Orchestra; SOCH: 9 July.
Mass no 5 in A flat – Schubert. c. Winther; Newcastle: 28 July.
Des Knaben Wunderhorn – Mahler. c. Shapirra; Melb.: 5 Aug.; Brisbane: 28 Aug.
Concert. p. Valler; Killara: 7 Aug.; *Mignons Lied* (Schubert); *Six English Lyrics* (Williamson).
Das Lied von der Erde – Mahler. c. Mackerras, t. Roden; SOCH: 16, 17 Aug.
Lux Christi – Elgar. c. Fredman; Adelaide TH: 7 Sep.
Bluebeard's Castle – Bartók – Judith. c. Hopkins, Melb. Symphony Orch.; Melb. National Gallery: 23, 24 Sep.
Concert. c. Divall; Melb. Dallas Brooks Hall: 22 Nov.; *Ruggeiro's arias* from *Alcina* (Handel).
Requiem – Verdi. c. Seymour; SOCH: 25 Nov.
Memorial Concert for W A Dullo. Syd. Mozart Society, p. Hutchinson; Willoughby Concert Hall: 28 Nov.; *Suleika I & II* (Schubert).
Missa Solemnis – Beethoven. c. Field-Dodgson; Christchurch NZ: 2 Dec.
Concert. o. Field-Dodgson; Christchurch Cathedral, NZ: 3 Dec.; *Benedictus* from *Missa Solemnis* (Beethoven).
Concert. p. Vance, va. Cik; Sydney University Great Hall: 1 Mar.; *Gestillte Sehnsucht / Geistliches Wiegenlied* (op 91 Brahms).

1979
Recital. p. Miller, va. Durie; SUIH: 16 Mar.; Lismore: 7 Aug.; Goulburn: 13 Aug.; Albury: 16 Aug;, Wagga Wagga: 17 Aug.; *Ach Herr, was ist ein Menschen Kind / Was Gott thut, das ist wohlgethan* (Bach); *Gestillte Sehnsucht / Geistliches Wiegenlied* (op 91 Brahms); *Le colibri* (Chausson); *Elégie* (Massenet); *Seven classical Spanish songs* (Obradors); *Folk Songs* (arr G Pikler); *Two Sonnets by Wm. Alabaster* (op 87 Rubbra).
Recital. p. Bouffler; Heidelberg, Germany: 11 Jan.; London Wigmore Hall: 20 Jan.; *Five Songs* (op 105 Brahms); *Charm of Lullabies* (Britten); *Seven classical Spanish songs* (Obradors); *Four divine poems of John Donne* (Le Gallienne); Debussy; Ravel.
Recital. p. Bouffler; London St Johns: 14 Jan.; *Suleika I & II / Am Grabe Anselmos / An die Musik / Aufenthalt / Ave Maria / Du bist die Ruh / Ganymed*

/ Gretchen am Spinnrade / Gruppe aus dem Tartarus / Heiss mich nicht reden / Jäger, ruhe von der Jagd! / Die junge Nonne / Kennst du das Land / Nur wer die Sehnsucht kennt / Raste, Krieger / So lasst mich scheinen / Was bedeutet die Bewegung? (Schubert).

Rhinegold – Wagner – Erda. c. Elder, Concert performance SSO; SOCH: 20 Mar.

Recital. p. Miller; SUIH: 27 Apr.; *Elégie* (Massenet); *Seven classical Spanish songs* (Obradors); *Folk Songs* (arr G Pikler); *Here let my life* (Purcell); *Two Sonnets by Wm. Alabaster* (op 87 Rubbra).

Bluebeard's Castle – Bartók – Judith. c. Hopkins; New Zealand; Auckland: 17 May; New Plymouth: 19 May; Wellington: 26 May.

Recital. p. Miller; SOCH: 9 June; *Five songs* (op 105 Brahms); *Charm of Lullabies* (Britten); *Seven popular Spanish songs* (Falla); *Three arias* from *Alcina* (Handel); *Four Divine Poems of John Donne* (Le Gallienne).

La clemenza di Tito – Mozart – Sextus. c. Divall; Melb. Princess Theatre: 7 July et al.

Concert. p. Miller, s. Bronhill, t. Stevens, b. Badcock; SOH: 5 Aug.; *Habañera* (Bizet); *Sextet* from *Lucia di Lammermoor* (Donizetti); *Che faro* (Gluck); *Mon coeur s'ouvre à ta voix* (Saint-Saëns); *Quartet* from *Rigoletto* (Verdi).

Symphony no 9 – Beethoven. c. Steinberg; SOCH: 25, 27, 28 Aug.

Petite messe solennelle – Rossini. c. Burstein; Brisbane University: 28 Sep.

Concert. c. Divall; Melb. Dallas Brooks Hall: 30 Aug.; *Two arias* from *Montezuma* (Graun); *L'amour viens rendre a mon ame* (Gluck); *Thamos King of Egypt* (Mozart).

Concert. c. Ancerl; Hobart: 13 Oct.; *Alto Rhapsody* (Brahms); *Gypsy Songs* (Dvorák); *Five Tudor Portraits* (Vaughan Williams).

Recital. o. Dudman, p. Winther; Newcastle: 28 Oct.; *Keep O my spirit this blessing / Prepare thyself Zion / Slumber beloved* (Bach); *Vier ernste Gesänge* (op 121 Brahms); *Frauenliebe und leben* (Schumann).

Shéhérazade – Ravel. Sydney Dance Company; SOH: 30 Oct., 4 Nov.

Concert. c. Llewellyn; Canberra: 10 Nov.; *Lucretia* (Handel/Nickson); *Stabat mater* (Vivaldi).

Elijah – Mendelssohn. c. Seymour; SOCH: 24 Nov.

Messiah - Handel. c. Fredman; Adelaide Festival Hall: 7, 8 Dec.

Christmas Oratorio – Bach. c. Divall; Hobart Odeon: 14 Dec.

1980

Recital. p. Hutchinson, cl. de Graaff; SUIH: 1980; *Seven popular Spanish songs* (Falla); *Lieder eines fahrenden Gesellen* (Mahler); *Sextus deh, per quest' istante solo / Parto, parto* (Mozart); *Frauenliebe und leben* (Schumann); *Six German songs with clarinet* (Spohr).

Lieder eines fahrenden Gesellen – Mahler. c. Serebrier; Syd. TH: 23 Feb.

Symphony no 3 – Mahler. c. Serebrier; Syd. TH: 27 Feb.

Petite messe solennelle – Rossini. c. Fredman; Adelaide St Peters Cathedral: 22, 23 Mar.

Concert. p. Winther; Newcastle: 29 Mar.; *An die Musik / Ave Maria / Die junge Nonne / Du bist die Ruh' / Gretchen am Spinnrad* (Schubert).

St Matthew Passion – Bach. c. Seymour; SOCH: 2 Apr.

Recital. p. Miller, va. Durie; SOH: 27 Apr.; *op 85 / op 100* (Bach); *Gestillte Sehnsucht / Geistliches Wiegenlied* (op 91 Brahms); *Le colibri / Le temps des lilas* (Chausson); *Elégie* (Massenet); *Seven classical Spanish songs* (Obradors); *Folk Songs* (arr Pikler); *Here let my life* (Purcell); *Two Sonnets by Wm. Alabaster* (op 87 Rubbra).

Concert. c. Cavdarski; Brisbane: 8 May; *Six songs for orchestra* (Sitsky).

Lieder eines fahrenden Gesellen – Mahler. c. Gill; SOCH: 17 May.

Poème de l'amour et de la mer – Chausson. c. Llewellyn; Canberra: 28 May

Mass in B Minor – Bach. c. Fredman; Melb. Blackwood Hall: 1 June.

Concert. c. Hobcroft; Syd. Con.: *Rückert Songs* (Mahler); 29 June.

Mass in B minor – Bach. c. Willcocks; Syd. TH: 30, 31 July.

Symphony no 2 – Mahler. c. Iwaki; Melb. Blackwood Hall: 27 Sep.; c. Mester; SOCH: 15, 16 Oct.; Syd. TH: 22 Oct.

Concert of Duets and Trios. p. Raschke, s. Berridge, t. MacDonald; Sydney Trinity Grammar School: 24 Oct.
Requiem, opus 9 – Duruflé. c. Cox; Bendigo: 15 Nov.; Melb. St Patricks Cathedral: 18 Nov.
Messiah - Handel. c. Seymour; SOCH: 4, 5, 6 Dec.
Messiah - Handel. c. Hopkins; Melb.TH: 12, 13 Dec.

1981
Concert of Duets. p. Baer, s. Berridge; Killara: 2 Mar.
The Dream of Gerontius – Elgar. c. Handford; Syd. TH: 7 Mar.
Recital. p. Winther; Canberra: 19 Mar.; *An die Musik / Ave Maria / Du bist die Ruh' / Gretchem am Spinnrad* (Schubert); *Frauenliebe und leben* (Schumann).
St Matthew Passion – Bach. c. Seymour; Syd. TH: 16 Apr.
Concert. p. Miller; 3 May; *Seven Early Songs* (Berg); *Songs and Proverbs of William Blake* (Britten); *Three Catalan Songs* (Mompou).
The Damnation of Faust – Berlioz - Marguerite c. Smart, Syd. Con. Choir & Orch.; SOCH: 17 May.
Poème de l'amour et de la mer – Chausson. c. Frémaux; Syd. TH: 29 May.
Sea Pictures – Elgar. c. Byrne, Western Sydney Orch.: 21, 28 June.
Recital. p. Miller; SUIH: 3 July; *An die Stolze / Salamander / Das Mädchen spricht / Maienkätzchen, erster Gruss / Mädchenlied* (Brahms); *Gypsy Songs* (op 103 Brahms); *Seven popular Spanish songs* (Falla); *Sea Pictures* (Elgar); *But hark, the heavenly sphere turns round / Iris, hence away / Then long eternity* (Handel).
Requiem K626 – Mozart. c. Seymour; SOCH: 18 July. Also *Les Noces* (Stravinsky).
Missa Solemnis – Beethoven. c. Hopkins; Melb. Dallas Brooks Hall: 12 Aug.
Recital. p. Schofield; Melb. Universal Theatre: 23 Aug.; *Seven popular Spanish songs* (Falla); *But hark, the heavenly sphere turns round / Iris, hence away / Then long eternity* (Handel); *Wesendonk-Lieder* (Wagner); *Mörike Lieder* (Wolf).
Die Walküre – Wagner – Fricka. c. Mackerras, MSO concert performance; Melb.TH: 25, 27 Aug.
Recital. p Miller; Syd. Con.: *Seven popular Spanish songs* (Falla).
Semele – Handel – Juno. c. Seymour; SOCH: 5 Sep.
Recital. p. Winther; Canberra School of Music: 14 Sep; *Mädchenlied / Therese Lieder* (op 86) / *Vier ernste Gesänge* (op 121) / *Gypsy Songs* (Brahms).
Government House Recital. p. Winther; Canberra: 15 Sep.; *Gypsy Songs* (Brahms); *Seven popular Spanish songs* (Falla); *Sea Pictures* (Elgar); *But hark, the heavenly sphere turns round / Iris, hence away / Then long eternity* (Handel).
Götterdämmerung Wagenr - First Norn. c. Mackerras, SSO concert performance; SOCH: 30 Sep., 3 Oct.
Recital. p. Winther; Canberra School of Music: 21 Oct.; *Wesendonk-Lieder* (Wagner); *Mörike Lieder* (Wolf); *Seven Early Songs* (Berg); *Rückert Lieder* (Mahler).
Sea Pictures – Elgar. c. Gill; Syd. Macquarie University: 31 Oct.
Symphony no 3 – Mahler. c. Decker; Melb. Dallas Brooks Hall: 7 Nov.
Requiem – Verdi. c. Cillario; SOCH: 19 Nov.
Messiah - Handel. c. Langbein; Adelaide Festival Hall: 4, 5 Dec.
Messiah - Handel. c. Fredman; SOCH: 10, 11, 12 Dec.

1982
Recital. p. Arnold, s. Hunter, cl. de Graaff; Syd. TH: 31 Jan; *Che faro* (Gluck); *Parto, parto* (Mozart); *Four Folk Songs* (Quilter); *Connais-tu le Pays / Gavotte* (Thomas); *Duet* from *Aïda / O don fatale* (Verdi); *Duet* from *Norma* (Bellini).; *O mio Fernando* (Donizetti).
Recital. p. Miller; Ascham School: 5 Mar.; *Au pays où se fait la guerre / Chanson triste / La Vie antérieure* (Duparc); *Che faro* (Gluck); *Love's Philosophy / Ye banks and braes* (Quilter); *Gretchen / Ständchen / An die Musik / Erlkönig* (Schubert); *Fussreise / Verborgenheit / Abschied / Auf einer Wanderung* (Wolf).
Recital. p. Miller; SUIH: 19 Mar.; *Gretchen / Ständchen / An die Musik / Erlkönig* (Schubert); *Fussreise / Verborgenheit / Abschied / Auf einer Wanderung* (Wolf);

Il segreto per esser felice (Donizetti); *Au pays où se fait la guerre* / *Chanson triste* / *La Vie antérieure* (Duparc); *Love's Philosophy* / *Ye banks and braes* / *Charlie is my darling* (Quilter); *Connais-tu le Pays* (Thomas); *O don fatale* (Verdi); *Sure on this Shining Night* (Barber).

Suor Angelica – Puccini – Principessa. c. Cillario; Melb. Princess Theatre: 13, 15, 19, 21, 24, 26 May.

Das Lied von der Erde – Mahler. c. Frémaux, t. MacDonald; SOCH: 29 May.

Il tramonto – Respighi. c. Harding; SOH: 10 June.

Symphony no 9 – Beethoven and **Serenade to Music** – Vaughan Williams. c. Thomas; SOCH: 1 July.

Symphony no 9 – Beethoven. c. Comissiona, opening of Melb.Concert Hall: 3 July.

Orphée et Euridice – Gluck – Orphée. Berlioz Paris Opera version, concert performance; c. Seymour; SOCH: 1 Aug.

Elijah – Mendelssohn. c. Hopkins; Melb.: 19 Aug.

Falstaff – Verdi - Mistress Quickly. c. Challender; SOH: 8, 11, 14, 18, 24, 30 Sep., 2, 7, 12, 23, 30 Oct.

Recital. p. Miller, v. Curby; Killara: 18 Oct.; *Parto, parto* / *Deh, per quest'istante* (Mozart); *Sea Pictures* (Elgar); *Schliesse mein herze* / *Erbarme dich* (Bach).

The Apocalypse – Goosens. c. Fredman; SOCH: 13 Nov.

Missa Solemnis – Beethoven. c. Burstein; Newcastle: 27 Nov.

Messiah - Handel. c. Hopkins; Adelaide Festival Hall: 7, 8 Dec.

Messiah - Handel. c. Lehman; Melb. Concert Hall: 10, 11 Dec.

Messiah - Handel. c. Measham; Perth Concert Hall: 17, 18 Dec.

1983

Concert. p. Miller, v. Kimber; Syd. TH: 28 Jan.; *Arias* from *Christmas Oratorio* & *St Matthew Passion* (Bach); *Seven popular Spanish songs* (Falla).

Alcina – Handel – Bradamante. c. Bonynge; SOH: 5, 9, 12, 16, 19, 22, 26 Feb.

Messiah - Handel. c. Divall; Melb. Concert Hall: 29 Mar.

Recital. p. Hutchinson; SUIH: 15 Apr.; *Les nuits d'été* (Berlioz); *Folk Songs* (arr. Britten); *Fac me vere tecum flere* / *O quam tristis et afflicta* (fr. Nelson Mass – Haydn); *All' mein Gedanken* / *Allerseelen* / *Cäcilie* / *Die Nacht* / *Morgen* / *Nichts* / *Traum durch die Dämmerung* (Strauss); *Orpheus with his Lute* (Sullivan).

Il trovatore – Verdi – Azucena. c. Bonynge; SOH: 25, 28 Jun., 2, 5, 8, 13, 16, 19, 22 July.

Semiramide – Rossini – Arsace. c. Bonynge; SOH: 5, 8, 13, 17, 20 Aug.

Concert. c. Mackerras; SOCH: 29 Aug. Arias - Handel & Mozart.

Die Walküre – Wagner – Fricka. c. Cillario; SOH: 4, 8, 10, 13, 19, 22, 25, 28 Oct.

Land of Hope and Glory – Elgar. Sydney Youth Orchestra; Mosman Prom.: 15 Oct; stand in for Hunter.

Mass in B Minor – Bach. c. Carolane; Melb.Concert Hall: 12 Nov.

Recital. p. McLaren, va. Gould; Ascham School: 25 Nov.; *Gestillte Sehnsucht* / *Geistliches Wiegenlied* (op 91 Brahms); *Two Sonnets by Wm. Alabaster* (op 87 Rubbra); *All' mein Gedanken* / *Allerseelen* / *Befreit* /*Cäcilie* / *Die Nacht* / *Morgen* / *Nichts* / *Traum durch die Dämmerung* (Strauss).

Stabat mater – Vivaldi. o. Heagney; Melb. St Francis Church; 1983.

1984

Recital. p. Miller; Syd. St Stephens: 19 Mar.; *Six Gellert Songs* (op 48 Beethoven); *Frauenliebe und leben* (Schumann).

Recital. p. Miller; SUIH: 29 Mar.; Beijing China: 4 Apr.; Shanghai China: 9 Apr.; *Six Gellert Songs* (op 48 Beethoven); *Chanson triste* / *L'invitation au voyage* / *La vague et la cloche* (Duparc); *We shall plan revenge* (Handel); *Mon coeur s'ouvre à ta voix* (Saint-Saëns); *Frauenliebe und leben* (Schumann); *In chains they bound her* (Verdi); *Erda's narration* (Wagner).

The Bells of Strasbourg – Liszt. c. Gee; Melb. CH: 30 May.

Siegfried – Wagner – Erda. c. Mackerras, concert performance; Melb. CH: 2 June.

Concert. c. Mackerras; Sydney University Great Hall: 11 June; *Three arias* from

Julius Caesar (Handel).
The Trojans – Berlioz – Dido. c. Mackerras, concert performances; SOCH: 30 June, 2, 4 July.
Symphony no 3 – Mahler. Israel Philharmonic Orch., c. Mehta; Perth: 9 July; Sydney: 14 July; Melb.: 21 July.
Julius Caesar - Handel - Caesar c. Langbein, concert perform. of arias; Adelaide TH: 13 Aug.
Julius Caesar – Handel – Caesar. c. Vaughan; Adelaide Opera Theatre: 25, 28, 30 Aug., 1, 4, 6, 8 Sep.; c. Divall; Melb. State Theatre: 15 Sep. et al.
Il trovatore – Verdi – Azucena. c. Vaughan; Adelaide Opera Theatre: 25, 27, 30 Sept., 1, 3, 6, 8, 10 Oct.
The Trojans – Berlioz – Dido. c. Divall, concert performances; Melb.CH: 29 Nov., 1, 4 Dec.
Paul Landa Memorial Concert. p. Winther; SOH: 16 Dec.; *Four Serious Songs* (op 121 Brahms).

1985
Il trovatore – Verdi – Azucena. c. Pido; SOH: 1985; c. Challender; Melb. State Theatre: 12, 15, 21, 27 Mar., 8, 11 Apr.
Aïda – Verdi – Amneris. c. Cillario; Melb. State Theatre: 9 May; Adelaide Festival Theatre: 27 May.
Recital. p. Miller; SUIH: 21 June; *Jesu lass dich finden / Jesu schlaft was soll ich hoffen* (Bach); *Seven Early Songs* (Berg); *Like to the Damask Rose / Shepherd's Song / Queen Mary's Song / A Song of Autumn / Rondel* (Elgar); David's three arias from *Saul* (Handel); *Rückert Songs* (Mahler).
Saul – Handel – David. c. Seymour; SOCH: 6 July.
A Masked Ball – Verdi – Ulrica. c. Agler; SOH: 17, 27 July.
Requiem – Verdi. c. Seymour; SOCH: 2 Nov.

1986
A Masked Ball – Verdi – Ulrica. c. Kamirski; SOH: 4, 7, 11, 14, 17, 27 Jan., 4 Feb.; c. Cillario; Melb. State Theatre: Mar.
Recital. p. Miller; Sydney Government House: 8 Feb.; SUIH: 1 May; *Six Castillian songs* (Guridi); *Four Irish Songs* (Hughes); *Les lettres (Werther)* (Massenet); *Connais-tu le pays / Gavotte* (Thomas).
Bluebeard's Castle – Bartók – Judith. c. Furst; Melb. Myer Music Bowl: 12 Feb.
Recital. p. Pommeroy; Shepparton: 16 Mar.; *Ave Maria* (Gounod); *Six Castillian songs* (Guridi); *God be in my head* (Hill); *Four Irish Songs* (Hughes); *Four Divine Poems of John Donne* (Le Gallienne).
Messiah - Handel. Phil. Soc. 200th performance; c. Blackburn; Melb. CH: 23 Mar.
Recital. p. Miller; Syd. St Stephens: 21 Apr.; *Vier ernste Gesänge* (Brahms); *Four Divine Poems of John Donne* (Le Gallienne).
Bluebeard's Castle – Bartók – Judith. c. Franks; Adelaide Festival Theatre: 28, 29 May.
Aïda – Verdi – Amneris. c. Challender; SOH: 16, 19, 23, 26, 29 July, 2, 6, 9 Aug.
Sea Pictures – Elgar. c. Reid; Melb. CH: 26 Sep.
Christmas Oratorio – Bach. c. Pyers; Melb.: 27 Sep.
Concert. c. Dommett; Canberra School of Music: 5 Nov.; *Parto Parto* (Mozart); *Symphony no 3* (Mahler).
Symphony no 9 – Beethoven. c. Challender; Sydney Town Hall: 16 Nov.
Concert. p. Kram, Willoughby CH: 18 Nov.; *Who is the mortal one* (Gluck); *O fatal day* (Handel); *Ständchen* (Schubert).
Recital. p. Miller; Syd. Everest Theatre: 13 Dec.; *Les nuits d'été* (Berlioz); *Die drei Zigeuner / Die Loreley / Du bist wie eine Blume / Es muss ein Wunderbares sein / Es war ein König in Thule / Freudvoll und leidvoll / Mignons Lied / Oh! Quand je dors / S'il est un charmant gazon* (Liszt).

1987

Symphony no 3 – Mahler. c. Hopkins; Auckland NZ; 4 Feb.
Requiem – Verdi. c. Rimmer; Perth: 15 Feb.
Recital. p. Miller; Lieder Society; Sydney Knox School: 28 Feb.; *Six Gellert Songs* (op 48 Beethoven); *Four Divine Poems of John Donne* (Le Gallienne); *Five Rückert Songs* (Mahler); *Six songs* (Strauss).
Concert. c. Dommett; Canberra: 7 Mar.; *Habañera* (Bizet); *Che faro* (Gluck); *Va tacito* (Handel); *Mon coeur s'ouvre à ta voix* (Saint-Saëns).
Symphony no 3 – Mahler. c. Turnovsky; SOCH: 11 Mar.
Chansons madécasses – Ravel. Australia Ensemble – 'Music & Heritage'; Waverley: 31 Mar.
Concert. p. Halstead; Lake Geneva, Wisconsin USA: 11 July; *Habañera* (Bizet); *Barcarolle* (Offenbach); *Mon coeur s'ouvre à ta voix* (Saint-Saëns); *Champagne song* (Strauss); *Ai nostri monti* (Verdi); *Quartet* from *Rigoletto* (Verdi).
Concert. Springvale: 20 Sep.; *How lovely are Thy dwellings; The Birds; The Holy City.*
Gurrelieder – Schoenberg. c. Iwaki; Melb.CH: 26, 28, 29 Sep.
Recital. p. Miller; Wahroonga: 16 Oct.; Springwood 6 Nov.; *Irish Folk Songs* (Hughes); *Six Castillian songs* (Guridi); *Four Divine Poems of John Donne* (Le Gallienne); *Rückert Songs* (Mahler); *Frauenliebe und leben* (Schumann).
Messiah - Handel. c. Blackburn; Melb.CH: 15 Nov.
Concert. p. Miller, cl. de Graaff; SOH Recording Hall: 27 Nov.; *E sempre inquieto / L'adorata* (Bononcini); *Six Christmas songs* (Cornelius); *From Sydney with love* (Strahan).

1988

Recital. p. Halstead; Syd. TH Foyer: 13 Jan.; *Rückert Songs* (Mahler); *Frauenliebe und leben* (Schumann); *Irish Folk Songs* (Hughes); *Six Castillian songs* (Guridi).
Serenade to Music – Vaughn Williams. c. Hopkins; SOCH: 17 Jan.
Symphony no 8 – Mahler. c. Farncombe; Melb.CH: 9 Apr.
Sea Pictures – Elgar. c. Hopkins; SOCH: 13, 14, 16, 18 Apr.
Recital. p. Miller; Syd. Hills Grammar School: 13 May; *Therese / Feldeinsamkeit / Nachtwandler / Über die Heide / Versunken / Todessehnen* (op 86 Brahms); *Charm of Lullabies* (Britten); *L'hiver a cessé / Nell / Aurore / Mandoline* (Fauré); *Music for a while / Mad Bess* (Purcell); *Suleika I / Suleika II* (Schubert).
Requiem – Dvorák. c. Grundy; SOCH: 21 May.
Recital. p. Miller, cl. de Graaff, ob. Nelson; SUIH: 10 June; *Therese / Feldeinsamkeit / Nachtwandler / Über die Heide / Versunken / Todessehnen* (op 86 Brahms); *Music for a while / Mad Bess* (Purcell); *From Sydney with love (excerpts)* (Strahan); *Blake songs for voice & oboe* (Vaughan Williams).
Missa Solemnis – Beethoven. c. Braithewaite; Adelaide Festival Theatre: 25, 26 June.
Das Lied von der Erde – Mahler. c. Litton, t. Lewis; Brisbane CH: 23 July.
Concert. p. Valler; Syd. TH: 3 Aug.; *Six Castillian songs* (Guridi).
Lieder eines fahrenden Gesellen – Mahler. p. Valler; Private Recital for Clare Stevenson; Chatswood: 29 Aug.
Concert. p. Tozer; Syd. TH: 21 Aug.; *Frauenliebe und leben* (Schumann).
Geoffrey Parsons & Friends. p. Parsons, s. Richardson, va. Morozov; Syd. TH: 4 Sep.; *Come ye sons of art: Sound the trumpet / What can we poor females do? / No, no, resistance is but vain* (Purcell); *Suleika I & II* (Schubert); *Spanish Songs* (op 74 Schumann); *Serate Musicale – La Regata Veneziana / La pesca* (Rossini); *Gestillte Sehnsucht / Geistliches Wiegenlied* (op 91 Brahms).
Symphony no 9 – Beethoven. c. Mackerras; SOCH: 22 Oct.
Mass in C – Beethoven. c. Grundy; SOCH: 7 Nov.
Requiem – Verdi. c. Field-Dodgson; Christchurch NZ: 19 Nov.
Messiah - Handel. c. Divall; Melb.CH: 9, 10 Dec.
Concert p. Valler, va. Todiscescu; Sydney Powerhouse Museum: 30 Dec.; *Gestillte Sehnsucht / Geistliches Wiegenlied* (op 91 Brahms).

1989
Symphony no 9 – Beethoven. c. Challender; Syd. TH: 28 Jan.
Recital. p. Tozer, va. Morozov; Canberra School of Music: 12 Mar.; *Gestillte Sehnsucht / Geistliches Wiegenlied* (op 91 Brahms); *Die drei Zigeuner / Die Loreley / Du bist wie eine Blume / Es muss ein Wunderbares sein / Es war ein König in Thule / Freudvoll und leidvoll / Mignons Lied / Oh! Quand je dors / S'il est un charmant gazon* (Liszt); *Allerseelen / Befreit / Die Nacht / Morgen / Nichts / Frühlingsfeier / Zueignung* (Strauss).
Concert. with string quartet leader Pini, cl. de Graaff, fl. Collins; Newcastle Con.: 21 June; *By Footpath and Stile* (Finzi); *Die junge Magd* (Hindemith); *Chanson perpétuelle* (Chausson - arr Butcher for flute).
Concert. p. Miller, cl. de Graaff, s. Thane; Trinity Grammar School: 25 Aug.; SOH: 15 Oct.; *Six Moravian Duets* (Dvořák); *Gestillte Sehnsucht / Geistliches Wiegenlied* (op 91 Brahms); *Guter Rat / Walpurgisnacht* (op 75 Brahms); *Serate Musicale – La Regata Veneziana / La pesca* (Rossini); *La nuit / Le réveil* (Chausson).
The Dawn is at hand – Malcolm Williamson. Poem Kath Walker, world premiere; c. Franks, Brisbane CH: 20 Oct.
Concert. p. Evrov, va. Todicescu; UNSW: 3 Sep.; *Gestillte Sehnsucht / Geistliches Wiegenlied* (op 91 Brahms); *Gypsy Songs* (Dvořák).
Stabat mater – Rossini. c. Pido; SOCH: 22 Sep.
Symphony no 9 – Beethoven. c. Bergel; Auckland NZ: 3 Oct.
Recital. p. Houston, other singers unknown; Auckland NZ: 4 Oct.; *Mon coeur s'ouvre à ta voix* (Saint-Saëns); *Barcarolle* (Offenbach); *Habañera / C'est Toi* (from *Carmen, Bizet*); *Quartet* from *Rigoletto* (Verdi).
Messiah – Handel. c. Franks; Launceston 7 Dec.; Hobart 9 Dec.

1990
Recital. p. Vorster; Melb. Melba Hall: 15 Feb.; *Les nuits d'été* (Berlioz); *Rückert Songs* (Mahler); *Five Cuban Songs* (Montsalvatge).
Serenade to Music – Vaughan Williams. c. Williams; SOCH: 10 Mar.
Beatrice and Benedik – Berlioz – Ursule. c. Mester; Adelaide Festival Theatre: 18 Mar.
Des Knaben Wunderhorn – Mahler. p. Miller, b. Pringle; Trinity Grammar School: 15 June; *Verlorene Müh / Revelge / Das irdische Leben / Wo die schönen Trompeten blasen / Des Antonius von Padua Fischpredigt / Urlicht / Lied des Verfolgten im Turme / Wer hat dies Liedlein erdacht / Der Tambourg'sell / Der Schildwache Nachtlied / Rheinlegendchen / Lob des hohen Verstandes / Trost im Unglück.*
La captive – Berlioz (arr. Bowen). p. Miller, cl. de Graaff; Trinity 15 June.
Concert. p. Miller, b. Pringle, cl. de Graaff; Art Gallery of NSW: 9 Sep. Same program as Trinity Grammar School 15 June.
Carmina – Butterley. c. Summerbell; Art Gallery of NSW: 24 Aug.
Concert. The Song Company, p. Miller; Pitt St. Uniting Church: 6 Oct.; *Il bacio* (Arditi); *Home Sweet Home* (Bishop); *Bless this House* (Brahe); *I want to sing in Opera* (David); *Ave Maria* (Gounod); *My ain folk* (Lemon); *Smiling Through* (Penn); *Ständchen* – w. male quartet (Schubert); *Danny Boy* (trad.).
Sea Pictures – Elgar. c. van Pagee, Geminiani Orch.; Port Fairy Festival: 13 Oct.
Recital. p. Vorster, Port Fairy Festival: 14 Oct.; *Gellert Lieder* (Beethoven); *Frauenliebe und leben* (Schumann); *Allerseelen / Nichts / Zueignung* (Strauss).
Schubert Recital. p. Miller; Albury Art Gallery: 3 Nov.; *Gretchen am Spinnrade / Frühlingsglaube / Ständchen / Gruppe aus dem Tartarus / Klärchen's Lied / Schlummerlied / Suleika I / Am Grabe Anselmos / An die Musik / Aufenthalt / Ave Maria / Du bist die Ruh / Ganymed / Gruppe aus dem Tartarus / Heiss mich nicht reden / Jäger, ruhe von der Jagd! / Die junge Nonne / Kennst du das Land / Nur wer die Sehnsucht kennt / Raste, Krieger / So lasst mich scheinen / Was bedeutet die Bewegung? / Erlkönig / Was ist Silvia / Wiegenlied* (Schubert).
Concert p. Valler, female chorus; University of Sydney Great Hall: 7 Nov.; *Ständchen* (Schubert); *Frauenliebe und leben* (Schumann).

1991

Ronald Dowd Memorial Concert. p. French; SOH: 20 Jan.; *Mon coeur s'ouvre à ta voix* (Saint-Saëns).

Schubert Recital. p. Miller; Penrith Joan Sutherland Performing Arts Centre: 9 Feb.; same program as Albury 3 Nov. 1990.

Recital. p. Miller, b. Pringle, cl. de Graaff; Sydney Con. of Music: 3 Mar.; *Des Knaben Wunderhorn* (Mahler); *La captive* (Berlioz arr. Bowen).

Schubert Recital. p. Vorster; Melb. Melba Hall: 18 Feb.; Brisbane Con.: 20 Mar.; same program as Albury 3 Nov. 1990.

Symphony no 9 – Beethoven. c Sinaisky; Melb. Myer Music Bowl: 20 Feb.

Elijah – Mendelssohn. c. Williams; SOCH: 16 Mar.

Concert. p. Hand; Leura: 27 Apr.; *Seven popular Spanish songs* (Falla).

Concert. Penrith: 5 May; Chamber group version of *Seven popular Spanish songs* (Falla).

Concert. Hazelwood Quartet, cl. de Graaff; Telecom Series; Sydney Con.: 26 May; *By Footpath and Stile* (Finzi); *Die Junge Magd* (Hindemith); *Chanson perpétuelle* (Chausson).

Concert. c. Downes; Adelaide TH: 13, 14, 15 June; *Wesendonk-Lieder* (Wagner); *Dido's Farewell* from *the Trojans* (Berlioz); stand in for Yvonne Minton.

Concert. Amadeus Wind Players; Sydney Con.: 18 Aug.; *Ariё Antiche* (arr. Bowen).

Symphony no 9 – Beethoven. c. Lehmann; Willoughby SO and Willoughby Choir; Willoughby CH: 6, 10 Sep.

Recital. p. Miller; Macquarie University: 7 Sep.; *Music for a while / Since from my dear Astrea's sight / Love quickly is pall'd* (Purcell); *Als Luise die Briefe / Abendempfindung / Dans un bois solitaire / Oiseaux, si tous les ans / Ridente la calma* (Mozart); *A Charm of Lullabies* (Britten); *Lieder eines fahrenden Gesellen* (Mahler); *Let us garlands bring* (Finzi); *Drink to me only with thine eyes* (trad.).

Recital. p. Vorster; Port Fairy Festival: 12 Oct.; *Music for a while / Since from my dear Astrea's sight / Love quickly is pall'd* (Purcell); a *Charm of Lullabies* (Britten); *Let us garlands bring* (Finzi); *Sun, Fun, and Other Disappointments* (Easton – premiere).

Les nuits d'été - Berlioz. c. van Pagee, Geminiani Orch.; Port Fairy Festival: 12 Oct.

Sea Pictures – Elgar. c. Franks; Melb. Symph. Orch.; Warragul: 22 Oct.; Sale: 23 Oct.; Morwell: 24 Oct.

The Feast of Euridice – Williamson. p. Miller; ABC broadcast; World premiere: 1 Nov.

Concert. p. Willems, cello Parry; Wahroonga: 3 Nov.; *Let us garlands bring* (Finzi); *Elegy* (Massenet); a *Charm of Lullabies* (Britten); *Serenade* (Gounod).

Advance Australia Fair unaccomp.; Inaugural Republican Movt. Dinner; NSW Parlt. House: 21 Nov.

Missa Solemnis – Beethoven. c. Brock; Newcastle: 30 Nov.

Messiah - Handel. c. Krug; Brisbane CH: 7 Dec.; Nambour: 8 Dec.

Sea Pictures – Elgar. c. Bowen; Gosford: 15 Dec.

Three Funerals - Bianca Vidor. 29 Oct; Rosalie McCutcheon: 24 Feb.'92; Werner Baer: 25 Mar. '92; p. Valler; *Fear no more the heat o' the sun* (Finzi); *Ich bin der Welt abhanden gekommen* (Mahler).

1992

Recital. p. Valler; Gargonza, Italy: 21 May; *Four Divine Poems of John Donne* (Le Gallienne); *Lieder eines fahrenden Gesellen* (Mahler).

Recital. p. Vorster; Melb. Cult. Centre Studio: 28 Jul.; *L'esule / Nell' orror di notte oscura / Stornello* (Verdi); *Chanson triste / L'invitation au voyage / La vague et la cloche* (Duparc); *Lieder eines fahrenden Gesellen* (Mahler); *Four Divine Poems of John Donne* (Le Gallienne); *Four songs from Shelley* – premiere (Powning); *Seven popular Spanish songs* (Falla).

Concert. p. Emmerson, va. Keir-Haantera; Brisbane Con.: 8 Aug.; *Lieder eines fahrenden Gesellen* (Mahler); *Gestillte Sehnsucht / Geistliches Wiegenlied* (op 91 Brahms).

Recital. p. Stevens, va. Gould; Orange Art Gallery: 30 Aug.; *Lieder eines fahrenden Gesellen* (Mahler); *Four Divine Poems of John Donne* (Le Gallienne); *Gestillte Sehnsucht / Geistliches Wiegenlied* (op 91 Brahms); *Seven popular Spanish songs* (Falla).

Duet Recital. p. Vorster, s. Haggart; Port Fairy Festival: 17 Oct.; *Sound the Trumpet / What can we poor females do? / No, no, resistance is but vain* (Purcell); *Five songs* (op 107) / *Guter Rat / Walpurgisnach* (Brahms); *Ici-bas!* (Fauré); *La nuit / Le réveil* (Chausson); *La Regata Veneziana – La pesca* (Rossini); *D'un coeur qui t'aime* (Gounod).

Concert. p. Kelly, s. Haggart, Port Fairy Festival: 18 Oct.; *O lovely peace* from *Judas Maccabeus* (Handel); *A perdona al primo affetto* from *La clemza di Tito* (Mozart).

Judas Maccabeus – Handel. c. Krel, Syd. Jewish Choir; Syd. Con.: 1 Nov.

Symphony no 9 – Beethoven. c. Bamert, ABC 60th anniversary; Adelaide Festival Hall: 12 Nov.

Messiah - Handel. c. Divall; Melb.CH: 11, 12 Dec.

1993
Recital. p. Brimer; Bermagui Festival: 11 Apr.; *Songs & Dances of Death* (Mussorgsky); *Sea Pictures* (Elgar); *Che faro* (Gluck); *Mon coeur s'ouvre à ta voix* (Saint-Saëns); *Habañera* from *Carmen* (Bizet).

Recital. p. Hidden P., va. Hidden S.; for Music & Heritage, and Community Aid Abroad; Paddington: 30 May; Chatswood: 30 July; *Gelobet sei der Herr* (Bach); *She never told her love / Shepherd's song* (Haydn); *Non t'accostare all'urna / In solitaria stanza* (Verdi); *El pano moruno / Nana / Canción* (Falla); *Gestillte Sehnsucht / Geistliches Wiegenlied* (op 91 Brahms).

Recital. p. Miller, cl. de Graaff; Albury Art Gallery: 26 Jun.; *To a sky-lark* (Pikler); *She never told her love / My mother bids me bind my hair* (Haydn); *Non t'accostare all'urna / In solitaria stanza* (Verdi); *Four songs from Shelley* (Powning); *Seven popular Spanish songs* (Falla); *Songs of a Wayfarer* (Mahler).

Langbein Memorial Concert. o. Dosser v. Kimber; St Peters Cath. Adelaide: 27 Jul.; *Tho I speak with the tongue of men and angels* (Brahms); *Erbarme dich* (Bach); *The strife is o'er, the battle done* (anon).

Recital. p. Vorster; Port Fairy Festival: 15 Oct.; *Widmung / Du bist wie eine Blume / Der Nussbaum / Waldesgespräch / Mondnacht* (Schumann); *Auf dem Kirchhofe / Immer leiser wird mein Schlummer / Klage / Verrat / Wie Melodien zieht es mir* (Brahms); *Allerseelen / Die Nacht / Morgen / Nichts / Heimliche Aufforderung* (Strauss).

Symphony no 9 – Beethoven. c. Tintner; SOCH Twentieth Anniversary: 22 Oct.

Recital. p. Brimer; CAA charity; Chatswood: 29 Oct.; *Widmung / Du bist wie eine Blume / Der Nussbaum / Waldesgespräch / Mondnacht* (Schumann); *Auf dem Kirchhofe / Immer leiser wird mein Schlummer / Klage / Wie Melodien zieht es mir* (Brahms); *Allerseelen / Befreit / Die Nacht / Morgen / Nichts / Heimliche Aufforderung* (Strauss).

1994
Ballad Recital. p. Ross; Albury Con.: 9 Feb.; *My ain folk / Danny Boy / Salaam / Connais-tu le pays / Homing / I'll walk beside you / Trees / I heard a forest praying / O peaceful England / Waltz of my heart / My dear soul / A summer night / When I have sung my songs.*

Elijah – Mendelssohn. c. Grundy; Philharmonia Choir & Orch.; SOCH: 23 Apr.

Farewell Sydney Recital. p. Brimer; Ku-ring-gai TH: 23 May; *Widmung / Du bist wie eine Blume / Der Nussbaum / Waldesgespräch / Mondnacht / Abendlied* (Schumann); *Auf dem Kirchhofe / Immer leiser wird mein Schlummer / Klage / Wie Melodien zieht es mir / Verrat* (Brahms); *Allerseelen / Befreit / Die Nacht / Nichts /Morgen / Heimliche Aufforderung* (Strauss); *An die Musik* (Schubert)

Alexander Nevsky – Prokofiev. c. Pisarek, Sydney Youth Orchestra; Syd. TH: 29 May.

Farewell Sydney Concert. p. Brimer, cl. de Graaff; Ku-ring-gai TH: 24 Jun.; *Song of Autumn* (Hyde); *Vier ernste Gesänge* (Brahms); *Parto Parto* (Mozart).

Recital. p. Vorster; Mietta's Melb.: 2 Aug.; *Gretchen am Spinnrade / Die junge Nonne / Ständchen / Klärchens lied / Ganymed* (Schubert).

Farewell Melbourne Recital. p. Dhar, va. Hazelwood J.; St Johns South Bank: 7 Sep.; *Widmung / Du bist wie eine Blume / Der Nussbaum / Waldesgespräch / Mondnacht / Abendlied* (Schumann); *Vier ernste Gesänge* (Brahms); *Allerseelen / Befreit / Die Nacht / Nichts /Morgen / Heimliche Aufforderung* (Strauss); *Gestillte Sehnsucht / Geistliches Wiegenlied* (op 91 Brahms).

Farewell Opera - *A Dinner Engagement* – Berkeley - Grand Duchess of Monteblanco. s. Haggart, s. Cole, b. Chard; designer Murphy, c. Stacey; Port Fairy Festival: 8 Oct.

Farewell Concert. c. Green; Port Fairy Festival: 9 Oct.; *Four Poems of St Teresa of Avila* (Berkeley).

Index to the Text

Works not listed in this index may be found
in the Catalogue of Performances